THE QUEST FOR MODERN IRELAND
THE BATTLE OF IDEAS 1912–1986

THE QUEST FOR MODERN IRELAND

The Battle of Ideas 1912–1986

BRYAN FANNING
University College Dublin

IRISH ACADEMIC PRESS
DUBLIN • PORTLAND, OR

First published in 2008 by Irish Academic Press

44, Northumberland Road,
Ballsbridge,
Dublin 4, Ireland

920 NE 58th Avenue, Suite 300
Portland, Oregon,
97213–3786

www.iap.ie

British Library Cataloguing in Publication Data
An entry can be found on request

ISBN 978 0 7165 2902 6 (cloth)
ISBN 978 0 7165 2903 3 (paper)

Library of Congress Cataloging-in-Publication Data
An entry can be found on request

Typeset by Carrigboy Typesetting Services
Printed by Biddles Ltd., King's Lynn, Norfolk

Contents

Acknowledgements

I owe a vast debt to Professor Tom Garvin for his encouragement, friendship and critical engagement with this and other projects of mine over the last several years. As the draft progressed I benefited from the admonishments and advice of academic friends and colleagues onto whose fields I have trespassed. The usual disclaimer is warranted. Any faults here are not theirs. In particular I wish to thank Dr Kieran Allen, Professor Angela Bourke, Professor Andrew Carpenter, Professor Patrick Clancy, Professor John Coakley, Professor Tony Fahey, Dr Andreas Hess, Dr Muiris McCarthaigh, Tony McNamara, Joan Maher, Professor Geraldine Meaney, Dr Tim Mooney, Professor Tom Inglis, Professor Michael Laffan, Dr Peter Martin, Professor Stephen Mennell, Dr Ronnie Moore, Professor Willie Nolan, Dr Susannah Riordan, John Sheehan and Professor Nicholas Williams.

I owe a considerable debt to the editor of *Studies*, Fergus O'Donoghue SJ, for his assistance. My preoccupation with Irish nation-building developed in the School of Applied Social Science at University College Dublin, where I teach social policy. As a newcomer to UCD I became intrigued by the legacy of Catholic thought and clerical politics on the Irish social sciences. A previous incarnation of the School (the Department of Social Science) during the reign of Fr. James Kavanagh features in this book. Patrick Clancy generously gave me the run of *Christus Rex* that he had inherited from his predecessor Fr. Conor Ward. In 2003 I co-edited with Tony McNamara the fiftieth-anniversary edition of *Administration* (published in book form as *Ireland Develops: Administration and Social Policy 1953–2003)*. This was useful groundwork for the chapter about that journal contained here. I found a near-complete run of *The Crane Bag* in Kenny's now-closed bookshop in Galway. It mattered to me that my encounters with most of the journals examined here was tactile, particularly in the case of *The Crane Bag,* where form as well as content communicated excitement about art and ideas. This book is dedicated to Denis Dillon, who introduced me to the shores of Lough Graney.

List of Abbreviations

CIÉ	Coras Iompair Éireann
ESB	Electricity Supply Board
GAA	Gaelic Athletic Association
GNP	Gross National Product
IPA	Institute of Public Administration
IRA	Irish Republican Army
NESC	National Economic and Social Council
NUI	National University of Ireland
OECD	Organisation for Economic Co-operation and Development
RTÉ	Radio Telefis Éireann
SJ	Society of Jesus (Jesuit)
SSIS	Statistical and Social Inquiry Society
TCD	Trinity College Dublin
UCD	University College Dublin

INTRODUCTION

Thinking for Ireland, 1912–86

Writing in *Studies* in 1961, having trawled the popular fashion and movie magazines of the time, Denis Donoghue noted that both were in their own way anthologies. The different items within each were 'all of a piece'; they were 'at home'. And this was to be expected: 'a competently edited magazine will tend to be diverse, but it will disclose or invent a "world" somehow its own, it will somehow enforce its own character.'[1] The five influential journals upon whose contents this book hangs each constituted such little worlds. Or, more precisely, each amounted to a distinct vantage point where the like-minded or those engrossed in particular debates pitched their polemical, scholarly or intellectual tents, even if some found themselves at home in more than one tent. Two of these are justly celebrated within the academic field of Irish Studies, *The Bell* and *The Crane Bag*, and three are generally not, *Studies, Christus Rex* and *Administration*. All five, taken together, give a broad sense of the intellectual politics that played out in Ireland after independence. The debates each nurtured were influential in the various battles for ideas that helped shape modern Ireland. *Christus Rex* sought to reproduce Catholic intellectual influence into the second half of the twentieth century through the social sciences. *Administration* articulated the developmental project of technocratic modernisation that came to define modern Ireland. *Studies*, because of its broad remit and its longevity, played a pivotal role in a number of debates. Each was the site, though not necessarily the sole stage, of important debates about concrete problems and issues affecting Irish society.

Although this book is not a history it covers a distinct period from 1912, when *Studies* was founded, to 1986, when its 300th issue was published. The year 1912 was a pivotal one in Irish politics, the starting date of political upheaval to come when Ulster unionism threatened violent resistance against the home rule sanctioned by Westminster.[2] The mid-1980s presented something of a fault-line between a period of societal fatalism, with high emigration that recalled the 1950s, and a later period of 'Celtic Tiger' confidence. The period examined in this book is almost the same as that covered by J.J. Lee's monumental *Ireland 1912–1985: Politics and Society*, a work that tried to address the dilemmas of the 1980s. Some of Lee's arguments against what he saw as the root causes of Irish economic fatalism were rehearsed in his contribution to a special issue of *Administration* entitled *Unequal Achievement: The Irish Experience 1957–1982*, itself an influential critique of Irish modernisation and its discontents. The period covered by Lee and examined here in the following chapters might be presented, to paraphrase Eric Hobsbawm, as a short Irish twentieth century, one book-ended by the events that precipitated the establishment of the Irish nation-state and by the challenges to its presumed autonomy attributed to globalisation.[3]

This book documents debates that, in various ways, intellectually sustained different influential nation-building projects that flourished in post-independence Ireland. The approach differs from influential works such as John Whyte's *Church and State in Modern Ireland 1923–1970* and, more recently in the same political science tradition, Tom Garvin's *Preventing the Future: Why was Ireland so poor for so long?*[4] Both emphasised the role of institutional factors and interest group politics. The focus of *The Quest for Modern Ireland* is mostly upon the software of influential ideas, ideologies and understandings. It furthermore differs from two previous noteworthy attempts to address Irish intellectual politics since independence. Maurice Goldring's 1993 examination of the role of intellectuals in the construction of the Irish nation-state focused on nationalism, class politics and class relations. In keeping with a French Republicanism vantage point, this relegated Catholic thought to the private sphere and offered no examination of the influence of liberal thought.[5] Liam O'Dowd in his 1996 edited volume *On Intellectuals and Intellectual Life in Ireland* emphasised a wider field of intellectual life but, overall, was more concerned with comparative taxonomies of intellectuals than with charting the historical breadth of Irish intellectual politics.[6] Here also Catholicism was viewed as the basis of ethnic-nationalist identity rather than as the bearer in its own right of ideological or ontological positions.

A key emphasis in a number of chapters in this book is on how Catholic thought, both anti-modernist and liberal, provided a conduit for broader debate. Secularisation, driven partly by Church authoritarianism, resulted in a degree of intellectual anti-clericalism in Irish universities. The generation of scholars that had struggled out from under clerical control inevitably sought a break with the past and, especially in the social sciences, the making up of lost ground. Yet no rounded account of intellectual politics in the Republic of Ireland can ignore the centrality of Catholicism and of Catholic journals as a clearing house for a wide range of ideas.

The project of a book on Irish intellectual debates is not, at face value, a promising one, notwithstanding a voluminous literature on Irish culture and national identity. Unlike in France, intellectuals are rarely lionised. Irish intellectual debates tend to be implicit rather than explicit. As put by Stefan Collini in his analysis of the British case, there is a need to address the 'absence thesis'. Collini argues that the frequently encountered claim that there are no intellectuals in Britain is generally advanced by those who, were they living in certain other societies, would unhesitantly be recognised as intellectuals.[7] Of concern here is the status of the term 'intellectual' – depending on the time or place it can be a derogatory one or not – and how intellectuals are defined, broadly or narrowly. As employed here it includes those who published essays and articles as a means of contributing to public debates on political, economic, cultural and social questions. It includes the foot soldiers as well as local leading figures in battles of ideas.

My approach was to rely as much as possible on what was expressed by contributors to the main debates within the journals, to let these breathe in how these were recounted and so try to capture the different worlds these constituted culturally, epistemologically and ontologically. The book attempts to break free from magisterial tendencies within Irish historiography and their equivalent within intellectual history to focus solely on pivotal figures.[8] This was necessary because the stall each journal set out in what Sean O'Faolain called 'the mart of ideas' was generally dominated by normative shared understandings rather than by the charismatic influence of key intellectual entrepreneurs.

Ireland's intellectual marketplace has relied on imports. The twentieth century depicted in Thomas Duddy's *A History of Irish Thought* is a glaringly impoverished one; the best-known figures he refers to are W.B. Yeats and, more tenuously, Iris Murdoch.[9] In truth only a handful of influential original Irish thinkers can be identified since George Berkeley and Edmund Burke outside the domain of English-language literature that now dominates Irish studies as an academic subject. The huge international appeal of Yeats and James Joyce partially explains the literary turn in the field of Irish studies represented here by *The Crane Bag*. Many who contributed to the five journals drew their status from institutions: the clerical and lay university professors – historians, classicists, economists and scholastic philosophers – who dominated *Studies*, the sociologist priests of *Christus Rex*, the university-based literary critics and philosophers of *The Crane Bag*, the civil servants and allied trades of *Administration*. Many of the main Irish figures who proved to be intellectually influential at home did so on the back of foreign recognition. International status became particularly important in the post-independence climate of censorship for writers such as O'Faolain. Otherwise, status and influence depended considerably on local institutional affiliations.

The book began as an effort to examine the intellectual tensions between *The Bell*, founded in 1940 by Seán O'Faolain, and *The Crane Bag*, set up by Richard Kearney in 1977. In the former, O'Faolain and his successor as editor, Peadar O'Donnell, practised a form of civic republicanism that emphasised the factual portrayal of everyday life as the antithesis of a prevalent romantic nationalism that was seen to legitimate cultural isolationism and censorship.[10] With the help of writers such as Frank O'Connor, Flann O'Brien and Peadar O'Donnell, O'Faolain sought to overcome prevalent nation-building myths that obscured the real problems of post-independence Ireland. *The Bell* under O'Faolain's editorship was a formidable achievement. Here established authors with international reputations pursued an anti-authoritarian intellectual project. O'Faolain mentored non-fiction contributions from many previously unpublished writers as part of an aim of reaching out to and reflecting the reality of Irish society.

The Crane Bag (1977–84) was no less of an achievement with strikingly high production standards and intellectual ambition. In *The Crane Bag* academics and literary critics promoted a mostly elite insider critique of what Kearney depicted as the Irish Mind. Kearney was still in his twenties when he founded *The Crane Bag*, and was already well on his way to becoming an intellectual star of Irish philosophy. His energetic approach to Irish intellectual politics was modelled on the French one. He obtained a doctorate in Paris under the supervision of Paul Ricoeur, whose work influenced much of what he wrote in *The Crane Bag*. As an academic he promoted the work of continental philosophers.[11] His co-founder Mark Patrick Hederman, a Benedictine monk, had also studied philosophy in Paris.[12] Kearney in particular brought a Gallic public intellectual flair to bear on Irish problems. The Cambridge-educated Seamus Deane, another major contributor, was both a poet and an academic literary critic. As the latter he went on to become a dominant influential figure in literary

Irish Studies. In *The Crane Bag* these and other contributors interrogated the extent to which Irish art and politics were intertwined within what Kearney depicted as the mythic structure of Irish nationalism.

The polarities represented by *The Crane Bag* and *The Bell* follow the contours of Ireland's primary post-colonial intellectual schism. The emergence of a nationalist school of Irish history was an important component in the building of the 'Irish nation'. After independence the 'greening of Irish history' placed heavy emphasis upon the struggle against British imperialism and landlordism, upon the dignifying of Irish Gaelic culture, and upon the positive, and often heroic, representation of the key figures of Irish nationalism and of nationalist struggle in general.[13] Since the 1930s a sustained conflict between what are commonly described as 'revisionist' and 'anti-revisionist' perspectives has persisted within Irish historiography, fanned by the Northern conflict and the political persistence of romantic idealist nationalism. Revisionists posed a political and epistemological challenge to the officially propagated histories of the post-1922 Irish Free State.[14] The conflict between O'Faolain and his own contemporary nemesis Daniel Corkery echoed those set in train by T.W. Moody and R.D. Edwards within Irish historiography.[15] Kearney retrospectively located the intellectual project of *The Crane Bag* into the anti-colonial tradition that includes Corkery.[16] Corkery's own vindication of the 'authentic' Gaelic culture in *The Hidden Ireland* was received as a justification for cultural decolonisation – as one enthusiastic 1925 review put it, for dealing with the mongrel upstart Anglo-Irish culture.[17] 'Revisionism', as Roy Foster put it in terms that fitted with what O'Faolain sought to achieve, was an attempt to recover methodologically and politically from the fantasy of folk mythologies.[18] The ontological conflict emphasised by O'Faolain was one between nation-building myths and Ireland 'as it is'. His critique of post-independence cultural politics was that the former obscured the latter to the extent that there was an overwhelming antipathy to discussing real social problems.[19] The task of *The Bell* was to discuss the real Ireland in plain terms.

This was very much in opposition to the approach advocated by *The Crane Bag* more than three decades later. Deane's literary criticism was explicitly in solidarity with Northern nationalism. Kearney's thesis was that one could engage with the atavisms of violent nationalism only from within. This required sympathy and empathy with the mythic components of national identity. These positions put both broadly within the anti-revisionist school that reacted to the explicitly empirical history promoted by Moody and Edwards and their successors. Anti-revisionism, in Brendan Bradshaw's summary, stood opposed to attempts at creating a 'value-free history' unsympathetic to the suffering and sacrifice of those who liberated the nation.[20] *The Crane Bag* preceded the big bang in internationalised academic Irish Studies from the 1980s, one driven by post-colonial theory. Here Deane has been a leading figure.[21] *The Crane Bag* itself made an important public intellectual intervention in the politics of the Northern conflict.

Arguably, the most important intellectual journal in post-independence Ireland proved to be the Jesuit-run *Studies*, whose first 300 issues from 1912 to 1986 (some 2,500 articles) provide the core of this book. This is not to say that at every given moment it was the best. *Studies* influenced and contributed significantly to many of the intellectual debates that featured in *The Bell*, *The Crane Bag*, *Christus Rex* and *Administration*. Unlike *Christus Rex*, *Studies* was not restricted by doctrinal censorship. It lacked the narrow editorial identity of other more focused journals. This elasticity contributed to its longevity but also to its being sometimes underrated alongside more short-lived ones.

From the outset *Studies* attracted leading Catholic academics and intellectuals from Patrick Pearse to Tom Kettle, the liberal Professor of Political Economy who died at the Somme weeks after the 1916 Rising. After independence it engaged with and explained Marxist ideas from a scholastic vantage point. In *Studies* corporatist alternatives to capitalism, deemed to be in accordance with God's natural law, were debated at length but eventually abandoned as politically impractical. *Studies* also offered a forum for economic liberals. In 1910 Tom Kettle, an early contributor to *Studies*, introduced George O'Brien, a later frequent one, to economics at UCD.[22] Other prominent contributors included O'Brien's protégé James Meenan, Patrick Lynch and Garret FitzGerald, who in turn taught economics at University College Dublin. O'Brien portrayed himself in terms that might be slipped unnoticed into Margaret Thatcher's autobiography:

> I breathed in my childhood the air of Victorian liberalism. My father worked his way up in the world from small beginnings entirely by his own thrift and energy. His undoubted personal virtues had resulted in a hard-earned material reward. He deserved his success and was entitled to hold what he had gained. That his profits should be confiscated by penal taxation would have appeared to him not only unjust but intolerable.[23]

O'Brien offered up this account of his formation to explain his own 'blindness' and 'insensitivity' to social problems such as poverty. But it was through O'Brien that *Studies* promoted the ideas of John Maynard Keynes as an intellectual antidote to economic isolationism. A complex and shifting intellectual engagement with economic and social liberalism evolved in the journal over time, one where clerics cited *The Road to Serfdom* by F.A. Hayek to support their opposition to the welfare state and where economists sometimes invoked papal encyclicals to do the same. Notwithstanding its complicity with literary censorship *Studies* gave occasional space to social liberals such as O'Faolain, whose non-fiction critiques of history and culture were taken seriously even if his fiction was shunned. From the 1960s *Studies* provided a platform for social liberals such as FitzGerald.

In 1953 *Studies* published Patrick Lynch's influential case for state-directed planning. This became the *raison d'être* of *Administration*, the Civil Service journal founded that same year. *Administration* stood for a technocratic modernisation and endeavoured to foster a public-sector expert intelligentsia. Its critique of the Irish public sector suggested that clerics were not the sole actors preoccupied with, as Tom Garvin put it, preventing the future.[24] Both *Studies* and *Administration* advanced the same recipe for economic development: the cultivation of enterprise, the abandonment of protectionism, the use of foreign capital and membership of the European Economic Community. Overall, Europe was viewed as a positive political influence on Ireland, a chance for economic and social uplift.[25] A debate in the 1960s, again led by Lynch in *Studies*, promoted the expansion of the human capital focus of education (at, potentially, the expense of religious social reproduction). A tendency to bend rather than break distinguished *Studies* from the rigid conservatism of Archbishop John Charles McQuaid. The focus of *Studies* shifted over time to reflect prevalent political, social, economic and cultural questions. Here, in the post-Vatican II era, scholasticism gave way to the revolutionary theology that fostered a leftist critique of Irish social and economic inequalities.

Christus Rex, on the other hand, reflected the dominant Church anxiety about social change, secularisation and loss of intellectual influence in the universities. Its project was an inherently conservative one, to some extent an anti-modernist one but also one of engagement with social change. Until 1969 it functioned as a last bastion of literary censorship on behalf of the Catholic clerical–university complex that dominated the Irish social sciences. Yet *Christus Rex* engaged with modernity through research and activism aimed significantly at addressing rural decline and emigration. Its model was that of European Catholic social action wedded to the rhetoric of neo-Thomism which, by then, had lost ground in *Studies*. It is perhaps difficult to grasp now the extent to which Thomism once stood as a proxy for Irish intellectual life. The 'secular' equivalent here was dialectal materialism under state socialism. Aquinas's natural law synthesis of Aristotle and Christian faith formed the basis of Catholic social thought. This in turn framed so much that was written by lay writers as well as clerics about social and economic questions. In *Christus Rex*, where most contributors were priests, and in Catholic-dominated universities, these were presented as unassailable 'sociological' truths. Clerical academics dominated fields such as philosophy and sociology until the 1970s. Here they resisted secular social theory but by championing narrow empiricism they were, no less than the lay technocrats they educated, the bearers of an uncritical modernity.

When it came to the study of shifts in social cohesion induced by modernity *Christus Rex* relinquished the conceptual tools that had been used by secular sociologists such as Auguste Comte and Emile Durkheim. The problem was an ontological one. Secular sociology depicted religion as a 'social fact' about society rather than as an eternal truth. Yet Irish positivists, both lay and clerical, true to the influence of Comte within the social sciences, understood their research as having something of a social engineering role.[26]

Administration reflected the developmental nation-building project that dominated the second half of the Irish twentieth century. Here, debates about the leadership role of civil servants resembled those amongst the priests of *Christus Rex*. The nation-building hero of Lee's *Ireland 1912–1985* was T.K. Whitaker, Secretary of the Department of Finance from 1956 to 1969. Whitaker's 1958 synthesis of Irish anti-isolationist thought since the 1930s, *Economic Development*, formally launched the new national developmental project and acquired the status of the papal encyclicals routinely invoked within *Christus Rex*. However, there was no overnight shift. The core ideas here were ones that had been debated in *Studies* since the 1930s.

The practical mission that *Christus Rex* fostered of preserving traditional (religious) social cohesion stood in contrast with de Valera's rural ideal expressed in his 1943 dream speech. What de Valera attempted in championing peasant virtues, Ernest Gellner suggests, was to present a mass politics of identity in the guise of cosy community as a form of ideological glue. Here, the phenomenon of *Gesellschaft* used the idiom of *Gemeinschaft*.[27] *Christus Rex* attempted something less abstract in seeking to promote viable rural planning and urban community development. Concrete institutions of community were seen as necessary to reproduce religiosity, and there was a degree of antipathy towards abstract nationalism for the same reasons as emphasised by O'Faolain in *The Bell*. As put in a 1959 article: 'Ireland is not just a shadowy abstraction, but men and women, children in slums, queues at the Labour Exchange, Teddy Boys, juvenile delinquents.'[28]

In *The Crane Bag* the notion of the Irish Mind as a Jungian collective consciousness was taken seriously. This was the opposite to the essentially sociological notion of nations as socially constructed imagined communities put forward by Benedict Anderson. Communities were *imagined* 'because the members of even the smallest nation will never know most of their fellow-members, meet them, or even hear of them, yet in the minds of each lives the image of their communion'.[29] Irish people could ponder the existence of an Irish Mind but not vice versa. For O'Faolain, presumptions that there could be a national *Geist* were themselves the problem. Whitaker, *Administration* and Lee emphasised the need to foster a shift in national psychology from a post-Famine peasant fatalism towards one conducive to economic growth, – in other words, a spirit of enterprise close to the Protestant ethic as depicted by Max Weber.[30] This tied in with a wider critique of post-colonial social, political and administrative conservatism that could not be reduced to clerical causes. In other words the problem was seen to lie with the inadequacies of Irish *Gesellschaft* (the legacy of cultural and economic isolationism) rather than with *Gemeinschaft*. Writing in the early 1980s Gellner and Anderson both emphasised the cultural politics of nation-building. The focus in this book is on how political and cultural factors intersect with social and economic ones. The light that the various debates examined here sheds on the Irish case reveals an inevitable interdependence between all four.

CHAPTER ONE

Taking the Fifth: *The Crane Bag*, 1977–84

Margaret Thatcher once angrily dismissed calls for Irish unity with the comment that the 'Irish thing was all metaphysics anyway' and hence incapable of resolution.[1] Fortunate then, for the cause of Irish peace, if not the one of Irish unity, that metaphysicians and indeed poets were on hand. *The Crane Bag* was founded in 1977 by Richard Kearney, an energetic young philosopher at University College Dublin and his former teacher, Mark Patrick Hederman, a Benedictine monk, with the support of Seamus Heaney and Seamus Deane, both Northern Catholics, both poets, the latter better known as an Irish literature critic and academic. These and other contributors wrote and sometimes responded to one another in cascading series of debates about art and politics, Irish nationalism, identity, mythology, minorities, Church and state and the Irish language.[2] These debates came back again and again to the Northern crisis. They were principally ones amongst and between Catholic nationalist writers and thinkers. For Kearney and Hederman the Northern problem, or, more precisely, nationalist thought and understandings, had to be addressed though grappling with communal myths. Understanding could come about only through a 'big tent' therapeutic engagement with atavisms shared across Catholic nationalist culture.

The one proposed was both family therapy and art therapy. Hederman, for the most part, wrote about art and literature, but his interview with the IRA Commander-in-Chief about the legitimacy of violence sparked an ongoing debate amongst contributors. Another editor, Seamus Deane, played post-colonial advocate for the Republican tradition. He questioned Heaney's political commitment and the authenticity of Yeats's Irishness. Kearney's articles, notably 'Myth and Terror', emphasised the need to transcend dangerous myths but also extolled the creative potential of mythic thought. Various shades of green grappled with various shades of grey. For many contributors

Conor Cruise O'Brien was Ireland's intellectual *bête noire*. O'Brien could be grudgingly admired for emphasising unpalatable truths but not for a 'liberal humanism' that was the antithesis of the critiques of disenchanted post-colonial modernity that predominated in *The Crane Bag*.

The Crane Bag had a distinct project of thinking for Ireland, described in the first issue through the concept of a 'fifth province' of Ireland. Mary Robinson, in her inaugural speech as President, subsequently borrowed the fifth province as a metaphor. For Kearney, it was always more than metaphor. It depicted the necessary break with a sectarian past in terms of metaphysical transcendence. The 'fifth province' was aptly summarised by Tom Paulin as an invisible province that offered a Platonic challenge to the nationalistic image of four green fields.[3] In *The Crane Bag*, then, one set of idealisms was to supplant another. The main intellectual and conceptual tools brought to bear were poetic and literary ones brandished, for the most part, by philosophers and literary critics rather than by social scientists or social researchers. Empirical questions about the condition of Irish society, what Kearney called 'the paralysing immediacy of facts', generally took a back seat to literary theory or visionary frameworks derived from metaphysics with a veneer of anthropology and psychology.

ART AND POLITICS

Kearney introduced the guiding metaphor of *The Crane Bag* in the first issue editorial. Modern Ireland, he wrote, was made up of four provinces, whose origins lay beyond the beginning of recorded history. And yet the Irish for province was *coiced*, which meant a fifth. This fivefold division, he continued, was as old as Ireland itself, yet the identity of the '*fifth* fifth' remained uncertain. Kearney sketched the notion of the fifth province as a mythic place, known only to druids and poets, as a non-political second centre that acted as a necessary balance to Tara, the political centre power. 'The balance between the two was guarantor of peace and harmony in the country as a whole.'[4] A restored fifth province, he argued, was needed given 'the present unhappy state of our country'. It could not be a political or geographical position. It was, he maintained, like a 'dis-position' to be discovered within each person by himself for himself. The purpose of *The Crane Bag* then was to 'promote the excavation of such unactualized spaces within the reader'.[5]

The first article in the first issue, written by Kearney, was entitled 'Beyond Art and Politics'. Art, he argued, implicitly negated politics. When, he noted, 'the late Romantics or Pre-Raphaelites dream their way into an aesthetic Eden of moons, sylphs and golden apples, they are expressing a fundamental refutation of the dissonant reality in which they live'.[6] Kearney named a roll-call of Irish critics, including Conor Cruise O'Brien, who had argued that art must stay aloof and neutral from the strategies of political power. For these, Kearney argued, 'Art must remain *unreal*. The fictions of aesthetic creativity are radically incompatible with the facts of brute existence.' They claimed, according to Kearney, that any attempt to translate the ideal fictions of the imagination into the real currency of politics must result in some form of totalitarianism.[7]

Kearney's response to Romantic idealism was appreciably less jaundiced than that of O'Brien, who connected it to emergence of fascism.[8] Kearney argued that a positive relationship between art and politics was attainable in a discussion of Walter Benjamin's anxiety about the translation of corrupt art into politics. Benjamin had argued in *The Work of Art in the Age of Mechanical Reproduction* that art had been corrupted by technology. Mass production had destroyed the uniqueness of response that had always been the traditional hallmark of genuine aesthetic experience. The resultant exploitation of human sensibility had resulted in an entirely new impersonal, even totalitarian aesthetic evident, from a High Culture perspective, in the vulgarity of television, radio and cinema. The possibility of individual aesthetic response had been replaced by anonymous voyeurism. From this perspective, Kearney summarised, art (with a small 'a') now served as whore to the highest bidding ideology.

Kearney then stepped back from Benjamin's preoccupation with modernity to his own central theme of the relationship between Art (with a big 'A'), myth, culture and the imagination. Imagination, 'the catch-all term for aesthetics, Platonic idealisms and faith', must be, he insisted, no less privileged than reason in making sense of the material world. It was central to existence. For Kearney, Art was the only power capable of reconciling the rift between the spiritual and the material precisely because it called for the suppression of the fallacious distinction between the two. The distinguishing mark of imagination was its 'dialectical' nature. This in a nutshell was its power to entertain the possibility of things being otherwise than they were:

> Each work of art is an attempt to say the world in a new way. As a model of the world it is therefore less an imitation than a creation. By recreating the world in language, the artist invites every man to discover his own freedom from the existing world and his potentiality to create an altogether new one. It is an open invitation. No one is excluded except those who exclude themselves by refusing to acknowledge the latent artist within.[9]

For Kearney, Benjamin's high culture fear of modernity weighed heavier than O'Brien's concern about the dark legacy of European Romantic thought. Kearney argued that 'Art' must open itself to politics and politics must open itself to the world of aesthetics, because 'Art without politics is superhuman. Politics without art is subhuman. Either without the other is inhuman.'[10] Kearney's artist was an idealised figure, somebody who 'renounced any temptation to dictate or impose a solution because he knows no one side can embody the totality which man must become'.[11] The fifth-province artist was someone who refused to take sides except, presumably, in the conflict between high culture and low culture.

The ghost of Benjamin haunted a number of articles in the first issue, whilst other contributions grappled with the central theme of Art and Irish politics. Read chronologically these built slowly towards this larger theme, even if some blocks fitted awkwardly within the overall design. A somewhat vitriolic but inconclusive article on cinema and television argued that much mass media was 'a distraction from the world, a process of making you a political eunuch, ballot-fodder for some demagogue'.[12] In Ireland, the *Seanachaí* who once held court in Irish homes had been supplanted by the 'indoctrination of the box in the corner'.[13] This cultural crisis was further pondered by Bruce Merry in an article entitled 'A Sense of Humour'. Both were misnamed. Merry reviewed the programmes and advertisements shown on a November Saturday in 1976 by RTÉ, the national broadcaster. These were seen to vindicate D.H. Lawrence's view that 'such mass entertainment was anti-life'. Merry surmised that the overall picture was bleak 'especially in Ireland, where there is no tradition of informed T.V. criticism and the newspapers and weekly summaries of coming programmes are totally lacking in speculative self-analysis'.[14]

The first culprit in the dock was the news programme followed the Angelus. The Angelus itself, a one-minute Catholic-specific television call to prayer broadcast at six o'clock each evening, escaped comment. Merry was exercised not by the actual weather forecast – rainy and drizzle – but by the inaccurate angle of Ireland in relation to England on the weather map. He discussed and disparaged the advertisements that recurred at fifteen-minute intervals, 'an Irish-interest programme in Gaelic', the evening film (*The 39 Steps*), a further news programme, *The Dick Emery Show* and a further weather report. This time he was exercised by the 'extremely unconfident weatherman' and the 'lexical redundancy' of his forecast of 'more extensive and eventually rather consistent' drizzle. There then followed a disparaging analysis of the 'pally patter' of *The Late Late Show*, RTÉ's highest-rated programme. Each of the imported programmes met with trenchant criticism. Greater rancour still was directed towards the mediocrity of each of the Irish-produced ones. The sole Irish-language programme, *Pobal*, was disparaged as cultural commodification:

> The title of this Gaelic programme was set against a woolly grey screen, hinting at wind swept sheep in an honest outback with deliberate *renvoi* to the Aran wool sweaters worn by sporty fathers and bank-financed infants in the middle-class environment of the standard commercial. Grinning in front of this rough and ready screen was a cloth-capped gentleman, who began to moralize and tell stories in Gaelic. He had an artless rustic face and was holding, *mirabile dictu*, a half glass of Guinness. Eventually he got round to introducing a well-scrubbed and long-haired blond Irish girl, singing a lament in Gaelic with bright excited eyes.[15]

If for Farrell the *Seanachaí* had been exiled from the Irish parlour by television, then in Merry's account they enjoyed an ersatz afterlife on Saturday evening primetime. Next up was 'A Marxist view of Art and Politics' by Peter Mew. This advanced two propositions; that 'the nature of a work of art can be explained ultimately by reference to the economic class position of its author', and that 'the value of a work of art is defined in terms of aptitude for promoting the revolutionary cause of the proletariat'. Mew filtered these propositions through the lens of Marxist critics such as Terry Eagleton and the 'French wizard' Louis Althusser and emerged with two further propositions. The first was that a work of art has value if it accurately expresses the tensions or 'contradictions' inherent in the ideological perspective of the author. The second was that the work has value if *in spite* of the author's ideological perspective it captures and brings clearly into focus the deep human experiential realities of its time. Mew briefly pondered the

Irish situation where, he maintained, the relatively poor and workers in mechanical uncreative jobs had an 'antipathy to moral, social, and political analysis'. These included nearly everybody amongst the middle classes and proletarians who did not happen to be working in a cultural or educational capacity. They were, he feared, 'ripe for escapism rather than critical questioning', incapable of cultural analysis, unable to access revolutionary art or think about literature in ways that might inform their own understanding of the world'.[16] The answer, for Mew, in so far as there was one, involved the overhaul of the educational system by Marxist literary theorists.

These stillborn criticisms of Irish popular culture reveal something of the contours of *The Crane Bag* as an intellectual project even if they fell well below the subsequent general standard. Ascetic arguments about Art and Culture fostered a bemused dismissal of everyday life as unauthentic, banal and unimportant. Such concerns were the province of social science and rather than the fifth province. Yet it was argued in two key articles, one by Hederman on Synge and another consisting of a dialogue between Heaney and Deane, that Art could and should eschew grand idealisms for the richness of ordinary life.

Hederman's article was on Synge's political role as an artist. *The Playboy of the Western World* had opened in Dublin in 1907 to a riot of protest against its presumed slur on Irish womanhood, the Irish peasantry and other icons of cultural nationalism. Synge, Hederman emphasised, was looking for real life at a time when the Catholic Church wanted saints and scholars and nationalists wanted a nation once again. As such he epitomised the conflicts between art and politics. The problem was that all three were looking in the same place for the genius of the Irish 'race'.[17] Yeats, the great transcendentalist, couldn't have been more temperamentally different from Synge who, he recalled, showed no interest in men in the mass, or in any subject that is studied through abstractions: 'Unlike those whose habit of mind fits them to judge of men in the mass, he was wise in judging individual men'.[18] Synge, then, was estranged from nationalist aspirations and beliefs. At a time, Hederman wrote, when so many were declaiming and hoping and portraying the 'ideal' Ireland and the 'real' Irishry in terms of nationalistic and religious patterns, Synge implied that none of it mattered a whit. He had claimed that the country people of the Western world were the authors of the play:

> I have used one or two words only that I have not heard amongst the country people of Ireland ... and I am glad to acknowledge

> how much I owe the folk-imagination of these people ... All art is a collaboration; and there is little doubt that in the happy ages of literature, striking and beautiful phrases were as ready to the story-teller's or the playwright's hand, as the rich cloaks and dresses of his time.[19]

Yeats maintained that Synge was hated because he gave the country what it needed. For Hederman this was an artistic account of the Irish soul, the Irish spirit, the Irish genius, rooted in the real music of Celtic language and heritage as Synge understood it. Yeats's understanding of Synge sets up a more complex nation-building dynamic, one whose national ideals are anchored in social reality. As put by Hederman:

> Once we have seen and heard and learned to love this reality, in the way that Synge knew and loved it, we can then set about rationalizing it, politicizing it, baptizing it, idealizing it or educating it to whatever other modality of existence we think fit. But none of these political attitudes of imposition of a form, whether that form be aesthetic or moral or social or political, can succeed until it grows out of the reality on which it is to be grafted. Without first of all understanding sympathetically the man we wish to change into an 'Irishman' or anything else, all our efforts are in vain.[20]

One of the central questions running through the *Art and Politics* issue of *The Crane Bag* was about the relationship between art and society as it pertained to cultural, hence, political, authenticity. The pivotal article here was Deane's interview with Heaney, published as 'Unhappy at Home'. This debated whether or not there was a recognisably Northern Irish group of poets (yes, thought Heaney, but it didn't include Deane), whether the emergence of this group had anything to do with Northern politics (no, according to Heaney, except for some common emotional ground arising from the Troubles) and whether tribalism was central to Heaney's own poetry. Heaney maintained that poetry was born out the watermarks and colourings of the self but that the self, in some ways, 'took its spiritual pulse from the inward spiritual structure of the community to which it belongs'. In his own case, he could acknowledge the 'slightly aggravated Catholic part' of his temperament.[21]

Deane put to Heaney O'Brien's description of the link between art and politics as an 'unhealthy intersection'. Heaney replied that he thought O'Brien was correct, but went on to suggest that any separation of the two was ultimately difficult to achieve.

> The community to which I belong is Catholic and nationalist. I believe that the poet's force now, and hopefully in the future, is to maintain the efficacy of his own 'mythos', his own cultural and political colourings, rather than to serve any political strategies that his political leaders, his paramilitary organisation or his own liberal self might want him to serve. I think that poetry and politics are, in different ways, an articulation, an ordering, a giving of form to inchoate pieties, prejudices, world-views, or whatever. And I think that my own poetry is a kind of slow, obstinate, papish burn emanating from the ground I was bought up on.[22]

He himself had thought and wrote along 'sectarian lines' but had become more and more anxious, in Deane's words, to refrain from taking any outright political stance in his poetry. In reply, Deane criticised the extent to which Northern Irish poets (other than himself) were influenced by the English poet Ted Hughes in their shared preoccupation with a 'well made poem', which Deane described as deliberately minor literature. 'Do you not think', he remonstrated, 'that a refusal by 'you and the Northern poets at large' to adopt a political stance on the troubles 'might lead to a dangerous strengthening of earlier notions of the autonomy of poetry'.[23] Heaney replied that most poetry was inevitably minor. But not deliberately so, Deane retorted.[24]

Deane then drew attention to the suppressed politics of Northern poetry and the violent atavisms he detected beneath the poise and balance of Heaney's own work. Deane sought to recruit Heaney to the cause of political Art. He also pressed Heaney to choose sides against O'Brien. Do you not think, he asked that 'the kind of humanism which Conor Cruise O'Brien sponsors is precisely that kind of humanism, totally detached from its atavisms, which, though welcome from a rational point of view, renders much of what he says either irrelevant or wrong. Particularly in relation to the North where bigotry is so much part of the psyche?' The obstinate voice of rationalist humanism, Heaney retorted, was important, for if that was lost everything was lost. He argued that O'Brien did an utterly necessary job in rebuking all easy thought about the Protestant community in the North: 'It is to be seen in this way: 7 or 8 years ago there was tremendous sentiment for Catholics in the North, amongst intellectuals, politicians and ordinary people in the South. Because of his statements O'Brien is still reviled by people who held these sentiments; yet now these people harbour sentiments which mirror O'Brien's thinking, and still they do not cede to the clarity or the validity of his position.'[25] But surely, Deane objected, did not O'Brien's 'bourgeois form of humanism' impose a rational clarity upon the Northern position that was untrue to the reality. Heaney replied that O'Brien's real force was in the South rather than the North: 'it is not enough for people to simply say "ah, they're all Irishmen"' when some Northerners actually spit at the word Irishman: O'Brien's contribution was an obstinate insistence on facing up to this kind of reality.[26]

Deane then changed tack. Could we not, he asked, refer to an Irish poetry tradition rather than the Northern one they had discussed? Yes, Heaney admitted: 'because there is a mounting confidence in the validity and importance of our ground. If only because people are killing one another. There is a strong sense in a number of poets that the cross channel tradition cannot deal any longer with our particular history.' Then Deane asked, was not Heaney intent on moulding his own psychic disposition onto a distinct Irish cultural landscape? Yes, Heaney accepted, up to a point. But there was a tension between mythical cultural schemes and a lyrical impulse rooted in ordinary everyday things. Yeats and Kavanagh, he explained, exemplified these contradictions, ones between: 'the search for myths and sagas, the need for a structure and a sustaining landscape and at the same time the need to be liberated from it'.[27]

The themes ineptly addressed by Farrell, Merry and Mew were revisited by the novelist Francis Stuart and the theatre director Peter Sheridan. Stuart's 'Literature and Politics' lamented the apparent absence of explicit ideological political inspiration for Irish artists: 'In a community like ours where there are no widely-held ideological concepts, either left or right, no political party with any real social commitment, where opportunism and the resulting mediocrity are the norm, there seems no temptation for the artist to feel anything but a totally negative attitude.'[28] In Stuart's account the zealous clergy and politics of a peasant materialist sub-culture displaced the other realities glimpsed by a few writers. Their successors were alienated, isolated 'internal exiles'. The isolation of the writer from the state, he argued, was a sign of social and political instability. The very idea, he argued, of a conversation between, say, Brian O'Nolan and de Valera was almost inconceivable. He could imagine it only in the context of some of the dialogue in *At Swim Two Birds*.[29] However, O'Nolan was hardly the example to prove Stuart's point. He was, by day, a prominent civil servant. As Myles na Gopaleen he lampooned the sacred cows of Irish society in a long-running *Irish Times* column.

For Sheridan, then director of Dublin's Project Arts Centre, the relationship between art, politics and the state was a complex one. In 'The Theatre and Politics' he described the decision by city councillors to cut the Project's grant as at least as political as any production of Brecht, Stuart's example of the politically engaged artist. The theatre, he argued, was all too often portrayed as a refuge, a place of safety from the stresses of the political milieu. The artist, he agreed, needed freedom from the philistines, but this 'alternative' reality depended on subsidy. The theatre of the recluse had become webbed in an ever-widening bureaucratic net. The politics of the theatre often amounted to presenting plays about the working class to a solidly middle-class audience. The challenge, he argued, was to overcome political naivety and to avoid polemical drama that encouraged predictable responses from audiences. His answer necessitated inference on the part of the audience as opposed to political statement to use the dramatic process to depict people in a true and realistic manner so as to engage at an 'emotive level'. Sheridan almost paraphrased Synge in describing his dramatic intent in *No Entry*, his own play about squatters: 'My method was to simply present the family in a true and realistic manner.'[30] If Synge was political in his indifference to political ideology, then Sheridan avoided it because his audience was indifferent to it. It wasn't, he argued, that polemics were bad but that political theatre predicated on left-right British politics didn't play well in Ireland. There was, he wrote, 'no such pleasant niche for a political theatre group here'.[31] Irish political theatre, then, had to engage with the emotions to awaken the political.

A SENSE OF NATION

The second issue, *A Sense of Nation*, began with an editorial that pondered Heaney and Deane's exchange about O'Brien's rebuke of prevalent nationalist thought. Being Irish, Kearney argued, involved something beyond the level of conscious decision. It was possible, he hypothesised, that there was a primitive atavistic layer of Irishness that 'would be much deeper than psychology and quite impossible to divest ourselves of'.[32] Hence the emphasis in *A Sense of Nation* upon archetypes of 'the Irish Soul' and what Tom Paulin described as Platonic idealisations of 'the Irish Mind'. Kearney argued that the sundry articles on these seemed to point to a deep-rooted schizophrenia in the Irish psyche, one caught between humanism and atavism, rationalism versus irrationalism, inner versus outer vision, singular versus plural consciousness, and so on.[33] There was no sociological component in this account of Irish society. Minds, it was suggested, imposed their ideas on other minds. Some of these ideas, it was proposed, were more authentic than others: these were the ones that tapped most closely into the deep-rooted, presumably innate, essences of authentic Irishness. What all this amounted to was an ontological theory of race and race memory with very much in common with earlier Irish-Ireland racial archetypes.[34] In essence Kearney proposed that bad ideals could be countered by more authentic ideals, but the debate was potentially a closed loop predicated upon myths of intrinsic Irish cultural authenticity. To put it another way, the fifth-province family therapy excluded those outside the family. To use the language of the social sciences, it outlined an ethnocentric and mono-cultural conception of social membership.

For O'Brien this emphasis on the authenticity of myth was so much Celtic mist. His sole contribution, 'Nationalism and the Reconquest of Ireland', eschewed any discussion of art in favour of a blunt rebuke to nationalist aspirations for the reunification of Ireland. O'Brien described a symbiosis between nationalist statesmen and the Provisional IRA. This allowed the former to draw political sustenance from the lethal actions they deplored.[35] If a military theoretician might categorise the fighting in Northern Ireland as a 'low-intensity operation' so too was Catholic nationalist politics. Few, he argued, gave much though to political unity, desired it passionately or would sacrifice much to achieve it: 'None the less the aspiration is there: diffuse, elusive, persistent, cryptic, lightly pervasive, a chronic mist.'[36]

For O'Brien, this mist prevented any practical engagement with the political aspirations of both Catholics and Protestants. If O'Brien stressed the need to see beyond the mist, *The Crane Bag* sought to converse with those caught up in it. The key article in the second issue consisted of an interview with Seamus Twomey, Commander-in-Chief of the Provisional IRA, by Mark Patrick Hederman.[37] Twomey described how, if this war was over, he would like to go back to his own ways: going to football matches and maybe placing a few bets on a horse. Hederman professed amazement to find his interviewee so 'human' and 'almost vulnerable', then asked Twomey whether he had qualms about killing other human beings. 'No,' replied Twomey, 'if I felt in my conscience I was right in doing it.' For most of the interview Hederman quizzed Twomey on his understandings of freedom and democracy. In essence Toomey denied the legitimacy of the Republic of Ireland as much as the status quo in the North. Pressed on the matter, Twomey argued that the way in which the IRA was organised exemplified good democratic practice. Everything, he argued, sprung from the grass roots. Volunteers at ground level picked delegates who elected the General Army Convention. In this Convention there were three ruling bodies: the army executive, the army council and GHQ staff. 'The army executive', he explained, 'remains the watch-dog of the movement in case we ever deviate from the path. The executive then chooses an army council who chooses a chief of staff. This, to me, is the true meaning of democracy.'[38]

The path in question, sometimes described as the struggle though not, in this interview as 'the cause', necessitated belief and certainty. In the struggle, Twomey explained, in reply to Hederman's question about killing others: 'You must have no thought whatever that what you are doing might be wrong.' There was no place in the Republican movement, he argued, for those who had even the tiniest doubt.[39] Those who struggled in a different sense with ideological certainty presumably faced the watch-dogs of revolutionary democracy.

Hederman's second contribution to the issue consisted of a meditation on Irishness, in the form of a personal response to David Lean's film *Ryan's Daughter*. Hederman quoted a 1971 review that described it as a film with a little theme that both portrayed Irish country girls in a disgusting immoral light and had little regard for the true situation of the 1916 period. In Ireland it had been received as an insult to both 'Art' and 'Irishry', as 'an outsider's view of Ireland' and though 'made with very beautiful pictures, its soul was no more Irish than its principal actors were'.[40] For Hederman, the greatness of *Ryan's Daughter* was its portrayal of the '*uaigneas*' of the Irish condition. *Uaigneas* translates imperfectly as wistfulness, loneliness or nostalgia. Hederman used the term to describe a characteristic Irish yearning for wild anarchical freedom, 'something more down to earth than Cathleen Ni Houlihan'.[41] Inevitably, Hederman suggested, *Ryan's Daughter*, like much Irish art and intellectual life, bordered on the brink of sentimentality. But the eponymous character, Rosie Ryan, railed against the exterior strictures of ideology and history. The image she provided for the Ireland of the 1970s, that of a young woman, huddled in a blanket, shorn and trembling just after she has been tarred and feathered, the victim of a punishment beating, was hardly whimsy.[42] Hederman maintained that Rosie Ryan stood against the ideological rigidity exemplified by Twomey.

MYTH AND TERROR

A number of contributors to *The Crane Bag* were preoccupied with Yeats's artistic and ideological legacy. One strand of debate emerged from John Hill's 'An Archetype of the Irish Soul' which attempted a Jungian analysis of Yeats's play *Cathleen Ni Houlihan*. Ireland, Hill argued, possessed no original psychology but it did have one of the largest mythologies in Northern Europe. Jung's work, for Hill, suggested that political problems might be solved through an understanding of the 'psychic roots' that 'make us who we are'.[43] Another strand began with a lengthy article on Yeats's artistic and political legacy by Seamus Deane that influenced some subsequent contributors but was much criticised by others.

Yeats, according to Deane, fostered mysticism to retain the consciousness of Irish culture. In Yeats's oeuvre metaphysics and spirituality stood in revolutionary opposition to modernity. This, Deane argued, quoting Theodor Adorno, was a conviction that had true revolutionary impact when we look at the disappearance from the Western consciousness of a sense of eternity.[44] Yeats's revolt was primarily one within himself but, as Deane observed at the beginning of his article, what Yeats did was invent an Ireland amenable to his imagination even if he ended by finding an Ireland resistant to it.[45]

Deane located Yeats alongside Nietzsche, Blake and Shelley in a European Romantic tradition which combined a revolutionary aesthetic with a traditionalist politics. He described Yeats's dominant theme as regeneration, as a means of emancipation from the manacles forged by a conspiracy between British empiricism and industrial capitalism. Yeats was therefore to be understood as a critic of modernity. For Deane, Yeats did for Irishness what Coleridge did for Englishness. He conjured up a Romantic Ireland that, like its English equivalent, pre-dated Locke, Hobbes and Bacon. Romantic Ireland was therefore set against the empirical tradition of the Enlightenment:

> Thus Berkeley's attack on Locke could be tied in with Swift's attack on the Royal Society and Burke's on the French Revolution. Between them they composed for Yeats an Irish Ascendency

> tradition of 'idealism' which he associated with the folk tradition in Ireland, claiming that each refuted science by its apprehension (although differently in each case) of mystery and death. The peasant and the aristocrat, kindred in spirit but not in class, united in the great Romantic battle against the industrial and utilitarian ethic.[46]

Yeats's politics, as described by Deane, were rooted in a conception of Ireland as a revolutionary country. Ireland was the only place in Europe where Romanticism might prevail, where the aristocrats and peasants had a fair chance of winning the great cultural battle against utilitarianism. He accorded Ireland's 'technological and economic backwardness the benefit of a spiritual glamour which had faded from the rest of Europe'.[47] The fly in the ointment was a middle class that, as portrayed in *September 1913*, could not but fumble in the greasy till. Deane depicted this disparagement of the middle classes as an inevitable social extension of Yeats's Romantic aesthetic. The middle classes stood condemned for their poverty of imagination. Yeats, according to Deane, emphasised the necessity of retaining a consciousness of death, something lost to the modern middle-class world, as a vehicle for idealistic rebirth. In Deane's account, Yeats's preoccupation with reincarnation, with Nietzchean notions such as eternal recurrence, and his fostering of imaginative nationalism rooted in ancient stories coalesced in the blood sacrifice of 1916:

> The men of 1916 had offered their deaths to history. In doing so they had broken the cycle of eternal recurrence. Their consciousness of themselves became the consciousness of the race. Irish difference, Irish uniqueness, the basis after all for the Gaelic-nationalist claim to independence, had been mediated through death. Yeats's aesthetic became then, more and more politicised under the pressure of the crisis which had afflicted his country. It could not but emerge as a conviction that the Irish had a crucial, redemptive role to play in the recovery of European civilisation from barbarism. Easter Week made the great war look like a mindless, despiritualised carnage.[48]

Mindless carnage could be contrasted with the presumably noble, justifiable, heroic carnage unleashed by the Easter Rebellion. The sacrifice of Pearse as rendered in *Under Ben Bulben* amounted to a new and specifically Irish version of modern existential heroism.

Deane's Yeats, then, was not a poet who might have given Seamus Twomey cause to have any qualms about killing for Ireland.

Deane then went on to argue that Yeats 'desperately' distorted the events of 1916. In depicting the rebellion as aristocratic he denied its essentially bourgeois character. Yeats the aristocrat found himself, so to speak, on the wrong side of Irish history and outside, even, the consciousness of the Irish 'race'. Yeats vindicated the nationalist cause but was also, Deane seemed to imply, to be discarded from the nation as doubly tainted for endorsing both colonialism and fascism. Deane's specific charge was that Yeats's 'so called fascism' was, 'an almost pure specimen of the colonialist mentality'. Yeats's Irish Romanticism, modelled on English poetic Romanticism, could indeed be a servant of nationalist ideology. However, in Deane's view, it should be ultimately repudiated by it as an alien attempt to re-create the degraded English motherland in an Irish colonial setting. Deane discovered in Yeats 'a complex act of colonial repossession, comparable to the sort of thing one hears in the blowsy rhetoric of Northern Irish Protestants or Rhodesians'.[49] Here, then, Deane moved far beyond a reading of Yeats's poetry, using, to some extent, the sort of criteria for judging art advanced in Mew's 'A Marxist View of Art and Politics'. Yeats's art was to be examined in terms of its nationalist revolutionary potential. It was to be understood as an expression of the contradictions inherent in the author's ascendancy perspective. Despite this perspective it was to be valued for its focus on the deep experiential realities of its time. Yeats, then, was permitted to cheer on the nationalist cause from the sidelines.

Deane's ambivalence towards Yeats might well be located in a historical reading of the gradual displacement of Protestants within Irish nationalism from the second half of the nineteenth century. S.J. Connolly, for instance, argues that the Gaelic revival was initially fostered by a Protestant elite anxious to reaffirm its place in Irish society at a time when an increasingly strident political rhetoric identified Irishness with Catholicism.[50] During the late eighteenth century it had been Protestant patriots who had first linked an assertion of Irish constitutional rights to an exalted vision of the Gaelic past. The Young Irelanders further developed claims to independence based on cultural identity and drew on Gaelic literary heritage as raw material for political symbolism and propaganda. Connolly further argues that the impetus for Protestant cultural nationalism was provided by threats of social and political modernisation which threatened its elite status within Irish society and was set in opposition to 'the contemporary reality of an unruly democratic politics and an upstart Catholic bourgeoisie'.[51] As such it provided a conservative ideology which drew upon idealisations of rural society and pastoral tranquillity as the authentic source of Irishness.[52] It also emphasised an 'elite harmony' that extolled the virtues of a society where aristocrat and peasant were bound by shared cultural values and mutual respect. In Deane's reading, Yeats, the Romantic extoller of aristocratic nationalism and presumed despiser of the (Catholic) middle classes, found himself on the wrong of a line that defined Irishness in terms of religion and social class.

The following issue of *The Crane Bag* elaborated on the topic of the Irish Mind. Hederman's article on James Joyce's *The Dead* advanced an account of myth that built on Hill's Jungian one in the previous issue. It also owed something to American pragmatist philosophy. Joyce, for Hederman, was the best teacher on the use of myth. 'Unlike the leprechaun-fanciers of the Celtic Revival,' Hederman quoted, 'Joyce did not seek forgotten beauty; he evoked the past to illuminate the present.'[53] He described Joyce's achievement as connecting what William James termed 'the stream of consciousness' to what Jung termed 'racial unconsciousness', beyond individual dream to collective myth.[54] Joyce and Jung, then, were the right men for the job of unpicking the Irish mind.

Deane's article on Yeats met trenchant criticism in Augustine Martin's 'What Stalked through the Post Office?' Martin argued that Deane was wrong on all counts about Yeats's attitudes to Ireland, revolution, death, poetry and class. He took no issue with Deane's account of Yeats as a Romantic who sided with Blake, Coleridge, Nietzsche against Swift, Burke and Berkeley, whose champions of light were the noble and the beggar, who saw the middle classes as slaves to materialism and disparaged their fear of death. However, he expressed deep unease about how Deane brought these positions to bear on Yeats's 'very complex reactions to the Easter Rising'.[55]

In the first place, Martin argued, Yeats's dismissal of the middle classes was overstated by Deane. Furthermore, Deane's 'Marxist inflection' suggested a reading of Yeats's poetry that the poet could not have intended. Neither Deane's emphasis on the 'middle class' nor his understanding of what Yeats meant by aristocracy stood up. *September 1913*, Martin insisted, was directed against the then present times and not against any particular social group. Yeats was preoccupied with a personal aesthetic of nobility rather than the social status of the aristocracy. Up to 1916 Yeats probably did not regard the

Irish middle classes as redeemable but his poems about 1916, especially *Sixteen Men Dead*, reversed that judgement. Martin furthermore objected to the appropriation of Yeats as a cheerleader for revolution by citing *Nineteen Hundred and Nineteen*, his great poem about the war of independence or, as Martin put it, the Black and Tan war:

> Now the days are dragon-ridden, the nightmare
> Rides upon sleep: a drunken soldiery
> Can leave the mother, smothered at her door,
> To crawl in her own blood, and go scot-free;
> The night can sweat with terror as before
> We pieced our thoughts into philosophy,
> And planned to bring the world under a rule,
> Who are but weasels fighting in a hole.

If then the events of 1916 changed his mind about *September 1913* then *Nineteen Hundred and Nineteen* can be read as a rethink of 1916, a rethink which was followed by further reconsiderations. Martin quoted *The Great Day*, a 1938 poem as an example of Yeats's antipathy to the glorification of violence and war:

> Hurrah for revolution and more cannon shot!
> A beggar on horseback lashes a beggar on foot.
> Hurrah for revolution and cannon come again!
> The beggars have changed places, but the lash goes on.

Martin argued that Yeats's attitudes to revolution shifted and shifted again as part of an unremitting life-long passionate dialectic meditation between self and soul and between truth and counter-truth. While Deane identified Yeats's great theme as one of regeneration (one that could be yoked to nations and nationalisms) Martin saw it as proccupation about the relationship between greatness (or nobility) and violence. Both qualities might be extolled in eulogies to Pearse or Cuchulain, but their costs then might be ruefully pondered in work concerned with the bitter consequences of real civil war. The Romantic celebration of myth could also be soured by reflection on the bloody consequences of heroic myth-making. Here Martin quoted *Meditations in Time of Civil War*:

We had fed our heart on fantasies,
The heart's grown brutal from the fare;
More substance in our enmities
Than in our love ...

Martin zeroed in upon Deane's fleeting reference to Yeats's 'so-called fascism'. This in Deane's article took the form of a fleeting reference to Conor Cruise O'Brien's 1965 essay 'Passion and Cunning' to disparage the authenticity of Yeats's Irishness. What O'Brien had done was to connect Yeats's presumed ambivalence towards fascism and towards nationalist violence. Deane's nationalist, anti-colonialist and somewhat Marxist stance allowed him to choose, somewhat disingenuously, not to engage with this argument. Martin responded with an examination of the later works that had put the poet in the dock as a fascist fellow traveller. He described these as yet another transitional phase in the poet's thinking to be viewed as a disreputable staging post to further different thoughts about the human condition. Yeats certainly provided a hostage to fortune when he wrote in his 1939 essay 'On the Boiler' that: 'The Fascist countries know that civilisation has reached a crisis' and that: 'The danger is that there will be no war, that the skilled will attempt nothing, that European civilisation, like those older civilisations that also saw the triumph of the gangrel stocks will accept decay.'[56] But this, Martin pointed out, was not the same as wanting to throw Ireland's lot in with European fascism. Why, wrote Yeats in a 1938 letter cited by Martin, should he trouble about communism, fascism, liberalism, radicalism when all were going downstream in the artificial unity that ended every civilisation?[57] Yeats's Romanticism envisaged Ireland or, more precisely, an indominatible Irishry as prevailing, ignoring or otherwise holding out from modernity and from Europe's mindless carnage. For Martin this was illustrated in the last stanza of *Under Ben Bulben*:

When Pearse summoned Cuchulain to his side
What stalked through the Post Office? What intellect
What calculation, number, measurement, replied?
We Irish, born into that ancient sect
But thrown upon this filthy modern tide,
And by its formless spawning fury wrecked,
Climb to our proper dark, that we may trace
The linaments of a plummet-measured face.

The custody battle over Yeats in *The Crane Bag* was the inevitable consequence of agreement amongst the main contributors about the relationship between art and politics. As fought between Deane and Martin it was one between sectarian and pluralist possibilities. Kearney weighted in with an article entitled 'Myth and Terror' that related questions about Yeats's legacy and the political symbolism of the 1916 uprising to the Northern conflict. Here Kearney attempted to flesh out his earlier emphasis on the role of myth. He distinguished between what he called a political hermeneutic, the basis of orthodox constitutional, economic and historical interpretations of the Northern Ireland Conflict and a sort of depth-hermeneutic that would be capable of detecting 'the more occult motivations operative in Ulster terrorism'.[58] Here he drew much on the work of his doctoral supervisor Paul Ricoeur. He quoted Ricoeur as depicting, in a study entitled *Civilisation and National Culture*, political nationalist movements as surface-signs which need to be deciphered. If terrorism was an articulation of political nationalism, then, it was suggested, this in turn was determined by some sort of cultural deep structure. To penetrate this, Ricoeur advised, one had to cut through to the layer of symbols and images that made up the ideals of a particular nation or national group.[59]

In particular Kearney focused on a claim by the Provisional IRA in 1970 that 'we take our inspiration from the past', which he related to Seamus Twomey's defence of 'the militant Republican tradition' in the first issue, the invocation of the Easter 1916 Proclamation of the Provisional Government of the Irish Republic, a profound identification with the heroes of Easter week. Like the 1916 Proclamation, the IRA legitimised the Republic in the name of the 'dead generations' who had sacrificed themselves for her nationhood.[60] Kearney traced the 'cultural deep-structure' of the Republican tradition to a mythical nucleus latent in the symbolism of Easter 1916, the reference of the Proclamation to dead generations, mythic heroes (Cuchulain and Cathleen Ni Houlihan), a mythos of blood sacrifice and renewal; Pearce had written of 'new generations' that had been baptised in Fenian blood, suggesting parallels between the Easter Rising and Christ's sacrifice. But, Kearney argued, the whole mythos of sacrifice found its clearest formulation in Yeats's poetic testimony of 'the Irish nationalist uprising'. In *Easter 1916*, Yeats professed astonishment at how such mediocre men as MacDonogh, Connolly and Pearse had been totally transformed by sacrifice: 'Now and in time to come / wherever green is worn / (they) are changed, changed utterly / A terrible beauty is born.'[61]

That same issue included an interview by Kearney with Paul Ricoeur entitled 'Myth as Bearer of Possible Worlds'. Prompted by Kearney, Ricoeur spoke of an opaque kernel beyond the self-understanding of a society that could not be reduced to empirical norms or laws. This kernel, was, he said, 'constitutive of a culture before it could be expressed'. It was 'reflected in specific representations or ideas'.[62] From this perspective, according to Ricoeur, myth could be subjected to hermeneutical analysis. Myths, he argued, had histories and were kept alive through processes of interpretation and re-interpretation. Societies, therefore had mythic nuclei. Here Ricoeur drew on conceptions of social structure advanced by Lévi-Strauss.[63]

Ricoeur argued that societal myths could be perverted and distorted. He gave the example of how European Fascist movements were characterised by a mythic glorification of blood-sacrifice and the hero-saviour and the revival of certain ancient rituals, symbols and insignia. Kearney pressed him on the question of the perversion of myth. Kearney had, in his 'Myth and Terror', sought to represent the mythic structures of extreme Irish Republicanism, such as its emphasis on the recurrence of blood-sacrifice, as deviant manifestations of an original mythical nucleus. These, he argued, needed to be demythologised as a resuscitation of genuine ones. Kearney elaborated by contrasting Yeats unfavourably with Joyce:

> In the Celtic Twilight literature of Yeats, Lady Gregory and others myth seems to have been appropriated as a 'chronicle' of the spiritual origins of the race. For this reason it often strikes one as suffering from a certain hazy occultism and introversion. Joyce on the other hand, used myth, and particularly the myth of Finn, in its 'wisdom dimension'; that is, as an Irish archetype open to, and capable of assimilating the rich resources of entirely different cultures. *Finnegans Wake* seems to me to be an exemplary synthesis of the particular and universal claims of myth.[64]

Ricoeur replied in somewhat more down-to-earth terms that the myths of communities could easily be perverted; for example, through chauvinistic nationalism or racism. Genuine myth, he argued, had a universal dimension. It had the potential to exceed the limits of any particular community or nation. It was, he argued, somehow characterised by a concern for the universal liberation of men. It could find expression in poetry or myth. Both were 'not just nostalgia for some forgotten world. They constitute a disclosure of new and unprecedented worlds, an opening onto other possible worlds.'[65] Hederman's article on Joyce in the same issue described him as having become 'the mouthpiece of the psychic history of his time'. This issue as a whole, Hederman argued, 'suggests that myth is one of the most important sources of enlightenment in our present situation in Ireland and that James Joyce is the person best suited to the task of teaching us how to use myth effectively'.[66] For both Kearney and Hederman the alternative ideal world was Joycean rather than Yeatsean.

THE RIDDLE OF SACRIFICE

The two issues of *The Crane Bag* published in its third year were edited by Deane. His opening editorial was somewhat disparaging of Kearney's fifth-province quest:

> No authoritative vision of Ireland has emerged in recent times to take account of the economic and demographic changes and the various forms of political crisis which marked or marred the last fifteen or twenty years. In this dishevelled and unattractive situation in which the 'Grocer's Republic' mentality struggles to survive in a consumer society, *The Crane Bag* introduces, mildly enough, some of the old questions, seeking new answers or seeking to acknowledge the impotence of the questions themselves.[67]

Instead, Deane emphasised the idea of an Irish tradition. The issue kicked off with an article by Declan Kiberd making the case for Irish Studies programmes. Kiberd emphasised the ambivalent status of the Irish language within the study of Irish literature. Irish Studies should, he argued, take both Anglo-Irish and Gaelic literature out of their respective quarantines and reassess writers in the context of the culture of the whole island, its politics and history, its folklore and geography. This required bilingual academics, teachers and programmes, no easy matter when at present, he argued: 'the denizens of our English departments patrol their corridors daily to ensure that no Gaelic expert penetrates the building, least of all a Gaelic scholar with the highest qualifications in English'.[68] Similar preoccupations emerged in a number of other articles on Ireland's literary traditions. One argued that a literature that included Yeats and Joyce was in no danger of neglect. These, together with Synge, Shaw, O'Casey, Wilde and Moore, ensured the viability of an Anglo-Irish literature academic industry.[69]

Deane's own 'An Example of Tradition' emphasised Matthew Arnold's revival of Edmund Burke's writings on Ireland and the centrality of Burke to nineteenth-century liberal thinking about Ireland; for instance, the repeal of Penal Laws and efforts to kill Home Rule with kindness. In 1867 his *Lectures on the Study of Celtic Literature* were published. In 1881 Arnold had produced an anthology, *Edmund Burke on Irish Affairs*, and argued in its preface for a degree of Celtic cultural independence.[70] Deane cast Arnold (and Burke by association) as parent to the subsequently prevalent archetype of the vitalic 'Celt as dreamer, imaginative, unblessed by the Greek sense of form, at home in wild landscapes', and so as the antithesis of European political and social modernity. Arnold's idealisation of the Celtic race, according to Deane, influenced subsequent Irish peasant archetypes from *The Playboy of the Western World* to the paintings of Jack B. Yeats. Yet, Deane argued, his call for a Celtic revival also informed a sectarian and even racial conception of Irishness. This, according to Deane, was distinct from the Anglo-Irish tradition that Yeats created out of Swift, Berkeley, Goldsmith and also Burke. It was distinct from the heroic revolutionary tradition that Pearse created out of Wolfe Tone and Robert Emmet. Through Arnold, Deane argued, a notion of Celtic Ireland had 'removed itself to Britain, encased in Burke's capricious reputation', to return later as an unlikely (and presumably inauthentic) influence on the Irish literary revival.[71]

The *Idea of Tradition* issue also included a reflection on Kearney's 'Myth and Terror' by Joseph Stephen O'Leary. This was entitled 'The Riddle of Sacrifice'.[72] O'Leary emphasised the 'creative or life-promoting function of sacrifice' from a theological standpoint but took issue with the legacy of 1916: 'Their sense of doing a glorious thing was not all delusion', but a narrow Gaelic tribal identity sat at odds with the broader horizons of Christian sacrifice. Their sacrifice imprisoned Gaelic identity in tribal self-worship. For O'Leary, Kearney's account of these myths of sacrifice missed out their value as a source of moral inspiration as 'just resistance to oppression'. The 'new primitivism' of the IRA found its contrast in the spirit of sacrifice amongst non-violent groups seeking to create a new society in Northern Ireland. It was possible, O'Leary contended, to draw positive inspiration from Pearse's dedication to his cause.[73]

Deane's postscript to the two issues he edited, *The Idea of Tradition* and *Anglo-Irish Literature*, proclaimed that the Ireland of 1979 sought its origins amongst the interpretations of those who helped to produce it – Yeats and Pearse, Burke and Parnell, Joyce and de Valera.[74] He restated the purpose of *The Crane Bag* as one of reappraisal of such figures and of the forces embodied in cultural and nationalist movements:

> In both these issues of *The Crane Bag*, the contributors have examined some of these forces and figures in a spirit of reappraisal, tending as a rule to the view that conventional notions of what the Irish tradition is or was are in need of some repair or are seriously outmoded.[75]

What specific repairs were needed remained unclear. We must learn, he chided, 'not to exaggerate the claims which a transient excitement or crisis might inspire us to make. There was no emergent, systematic or organic reformulation either of Irish tradition, Irish dilemmas, of Irish problems.'[76] He argued that in the larger scheme of things the two literary issues of 1979 warranted a less than benevolent response. It could be argued that such literary emphasis was a form of evasion and a covert expression of conservativism in the face of the critical questions on the Irish table. Deane concluded, from his own nationalist vantage point, that the *Crane Bag* project was a conservative one:

> Ireland, by which in this instance I mean the Republic, may now be reaching that point where defending her way of life is more important to her than dreaming towards that yet to come. The year 1972 saw a very definite turn on the part of the republic from its earlier attitude to Northern Ireland. Despite Bloody Sunday and the prolonging of Stormont, Dublin was politically muted. The burning of the British Embassy was no more than a gesture, an allowed release of energy after which attention returned to the real consequences of those late January days – the effects upon the Republic's trade and tourism. This is all very deflationary towards any heroic ideal and very far removed from either Jack or W.B. Yeats's Irelands. But it is perhaps that very defensive practicality and conservativism which, in disguised form, operates here in *The Crane Bag* also. Perhaps we are as willing to go so far as to say in literature we are one – almost. Perhaps we are rephrasing Burke's magnificently deployed arguments in favour of traditional complexity against the *simplisme* of revolution. This may be so.[77]

The 'Grocer's Republic', as Deane disparagingly put it in his previous editorial, had possibly won. Yeats' lines in *September 1913*, written before 1916, 'Romantic Ireland's dead and gone / it's with O'Leary in the grave' could be read literally. The myths of 1916 could be set aside. Whether to do so was a covert manifestation of conservatism, an act of insidious conservation or a courage to demystify was open to interpretation. Deane's postscript to his second issue as editor concluded that he would prefer to think the latter and ended by quoting Bertolt Brecht as saying to Walter Benjamin: 'do not build on the good old days but on the bad new ones'.[78]

THE TALKING CURE

The Crane Bag ran until 1984 when, exhausted by the effort, Hederman and Kearney laid it to rest.[79] From 1980 onwards the themes addressed became broader. The first issue in 1980 was entitled *Images of the Irish Woman*. It contained the expected admixture of articles on women in Irish mythology, art and literature but also, unlike previous issues, articles with a strong empirical focus. These included '10 Years of Progress? Some Statistics' by Betty Purcell and 'Women in Higher Education in Ireland' by Eileen Breathnach. The issue reflected the struggles and achievements of Irish feminists during the 1970s when many overt gender inequalities in employment, law and welfare were challenged.[80] It included a dialogue between two subsequent Irish Presidents, Mary Robinson and Mary McAleese, on divorce, contraception, abortion, child care and law reform. The guest editor, Christine Nulty, and most of the contributors, were women.

The second 1980 issue, entitled *The Northern Issue*, again had empirical content and political commentary unmediated by art or literature. This included 'A Register of Northern Ireland's Casualities' by Michael McKeown, 'The Class Structure of Ulster Unionism' by David McKittrick and an analysis of British commitment to retaining the North as part of the United Kingdom by Michael McDowell. There was, then, in both 1980 issues, a sense of acting on Deane's conclusion that the bad new days must be addressed directly. The editorial of *The Northern Issue* emphasised an indifference to the North in the Republic. Having sought to wean (Southern) nationalists off the 1916 tradition of nationalist myth ('negative nationalism' as Barre Fitzpatrick's editorial put it) the emphasis was now to be upon practical dialogue, political re-engagement and an unflinching look at the dynamics of the Northern conflict. The issue inevitably considered intellectual interpretations of these dynamics. An article by Percy

Allum surveyed different historiographical interpretations of 'The Irish Question'.[81] Historiography has been, perhaps, the most evident cleavage in Irish intellectual life.[82] To no little extent the conflicts between Green and so-called 'revisionist' interpretations of the Irish historical past match the contours of the readings of national myth and literature that preoccupied *The Crane Bag*.

For Kearney the problem was not essentially about the empirical past or even the empirical present. Any hopes that the blood-sacrifice mythos of 1916 had been laid to rest unravelled in the face of the H-Block dirty protests and hunger strikes. Kearney's 1980 article 'The IRA's Strategy of Failure' maintained that the hunger strikes had become invested with the sanctity of a sacrificial rite:

> The sacrificial victim must undergo his passion and crucifixion before arising to liberate his community from its bondage. By commemorating the violence of their Fenian forebears, the IRA seem to be operating on the prerational and atavistic conviction that they can fulfil the redemptive promise of their martyrdom.[83]

Kearney argued that although the IRA could not achieve military victory it was pointless to view the conflict, as British governments did, as one that would result in their defeat. The IRA campaign had acquired a sacrificial mystique. Yet the sacrificial victories of the IRA necessitated the conspiracy of a oppressor willing to oppress. British policy had added much grist to the sacrificial mill. Nowhere, he argued, in Republican 'theology' was sacrifice more evident and effective than in the current H-Block blanket process. Prior to the hunger strikes the IRA had become a spent and discredited force. Now it was a Christ-like one reborn in sacrifice. The 'patriot game', then, consciously invoked mythologies of past endurance and self-sacrifice and set new ones in train. The myths in question were communal and vicariously shared between martyrs and the broader community.

In the 1980 *Northern Issue* Hederman recalled his initial hope that *The Crane Bag* would help in a small but specific way to clarify the problems that have 'haunted every Irish person for the last two decades'.[84] He recalled the critical uproar that had emerged in response to publication of his Twomey interview. In the Republic Conor Cruise O'Brien as Minister for Posts and Telegraphs had introduced legislation preventing the IRA from accessing state (RTÉ) radio and television stations, denying them what Margaret Thatcher once called the oxygen of publicity. There had been a House of

Commons debate about funding of *The Crane Bag* by the Arts Council of Northern Ireland. Hederman admitted that the Twomey interview might have given the IRA a critical boost, but argued that O'Brien's tactics were wrong. He recalled Heaney's assertion in the first issue that O'Brien, as an intellectual, 'did an utterly necessary job' in rebuking all easy thought about Ulster Protestants but suggested, in quoting Heaney, that such censorship also fostered facile thought about the problem of Irish nationalism:

> The kind of humanism which Conor Cruise O'Brien sponsors is precisely the kind of humanism, totally detached from its atavisms, which though, welcome from a rational point of view, renders much of what he says either irrelevant or simply wrong, particularly in relation to the North where bigotry is so much part of the psyche ... The very clarity of O'Brien's position is just what is most objectionable. It serves to give a rational clarity to the Northern situation which is untrue to its reality. In other words, is not his humanism here being used as an excuse to rid Ireland of its atavisms, which give it life even though the life may be in some ways brutal?[85]

The approach of the *Crane Bag* editors had been to question the capacity of such rational humanism to address the Northern problem and to argue for another form of understanding. However, Hederman recalled, it was first necessary to consider such arguments seriously. In June 1977 Hederman wrote to O'Brien and put his cards on the table:

> The Heaney/Deane interview in the first issue of *The Crane Bag* discusses you in terms of the rationalistic rejection of the atavistic adherence to roots that defy logical endorsement. Mary Holland in *The Observer* suggests that you are trying to teach us a history lesson too early after the history has happened and suggests that you are wrong. When I heard your lecture on Simone Weil it did strike me that you were perhaps a privileged kind of person, more cosmopolitan and European than the ordinary Irish person, and you could afford to exchange the 'nationalism' in your life and your blood for something like 'culture' or 'mysticism'. On the other hand, there would seem to be an Irish set of Archetypes, which form part of that collectivity unearthed by Jung, from which we cannot escape. Your desire to demythicize us is, perhaps, an impossibility, and one which can only serve to drive the 'reality' even more deeply and dangerously underground.[86]

O'Brien had given a lecture on the French philosopher Simone Weil on 21 Feburary 1977. Hederman, writing in 1980, explained why this intrigued him. Weil's philosophy was, as he put it, an unusual and highly personal form of mysticism, one which Hederman, a Benedictine, one of the monks of Glenstall, was well placed to appreciate. Why, he pondered, was O'Brien, the rational humanist, devoting attention to Weil? He was at that moment a man of many parts: Cabinet Minister, influential intellectual but yet isolated from the collective Irish 'us' that Hederman and Kearney sought to identify with. O'Brien, for Hederman, was preoccupied with a different form of martyrdom, one that excluded him from the various but intertwined shades of Irishness that made up *The Crane Bag*:

> While he was talking it became apparent to me that although his subject was Simone Weil, he was really using her to describe his own isolated position in Irish politics. Her unusual and highly personal philosophy which had led to her political martyrdom, was almost like a mirror image of his own. As events later unfolded, this comparison took on something of a prophetic quality. Before that year had ended Conor Cruise O'Brien had been rejected by his constituents and forced into exile in England, where he became an Editor-in-Chief of *The Observer*.[87]

For Hederman, O'Brien's actions were of little significance compared to ones anchored to communal myth. This was both a pragmatic observation – nationalist sacrifice had grave consequences whilst self-mythology did not when it emanated from someone who placed himself outside the tribe – but it also seemed that Hederman could not envisage a sense of Irish identity that was not beholden to communal myth. Or, did not want to. It made no sense then not to talk to the IRA. Twomey's interview could be justified because he represented for *The Crane Bag* a symptom of how the most pathological manifestations of Irish consciousness were exaggerations of those contained within the norm:

> He is a child of that psychic hinterland, made up of history, religion, education, culture and mythology, which is one that most Irish people share with him. Unless we are able to go behind his words, as effects, and examine the causes which produced them, we will never be able to root out the evil which lurks at various depths within the psyche of us all.[88]

Twomey was, then, no isolated exception to be dealt with in the way in which terrified medieval communities dealt with witches. He could not be locked in the attic, as Hederman put it, like Rochester's mad wife in *Jane Eyre*.

How then could Irish atavisms be faced? For Hederman, Joyce could be held up as someone who sought to extricate himself from the inevitable clutches of his own psychic atavisms rather than deny their existence.[89] He had criticised Heaney for being a reluctant poet.[90] This, he now emphasised, was a philosophical criticism rather than a literary one 'of Heaney's reluctance to serve as a guide to the psychic underworld of Northern Ireland'.[91] Politics, he stressed once again, should not be elevated at the expense of poetic authenticity. Yet what he asked of Heaney overlapped with Deane's insistence that the unwillingness of the Northern poets at large to adopt a political stance on the Troubles amounted to a denial of communal atavism.

An article by O'Brien the following year suggested that nationalist family therapy needed to look outwards as did others in the *Minorities in Ireland* issue. O'Brien examined how politicians in the Republic addressed Northern Protestants in speeches that advocated a united Ireland. Inevitably these were, he argued, addressing 'imaginary Protestants' as their audiences were overwhelmingly Catholic. In reality, he observed, Northern Catholics would be less easy to assimilate into the Republic than Southern Protestants had proved to be.[92] In the same issue Garret FitzGerald emphasised the need to pluralise the 1937 Irish Constitution as a necessary prelude to making the case for Irish unity. There was a need to reassure Northern Protestants that the Republic could be a state that they could feel at home in. This prefigured his subsequent abortive Constitutional Crusade as Taoiseach.[93] Other articles emphasised the need to address social and demographic change, poverty, 'racialism' against Travellers, homosexuality and the marginalisation of Protestant minorities.

THE NEW GOOD MYTH

The Crane Bag loosely reflected the sort of critique of Western rationality that Theodor Adorno and the Frankfurt School developed from the work of Max Weber. This suggested that that the ontological and material oppressions of disenchanted modern systems fostered oppression and inhumanity. The consequences of modernity for Weber and his successors included the rationalisation and disenchantment of life. If *The Crane Bag* stood against anything it stood against disenchantment. Crucially, Heaney described O'Brien as the obstinate voice of rationalist humanism. Being obstinate and isolated hardly constituted a position of dominance. Yet nothing, Deane had written, in 1979 sounding almost like O'Brien, was more monotonous or despairing than the search for the essence which defined a nation: 'The nineteenth and twentieth centuries have managed to outwear the patience of most rational people with this issue.'[94] From this perspective, what *The Crane Bag* generally referred to as rational humanism constituted not so much an oppressive denial of the broader non-empirical conceptions of reality coveted by poets and Romantic idealists as a 'deracinated' one. Yet Kearney and Hederman were uncomfortable about the prevailing sense of Irish identity and its governing myths. For Kearney, the fifth province aimed to trump bad myths with good ones. For Hederman, it was about a poetic wild anarchic individual freedom against a tyranny of oppressive nationalist ones.

However, the mythic bulwark of Irish archetypes and ideals cherished within *The Crane Bag* was in the main a nationalist one. It was ultimately an exclusionary bulwark in that it posited the notion of an Irish soul or an Irish mind and indeed an Irish race that was somehow intrinsically authentic and distinctive. From this perspective even Yeats, the high priest of national myth, could be excluded from the tribe, or O'Brien's deracinated cosmopolitism dismissed as inauthentic. The dialogues in *The Crane Bag* were green on green. That was their strength and their weakness. The *Crane Bag* project was a culturally bounded one; it was a family affair. However, against any tendency towards parochialism stood the influence of James Joyce, highlighted in particular by Gerald Goldberg's seminal article on Irish anti-Semitism, 'Joyce and the Arts in Ireland'.[95] Goldberg discussed the Citizen character in *Ulysses* as a composite of a number of actual prominent nationalists, most notably Michael Cusack and Arthur Griffith, founder of Sinn Fein. Goldberg outlined how Joyce's fiction drew upon a detailed factual awareness of anti-Semitism in the Ireland of 1904. Kearney and Hederman advanced Joyce as the antidote to the intemperate myths 'brilliantly curated' by Yeats.

The idea of a fifth province introduced in the first issue of *The Crane Bag* by Kearney and Hederman was never really engaged with by other contributors and the various guest editors, even if Seamus Heaney subsequently lent it his eloquence. To a considerable extent, though, *The Crane Bag* itself fulfilled the fifth-province manifesto as an act of literary choreography cum political reappraisal. As Deane put it in 1979, there was a curious tension between the imaginative achievement of Irish literature and the more limited one of Irish political culture.[96] No wonder, then, that literary criticism became a vehicle for political discourse. *The Crane Bag*, like many such journals, had a limited circulation, two thousand or so, but it did prove influential. Kearney, Deane and Kiberd became significant academic figures and influential public intellectuals. The 1984 edition *Ireland: Dependence and Independence* consisted of lectures that had been previously televised. Kearney, in particular, persisted with his fifth-province project.[97] It was subsequently adopted symbolically in the area of clinical and research work on sexualised abuse in Dublin's Mater Hospital by the Fifth Province Associates during the 1980s to refer to therapeutic goals of disqualifying no voices, including those of abusers.[98] Kearney had a hand in Mary Robinson's inaugural speech as President.[99] She regurgitated whole chunks of his original 1977 editorial in explaining to the electorate how her presidency symbolised a fifth province.[100] This, she said, expanding on Kearney's imaginary space, included the 70 million or so people of Irish descent around the world – as Yeats had put it: 'wherever Green is worn'. In such terms the fifth province remained green on green, a metaphor for extended family therapy rather than any broader pluralism.

Of the five journals examined in this book *The Crane Bag* most self-consciously adhered to what might be regarded as the archetype of the intellectual journal. Its main contributors strove to be entrepreneurial and influential within Irish intellectual politics. Kearney and Hederman related their philosophical preferences to nationalist debates about the Northern conflict with considerable flair. Their ability to do so contrasted favourably with the often incoherent efforts of fellow contributors to apply then fashionable Marxist literary theory to modern Ireland. Overall, *The Crane Bag* had a coherent political project related to a specific ethno-nationalist imagined community. This sense of its audience was the key to its success. Yet much of what was written about what Kearney called the 'Irish Mind' was in the grip of earlier phases of cultural nationalism. In *The Crane Bag* the intellectual battles of the Celtic Twilight were retold and re-fought. If Kearney emphasised a need to engage with the myths and martyrs of 1916 Deane was compelled to re-challenge the arguments of Matthew Arnold and the authenticity of the Irishness of Edmund Burke or W.B. Yeats in a fashion that restaged 1930s literary debates.[101] Taken alongside earlier advocacy of Romantic nationalism and cultural isolationism (considered in subsequent chapters on *The Bell* and *Studies*), the nation-building project of *The Crane Bag* appears quite old-fashioned, one anchored to conceptions of national identity debated and challenged by Irish intellectuals even prior to 1916; hence the decision to locate this chapter at the beginning of this account of Irish twentieth-century intellectual politics.

CHAPTER TWO

Out of the Mist: *The Bell, 1940–45*

Thirty-seven years before *The Crane Bag* was hatched a very different journal with a mission of thinking for Ireland was launched. The first issue of *The Bell* was published in November 1940. Sean O'Faolain named it after *Kolokol*, a nineteenth century anti-government, anti-censorship and anti-isolationist Russian journal edited-by Alexander Herzen.[1] *The Bell* published new Irish fiction and poetry, but these were ancillary to its main intended purpose of documenting life in Irish society. O'Faolain's second editorial was something of a manifesto. He enjoined future contributors to note how writers in the magazine drew on actual experience. There was, for example, a first-hand account of a local theatre. There was one on life in a teacher training college rather than an opinion piece on whether teachers were properly trained. An article on the need for prison reform was based on a detailed account of prison visits by the author. Two further articles, 'Orphans' and 'I Live in a Slum', were documentary 'pieces from real life'. Do not, O'Faolain begged, write articles on abstract subjects. The mission of *The Bell* was simple but radical. We are, O'Faolain wrote, 'writing about our own people, our own generation, our own institutions' in a 'decent, friendly, possibly hot-tempered, but always polite and constructive way'.[2]

Subsequent editorials reiterated the goal of keeping both feet on the ground – 'life about us put down clearly and faithfully' – and of avoiding controversy for its own sake: 'the sort of thing that goes on, and on, night after night, in pubs and back kitchens and front parlours and never gets us anywhere'. The business of describing Irish life honestly and plainly was vital if slavish imitation of other nations was to be avoided: 'When Ireland reveals herself truthfully, and fearlessly, she will be in possession of a solid basis on which to build a superstructure of thought; but not until then'. This, he claimed, had never been attempted before in Ireland: 'There were plenty of other magazines that dealt with abstractions. There should be room for one that concerned itself with facts.'[3]

O'Faolain was somewhat disingenuous when he wrote in September 1941 that the editors: 'simply *do not know* where *The Bell* stands with reference to all sorts of questions such as Politics, England, America, the Church, Clericalism, Education, The Gaelic League, the Irish Language, Compulsory Irish, Socialism, Democracy, Agriculture'.[4] O'Faolain was hardly an ingénue and far from detached from the controversies he hoped *The Bell* might eschew. He was polished by three years as a graduate student at Harvard. He had lectured in England. He had been at the fore of controversies about cultural nationalism since the 1920s. Much of his fiction had been banned in Ireland. As a short story writer, he held his own alongside Frank O'Connor and Liam O'Flaherty. Some of the arguments in *The Bell* were expounded at greater length and rigour in books such as *King of the Beggars*, his 1938 life of Daniel O'Connell, *The Great O'Neill* (1942) and *The Irish* (1947). A reworked edition of *The Irish* published in 1969 summed up the critique of Irish cultural nationalism that he had been developing since the 1920s, when he broke with mentors such as Daniel Corkery and the IRA he fought for during the civil war:

> Nowadays I sometimes say, to tease my fellows, 'You are all men of the twenties.' Their eyes glow, recalling our glorious twenties. 'I mean,' I add, 'of the eighteen-twenties' – as Yeats (Shelley and all that) was unto his dying day. Not that, with one proviso, there is anything wrong with being a romantic, as Yeats proved. The proviso is whether the world about us will play ball with our romanticism. Otherwise it is like playing tennis with a ghost. Yeats was so lucky! He had the Irish folk world, now taken over by tourism and T.V.; Irish mythology and hagiography, now and none too soon, in the hands of sceptic scholars ... [5]

The problem was how to cut through the mist of romanticism and ideological nationalism that enveloped and stymied modern Ireland. The job of *The Bell* was to nurture sceptical scholarship and factual enquiry. O'Faolain's battle with the dominant strands in Irish intellectual life was an epistemological one. *The Bell* emphasised the need for empiricism in the plainest possible terms. What O'Faolain proposed, without recourse to the language and terminology of social theory, amounted to a radical intellectual challenge: 'To see an object clearly – *voir clair* – that is all we ever have asked for here. The great romantic period of Yeatsian glorification must find this idea most unexciting; though our experience it is, apparently, to ask for a great deal more than we shall easily get.' His attacks upon such idealism became more and more splenetic. The enemy of 'national and individual liberty' identified in one 1944 editorial was 'a sort of cloudy transcendentalism much hawked about by gentlemen of leisure whose role seems to be to disintegrate every natural human instinct with their metaphysical little dissecting-knives'.[6] The problem for O'Faolain was a practical one: 'Most of our inherited ideas about ourselves are born of patriotism and propaganda, and most of our pictures of life are pictures either drawn from the outside, or about a period and conditions now past.' Ireland, he argued, was choked with 'ideas and idealisms; mainly anachronistic, and almost wholly unadaptable to life as it is lived'.[7]

He described *The Bell* as 'the only native periodical open to everyone'.[8] His editorials chided and hectored the prospective authors he hoped were amongst his readers. His February 1941 editorial took 'Irish thinkers and students' to task. The intelligentsia – he did not use that word – 'those to whom every country looks for guidance', had proffered 'vague woolly articles, all personal opinion and no study. When we try to pin them down for facts they give us some such excuse as, "But that would mean a lot of work". If *The Bell* were to fail it would be because of a lack of suitable material. There was, he emphasised, a shortage of suitable articles for future issues on Irish social and political problems.[9] Even when the material was up to scratch there was an absence of engagement with what was being written about modern Ireland:

> We encouraged articles on a great many social and economic questions – Jails, Illegitimacy, Crime, Workhouses, Hospitalisation, Fisheries, Canning, Public Libraries, Jockeys, Mental Defectives, Housemaids, Other People's Incomes, Pawnshops, Flower Shows, T.B., Slums, Turf Cutting and so forth. They did not produce a whimper of comment. Does this mean that the people are eager to respond to any declaration of faith in the uptapped vigour of the nation and unexhausted idealism of the nation but are as yet inarticulate or unstudied when it comes to method and detail? Or does it mean that there is a weight of inertia, some large psychological frustration all over the nation, and that until it is removed the energy cannot be released? More and more I feel driven to that last conclusion.[10]

By 1944, after more than forty issues, only three contributions from Irish academics had been published: one from the National University and two from Trinity College.[11] In this intellectual vacuum he saw a general tendency to rely on imported ideas: 'Are we to imitate the Civil Servant mentality (which knows the answer to everything) and impose another set of *a priori* ideas on our fumbling democracy? Are we, I repeat, to know better than our people?'[12] The people, the flesh-and-blood inhabitants of Irish society, were central to O'Faolain's patriotic and anti-establishment project for *The Bell*:

> That the vast majority of the people here are Catholic is a matter of mathematics. That the country is in the main Nationalist is equally obvious, and that it has Isolationism in its blood must be evident to anybody who has even heard the words Sinn Féin ... 'Nationalist, Democratic, and Catholic then: that appears to be the sum of what it is clear in the picture of Life here.'[13]

O'Faolain cited the inspiration of Daniel O'Connell, whom he credited with moulding the craven helot peasants of the early nineteenth century into individuals capable of advancing democracy in Ireland. In essence, the thesis of his O'Connell biography was that the peasantry found their revelation in the Enlightenment, as interpreted by their leaders, rather than the old Gaelic order: 'The literature of the French Revolution, the English radicals, Godwin, Tom Paine, the French Deists, Adam Smith, Mary Wollstonecraft – these assimilated and adapted by O'Connell, put into words of one syllable, were what really interested the poor people of Ireland.'[14] There was a gulf between the intellectuals and the masses. O'Faolain argued that the rebel leaders who were inspired by the Enlightenment, Tone, Mitchel, even O'Connell, found their encounters with the common people repulsive. They were compelled to struggle in an anti-intellectual milieu at considerable personal cost:

> What was it the Irish rebel sacrificed? The better part of his life? Far worse, far more exhausting, harder far to bear, he sacrificed the better part of his mind. Men like Tone, Mitchel, Doheny, all of them, had smothered talents. They were presumably men with as much human ambition as anybody else, and more sensibility than most. It was a drudge to them to 'go down into the cabins of the people'. How bored Tone was by these talks and meals with dithering, half-educated, Catholic tradesmen and farmers;

> and he was the last man to whine or complain ... All these men deprived themselves, and Ireland, of as much as they gave: they choked the critical side of their minds, they were good rebels in proportion as they were bad revolutionaries. Their passion for change and their vision of change never pierced to organic change, halted dead at the pure modal and circumstantial. It has to be that way since they devoted their lives and all their being to passion rather than thought, or in Arnold's words describing the French Revolution 'had their source in a great movement of feeling, not in a great movement of mind'.[15]

The first part of this quotation said as much about O'Faolain's own state of mind and intellectual isolation as it did about the likes of Tone. The second part got at a distinction between the emotional impact of the French revolution and any political or intellectual programme grounded in Enlightenment ideas. An emotional response to these ideas, rather than an intellectual one, rendered Ireland unable to cope in a world shaped by the Enlightenment:

> The result is that the whole of Irish patriotic literature ever since has either concerned itself with matters of sentiment rather than thought; or with interim solutions of immediate problems that time has since dealt with otherwise. Irish political thought is, to this day, in its infancy.[16]

O'Faolain's antidote to the 'arid traditionalism' that came (in his view) to dominate Irish thought was an admixture of intellectual pragamatism and necessary faith in Irish democracy.[17] His methodology in attaining such intellectual accountability was a homespun empiricism capable of expressing social issues in straightforward clear-cut terms.

TRUE STORIES

Early issues of *The Bell* contained some non-fiction articles that played by the house rules laid down by O'Faolain. In particular, two by Edward Fahy, in the second and third issues, set the standard. The first of these, 'The Prisons', was the first examination of the Irish prison system. It described the organisation of prisons, the operation of prison workshops, the severity of regulations, prisoner diet, and health and education issues. It concluded that while there was nothing disgraceful about the treatment of the Irish prison population much about life within prison walls was unnatural, illogical and unwise. Fahy concluded that many of the restrictions imposed on prisoners were 'irksome and useless, tending only to humiliate the prisoner and destroy his individuality'. Not one of the restrictions – these included being allowed to write but one letter a month – was essential to good order or discipline. The evidence suggested that such practices failed miserably to deter further crime. Fahy's second article, 'The Boy Criminal', was similarly exact, if dependent in its opening section on what academics would call the secondary literature. It concluded that management of the Irish Borstal system was 'absurd and mischievous' given that it was meant to be an alternative to prison. The conditions experienced by Borstal boys were typically worse than those in adult prisons. The case for urgent reform was anchored in precise yet evocative description. Of his visit to Clonmel, where the average detention period was in the region of two years, he wrote:

> Inside the main gates – and there are two of these, one inside the other – is a small patch of ground not much bigger than the lawn of a fair sized residence. Anything less like a lawn, however, would be difficult to imagine: the surface of this patch consists of very fine gravel and dust – mostly dust, in summer time, at any rate, and surely unadulterated mud and slush in winter. But this is the only available space in which the boys – about 64 in number – can exercise.[18]

Another 1940 article, *The Decline of English*, anonymous this time, examined how English language was taught in Irish schools. The aim (O'Faolain's editorial touch was evident throughout) was 'to give the reader a clear picture of what was happening'.[19] Some 84.7 per cent of girls passed the Intermediate certificate in 1940 compared to 75.4 per cent the previous year. The article combined precise description of required standards and marking procedures with specific impressions obtained from preparing girls for the English exam in two schools. Exam results, it was explained, were not necessarily proof of successful teaching. Indeed, the author maintained that that the examination pass standard was unnecessarily low, citing a Department of Education rule that no more than 15 per cent of pupils could be failed. This, it was explained, contributed to poor standards: 'I have seen my friend, who acted last year as an examiner, fail students; and then, having done a sum to see what percentage she was failing, go rapidly back, and Pass those students so as keep the final number of Passes high.'

The article provided examples of specific problems pupils had in grasping English grammar. The influence of Irish on how English was spoken, written and spelt remained strong. Essays typically contained a hotchpotch of half-English and half-Irish words. Misspelling centred on the common mispronunciation of English ones. Nineteenth-century hedge-schoolmaster eloquence was not uncommon. One child wrote of a proposed visit to a big city: 'I would be anticipating for several days premonition seeing the vehicles of locomotion going through the great squares of traffic.' The view of the author was that such expression was in part fostered by the absence of modern texts about Irish society within a curriculum shaped by ideology. Everything seemed to have ended with the 1916 Rising; nothing had begun:

> The long line of Irish patriots is crowned by Pearse, who is thought of as a saint and king of all Irish martyrs and heroes. One hardly ever hears mention of post-1916 figures. I cannot help think that this attitude explains the 'Emerald Isle' style of writing, i.e., the lack of simple concreteness, of what *The Bell* would probably call realism. The mind is turned backward, and inward. It is hard to blame the kids. They do not read about Irish life today. There is very little for them to read.

The article ended with two concrete suggestions: one for an administrative reform of the grading, the other that the Minister of Education invite (and pay) modern Irish writers to prepare set textbooks and novels about modern Irish life which boys and girls could read.

Flann O'Brien contributed a number of articles, beginning with 'The Dance Halls' (1941). Here, a factual account of such venues was marshalled to counter prevalent hyperbolic claims about 'vestibules of hell' fuelled by clerical preoccupations with sexual immorality. The article distinguished between various types of rural and urban dance events, their organisation and, not without humour, the ways patrons got round the prohibition of alcohol in many venues. O'Brien quoted a number of court and newspaper accounts of the presumed relationship between dance halls and the emigration of young women. One Father Devane was reported as being anxious to know how far dance halls 'set up a restlessness that causes girls to emigrate'. Why, he asked, were there so many dance halls in Donegal? Emigration, a letter to the *Irish Press* explained, was not caused by dancing: 'Many

Donegal girls come to Dublin. Some get good wages. But they don't stay in Dublin though Dublin has dance halls galore. They feel lonely in Dublin, so they go to Glasgow where hundreds of neighbours have made their homes.'[20] The article sought to engineer a debate about emigration: the *Irish Press* letter cited by O'Brien was from Peadar O'Donnell, a co-founder of *The Bell.*

The topic of emigration was revisited in subsequent issues. A 1942 piece by O'Faolain lambasted the response to emigration of *An Glór*, a fortnightly periodical published by the Gaelic League. This he described as an example of 'sentimental sludge', 'full of the old sentimental rhetoric, but too lazy to make one single constructive proposal of any kind – beyond calling on the Clan of Gaels to answer the voice of Eire in her misery with the "fiercely national spirit".[21] A 1943 article by O'Donnell on the conditions experienced by emigrants called for the establishment of Irish centres in British cities.[22] *The Bell* also published 'I Wanted to be a Nurse', an anonymous account by a 21-year-old Irish woman of her experiences in British hospitals.[23] It revealed that young emigrant women had more on their minds than dancing. The author describes a dying patient: 'I think she knew she was tubercular because at night when the bombs started to fall she didn't care if she were hit or not.'

For the most part non-fiction articles restricted comment to the specific matter being considered. Events that took place off-stage, in particular the Second World War, were presumed to be no less out of bounds than opinion for opinion's sake. To some extent this fed the very isolationism and provincialism that *The Bell* opposed. A 1943 editorial noted that when Mussolini resigned and the battle of Sicily was at its height the first item on the Irish radio news concerned the pilgrimage of 10,000 people to Croagh Patrick. The second gave account of a Muintir Na Tíre conference in Cork. O'Faolain commented that: 'Not until these things were given their pride of place did we turn to the war of the world. It was impressive and touching incident: it was maddening too.'[24]

There was but just one incidental reference to what the Irish called the Emergency amongst the early issues. 'I Live in a Slum' (1940) described a day in the life of an unemployed man. It recounted a conversation that touched on larger events: 'The men get together at night too. We talk politics. Now it's the war. The I.R.A ... and what is to come ... Next thing it's time for the news on the wireless. We gather around a window in the next house where a fellow has one; into the hall if it's wet and he leaves the door to his room empty. We never talk much after the news.'[25] What was not spoken or described remained for the most part out of bounds.

Each issue of *The Bell* contained fiction and poetry. To some extent its non-fiction was moulded from the observational template of the short story. In the early days Frank O'Connor contributed both fiction and non-fiction. Other non-fiction contributors, such as Flann O'Brien and O'Donnell, were novelists. Some of the reportage collated by O'Faolain had all the art of the short story. An April 1942 piece by an unnamed unemployed man recounts fleeting conversations at night in a city centre tenement hostel. The author records a fragmented conversation about ghosts. He alludes to homosexual encounters on the street below: 'Two men pass by arm in arm talking; for a second they pause and point across the river, then laugh. Their high-pitched voices are unreal in the heavy darkness seeking some darker place.' Conversations about the war, it seems, were no less surreptitious than homosexual sex:

> From behind me in a room I hear the man talking ...
> 'The Germans are great'
> 'Why?' I ask.
> 'Look at all they've got'
> 'Well, is it theirs?'
> 'It doesn't matter. They've shown the world some-thing'[26]

O'Faolain was first and foremost a writer of stories about the human condition. His advice to contributors overlapped with advice he gave to would-be fiction writers in a 1942 series of radio talks. This was repeated in a 1944 article for *The Bell* on the craft of the short story: 'I think that it is safe to say that unless a story makes this subtle comment on human nature, on the permanent relationship between people, their variety, their expectedness and unexpectedness, it is not a story in any modern sense.'[27] The business of describing life in Ireland did not have to be a turgid one. *The Bell*, he declared, was a magazine for people 'more sensitive to the Human Comedy, more shrewd about character, more responsive to all its vagaries and subtleties, than many far more cultivated people who live in the kind of society where natural personality has been ruled by convention'. Non-fiction, no less than fiction, needed to look beneath the surface of life.

At its best *The Bell* presented compelling snapshots of Irish society. It grappled with a series of taboo issues such as birth control, freemasonry, the Knights of Saint Columbanus, unmarried mothers, illegitimacy, divorce, homosexuality, mental illness and prostitution.[28] There was a recurring focus on poverty and its consequences. February 1941 saw the publication of 'The Delicacy', a colloquial term for TB, by Dr Robert Collis, a child specialist remembered amongst other things for his efforts to have Jewish refugee children admitted to Ireland. Collis described the disease as 'a lurking terror in the national mind; an evil thing; something best not spoken of, a shame which must be denied and hidden'.[29] Collis's piece was complemented by 'Two Years in a Sanatorium', which described the routine of a patient, Charles Woodlock, being treated for the disease.[30] Both articles employed clear description to dispel prevalent myths and fears about the disease. Woodlock's story made it clear, Collis argued, that the problem of tuberculosis was more than a matter of germs. Its solution could only be found by taking account of 'national psychology' – societal willingness to address the problem – as well as individual fears. Patients regularly infected several others before being diagnosed. At that stage it was too late for any treatment except palliative care. Collis didn't pull any punches:

> In the meantime, if he belongs to a Dublin family, and lives in one room with his family, he will be given first preference for a new house at Crumlin or Cabra. In the new house he gets a room to himself, but now he is out of work, the rent is higher, the food is dearer. He continues to go down-hill, infecting others as he goes. If he is very unselfish and sufficiently intelligent to realise what a frightful danger he is to others he may give up his sole little bit of security – the companionship of the only people who love him – and submit to being isolated in a home for the dying, or in the Pigeon House Sanatorium. If he does this he is a very gallant man, for the Pigeon House Sanatorium, built on the end of a windy pier, chiefly of corrugated iron and wood, is a horribly bleak and lonely place in which to face death.[31]

Tuberculosis, he explained, could generally be successfully treated if caught in time. Yet 90 per cent of patients came to the doctor too late for the then most effective treatments to be used, and the majority too late to be cured. Collis's activism was part of a broader reformism headed up by James Deeny, who became the Chief Medical Officer in 1943.[32]

'Off the Dole' (1941) gave a first-person account of a visit to a Labour Exchange by an unemployed journalist.[33] 'Illegitimate' from the same year observed the treatment of women in court. It described the experiences of women from different social classes and conditions in institutions for unmarried women. 'Will you go back to your people?' the judge asked a woman in the dock:

> 'They don't know about the baby, sir, they wouldn't take me.' Breaking down she pulls the shawl over her face and the half-seen child. The crowd has ceased to shift and whisper and even the shiny-haired pressmen are embarrassed under their all-in-a-day's work composure as a guard leads her once more out of court, placed on remand until further enquires are made.[34]

The widespread institutional abuse of such women remained undiscovered, but shortcomings identified in the five homes examined were described. There was, the author wrote, no use in pretending that they did not badly need improvement, supervision and co-ordination. They were described as miserably comfortless, generally incapable of meeting the long-term needs of unmarried women and, most importantly for the author, unable to prevent a needless level of infant mortality because of the lack of resident doctors.

Some proposed articles never materialised because the practical difficulties or expense proved too great.[35] One notable success was a series of articles that examined the lives of families in different income brackets. The series began with an account of the household budget of a well-to-do solicitor family on £850 per annum centred on expenditure for May 1943.[36] The article noted that expenditure on grocer's bills alone for this family approached the total income of many artisan families. This point was put to the interviewee. She said, 'I don't know! I just don't know how they live.'

The second article examined the household of a 45-year-old civil servant with £400 a year.[37] The third described a couple with no children living on £300 per annum. The fourth and final article documented the case of an unemployed labourer, his 33-year-old wife and their six children living on just £100 per annum. This family lived in a two-roomed Dublin tenement without gas or water. They shared a lavatory with five other families. In the winter they purchased one candle per week, their only form of lighting. Their diet was described as barely adequate: 'No fruit, no vegetables, no cheese, no eggs, no variety whatsoever.' They depended on school dinners, The St Vincent de Paul Society, the Parish Clothing Guild and State Home Assistance payments and food vouchers.[38] Significantly, all the interviewees were women. In each case, the woman was in charge of the family budget.

A number of articles about poverty transcribed women talking about their lives. 'Slum Pennies', from 1941, could well have been so authored by the woman getting by on £100 per annum in 1944.[39] She focused on issues that she considered would be of most interest to readers of *The Bell*: the use of docket systems and moneylenders to buy clothes for her six children and having to lie about her husband going to mass and her own Legion of Mary attendance to get help from the St Vincent de Paul Society. 'I Live in a Slum' (1940) transcribed an interview with an unemployed man who could well have been this woman's husband.[40] It covered the same ground of providing for the children, coping with moneylenders and getting around the Vincent de Paul. He describes how his wife sometimes stole from stalls in Moore Street: 'She's a great hand at it. Now and then she pinches something. So do I, but very rarely. We never let the kids know. We try hard to train them to be honest.' He wonders what it would be like to have secure employment: 'I think I would never have a worry if I had work, for I'm strong and my wife is strong and we get on terrible well together.' The woman interviewed for the 1944 article said of her husband: 'He'd take the stars down out of the sky for me – never a word out of place since the day we got married.' *The Bell* hardly romanticised poverty, but it found space to note romance amongst the poor.

TWO HIDDEN IRELANDS

In many respects *The Bell* was hardly breaking new ground in its accounts of such poverty. These could be located in the social explorer tradition of writing that included Jack London's *People of the Abyss*. There were commonalities too with George Orwell's *The Road to Wigan Pier* (1937). Orwell's narrative was in the tradition of Charles Booth's earlier studies of British poverty.[41] In the Irish case, hundreds of detailed transcripts of the circumstances of Irish paupers had been collated by the 1833 Royal Commission established under Dr Whately, who was both Protestant Archbishop of Dublin and a political economist. Whately's remit was to inquire 'into the conditions of the poorer classes in Ireland, and into the various institutions a present established by law for their relief'.[42] Subsequently, hundreds of coroners' reports described the conditions of those who had died in the Famine. Earlier again, in 1825, O'Faolain's hero Daniel O'Connell provided evidence to a House of Lords Select Committee on the State of Ireland.[43] Poverty in Ireland was 'discovered' generation after generation. *The Bell* formed part of a longstanding tradition of empirical writings that sought to draw attention to social problems caused by poverty.

The secret Ireland revealed by *The Bell* was, for O'Faolain, obscured by a dominant Romantic idealism incapable of examining the real conditions of Irish society. Corkery's *A Hidden Ireland*, first published in 1925, exemplified the sort of thinking he had in his gunsights as editor of *The Bell*. The hidden Ireland that preoccupied O'Faolain was the 'silent Ireland' of the 1940s.[44] The young O'Faolain was Corkery's protégé, the 'best friend' who was allowed to look at a copy of *Ulysses* which Corkery kept in a locked drawer.[45] When *The Hidden Ireland* was published in 1925 O'Faolain objected to Corkery's idealisation of uneducated peasant culture as the model for independent Ireland when, in his view, Ireland had its own cosmopolitan European tradition and a place in world literature to build upon.[46] During the 1930s he and Frank O'Connor criticised Corkery in literary journals such as the *Dublin Magazine* and *Ireland Today*. Their concern was that Corkery was helping to popularise a myth of Irish purity that lent false credibility to the 'immunisation' work of the Censorship Board.[47] O'Faolain's subsequent writing, notably his O'Connell and O'Neill biographies, sought to refute factually ideological premises advanced by Corkery about Gaelic culture.[48]

Corkery's book promoted a rediscovery of the Gaelic poetry tradition as an antidote to an Irish language revival tainted by colonialism: 'What pains one', he wrote, 'is to come upon an Irishman who cannot speak either of the Irish language or Irish literature or Gaelic history except in some such terms as the Ascendancy in Ireland have taught him. In his case the Ascendancy have succeeded; they have created in him the slave-mind.'[49] Corkery's project was one of cultural nationalism, to unearth what he believed to be the nobility of Gaelic culture, to challenge pervasive English-language accounts of the Irish past in novels, travelogues and histories.[50]

The actual conditions of the peasantry that these described were not rejected by Corkery. Indeed, his descriptions of peasant poverty would not have been out of place in *The Bell*. For example, 'Every hut had its dung pit in front of the door', 'House and dress were so miserable that food was almost the only expense', or 'Seldom was there a lease, either on house or land; and to improve either led to an increase in rent, perhaps an eviction.'[51] The result, according to Corkery, was that civic life and institutions that might find a place for art had been wiped away.[52] Yet, Corkery argued, the nobility of the Munster Gaelic tradition, exemplified in its poetry, survived under the emaciated conditions of the Penal Law. The eighteenth-century peasant poets were the lineal descendants of the old bardic line, the proud possessors of an aristocratic tradition of literature. This, he maintained, was proof of an indomitable Irishness.

O'Faolain did not object to much of what Corkery had to say about the persistence of the Gaelic bardic tradition in this impoverished setting. However, he vehemently disagreed with how Corkery depicted the erstwhile Gaelic aristocracy that had sustained the bards through their patronage. These Gaelic houses, according to Corkery, were in some ways similar to Planter ones yet possessed certain notes of their own: 'freer contact with Europe, a culture over and above that which they shared with their neighbours, a sense of historic continuity, a closeness to the land, to the very pulse of it, that those Planter houses could not even dream about'.[53] Corkery proclaimed the native superiority of the bardic schools to the European type of university, where the main study was of Roman Law – 'the relic of a dead empire' – and the literature of dead languages. By contrast, the history that was taught in the bardic schools was 'that of Ireland, namely the Brehon Law system; the language was that of Ireland, the literature that of Ireland – and through the medium of the native language were all subjects taught'.[54] O'Faolain disagreed. In *The Great O'Neill* he demonstrated that the Gaelic past was never so neat and tidy. The claims about Gaelic aristocraticic cultural purity advanced by Corkery did not hold up.[55]

O'Faolain argued in *King of the Beggars* that the bardic tradition of the eighteenth century was intensely anti-realistic. Their poetic convention was one of exaggerated effusive praise of patrons, their palaces and the gifts they bestowed. It was never for things like pennies or bacon, which the poets would be lucky to get, but for 'silks, wines, jewels, steeds, cloaks, gold in abundance, silver and arms for heroes'. Later it became one that bewailed the loss of patronage. The cast of these poems, O Faolain emphasised, the bards themselves and the aristocrats they identified with, but 'never once a peasant'.[56] The bards praised by Corkery were, at best, hapless men out of tune with their times.[57]

At their worst, they were a craven lot and fantasists to boot. While his people starved in windowless hovels the poet O'Rahilly fantastically listed, over and over, the glories of erstwhile great houses: 'glories in which we do not find one homely detail, a thing we could take for fact, one item to make us feel that we are not been taken by the hand into a complete dream-world'.[58] The literary value of such poetry was not at issue, but it had nothing to say about the actual culture within which it was produced:

> It means either that these semi-popular poets had nothing to say to the people that was related to their real political and social condition; or else it means that the people were themselves living in a conventional attitude of mind, asked for and desired no realistic songs, had no wish for a faithful image of their appalling conditions – were, in one word sleep-walking.[59]

O'Faolain marshalled this argument in *King of the Beggars* to illustrate the scale of O'Connell's achievement. In O'Faolain's version the peasants of *The Hidden Ireland* were badly in need of a realistic political leader but hardly ready for one that they got in O'Connell.[60] His analysis of the poets translated and cited by Corkery holds for the most part. The few exceptions were amongst the 'minor poets' rounded up in one of the later chapters of *The Hidden Ireland*. There, just one poem cited by Corkery addressed the treatment of tenants by a landlord might, barely, have passed O'Faolain's test. This 'Jacobite poem' by Sean MacDomhnaill said of one Colonel Dawson of Aherlow: 'He hitched Hunger to the people / forcing them to obey.'[61] More generally, what realism there was focused on the reduced circumstances of impoverished poets forsaken by their patrons. The now destitute last official poet of one family writes:

> My craft being withered with
> change of law in Ireland,
> O grief that I must henceforth
> take to brewing!

Another replied:

> O Tadgh, understanding that you
> are for the brewing,
> I for a space will go skimming the milk.[62]

O'Faolain looked at such poems from the perspective of a political historian. He argued that *The Hidden Ireland* 'sinned from over softness and romanticism' but acknowledged that *King of the Beggars* 'sins, perhaps, from harshness, or impatience, due to a deliberate insistence on political realism'.[63] O'Faolain's criticism of the Munster poets here was much the same as his criticism of W.B. Yeats in *The Irish* (1947). Yeats, according to O'Faolain, had a weakness not shared by his immediate Irish successors. These – O'Faolain's generation – were mostly writers of novels and stories, all observation, all eyes, avid for realism (even if they were never to achieve it), preoccupied with what Stendhal called 'the little actual facts' – those details and precisions which accumulate as well-imaged reality. In their sense, Yeats did not have an observing eye. He could evoke like a magician; he could not draw a picture.'[64]

O'Faolain and Corkery, inevitably, had different tastes in Gaelic poetry. *The Hidden Ireland* gave a chapter over to the work of the Clare poet Brian Merriman whose one great poem, *Cuairt an Mheadhon Oidche* (The Midnight Court) was a fantastical bawdy satire on peasant society, its priests and its cuckolds. Corkery lambasted Merriman's lack of bardic refinement. 'It had no luxuriance in it, nothing flowing, sinuous, gentle or efflorescent. Its accent is, rather boorish, abrupt, snappy', even if it was 'taut and well-articulated'.[65] For Corkery, its distance from the Munster bardic tradition he admired (which he called the living Court of Poetry) was exemplified by 'its description of the peasant's hut or the implicit contrast it makes between the fanciful Midnight Court and the court the people had to do business with'.[66]

Corkery maintained that *The Midnight Court* lacked a true lyricism capable of dealing with nature. Indeed, Merriman was not a Nature poet. His main topics, sex, marriage, inheritance and women's rights, were advanced through satire. Corkery judged Merriman's much-praised opening descriptions of east Clare to be commonplace: 'we get no passage of any length sustained in that high style'.[67] This is less than fair to the wonderful animistic vista executed by Merriman at the beginning of the poem. Consider the following two translations, one by Frank O'Connor first published in 1945:

> When I looked at Lough Graney my heart grew bright,
> Ploughed Lands and green in the morning light,
> Mountains in ranks with crimson borders
> Peering about their neighbour's shoulders.

Or, as rendered in J.N. Fahey's 1998 translation:

My heart would brighten Loch Graney to spy,
And the country around it, to the edge of the sky.
The serried mountains were a delight to the beholder
Thrusting their heads over each other's shoulder.[68]

O'Connor took huge issue with Corkery's 'sneer' at Merriman as 'a coarse jester'.[69] He depicted him instead as an independent intellectual who drew on contemporary English verse to produce an authentic piece of Gaelic literature rooted in the society he came from:

> His language – that is its principal glory – is also a complete break with literary Irish. It is the spoke Irish of Clare ... What Merriman aimed at was something that had never been guessed at in Gaelic Ireland; a perfectly proportioned work of art on a contemporary subject, with every detail subordinated to the central theme.[70]

Yet Merriman, 'the intellectual Protestant' and schoolteacher-farmer who somehow 'knew as much about Lawrence and Gide as he knew of Savage, Swift, Goldsmith and most of all Rousseau', had no influence on Irish life or Irish thought. This was evident, according to O'Connor, in the subsequent triumph of 'Puritanism' over the sensuous eighteenth century society evoked by Merriman. O'Connor felt constrained when translating *The Midnight Court*; he sought to evoke rather than directly translate Merriman's 'perfect crescendo of frustrated sexual passion'.[71] There are less inhibited translations, yet the tremendous physicality of *The Midnight Court* is evident in O'Connor's:

Down with marriage! Tis out of date,
It exhausts the stock and cripples the state.
The priest has failed with whip and blinker,
Now give a chance to Tom the Tinker,
And mix and mash in nature's can
The tinker and the gentleman;
Let lovers in every lane extended,
Follow their whim as God intended,
And in their pleasure bring to birth
The morning glory of the earth;[72]

The twentieth-century secret Ireland – where frank translations of Gaelic poems might be censored alongside literary depictions of modern society – was, O'Faolain argued, obscured by the ideology of *The Hidden Ireland*. O'Faolain and O'Connor, like many Irish writers of their generation, enthused about the Irish language, peasant lore and country tradition. *The Bell*, for instance, published a series of extracts from Tim Buckley's *The Tailor and Ansty*, an irreverent account life of country life. These stories of the actual people of Gougane Barra, where O'Faolain, O'Connor and Corkery went to study the Irish language, fell foul of the censor.

THE MART OF IDEAS

The pressures of putting out *The Bell* while pursuing a parallel writing career took its toll. When he stepped down as editor it was as much due to exhaustion as anything else.[73] He and O'Connor fell out following a series of spats, for reasons not uncommon to writers who were both friends and rivals. O'Connor disparaged him as a lover of the second-rate. O'Faolain, wearing his editor hat, defiantly admitted as much:

> We have printed things, at times, that were not of the first literary standard because they were real and true, and we would always lean primarily towards reality and veracity rather than towards a superficial literary perfection. What he asked had been the result? 'Irish Life has licked us into shape. It has given us an Attitude.'[74]

There was a two-fold problem. Intellectuals needed to address the world as it was. Only by doing so could a viable intellectual Irish project be sustained. At the same time, it was not enough to listen:

> A confession. We have not been either entirely successful or honest about letting life speak for itself. We have found that a good deal of life is, for one thing, sadly inarticulate. We found that we could not just simply 'let' Life speak for itself, for the simple reason that it often does not know how to speak at all. It has becoming a question of *making* Life speak, of teaching it how to speak. Only the editorial board knows how often we had to cure Life of lockjaw. There have been, for example, articles in *The Bell* which bore no authors name: someone had to go out with a notebook and listen, and encourage, and make a record. The poor would for ever remain silent if people did not, in this

> way, wrench speech out of them. There have been articles which have been built up, laboriously, in a form of collaboration between the editor and unpracticed contributors.[75]

O'Faolain was frustrated both by such practical difficulties and by what he saw as the indifferent reception to such reportage. His editorials became more and more akin to the opinion essays he rejected from others. The folksy simplicity of the first year or so, essentially come-ye-alls aimed at potential contributors, gave way to frequently bitter essays. Yet, collectively, essays such as 'Attitudes', 'Sex, Censorship and the Church' (1941), 'The Mart for Ideas', 'What Possible Future', 'New Wine and Old Bottles' (1942) and 'The State and Censorship' (1943) mapped out a distinct intellectual project.

'The Mart of Ideas' posited the need for an intelligentsia and free intellectual exchange against the black market produced by literary censorship. Censorship stymied debate on numerous important issues. Not only that, censorship 'policy' was imposed 'without rhyme or reason'.[76] 'Sex, Censorship and the Church' outlined Catholic arguments in favour of censorship in an effort to promote debate.[77] *The Bell* examined the actual workings of censorship rather than just opposing it on libertarian ideological grounds. It printed lists of censored authors and works.

The Bell emphasised the importance of ideas but rarely discussed ideas per se. As a rule, references to political and social theorists were fleeting ones that, at best, offered clues about the intellectual hinterlands of contributors. So, when O'Faolain wrote of the importance of Ireland's much-derided intelligentsia, the specifics had often to be taken on trust.[78] The ideas most overtly discussed in *The Bell* tended to be those derided as bad ones. The classic example was Frank O'Connor's article on Yeats, written after the poet died in January 1939. Here, O'Connor contrasted Yeats with Æ. There was an old feud between the two. O'Connor's loyalty, he made clear, was totally with Æ, who, in old age a least, stood for rationalism, humanitarianism, democracy (with leanings towards communism) pacifism, internationalism and hatred of tradition and class. Yeats he described as a polar opposite:

> Yeats was a rabid Tory; he professed himself a member of the Church of Ireland, though he had much more of the Catholic in him; he was a fascist and an authoritarian, seeing in world crises only the break-up of the 'dammed liberalism' he hated; an old

> I.R.B. man, passionate nationalist, lover of tradition; hater of reason, popular education and 'mechanical logic.'[79]

So very much of the charge popularised by Conor Cruise O'Brien a quarter of a century later in *Passion and Cunning* was laid down in 1941 by O'Connor:

> He admired Mussolini, Hitler and Stalin, and believed the dictatorships might be the beginning of a rebirth. He wrote marching songs for O'Duffy's Fascists. He felt himself lost in a world where the poet has no place and clung to his boyhood belief that matter is nothing, that whatever has existed, that whatever has existed still exists and that he 'could be its servant though all are underground'.[80]

O'Connor became director of the Abbey Theatre. They fought over a production of *Coriolanus* 'being produced as Fascist propaganda'. They had long wandering discussions about Hegelianism, pacifism, communism and, shortly before Yeats's death, eugenics. These frequently left O'Connor abashed and miserable as someone on the side of liberals, rationalists and humanitarians. Yet he was 'taken in his country blood' with some of Yeats's plays and felt somewhat ashamed about his own detachment from Yeats's 'blunderings in religion, philosophy and art'. As for the Hegelianism and late preoccupation with eugenics, these O'Connor read as excuses to believe in the imminent destruction of civilisation and the death knell of progress. 'It seemed to me', he wrote, 'that towards the end he was looking forward with fiercer and fiercer gusto to the crash. To him our realism, naturalism, humanitarianism, popular education and Book Societies were only signs of the end.'[81]

The connections made by O'Connor between Hegelism and fascism paralleled those emphasised by Karl Popper in *The Open Society and its Enemies* (1945).[82] This influential critique of the thought of Plato, Hegel and Marx argued that idealist philosophies had contributed to political authoritarianism and totalitarianism throughout the history of the West.[83] Popper's critique of political authoritarianism and totalitarianism was to some extent anticipated by O'Faolain in 'Ireland and the Modern World' (1943). O'Faolain, however, was more preoccupied with the malign influence of nationalism than with dangers of fascism. Here, like O'Connor, he described an intellectual debt to Æ:

> Æ used to say that this rise of the State as watchful father was largely due to Hegelianism. Hegelian philosophy spread the idea that history was, loosely speaking, not so much a free process as the procreation of the Divine Will in human terms (Which is almost as determinist an idea as the Marxist theory that history is the inevitable projection of economic forces.) Once God and the Nation were put on equal footing it was obviously only a matter of time before the Absolute Spirit was born – the State masquerading as God Almighty. It is said that when Hegel saw Napoleon in the streets of Jena, he declared: 'I have seen the World Spirit go riding out'. What he was duped into admiring was a complex of extreme nationalism, despotic absolutism, and ruthless imperialism.[84]

His case against extremist nationalism – one that would 'assail the Jews or outlaw the Protestants or gag the writers' – referred to Peadar O'Donnell's essay in the same issue on anti-Semitism.[85] That such nationalism was institutionalised in Ireland he had little doubt. It was evident in school textbooks and in the very history ('complete fairy-tale', 'fanciful Celtophilism') being pumped into Irish schoolchildren:

> The main notion of it is that we have since the dawn of our history been united here in our efforts to reject all foreign ways, peoples, manners, and customs – which is, of course, arrant nonsense: on this fancy there has been piled up a gospel of the sanctity of the West and the evil of the East, the generative power and utter purity of all native custom and tradition, saints and heroes; a thirst for not only what little remains of this custom and tradition but for the revival of what is actually dead or obsolescent, a drive towards authoritarianism to enforce these ideas and a censorship of cold-blooded economic pressure (which we all feel, and which business-men carefully watch) to down everybody who opposes them. This farrago is called Nationalism.[86]

Further parallels, both political and ontological, were to be found with the Vienna School, the group of empirical philosophers that at one stage included Popper. During the 1930s it railed against the then locally dominant Hegelian and Kantian tradition of German metaphysical idealism that proclaimed the duty of philosophy to advance the cause of religion, morality, the *Volk* and the organic nation-state.[87] As A.J. Ayer recalled:

> There was at that time a bitter struggle between the Socialists and a right wing clerical party, headed by Dollfuss; and the opposition of the Vienna Circle to metaphysics was in part a political act ... they were against what we might call the German past. They were against the romanticism of German philosophical thought which had existed since the early nineteenth century. They were against the followers of Hegel, or rather the idealist followers of Hegel: they weren't of course, against Marx.[88]

The logical positivism of the Vienna School employed the logic of science and commonplace observation as a means of refuting idealisms.[89] Logical positivism restricted the ontological remit of philosophy to verifiable logical or scientific claims. Philosophy was redefined as the means by which the meaning of statements was defined as either true or false. This, of course, excluded statements about ethics and morality that could be categorically proved as true or false.[90] O'Faolain's challenge to Irish society in 'Why We Don't See It' (1942) advanced just such an ontological perspective:

> Before me on my desk is a pewter mug, which, I regret to say, I debase as an ash-tray. If I handed this mug to the average would-be contributor and said 'Describe that!' – I can see the glaze coming over his eyes, and the fumes of some *a priori* ideas coming between him and the object, and I can hear him say – 'Well now, of course, that mug isn't made in Ireland. Now the Irish people ...' etc. etc.[91]

The premium that *The Bell* placed on facts was one thing. The pervasive humanism in how these were presented, often with the psychological craft of a short story, was another. For O'Faolain, the Irish difficulty with sticking to the facts was a problem of temperament. Irish emotionalism, he argued, was splendid for fighting, oratory or drama, but it did not shed light on actual social conditions.[92] Yet the very emotionalism that he distrusted was part of his own makeup. As he put it in a 1948 letter, he was cursed by being born emotional amongst a race mad with emotionalism: 'driven to being an intellectual without any qualifications and wholly against my grain in the worst country in the world for intellectuals'.[93] Again and again O'Faolain saw in himself the shortcomings he identified in Irish society.

In 1943 he wrote: 'Our more humane leaders, from Collins to O'Connell, established the nearest thing we have to a broad, humanist tradition in politics. Our idealists interrupted it with something almost sectarian; so that, however lofty in the abstract, their course has been to dehumanise and disrupt.' O'Faolain's response to such dehumanisation was an essentially Catholic one. O'Faolain's return to Catholicism coincided with the end of his editorship of *The Bell*. His biographer Maurice Harmon times it to a visit to Italy in 1947. He had not been to confession since he was excommunicated during the Civil War.[94] However, he had long wrestled spiritually with the influence of Jansenist Catholicism; notably with a fear of predestination.[95] His Catholic intellectual hinterland was evident in his choice of topics for a 1954 series of lectures at Princeton, later published as *The Vanishing Hero*.[96] Richard Ellman, the biographer of Joyce, had urged him to change the titles of two: 'Greene: The Jansenist Fallacy' and 'Hemingway: The Pelagian Vertigo'.[97] Pelagius was the early Church theologian who unsuccessfully opposed St Augustine's account of original sin, which subsequently influenced Reformation and counter-Reformation beliefs about predestination.[98]

Little of this crept into *The Bell*. However, in a 1943 editorial, O'Faolain endorsed the Catholic humanism of Jacques Maritain.[99] After the First World War Maritain authored a number of textbooks on philosophy, logic, psychology and metaphysics for use in Catholic colleges and seminaries. For the most part these advanced orthodox readings of the thought of Thomas Aquinas favoured by the Church. This neo-Thomism, rooted in Aristotlean concepts of natural law, became central to twentieth-century Catholic social thought. Maritain had considerable influence in promoting the acceptance of liberal democracy, religious pluralism and human rights by European Catholics and by the papacy. He portrayed the modern secular democratic state as ultimately more faithful to the principles of Christianity and natural law than the corporatist politics favoured by the papacy.[100] Maritain described his Christian humanism as opposed to communism, totalitarianism and racism because these sacrificed the dignity of the person.[101] When it came to human rights he suggested that Christian humanism could draw an absolute line in the sand between right and wrong in a way that secular democratic ideals could not:

> The mistake of bourgeois liberalism has been to conceive democratic society to be a kind of lists or arena in which all conceptions of the bases of common life, even those destructive to freedom and law, meet with no more than the pure and simple indifference of the body politics, while they compete before

> public opinion in a kind of free-market of mother ideas, healthy or poisoned, of political life. Just as it had no real *common good*, it had no real *common thought* – no brains of its own, but a neutral, empty skull clad with mirrors: no wonder that before the Second World War, in countries that fascist, racist or communist propaganda was to disturb or to corrupt, it had become a society without any idea of itself and without faith in itself, without the *common faith* which could enable it to resist disintegration.[102]

O'Faolain rarely cited Maritain directly but Maritain's influence was evident in some of his editorial pieces, notably in 'What Possible Future' (1942), which presented Aristotelian and Thomist arguments, about human dispositions and about persons as inviolable ends in themselves, as the ethical basis for the good society:

> In other words we must agree that no view as to the possible splendid development of our country can dispense with the humanist concept of life – with man's natural ambition to participate in all that can enrich him in nature and in history, with man's efforts to exploit all him human potentialities, to make the powers of the physical world the instruments of the physical world the instruments of his freedom, to develop his reason and employ his creative powers to the utmost.[103]

Both Maritain and O'Faolain opposed state authoritarianism. Yet for both the state had a necessary role to play in realising human potential. In 1942 O'Faolain argued that state control should be welcomed when 'it transfers the responsibility for all public troubles – say Hunger, Poverty, or Disease – to the shoulders of Government, i.e. to us, the public, through our representatives'.[104] He railed against the campaign against the Beveridge Report, the wartime blueprint for the British welfare state, by the Catholic media. His perspective, however, was more that of a liberal Christian Democrat than that of a social democrat or socialist.

Some parallels with the work of George Orwell might be identified between the themes advanced by *The Bell* and O'Faolain: not least the call for essays documenting life in general and exploring the social conditions of the dispossessed. What O'Faolain sought from his contributors was often to be found in the work of Orwell. Both were patriots. Both were ambivalent about the intellectual elites they belonged to, even if there were crucial differences in how this ambivalence played out. O'Faolain saw himself as an improbable intellectual starved of intellectual companionship. Setting up *The Bell* was in part a quest for intellectual company. Even if he positioned himself outside the Irish intellectual elite, and even as a banned writer, he was very much part of the Irish literary establishment. Along with the elderly Yeats he was a founding member of the Irish Academy of Letters. If there was antagonism there had been friendship too. Older writers, such as Yeats and Æ, had nurtured, helped and passed the batton to the post-independence generation of realists that included O'Faolain and O'Connor.[105]

Almost four decades after the launch of *The Bell* Richard Kearney acknowledged O'Faolain's influence.[106] Kearney framed his essay 'Myth and Terror' (1978) with a quote from O'Faolain's autobiography where the latter recounted how, as a young man, he was caught in a labyrinth of nationalist symbols:

> And so blinded and dazzled as we were by our Icons, caught in the labyrinth of our dearest symbols – our Ancient Past, our Broken chains, our Seven Centuries of Slavery, the Silenced Harp, the Glorious Dead, the tears of Dark Rosaleen, the Miseries of the Poor Old Woman, the Sunburst of Freedom that we almost always believed would end our night and solve all our problems with the descent of a heavenly human order which we would immediately recognize as the reality of our never articulated dream ... I had nothing to guide me but those flickering lights before the golden Icons of the past ... the simple pieties of Old Ireland.[107]

O'Faolain's sojourn in this labyrinth was, at best, temporary. He recalled growing up in Cork with 'no consciousness of Ireland as a separate cultural entity'.[108] A temporary attachment to revolutionary republicanism and its Irish-Ireland hinterland came later.[109] From his time at Harvard during the 1920s he could present himself as a sort of citizen of the world. His literary successes were, in the first instance, international ones. During the 1930s he contributed essays and reviews to the likes of The *Spectator* and the *New Statesman*. He kept cosmopolitan company. For instance, in 1937 he travelled with Elizabeth Bowen to the Salzburg Festival together with Isaiah Berlin and Cyril Connelly.[110] He remained an adroit international networker. Irish recognition was impeded by censorship but some degree of distance from what he termed parochialism was perhaps inevitable, even if he eschewed the voluntary exile of a Joyce or a Beckett. The thread he followed avoided cosmopolitanism for its own sake. He was fond of quoting Æ as saying that a nation is cultivated 'only in so far as the average man, not the exceptional person, is cultivated and has knowledge of the thought, imagination, and intellectual history of his nation'.[111]

In 1953 he became the founder President of the Irish Council for Civil Liberties. In 1956 he was appointed Director of the Arts Council by the then Taoiseach, John A. Costello. Subsequently Costello tried to withdraw the offer under pressure from Archbishop John Charles McQuaid and right-wing Catholic groups such as Maria Duce; the reason being that, as President of the Irish Association of Civil Liberty, he had contested the censorship of 'immoral' literature and therefore was unfit to preside over the Irish arts.[112]

That McQuaid failed to block O'Faolain's appointment suggested that the social liberalism and anti-authoritarianism promoted by *The Bell* had gained ground. Chapter Six examines how this occurred in the face of apparent monolithic Catholic conservatism. However, the main intellectual battles that O'Faolain fought in the era of *The Bell* ended at best in a stalemate. Subsequently *The Crane Bag* reflected the extent to which the idealist nationalism he attacked proved to have an enduring appeal. The complexity of this appeal is partly the subject of the next chapter.

CHAPTER THREE

Unfinished Revolution: *Studies*, 1912–39

Studies was launched in March 1912. It was, and still is, published by the Jesuits. A catholic intent was signalled by its subtitle: *An Irish Quarterly Review of Letters, Philosophy and Science*. The stated object of *Studies*, set out in a foreword to the first issue, was to 'give publicity to work of a scholarly type, extending over many important branches of study, and appealing to a wider circle of cultured readers than strictly specialist journals could be expected to reach.'[1] Specifically, it sought to address general modern literature, comprising both critical and original work: Celtic, Classical and Oriental subjects; historical questions that had some bearing on religious and social issues; philosophy, sociology, education and the experimental and observational sciences. *Studies* was initially conceived as a review for University College Dublin, control of which in 1909 was handed over by the Society of Jesus to the National University of Ireland.

The Jesuits stayed on in academic posts and remained influential. Timothy Corcoran SJ, the first short-lived editor, was Professor of Education at UCD. Corcoran was also unofficial leader of the Sinn Féin caucus at the university.[2] He was close to de Valera, a mentor to the future Archbishop John Charles McQuaid and, later, also involved in the *Catholic Bulletin*.[3] Corcoran was described in a 1943 obituary as 'the master-builder after independence of the Primary and Secondary curricula'.[4] He was briefly succeeded by Thomas Finlay SJ, who went on to become UCD Professor of Political Economy. The third editor, Patrick Connolly SJ, remained in post from 1914 to 1950. Finlay's protégé and successor at UCD, George O'Brien, published twenty-six articles in *Studies* from 1923 on economic policy. O'Brien metaphorically and literally brought John Maynard Keynes to Ireland. In 1932 he invited Keynes to give the first Finlay memorial lecture at UCD in the presence of de Valera and his Cabinet. This was then published in the journal. A further member of the original editorial board, Alfred

O'Rahilly, Professor of Mathematics and later President of University College Cork, left the Jesuits before ordination but contributed thirty-seven articles between 1912 and 1961. The most prolific contributor to *Studies* was Michael Tierney, Professor of Greek, TD, Senator and later President of University College Dublin. He published fifty-five articles between 1922 and 1953.

Studies attracted contributors from the pinnacle of Irish Catholic academia. Occasional or one-off contributors cut across the mainstream of Irish intellectual and cultural life. These included Patrick Pearse, George Russell (Æ), Daniel Corkery, Sean O'Faolain and Daniel Binchy. *Studies* provided an important scholarly outlet for Irish academics though not, usually, for those at odds with the Catholic establishment. The first mention of the Jesuit-educated James Joyce in 1927 (by Tierney) disparaged the 'modernist incoherences' of his writings.[5] The first full article on Joyce did not appear until 1956. A self-critical internal assessment of the journal one year after its launch noted that it was mistaken to call it a review of either literature or science, given the kinds of articles it was attracting.[6] That *Studies* did not develop as a journal of literary criticism until the 1950s is unsurprising given the pro-censorship stance it developed during the 1920s. Nor, with a couple of early honourable exceptions, did *Studies* pay much heed to scientific debates. Most issues published in the first several decades included some emphasis on theology, comparative religion or history. The first issue, for instance, included articles entitled 'Tradition in Islam' and 'Athenian Imperialism'.[7] Themed issues debated cultural nationalism, the applicability of Catholic social thought, economic isolationism and censorship.

It was perhaps crucial that the core founders of the journal had been educated outside Ireland. They were more confident about continental efforts at social reform than the mostly rural Irish-trained clergy, who were not intellectually equipped to be 'anything other than reactionary'.[8] Several Jesuit contributors to *Studies* were well versed in socialist literature and ideas. Peter Finlay SJ, brother of the editor, drew praise from James Connolly for his understanding of Marxism.[9] *Studies* proved more intellectually open than other Irish Catholic periodicals. It exhaustively articulated a set of mainstream nation-building projects in post-independence Ireland. Its importance lay in how these were thrashed out and found wanting. These amounted to a series of thought experiments concerning the applicability of Catholic anti-modernism to the Irish twentieth century, political alternatives to liberalism and socialism, religious socialisation, cultural nation-building, constitutional reform and economic isolationism. The paradox was that positions outlined in *Studies* became more and more conservative into the 1930s while also facing a series of harsh truths, not least that few Catholics, lay or otherwise, intellectually grasped the philosophical and theological arguments against secularism.

AQUINAS FOR IRELAND

Between 1912 and 1939 the principal intellectual point of departure for much that was written in *Studies* about Irish society was the neo-Thomism that had become prominent within the Church from the late nineteenth century. It was initially mobilised against modernist dissidents within the Church as part of an ontological attack on the Enlightenment. In particular, the physical and social sciences were seen to pose challenges to Church doctrine. Only subsequently did more elastic appropriations of Thomas Aquinas's thought allow for engagement with modernity. Here the key texts were the 1891 papal encyclical *Rerum Novarum* and its 1931 successor *Quadragesimo Anno*. Both employed conceptions of natural law devised by Aristotle and Christianised by Aquinas to engage with liberal and socialist conceptions of the good society.[10]

Their core premises warrant summary here because of their centrality to the nation-building aspirations outlined in *Studies*. Drawing on Aristotle, Aquinas maintained that natural science abstracted unchanging rules from the study of changing matter and, in doing so, gave human beings knowledge of the material things that existed outside the mind. This included knowledge of human nature. Aquinas understood mankind's ability to grasp rules derived from such knowledge through the exercise of reason as the starting point of understanding natural law.[11] Here he quoted from Aristotle's *Metaphysics*: 'By means of my general rule about what constitutes a human being, I can make judgements about this and that human being. Now general rules don't change, so in that respect all science studies what must be so ... Though the general doesn't change it expresses a rule about things that do.'[12] To this Aquinas added: 'The vulnerability to change common to all creatures is not some natural tendency to change, but a dependence on God, without whom, if left to themselves, they would lose their hold on existence.'[13]

Aquinas understood the natural world to be governed by a natural law which concerned the rational human apprehension of those principles of eternal law that affected human nature and its natural ends. To seek to understand the natural world was to develop an understanding of God. Man had a body and a soul. Material existence was important because it was God's creation. Aquinas took from Aristotle an emphasis on the social nature of mankind and on the necessity of mutual co-operation on the conditions of the fulfilment of man's needs on every natural level. Government, as such, was recognised as a natural necessity if the activities of all were to be organised so that the good and sufficient life could be realised for everyone.

What this could mean in practice had yet to be worked through in the Irish case when *Studies* began in 1912. In an assessment published in *Studies* in 1981:

> Clerical analysis of the situation tended to be rather abstract and this is amply demonstrated by the fact that *Rerum Novarum* and other papal documents were being constantly put forward as solutions to the social problem. Many failed to see that these documents were, by their very nature, general in their principles and that these same principles needed to be applied concretely to the local situation. This, of course, both demonstrated and reinforced a very common phenomenon – the fact that religion and social life followed parallel paths but did not coincide. This meant that work and social responsibilities were not imbibed with a Christian motivation, that Catholic social principles did not relate to work and to the social problem generally. Religion was a private affair of the individual without any social consequences or, as Alfred O'Rahilly phrased it 'we in this overwhelmingly Catholic country have come to accept a condition of public life which is practically uninfluenced by Catholic principles'. The result was that the social question remained outside the sphere of the influence of religious conviction, a situation that is still evident in Irish life today.[14]

O'Rahilly was speaking in 1917. Independence brought with it a partial institutionalisation of Catholic ideals, but not quickly enough to satisfy clerics. In 'Divorce in the Free State' (1924) Peter Finlay SJ claimed that when the 1922 Constitution was being drafted, 'the Government, 'pressed with many cases and much grave anxiety at the time', was 'unwilling to create unnecessary controversy'.[15] However, Cosgrave had been genuinely anxious to reconcile Protestants to the new state. His Attorney-General, Hugh Kennedy, favoured a right to divorce for those who approved of it.[16] In 1926, with a prohibition on divorce now pending, Finlay argued that it was not necessary to consider the case of unbaptised persons – Gentiles or Jews: 'Their marriages would seem, indeed, to be indissoluble by natural law and by positive divine instruction.'[17] Finlay acknowledged that a prohibition on divorce would impose religious disabilities upon minorities but insisted on the Catholic view that there could be no right to what is sinful or immoral.[18] This was essentially the argument that the hierarchy forcefully put to Cosgrave's government.[19]

Catholic teaching and interpretations of natural law endorsed a prohibition on divorce, but when it came to alcohol *Studies* endorsed a relatively libertarian position. 'Prohibition in Practice' (1925) was clear that prohibition could not be justified under natural law. To argue that matter, be it alcohol, wheat or water, was evil recalled the Manichean heresy. It was the abuse of alcohol that was bad. Prohibition, as defined under the Eighteenth Amendment to the Constitution of the United States in 1919, had, it was argued, led to rise of a sinister and vile aristocracy with considerable political power and to the demoralisation of public life through bribery and widespread corruption.[20]

The emergence of neo-Thomist orthodoxy had been marked by trenchant conflicts with modern knowledge. Just a few years before the foundation of *Studies*, in 1908, Cardinal Mercier, the Primate of Belgium, publicly denounced George Tyrell, an Irish-born Jesuit priest, as a leader of the Modernist heresy.[21] Tyrell published a book-length reply entitled *Medievalism* later the same year. In it he defined Modernism as acceptance of the methods and results of science.[22] He argued that Church doctrine was specifically challenged by historical evidence: 'The Bible and the Church were not created by a Divine *fiat*, that they have grown with the growth of man.'[23] Tyrell observed that various orthodoxies, including papal infallibility, had emerged from long and bitter controversies within the Church. Tyrell's dissident position exemplified the conflicts which racked the Church's engagements with modernity. As a Thomist theologian he initially welcomed the revival of Aquinas's thought. However, he subsequently objected to its mobilisation for narrow doctrinal purposes. For Tyrell, faith was the only rock upon which the Church could survive. Facts, he wrote, were stronger than cardinals.[24] Tyrell drew a fundamental distinction between faith on one hand and the changing human synthesis of reason, science, and theology on the other. He advocated scientific freedom in the area of biblical criticism. As he put it: 'Religion cannot be the criterion of scientific truth, nor science of religious truth. Each must be criticised by its own principles.'[25]

It was Tyrell's approach to epistemology – not the doctrinaire anti-Modernism he criticised – that featured in the first issues of *Studies*. This could be seen in O'Rahilly's 'The Meaning of Evolution' (1912), which advanced a favourable critique of Charles Darwin's *On the Origin of Species by Means of Natural Selection* (1859) and of Darwin's subsequent evolutionary theoretical work.[26] Much of what O'Rahilly had to say might incense twenty-first century proponents of intelligent design:

> Darwin introduced his simple hypothesis into the supersaturated mass of biological observations; and at once the facts began to crystallise out in orderly array, clicking into their places, ranging themselves in harmonious sequence. Instead of being confronted by an amorphous heap of Baconian instances, men of science had now an object in working, a definite scheme to be proved or disproved. Thus, Darwinism provided the necessary psychological cue for action; by an ideal simplification of the problem, it allowed provisional schedules into which otherwise intractable facts could be classified.[27]

O'Rahilly's take on evolutionism was grounded in natural law. Evolution suggested 'the time expansion of God's purpose, the unfolding of an eternal plan'.[28] What came to be known as social Darwinism was contested in a masterful and even-handed 1914 article on Friedrich Nietzsche's legacy. 'The Gospel of the Superman' considered the influence of Darwin on Nietzsche's thought.[29] Nietzsche, O'Rahilly, suggested, 'out-Darwins Darwin' in his conclusion that life was essentially amoral: 'Darwin is emphasising the fierce gladiatorial warfare of nature; struggle for existence is not enough, it is a struggle for power, for more and more existence; beings not only want life, they want it more abundantly.'[30]

However, the two thinkers had deep differences in their understandings of human society. Darwin's *The Descent of Man* suggested that tribes willing to co-operate, help and defend their members were more likely to survive than those without such attributes. O'Rahilly's account of Nietzsche drew on a complex and sympathetic reading of the complexity of his *oeuvre*. It was not, for instance, to be blamed, O'Rahilly insisted, for the excesses of German nationalism, because Nietzsche clearly opposed such nationalism. Nietzsche's argument in

Thus Spake Zarathustra and *Ecce Homo* that Christianity was a slave religion was clearly explained. The intellectual importance of Nietzsche's 'lucid brutality' was emphasised.[31] O'Rahilly outlined Nietzsche's verdict on Thomist natural law and the Aristotelian concept of dispositions common to both (so as the acorn is disposed to become the oak, so do humans have dispositions to attain good ends) as *ad hominem* reasoning. In an age when 'time-worn phraseology is denuded of its meaning', when 'Christless philosophy is baptised word-deep in Christianity', there were times, O'Rahilly asserted, when 'one misses a man of Nietzsche's calibre, who calls a spade a spade and does not try to put a halo around a shovel'.[32] That said, O'Rahilly insisted that the influence of Nietzsche was a brutalising one. It lay at the heart of the cult of power (at the levels of the individual and of the state) that had penetrated modern life. Eugenics, a revolting renunciation of human nature, was an example of this.[33] Christianity, he insisted, retained a sociological value.[34] By this he meant that God-given natural law could be understood by the power of human reason and applied to earthly societies.

WRESTLING WITH SOCIALISM

The first issue in 1912 contained an article, 'The Future of Private Property', by Tom Kettle, who became something of an iconic figure amongst the liberal economists who wrote for *Studies* in the decades after his death in 1916. Arthur Cleary's obituary in *Studies* described him as 'the most brilliant mind of a generation, the generation that succeeded Parnell and Yeats'.[35] Kettle, Cleary emphasised, was 'at all relevant times a constitutionalist, a parliamentary nationalist, but with a highly developed dramatic sense', rooted in the orthodoxy of the Irish Party of Davitt and Parnell, but also part of a cosmopolitan movement that existed as an undeveloped alternative to the 'Irish-Ireland' ideology of which D.P. Moran was the prophet. A casual observer, Cleary argued, would describe this incorrectly as 'socialistic'. What this amounted to was 'an effort to apply cosmopolitan ideas of regeneration (often without any clear idea of what they were)' to social conditions – 'in fact, an aspiration towards modern "progress" of the less brutal kind'.[36] Kettle had once said, in a celebrated phrase, that he agreed with everything in socialism except its first principle. His disposition towards things 'liberal' was so strong that: 'if he had been brought up in a different religion, or perhaps even in a different country, he would not improbably have been a Free Thinker'.[37]

Kettle became an Irish Party Member of Parliament and then Professor of Political Economy at UCD. His 1912 article concluded that private ownership had indeed a future in twentieth-century Ireland and in Western societies more generally. The substance of it traced the appeal of socialist ideas in the face of nineteenth-century industrial and agrarian despotism: 'The French revolution made men drunk with the dream of freedom, though hardly with the fact of freedom, equality and fraternal love. The Industrial Revolution taught them, by harsh experience, that the first gift of the new science was slavery.'[38] This, together with the 'atomism' of the nineteenth century, was a 'new sociological context' that lent appeal to Marxism:

> Rich and poor, capitalist and worker, were regimented into two camps with an ever-sharpening conflict between them. To him that had was given, from him that had not was taken away even that which he had. It is not surprising that against a system that seemed to involve a progressive pauperisation of labour a literature of denunciation, passionate rather than constructive, hospitable to any idealistic solution, however unworkable.[39]

Kettle addressed what he saw as problems with socialist collectivism through the lens of Irish reforms. The Land Acts, he argued, were denounced by some as communism but by broadening the basis of private property they made that institution 'for all time impregnable in rural Ireland'. This was Kettle as Irish Party constitutional pragmatist. He closed his article with a passing nod to the relevance of Catholic social thought. However, most of what Kettle had to say amounted to a liberal reformist critique of collectivism, trenchantly and polemically critical of the viability of socialist ideals:

> Propagandists assure us that Socialism is a poetry, a religion. Whether it is a good or bad sort of poetry is a question for poets; certainly it is a miserable doctrine; it is a miserable religion. But it is in essence an economic doctrine; it is neither more nor less than a critique of private property ... Collectivism recommended itself to the affections of mankind with bombs and daggers; individualism with prison cells, knouts and halters. What has been the results of this long conflict of ideals? As is usual in all great material struggles, both sides have won, and each side has been beaten. The idea of private property survives, unshaken, and now proved impregnable; but profoundly modified. In other

> words, Socialism, as a constructive theory of the State, has been judged and set aside. This is not to say that it is impossible to imagine a society established on a Collectivist basis. It is not only possible but easy to conceive a static Socialism; it is not only difficult but impossible to conceive a dynamic socialism. Socialism is like a bundle of plans and drawings for a new mechanism. On paper they are at once highly logical, and indeed poetical. But if, out of that material at our disposal, namely human nature, we were to build the machine, it might possess every other virtue but it would not work.[40]

Kettle's certainty that socialism would not succeed was by no means initially presumed by Henry Somerville, author of two dozen articles on the subject between 1912 and 1931. His first, 'The Variations of Socialism', distinguished between the utopian tradition exemplified by Robert Owen, scientific and deterministic variants of Marxist theory and more recent reformist or revisionist socialism.[41] Somerville discussed the electoral failures of doctrinaire Marxism with its contempt for palliative legislation. Here he drew on an analysis of Bismarck's political success against the socialists in 1884. Bismarck's social reformism had in effect stolen the clothes of the left. As a consequence of such practical politics Somerville considered that socialist politics had become so compromised as to defy all definition. This, he concluded, was a good thing.[42] 'Socialism and the War' (1914) assessed the impact of internationalism though an examination of the response of socialist parties in different European countries.[43] Somerville's approach again was to offer a detailed account of positions and manifestos adopted by different European socialist parties. German socialists, he argued, always affirmed their readiness to defend the Fatherland, and were careful not to embarrass seriously the military position of the government. By contrast the avowedly 'anti-patriotic' anti-militarism of French socialists demonstrated a commitment to internationalist ideals. Somerville argued that the war itself demonstrated the 'fatuousness' of socialist propaganda that 'pretended that wars were caused only by a certain class for their own class interests'. They ignored the 'factor of nationality'.[44] Somerville concluded, without regret, that internationalism was a spent force.

But he argued that the class war between workers and capitalists was in some places at a 'very advanced stage'. In wartime South Wales the miners were 'the most restless and revolutionary of workers'.[45] That such workers were treated unjustly must be accepted. The root of labour difficulties lay in immoral business practices.[46] But this did not justify socialism. As summarised in a 1914 book review by another contributor, 'Socialism is undesirable economically and morally. The solution to our world-problem must be sought in Christian Democracy, with its harmonising of the claims of liberty and authority, with its assertion of the duty and just limits of State interference, with its emphasis on the duties of Capital to Labour and of Labour to Capital, and especially with its demand that the workman be given a "living family wage" and granted full liberty ... in pursuit of this end.'[47] In other words, mostly the same words, what was stated in Leo XII's 1891 encyclical *Rerum Novarum*. A number of articles advocated copying Continental European Catholic Social Action and Catholic trade unions. There was no point, insisted a 1915 article, in priests forbidding Irish workers to join socialist trade unions, unless there was a viable alternative.[48] This again was the argument of *Rerum Novarum* and explained the support of the Archbishop of Glasgow for strikes by Clyde engineers in 1915 and for South Wales miners seeking a just wage.[49]

Debates about socialism often remained abstract or theoretical. They rarely touched on Irish conditions and, if they did, they struck more conservative positions than did the Archbishop of Glasgow. A 1919 article, 'Socialism and Catholic Teaching', by Finlay maintained that the programme that the Irish Republican Socialist Party recommended to Irish workers from its headquarters in Liberty Hall was one that Leo XIII had explicitly condemned.[50] Here the argument consisted mostly of theological arguments against socialist collectivisation.

The more important question for Somerville was whether collectivisation would work better or worse than private ownership. Somerville's view was that it needed to be considered on a case-by-case basis. As he put it: 'The nationalisation of railways does not justify the nationalisation of farms; the failure of Government operation of the telephone service does not discredit the Government carrying of letters. Some industries may be suited to public management and others left to private enterprise.'[51] After weighing up the experiences of various countries Somerville concluded that the case for public ownership applied most strongly to natural monopolies such as railways, gas and waterworks.

Other contributors, notably Lambert McKenna SJ, scrutinised the Bolshevik Revolution. In 'Character and Development of Post-War Socialism' (1920) he argued that the Dictatorship of the Proletariat would not wither away; 'for history shows us no case of a dictatorship resigning or "withering away."'[52] In 'The Bolsheviks' (1921) he called the inner cadre of the Communist Party 'Mullahs who lead the Faithful of this new Islamism'.[53] Such disparagements were leavened with a degree of admiration. Although the Bolshevik experiment had 'proved to be a hopeless failure' there was 'something splendid about it'.[54] In 1926, 1929 and 1932 *Studies* published reports by visitors to Soviet Russia. In 'Two Months in Soviet Russia' Violet Connolly described a delightful 'pulse of life' behind the shabby character of day-to-day existence, noting only in passing that prospective émigrés recounted alarming stories about 'the latest communist enormities'.[55] In 'Reflections After Visiting Russia' (1929) Somerville came away by no means certain that communism would be an economic failure.[56] In 1932 the economist John Busteed insisted that the Soviets had accomplished colossal tasks.[57]

Somerville returned from Russia shaken out of his previous complacency that socialism in practice tended to become watered down and compromised.[58] His main observations in *Studies* concerned the state suppression of religious instruction and the workings of Soviet divorce law and maternity benefits. He professed to be shocked by the lack of revulsion amongst English-speaking people he met in Moscow for unconditional divorce ('if two people are no longer happy together, it is a tyranny to refuse them a divorce'), social insurance that allowed mothers four months' paid leave from the employment they were expected to return to and widespread childcare outside the home.[59] Bolshevik Russia's biggest danger was that it represented the triumph of a materialistic philosophy of life.

Studies, as such, examined socialism as a serious threat that warranted serious alternatives. Somerville's 'An Alternative to Capitalism' (1925) outlined what he had being trying to achieve by his own Herculean labours:

> For nearly twenty years I have been strenuously engaged in the propaganda of Catholic social teaching amongst Catholic working people. I have condemned Socialism, as I felt obliged to do unless I made nonsense of the *Rerum Novarum*. At the same time I have maintained that the Church condemns Capitalism as well as Socialism. I will not stop to justify my attitude on this point, for I have no reason to suppose that it will be challenged by instructed Catholics. I can say from experience that anti-Socialist propaganda which had the appearance of pro-Capitalist propaganda would be resented amongst Catholic working people and would do more harm than good.

> For quite a considerable period one can carry on propaganda by impartially denouncing both Capitalism and Socialism and making the general assertion that the remedy for social evils lie in the application of Catholic principles. The time comes, however, when your audiences begin to ask you for something more constructive and detailed. What are the actual reforms that Catholics would propose? The question cannot be indefinitely shelved. It is not adequately answered by making a selection of reforms that figure in the programmes of various political parties. Some of those reforms are capitalistic in the sense that they are intended to make capitalism more secure; others are socialistic in the sense that they are intended as steps to Socialism. It is very unsatisfactory for us to be denouncing our opponents at the same time we are dressing ourselves in their clothes.[60]

Somerville insisted that there was no viable anti-modern alternative to socialism: 'This reactionary utopianism has its attractions for all of us, especially in our moments of weariness, but it has no chance of being accepted as a solution of our social problems.'[61] Instead, he advocated a kind of Guild Socialist system of worker control, one proposed by a number of others in *Studies*.[62] Such co-operative societies would deprive capitalists of control but not deprive them of dividends. Wages were to be fixed at the lowest levels compatible with justice until the liabilities of capital had been met.

However, responses to Somerville disparaged the practicality of his scheme. Joseph Canavan, a Jesuit Professor of Ethics, insisted that Catholics were not bound to demand an alternative to capitalism. Professor John A. Ryan, who had written on profit-sharing in 1920, maintained that the Church could make moral judgements but that pragmatism was needed when evaluating the viability of profit-sharing schemes.[63] George O'Brien argued that Somerville's proposal suffered from the defects inherent in every socialistic or semi-socialistic Utopia. Capitalism was the only method of organisation by which modern industry could be organised. Echoing Kettle, O'Brien insisted that the glaring evils that had disfigured capitalism in the nineteenth century – child labour and the like – had already been abolished in most civilised countries. Nowhere in the world was a pure and undiluted form of capitalism to be found. A depressingly great deal of reform was still necessary, but the promotion of a new (Catholic corporatist) mentality would only serve to distract attention from more practical, if less romantic, remedies for particular evils.[64]

Similarly, the Revenend John Kelleher, a Professor of Theology, argued that capitalism may be 'shaken and discredited' but still held sway. Neither natural law nor Supernatural Revelation required the establishment of an alternative to existing economic systems. The ethical requirements of these had, in fact, never been met by any previous human economic systems. Slavery, feudalism and capitalism had all existed in Christian countries and had been tolerated by the Church. What Somerville proposed would be 'more of a hindrance than a help'. It would be perceived as a timid variant of socialism. Somerville, in his view, appeared to be fixated on finding alternatives to state or public ownership. Under his scheme, owners of capital would lose control but be compensated. Under socialist collectivisation they would lose ownership but be compensated. To the ordinary mind this was hair-splitting. Full-blooded socialism was simpler and more intelligible. Capitalism, as such, badly needed to be reformed.[65]

What is striking about such responses is the extent to which the possibility of a Catholic alternative to capitalism and socialism was dismissed even as Catholic vocationalism was coming to the fore in Europe. Only Hilaire Belloc (who had earlier contributed a series of articles on the treatment of Catholicism in Gibbon's *Decline and Fall of the Roman Empire*) saw what Somerville advocated as a step in the right direction. His bottom line, however, was that the enormous evil of capitalism could be tamed only by the re-establishment of the Church as the moderator of European civilisation.[66]

A 1926 review article by O'Brien praised R.H. Tawney's *Religion and the Rise of Capitalism*. Tawney's book was compared to Max Weber's critique of the role of Protestant aestheticism in understanding the rise of capitalism. Tawney, O'Brien argued, offered a more sophisticated account of the different branches of Calvinism than Max Weber and addressed the significance of non-religious factors in the rise of individualism and capitalism. O'Brien took some umbrage at the dichotomy implied by Weber and, to a lesser extent, by Tawney between progressive Protestantism and backward Catholicism without challenging the core argument that the modern industrial spirit was brought into being by the Reformation.[67] Merely to plead, then, that a religious reaction was all that was needed for the survival of Europe was to shut one's eyes to the reality of the situation. There was, O'Brien insisted, no feasible third option distinct from 'the Scylla of godless business and the Charybdis of the godless State'. If it came down to it, it was a matter of choosing the lesser of two existing evils.[68]

The problem, Somerville admitted in 1931, was that Catholic aspirations for a 'third way' could be realised only in a society dominated by a 'real Christianity', the bucolic Christendom yearned for by Belloc, as distinct from one merely comprising flesh and blood Catholics.[69] In a dismissive assessment of *Rerum Novarum* (1891), on the occasion of its successor *Quadragesimo Anno* (Forty Years Later), John Busteed questioned how many of the 150 legislators in the Dáil Éireann had ever read it ('setting forth, remember, fundamental and unchanging economic doctrine for Catholics'). 'If there are four or five, I would be surprised.'[70] Even if all had read *Rerum Novarum* and taken it to heart, Busteed implied, Irish economic policy would continue to be inevitably shaped by the 'unchristian liberalism that dominated the world economic system'.[71]

Yet, Busteed argued, capitalism was seriously flawed and economic planning would always have advantages over the 'anarchy of *laisser-faire*'.[72] It was not enough 'for the West of hunger-marchers and silent factories' to decry Bolshevik efficiency in the materialist sphere. Communism, he insisted, was driven by a clear-headed logic, something materialist capitalism could not claim. For a Catholic community to insist, on the basis of prejudiced evidence, that communist industrialism must crash was, he argued, criminal folly. It was not enough 'to meet the threat by negation, suppression or denunciation, by platitudinous references to an unread *Quadragesimo Anno* or by pious approval of movements that do not move'.[73] Busteed typified the dominant position in *Studies* at the time, even if Somerville doggedly insisted that co-operative ownership and profit-sharing schemes, as an 'alternative to capitalism', were possible and practical. However, if Somerville could not win support from a handful of colleagues what hope was there for winning Irish hearts and minds?[74]

Support for European vocationalism also proved qualified. 'Italian Catholics and the Economic Problem' (1923) praised non-socialist experiments in establishing factory councils that adhered to Catholic social teaching. Political changes in Italy were presented as a great success of Catholic politics and as an example to Irish Labour.[75] Other accounts of the Italian experiment were more pessimistic. Virginia Crawford's 'The Rise of Fascism and What it Stands For' (1923) noted the apparently successful corporatist restructuring of trade unions and the establishment of vocationalist councils, all along lines mooted by Catholic thinkers. However, this was leavened by a scathing account of Fascist terrorism:

> The trained bands of Fascisti, organised on a strict military basis, and containing many ex-service men in their ranks, were let loose, by Mussolini's command, on their Socialist fellow-countrymen. The methods pursued can best be explained to Irish readers by saying these were those of the Black and Tans. Lorries filled with armed Fascisti would concentrate at a given signal on a Socialist municipality, setting fire to Labour Halls and Co-operative Stores, destroying and looting property unhindered.[76]

Mussolini, she reported, had restored religious teaching in the schools ('not that he is a practicing Catholic but he accepts Italy as a traditional Catholic country and believes that religion is beneficial for the masses'), but all (including prospective Irish admirers), she argued, would be wise to copy the extreme caution of the Vatican in its dealings with the new Italian state.

EDUCATION AGAINST UTILITARIANISM

In the first issue of *Studies* Timothy Corcoran SJ attacked the usually venerated Cardinal Newman, architect of the Catholic University of Ireland. In 'Newman's Ideas and Irish Realities' (1912) Corcoran, then Professor of Education at UCD, argued that Irish realities were at odds with Newman's Oxford-derived vision.[77] What 'Ireland and the Irish race' had needed in the middle of the nineteenth century were professional schools of law and medicine together with newer disciplines not known to Oxford at that time aimed at reversing 'the evil results of the Penal Laws on their social position and their right to work'.[78] Their due places in the law, in medicine, in engineering, in the industrial arts, in commerce, 'all these had to be asserted or won back'.[79] In 'Social Work and Irish Universities' (1912) he criticised the disdain of Oxford and Cambridge tradition for degree courses in areas such as engineering, metallurgy, commerce and architecture as a bad model for Ireland.[80] However, he argued that the separation of intellectual training from experience and practical duties was 'one of the evil results of the miscalled liberalism of the Renaissance'.[81] Economics, for instance, had, at one stage, become abstracted from the economic realities; pleas to 'mitigate flagrantly inhuman treatment of child operatives in the North of England' would be 'non-suited in dignified language by the classical Economists of England'.[82] Economics and sociology were fine as long as these were not detached from social reality as understood by the inviolable truths of God-given natural law.[83]

Corcoran advocated the development of applied social work courses within the National University of Ireland. These should replicate much of the curriculum of British social work courses but substitute Catholic social thought for social philosophy as these would have understood it. The NUI, he argued, would have 'no difficulty in building its superstructure of applied sociology upon Papal encyclicals such as *Rerum Novarum*'.[84] A programme modelled on the Central Labour College in London could to build Irish outreach programmes in philosophy, sociology and commerce.[85] Similarly, Somerville's 'A Catholic Labour College' (1921) emphasised the role of education in winning hearts and minds.[86] Catholic organisations should, like the British Labour movement, put forward their 'picked men'. These would not necessarily be the most intellectually able. There should be tests in 'mental alertness, in Catholic and public zeal, in community spirit and initiative, not merely book knowledge' – tests used by the Catholic Summer School at Oxford in 1920.[87]

Education, Somerville argued, was 'the means to power which churches, nations, parties, classes and this world neglect at their peril'.[88] Something of a Marxist conception of social structure, with a consequent denigration of the power of human agency, was evident in his opening argument. To speak of 'freedom of thought' to someone who knew modern life was to invite derision:

> The whole of the periodical press is doctored, the text books in all the schools are doctored, and the films shown at cinema entertainments are doctored by those who for political, religious or economic reasons are interested in emphasising some facts and suppressing others, in insinuating some beliefs and destroying others.[89]

Somerville's critique of modernity anticipated themes associated subsequently with later secular sociologists such as Theodor Adorno in *The Authoritarian Personality* and Herbert Marcuse in *One Dimensional Man* and also popular critiques of totalitarianism by writers such as George Orwell and Aldous Huxley.[90] The propaganda experts of the state, the market and, by implication, the Church relied on the force which mere suggestion exerts on half-trained minds such as were ordinarily produced among the masses of the people by the modern school system. Somerville was struck by and quoted *The*

Social Direction of Human Evolution by the American Professor William E. Kellicott. Here Kellicott anticipated the future prevalence of eugenicist propaganda. The same techniques that sold pills and pickles, that made free trade or tariff reform a national issue, 'when linked to Eugenic proposals ... [would] in a few years make these proposals a living force to the common man'.[91] The stakes in the future propaganda wars anticipated by Kellicott and Somerville were high.

Corcoran's advocacy of Catholic social thought as the true sociology and Somerville's argument that this could replace the secular ideas that fostered socialism both placed the education system at the front lines of the battle against secular modernity. Both argued that practical and professional and advanced education could be harnessed to natural law metaphysics. In practice, educating Irish minds against the epistemological challenges of modernity proved no easy matter. There was a tendency to fall back on the hard-line restatement of dogma and a preference for catechisms above intellectual argument.[92]

In 'The Present Crisis of Intelligence' (1937) Arthur Little, a Jesuit Professor of Philosophy in Tullamore, argued that a Catholic social order could not succeed unless Thomist metaphysics were extended to finance, economics, education and science, as well as to religious education.[93] Little made the case for bringing Scholastic philosophy into Irish secondary schools.[94] In a second article, 'The Case for Philosophy in Secondary Education' (1938), he argued that Irish Catholics were incapable of withstanding intellectual attacks on their faith.[95]

However, a lack of philosophical rigour in Little's article exercised Michael Browne, Bishop of Galway.[96] He did not take warmly to Little's criticism of existing religious instruction of secondary school pupils. Browne doubted whether their minds and even the minds of clerical students were mature enough for philosophical speculation. Little had maintained that Immanuel Kant, Gootfried Wilhelm von Leibnitz and René Descartes were unable to grasp Thomist metaphysics. If this was so, what chance then had Irish boys and girls? O'Rahilly too doubted that the secondary system could handle Scholasticism. Like Browne he argued that Catholic philosophy must become a compulsory subject for degrees in the arts, medicine and law, as was the practice in the Catholic University of Louvain. O'Rahilly detailed how this was beginning to be done at University College Cork:

> Here in Cork we have made some little headway. We have started a course in sociology – the papal encyclicals are for the first time

> prescribed as official texts. It is obligatory for students in commerce. It may be capable of extension so that all our students during their course may learn something about the living issues – family, state, communism, fascism and so on – on which they read about in newspapers and see in the cinema... this year there has been another experimental innovation – the introduction of the 'elements of psychology, ethics and sociology' into the pre-medical year. It comes a bit early in the course, but it is the only place where it can be fitted (I am told that some of the parents resent it; their little darlings must not be diverted from bread and butter subjects).[97]

For Tierney, as for other contributors to the 1938 symposium on philosophy in schools, the real threat was a pervasive materialism that would reduce education to a machinery for getting boys and girls into jobs – a 'shoddy edifice of commercial, technical and pseudo-professional courses'.[98] What was needed, he insisted, was not just a Catholic restoration but a Gaelic one. Both were required to counter 'the great heresies of the last three hundred years'. Here Tierney's position combined something of the nostalgic Catholic medievalism of Belloc with the idealised Gaelic medievalism of Daniel Corkery in *The Hidden Ireland*. In drawing such connections in 1938 Tierney articulated a common cause between cultural isolationism and Catholic conservatism. Here, education was the crucial battleground.

CULTURE AGAINST DEMOCRACY

The hope that the Catholic restoration of Ireland would also be a Gaelic one provided the basis for a compact between Thomists and cultural isolationists. The culture that Tierney would restore was the European one that preceded the Enlightenment. Ireland's ruined Gaelic order constituted a vacuum into which the utilitarian English-speaking nationalism of Daniel O'Connell had successfully poured. The now-dominant culture was an English-speaking materialism destructive of both high culture and religion. Tierney's roll call of 'heretics' who had 'crippled and perverted all the arts' took in Réne Descartes, John Locke, Jean Jacques Rousseau, G.W.F. Hegel, Karl Marx, Friedrich Nietzsche, Jeremy Bentham and J.S. Mill. Newspapers carried their 'intellectual and moral diseases'. Politicians imbibed their ideas without ever having read a line they wrote. Cultural renaissance, for

Tierney, involved much more than a revival of the Irish language. Tierney's reconstruction would exorcise the alien secular ideas of the Enlightenment that, he admitted, had been the very building-blocks of Irish independence.

The extent to which post-independence Ireland could or should overthrow Enlightenment ideas became a running debate in *Studies*. In 1919 Corcoran had looked forward to an independent Irish education system that would cast off the 'alien misdirection of education effort' that had prevailed since Ireland's 'democratic clan-system of Education was crushed in the sixteenth and seventeenth centuries'.[99] Other contributors also anticipated the argument of Corkery's *The Hidden Ireland*. As put in an anonymous article from 1918:

> By long tradition of preserving resistance to aggressions on their national life; by the possession of a distinctive culture and social order; by their corporate unity; acknowledged since the dawn of European civilisation; by the ample proof of political wisdom and comprehensive tolerance that they have always shown; by their spiritual and social development from within, manifested most of all in the last hundred years; by their moral courage amid severest trials, the people of Ireland have established beyond question their possession of all the qualities and attributes of a free nation.[100]

'Lessons of Revolution' (1923) by Æ offered a pessimistic assessment of the failure of the revolution to overthrow the British legacy. Free State Ireland had 'hardly deflected a hair's breath from the old cultural lines'. Preoccupation with material reconstruction would, he argued, thrust all spiritual and cultural ideas out of sight.[101] The champions of physical force, he continued, had unintentionally poisoned Ireland. They had squandered a spirit created by poets, scholars and patriots: 'spending the treasure lavishly as militarists in all lands do', to give 'a transitory gilding to their propaganda'. Ireland seemed immeasurably further away from a spiritual nationalism than it was in 1914.

The same 1923 issue debated the future of the Irish language. The lead article maintained that literary Irish could be viable only if differences between dialects were suppressed.[102] Native speakers had kept the language alive, but they could not save it in a modern world. Irish could not survive as 'an adornment of some sleepy fairyland which, in these prosaic times, the rough hand of reality so easily and ruthlessly shatters'. If the language was to be rescued it must be as a vehicle for the expression of every idea and thought which the nation required. One of two things was needed. One was the emergence of some literary genius who would do for Irish what Shakespeare and Dante respectively did for English and Italian. However, literary geniuses were not made to order. The only other way was through the willpower of a language dictator: 'The unhappy dictator will be despised in the *Gaeltacht*, reviled in the Dáil, caricatured in the newspapers, loftily refuted in university lectures. But if he has good sense, courage and perseverance he will do a noble day's work for the language and for Ireland.'[103] All, seemingly, that could be done was to hold out for a hero or a despot.

The overall tone of the 1923 language debate was pessimistic. As one put it, the 'struggle of a people drugged with Anglicisation' to save the language would 'thoroughly test the grit of the Irishman'.[104] Another was more optimistic. Now, after thirty years of propaganda public opinion, the schools and government were on side. But if Irish was to survive it must be in a new form. Languages changed rapidly when taken over by new populations, especially when the new speakers outnumbered the old. Already 'learner's Irish' had its *Lautverschiebung*, every sound was a bit wrong.[105] Another contributor pointed out that much of the existing bilingual population spoke English habitually and by preference. Many of those who had held on to it did so not from love or out of patriotic pride but because they could not help it.[106] All concurred that state action to institutionalise Irish was required, but stopped short of endorsing the proposed language dictator. The only such dictator needed was someone who would make it his business 'to see that in every Irish-speaking district Irish shall be petted and English discouraged'. The petting was to be a financial one: 'parents will speak Irish to their children when Irish spells bread and butter, as English did in the past'.[107]

1927 saw a further symposium on the revival of Irish. Tierney's lead piece argued that failure would render worthless the sacrifices made to attain independence. Shannon hydroelectric schemes, sugar factories and other efforts at reconstruction meant little by comparison.[108] The two enemies of success were blind antagonism amongst some elements of the intelligentsia and blind optimism in other quarters. Tierney advocated a pragmatic approach within schools. All things about Ireland should be taught through Irish at all stages. The Sisyphean toil of producing science, mathematics, Classics and language textbooks in Irish should be avoided. However, the cost of substituting for Ireland's English-language literature was warranted. He advocated a modern form of patronage by nobles of poets in Ireland's medieval period. That the likes of James Joyce were undeserving of support was made clear.[109]

Three reply articles agreed that Irish, as things stood, depended for its survival on the *Gaeltacht* and that the *Gaeltacht* needed more economic support if native speakers were not to emigrate. The problem with this was that economic development had, so far, extended the use of English.[110] One pointed out that the Irish aristocratic culture favoured by Tierney – 'Medieval because Ireland for good or evil escaped the Renaissance' – was three hundred years dead.[111] Another, by General Richard Mulcahy, cited data on the revival of Finnish to make the case for teaching all subjects through Irish.[112] He insisted that the will of the people was behind the revival of Irish. The day would come when there would be no need 'to fall back on any other medium for instruction in sciences or for the expression of any part of the National Mind'.[113] However, the Finnish data he referred to suggested that this optimism might be misplaced. The Finnish revival dated from 1821. The figures for 1916 quoted by Mulcahy identified just six out of a total of twenty-six Physics and Mathematics Professors as lecturing in Finnish. A further three taught in both Finnish and Swedish.[114] Mulcahy's article was attributed to Risteard Ua Maolchatha, but the unmentioned elephant in the corner was that debate on the revival of Irish had to be conducted in English.

As put by Tierney in 1938: 'in spite of our modern preoccupation with Gaelic culture, only those who care little for the meaning of what they have to say can apply the phrase to anything very living or effective in Ireland at present'.[115] The context here was a symposium on Sean O'Faolain's biography of Daniel O'Connell, *King of the Beggars*. A modern Irish culture, Tierney argued, could be built on the old Gaelic culture but a viable political system could not. The nation-state, he explained, was a nineteenth century invention that 'coincided with the decay and gradual disappearance of the native ways of thought, life, and expression'.[116] Tierney drew a parallel between the present disjuncture between Irish culture and politics and what occurred when the Normans became Gaelicised: 'cultural absorption coincided with a calamitous failure to create or even conceive of a Gaelic state'.[117] O'Connell's contribution to the modern Irish nation was, Tierney argued, a philosophically utilitarian one that readily discarded this legacy.[118] The English language and the ideas it communicated ('the whole complex of Puritan and Utilitarian anti-culture') were now integral to the Irish nation.[119] However, these needed to be understood as part of a broader process of pre-independence modernisation and nation-building. As summarised by Tierney:

> The link, forged by O'Connell and still strong today, between Irish nationalism and English radicalism. Middle-class liberalism, manhood suffrage, and the land Acts, have between them created an Ireland as different as anything could well be from the Ireland which slowly but inexorably collapsed between the Battle of Kinsale and the treaty of Limerick.[120]

The problem for Tierney, then, was not merely a linguistic problem: 'a mere change in language might now hardly have any effect' on the dominant, as he saw it, Irish culture. Tierney's thesis was that the Irish Revolution had politically internalised that which it supposedly stood against. His underlying presumptions here warrant quotation:

> The truth that political nationalism in itself, while it may be an excellent vehicle against English government, cannot by its very nature be of any use against Anglicisation. There are two reasons for this: first the obvious one that you cannot quarry rocks with razors; and second, the less widely realised fact that nationalism, even in Ireland, is itself for the most part a thing of English origin. Its real home is the Dublin of the ascendancy, and almost all its heroes belonged to the type of Ascendancy younger sons who for one reason or another could not fit into the system and who in thoroughly Puritanical style revolted against it and brought a reinforcement of English and French radical ideas to justify and strengthen their revolt.[121]

Implicit in Tierney's critique of how alien ideas filtered into Ireland was the absence of native political intellectual tradition.[122] The nation-building foundations laid down by O'Connell; the roots of Irish democracy from Catholic emancipation through later extensions of suffrage were ones that had filled an indigenous vacuum: O'Connell's Benthamite ideas justified the abandonment of Gaelic for the 'superior utility of the English tongue'. This did not validate, Tierney insisted, a rejection of the linguistic revival even if irritation with some of the crude measures for reviving the Gaelic language was justifiable. That O'Connell's democratic nation-building occurred alongside Gaelic cultural decline was to be regretted. As Tierney put it, 'Democracy is no substitute for culture.'[123] This held even if the culture being revived was inauthentic. Many successful civilisations were built, Tierney explained, on attempts to 'recover literary, linguistic and artistic traditions that were not always genuinely ancestral to them'.[124] The vanished Gaelic past, however unreal, was a necessary ideological bulwark against the cultural void of individualism and utilitarianism.

Tierney, then, had no real quarrel with O'Faolain's account of the genesis of the modern Irish nation in *King of the Beggars*. Gaelic League platforms were built on 'faked tradition' but this did not, he argued, warrant a denunciation of the older Gaelic order of society that preceded the political Irish nation.[125] But here Tierney returned to his earlier point: a cultural restoration did not fulfil the institutional needs of a nation-state. The revival of 'faked tradition' should be abandoned for the English-speaking seven-eighths of the country. Efforts should be concentrated on the rapidly dwindling areas where Gaelic was still spoken, where it was not 'fake'. He concluded that 'a sane and honest policy in regard to Irish in our day is an even more fantastic dream than was the hankering of the poets of the eighteenth century after the vanished Ireland of their fathers'.[126] Tierney tried to have it both ways. His reading of the politics of cultural nation-building was astute. The invocation of a mythic past sometimes worked as symbolic politics but not as a basis of policy-making.

O'Faolain's reply took issue with Tierney on a number of points. His use of the term 'Puritan' betrayed a Catholic chauvinism that his essay would have been better off without. Tierney championed Gaelic culture for the Catholicism it had for centuries cherished as a 'nationalised religion'. However, this was a Church 'which never produced any articulate philosophy, whose hagiography was without merit' even if it copied some fine manuscripts.[127] In other words it was arguably no more vibrant than the Gaelic court poetry O'Faolain thought so little of. Tierney's prioritisation of culture (real or imagined) over democracy in the politics of nation-building was one that O'Faolain opposed.

THE POLITICS OF LITERATURE

Studies, for the most part, sidestepped the politics of literature for its first decades. It published little on the literature of the Celtic Twilight – no full article on Yeats appeared until 1934 – and ignored the banned generation of post-independence Irish writers. In 'Some Types of Irish Character' (1912) William Boyle dissected portrayals of national identity in modern Irish literature. The author admired the greatness of Yeats, but not his grasp of reality and his Celtic Twilight imitators, concluding that: 'One Yeats is enough for Ireland.'[128] A 1934 article by Francis Shaw SJ disparaged the anti-Christian dream world evoked within Yeats's treatment of the Irish sagas, Druidic themes and the Celtic Twilight in general. His poetry was criticised as expressing the character of the Celt as rendered by Matthew Arnold: 'the ineffectual, romantic dreamer who lives in a constant state of reaction against the despotism of fact.'[129] O'Faolain made it into *Studies* as a historian rather than as a writer of problematic fiction which addressed topics that fell foul of the censor.[130] In its early years *Studies* endorsed, though mostly posthumously, the poet-scholars of the 1916 Rising. In 1913 Patrick Pearse's 'Some Aspects of Irish Literature' had claimed greatness for the Gaelic epics whilst disparaging the court poetry revived by Corkery a decade later.[131] Pearse's benchmarks for greatness were both Classical (he claimed the Tain exceeded the Greek) and modern (Gráinne was the Hedda Gabler of Irish literature). His stated opposition to sentimentality in later Irish literature made him an unlikely bedfellow of O'Faolain:

> One finds it in the later literature, especially in the later poetry, bad taste of various kinds, but never that particular kind of bad taste. The characteristic faults of the later poetry spring from various causes. First, the metres which had been elaborated on became a snare. And secondly, Irish poets, most conservative of races, retained an obsolete machinery and an outworn set of symbols long after the machinery had become unnecessary and the symbols had ceased to be convincing. There is a place for symbols in literature, but there can be no excuse for using symbols in which you do not yourself believe.[132]

Studies responded to the Easter 1916 Rising with a series entitled 'Poets of the Insurrection'. Praise for their poetry was measured. Praise for their characters was unstinting. Thomas McDonagh's patriotism, as evident in his poems, was described as a 'furnace glow of passion'.[133] Joseph Mary Plunket drew admiration for proclaiming that he was dying for God and the honour of Ireland.[134] John F. MacEntee was described as 'a genuine if immature poet', who hated 'all that the word "England" means to an enlightened and patriotic Irishman', yet was passionately fond of English literature, architecture and art.[135] Each was described as an exemplar of Catholic piety and true patriotism.

McEntee, who survived 1916, changed his first name to Seán and gave up on poetry for a long career in politics. The summer 1916 verdict on Patrick Pearse was that he was a better short story and prose writer than he was a poet. Some of his poems were 'so simple that one may not say much about them'.[136] However, he was portrayed as a brilliant educationalist in his use of school pageants to foster simultaneously a patriotic and religious spirit amongst his pupils:

> Two great exemplars were always kept before the eyes of his pupils – the youthful hero Cuchulainn and the Divine Boy who lived subject to His parents at Nazareth. From the study of these exemplars he hoped they would get that gallant inspiration which was to help them to overthrow the forces of evil with which they would have to war outside. Miracle-plays and pageants were to help in producing this inspiration. The boys who were to take part in the Cuchulainn Pageant, and in the Irish Passion-Play, were not likely to forget the great lessons taught by characters they personated, and the parts they played. It might seem a daring experiment to have the sacred characters of the Passion represented by schoolboys; but the simple sincerity of the boys, and the reverent training of the master, secured that religious atmosphere which was necessary for suceess.[137]

Studies, then, was quick to represent the 1916 insurrection (not yet the Rising with a capital 'R') in terms that anticipated the juxtaposition of Christ and Cúchulainn later marshalled by Yeats.

However, *Studies* also celebrated a broader church of Irish patriotism. A eulogy for Thomas Kettle appeared in December 1916 alongside the one for Plunkett. Kettle died at the Somme just weeks after the executions that followed the 1916 Rising. Arthur Cleary described meeting Kettle in Dublin following the executions: 'his whole conversation was of MacDonagh and the others who had been put to death in Low Week, of the fortitude they had shown. He felt very bitterly ... He died in a different way for a different cause.'[138] In 1920 *Studies* published an article by Henry Gill SJ, a much decorated former member of the Irish Guards (DSO and MC) which described his unsuccessful efforts to retrieve the flag of the Irish Brigade from the Convent of Les Dames Irlandaises in Ypres, at the time a deserted ruin 'being heavily bombarded by gas shells almost every night'. The flag in question was a 'relic' of the Irish brigade which had fought in the Battle of Ramillies in 1706 under Lord Clare. Irish regiments fought on both sides of the 1706 battle. Clare's brigade fought against the British.[139] His account of his quest referred to the death of another Jesuit chaplain to the Irish Guards, a fellow aficionado of the history of Irish regiments.

Debates in *Studies* on censorship promoted cultural isolationism as well as the preservation of Catholic morality. In 1918 *Studies* published an article, 'The Cinema Peril', that advocated extending existing censorship.[140] The author, John Ryan, was clearly entranced by the wonders of cinema but pointed to the dangers resulting from its brilliance as a means of communication. 'We cannot', he argued, 'afford to barter away the Irish ideals of humour and virtue for those that obtain in the busy marts of England, of America, or upon the Continent of Europe. Better to remain in our ignorance; better not to know the machinery of other lands; better to be content with our innocent mirth than to participate in the cosmopolitan gaiety of sin.'[141] The example he gave was of a tendency of American films to include bedroom scenes and lightning marriages 'which take place anywhere and everywhere, in spite of *Ne temere* or other impediments'.[142]

Ryan argued that British censorship was not robust enough to meet the Catholic view (nor that of High Church Anglicans and the bulk of evangelical Christians).[143] He recalled seeing a picture-house representation of a number of young women who were supposed to be unclad that had been passed by the British Board of Film Censors (although he had no doubt that they were covered with some thin fabric not likely to be noticed by young people). He advocated parish priests taking responsibility for recommending suitable cinemas in their areas ('and giving a lead in denouncing what may be wrong') as an addition to inadequate censorship and industry self-regulation. A later 1926 article on American cinema censorship described the workings of the Hays Code, which policed Hollywood movies.[144] Catholic censorship, as such, became internationalised.

ON RACE AND NATION

A 1918 piece, 'Irish Fiction for Boys', surveyed and classified stories with Irish characters and settings.[145] Not much was available in the area of school stories. The atmosphere, tone and spirit of English school life as presented in most of these stories was, according to Stephen Brown SJ 'wholly alien to that of our Catholic schools at home' even if most were 'morally healthy in tone'.[146] Brown began his survey with a warning against the promotion of 'narrow nationalism', one that would 'shutter up the face of the youth of any country all the windows that look forth upon the great world in order to capture their whole minds for the country of their birth'. Such nationalism, he cautioned, 'would in the long run be doomed to failure'.[147]

Earlier, in 1913, Brown published two articles that launched an ongoing debate in *Studies* about nationality and national identity: 'What is a Nation' and 'The Question of Irish Nationality'.[148] The former opened with a series of quotations, one from Tom Kettle's *The Open Secret of Ireland*: 'The open secret is that Ireland is a nation.'[149] Brown then outlined and discussed the extent to which the Irish case fitted criteria for nationhood identified by 'anthropologists and sociologists' in the 'truly vast body of literature dealing with the connection between national character and *race*'.[150] The specific criteria outlined – physical environment, race, language, custom, religion, common interests, history – were broadly equivalent to those evoked in the late twentieth century in definitions of ethnicity. Ethnicity is a term that only gained currency from the 1970s.[151] 'Race', as used by Brown with some degree of equivocation, referred to presumed national characteristics rather than those presumed to relate to genetic phenotype.[152] Brown identified custom, the unwritten and traditional codes which rule the habits of people and 'by long iteration, furrows deep traits in its character' as a 'nation-building force'.[153] Linguistic distinctiveness too could have a nation-building role.

However, Brown emphasised that the boundaries of language and national belonging were by no means the same even if a common language – here he was thinking of the United States – had the power 'to weld into some sort of oneness' the 'jumble of races as is to be found within its borders'.[154] Religion, he argued, was 'the strongest and most important of the elements which go to constitute nationality'.[155] He instanced the power of Mohammedanism 'to bind its votaries into a kind of national exclusiveness'. Before the Reformation, he argued, the idea of a common Christianity was stronger that that of loyalty to separate nationalities: 'The enemies of Christianity were, so to speak, the national enemies of all.'[156] Since the Reformation, religious differences had prevented devotion to a common country but the experience of modern nations had shown 'the absurdity of the notion that there can be no national unity without religious unity'. Brown emphasised the role of historical consciousness – of Fatherland as 'the patrimony of memories that unite us to our fathers and in terms of an understanding of common origin' – as the crucial block of nation-building.[157] Nations were held together by common memories:

> A nation looks back on its past as a lesson for its national life in the present, and as a justification of its continued national life in the future. Common memories are the nourishment of patriotism, the foundation of national consciousness and by the common hopes and aspirations that sprung from these.[158]

Taking these elements together, 'race', language, custom, religion and common understandings of history, Brown drew a few conclusions about what constituted a nation. A nation consisted of a relatively large group living together in common territory in organised social relations held together by a peculiar kind of spiritual oneness. There was, he insisted, nothing mystic about this sense of oneness. National consciousness consisted 'of common memories of historic things wrought in common and suffered in common in the past, and secondly the actual consent to carry on that common life, as a distinct people, master of its destinies, shaper of its future.'[159]

Other articles on nationality engaged with Brown. 'The Problem of Nationality' (1913) disagreed with his depiction of 'race' as a factor contributing to nationality.[160] No nation, C. Jocelyn O'Hehir argued, 'is now composed of a single race, but in each a *predominant* race actually exists'.[161] O'Hehir distinguished between nation and state, thinking not so much about the Irish case (an Irish nation within a British state) but as a set of ideals and institutions that could change and reform – he gave the example of shifts from monarchism to republicanism in France – whilst being contained by the nation.[162] The state institutionalised the nation as: 'the concrete expression of phases of a nation's spiritual life'.[163] What nation or nationality meant was inevitably unclear even if constituent elements could be listed, as Brown tried to do. Nationality meant, O'Hehir argued, different things to different groups and classes. In 'Class and Nationality' (1914) he examined the roles of different social classes in national movements.[164] He outlined a general typology whereby the leader was surrounded by a small group of lieutenants 'all animated by a feeling of pure patriotism' and a mass of followers 'actuated almost exclusively by a lively sense of personal wrongs to be righted and economic oppressions to be relieved'. Most leaders, he argued, however pure and disinterested their patriotism, find it expedient to appeal more or less to this instinct.[165]

Brown's 'Recent Studies in Nationality' (1920) addressed the problem of using the terms 'race' and 'nationality' interchangeably. [166] Here, in the absence of the concept of ethnicity, he sought to explain how the term 'race', as used by anthropologists, acknowledged no racial distinctions between Europeans.[167] Race understood as nation admitted 'absurd and often unjust explanations' of the inherent qualities of different types: 'the Latin decadent, the Slav politically incapable, the Irish lazy and mendacious', and so on. Brown's literature review examined the use of abstractions such as the Teutonic, Anglo-Saxon or Celtic races. It cited refutations of the German idea of nationality, which was understood to be 'based on the ethnographic or race theory'. Brown's account, to use a later terminology, was sceptical of accounts that presumed intrinsic characteristics of any race as nationality. Yet Brown presumed a psychology of national character.[168] Different peoples (Brown used the term 'race' for want of an alternative) cultivated distinctiveness. Distinctions in the Irish case between culture and phenotype had emerged in a 1919 article as pejorative ones. Here John Horgan quoted Erskine Childers on the distinctiveness of Irish claims for national self-determination:

> Ireland is now the only white nationality in the world (let us leave coloured possessions out of the discussion) where the principle of self-determination is not, at least in theory, conceded.[169]

The white Irish, he argued, deserved parity with other white nations and colonial powers.

A number of articles preoccupied with national character emphasised the role of the German state in promoting national culture. '*Kultur* and Our Need of It' (1915) fixated on the achievements of the German state.[170] *Kultur* was defined in the following terms:

> *Kultur* is not primarily an attribute of the individual, as culture is, but of the group, and especially of the nation. It is what makes a nation a state, it is its organic life. It consists, in a word, in ordered co-operation. Its scope is not merely intellectual, but is moral, spiritual and material as well. It is the action of the state in stimulating and guiding the energies of its subjects and in co-ordinating them with one another for a common purpose, and the reciprocal devotion of the citizens to the state. It is the product of education; perhaps the most wonderful of its products, for it implies the universal, willing, and above all, intelligent acceptance of a common ideal.[171]

A watered-down version of *Kultur* was advocated in the Irish case, although the mechanisms for achieving it were hardly in existence. It was noted that the Local Government Act had restored a measure of control over destiny into Irish hands and soon, it was to be hoped, this would be extended through Home Rule. Ireland, it was concluded, had much to learn from Germany. A fascination with all things German is visible during the early years of *Studies*.[172] German education, with its emphasis on science and technology, was posited as an alternative to the Scholastic model preferred by many contributors.[173] Most articles on German *Kultur* were critical. For O'Rahilly it was essentially warlike. He blamed this, to a considerable extent, on the influence of German Idealist philosophy.[174] Behind the reasoned Kant of the categorical imperative O'Rahilly discerned a more chauvinistic one who depicted war (in some instances) as enobling the character of the nation.[175] State-idolisation, he observed, citing Hegel and Johann Gottlibe Fichte, seems to be an integral part of the philosophic legacy of Germany's classic thinkers. For Hegel, 'The Nation (*Volk*) as State is the Spirit in its substantial rationality and immediate actuality, and therefore it is the absolute power on earth.'[176] Fichte's writings, he argued, demonstrated 'how thoroughly philosophy had co-operated with the State in the pedagogical dragooning of the people'.[177]

In Germany, O'Rahilly noted in 1915, 'culture bears a government stamp, it is a state product, manufactured in school and camp. The result is that, at least in academic circles, legitimate pride in German science and method has become a veritable obsession, and has swollen into intolerable and intolerant conceit.'[178] From a Catholic perspective, the notion of a state monopoly in nation-building was an anathema.[179] Brown in 1923 outlined a Catholic natural law critique of nationalism from the perspective of the universal Church. This allowed the legitimacy of maintaining the 'indispensable diversity of nations'. National autonomy could be in accordance with natural law. Where the state already existed nationalism, he argued, had a positive role in placing the interests of country above party. But it was not without its dangers. Whatever might be thought of in the abstract, it could be difficult to love its concrete manifestations. Brown wrote: 'In my own country extreme nationalism has broken the unity of the Catholic forces; it has spoilt vocations to the priesthood; it has propagated anticlericalism; it has cooled religious enthusiasm. Elsewhere it gives rise to rapine, murder, incendiarism.'[180] In the specific Irish context extreme nationalism was to be condemned for undermining the legitimacy of Church and Free State.

A 1925 article, 'Nationality as a Claim to Sovereignty', by UCD Professor of History and soon-to-be Minister of Education John Marcus O'Sullivan, echoed much of Brown's argument.[181] The nation, O'Sullivan maintained, had a quasi-personality: 'There is a feeling of oneness, a will to be and to act as one; a distinct culture has been evolved, which at least tends to desire and even create its own governmental machinery. Its members have grown together, so as to have developed a corporate consciousness, a spiritual oneness, a feeling that they can live happily when they live together, unhappily when forcibly separated or subordinated to others.'[182] O'Sullivan accepted that a vigorous national feeling combined with a strong spirit of independence was perhaps one of the most solid foundations that a state can have. However, it could be taken too far. Extreme forms of nationalism were not to be condoned. In the end nationalism, as an ideology, rested upon abstraction and as such differed, or should differ, from the real loves people could have for individuals or family. O'Sullivan's main theoretical standpoint was again grounded in natural law conceptions of social order.

In 1933 Professor Daniel Binchy, the Irish Minister to Germany from 1929 to 1932, published an astute article on Adolf Hitler immediately after his rise to power.[183] Binchy had first heard Hitler speak in Munich in 1921. He had read *Mein Kampf* ('Written in a maddeningly wooden style, in which hackneyed *clichés* alternate with windy rhetoric, full of rambling digressions and hysterical denunciations') and closely followed Hitler's rise. His article detailed the role of anti-Semitism in building the National Socialist movement from 1920 onwards. Hitler's race theories ('Hitler does not seem to know the meaning of the word Aryan: indeed he is not even sure of the meaning which he intends to attach to it') built on ideas 'made fashionable by pseudo-ethnologists of the last century'.[184] Binchy took care to refute various anti-Semitic claims noting, for instance, that thousands of Jews (denounced by Hitler as traitors) had fought bravely for Germany during the Great War and the self-contradictory claims that Jews were at once 'the leaders of international capital and of the Bolsheviks who seek to destroy it'.[185] Binchy detailed plans, outlined in *Mein Kampf*, for the withdrawal of citizenship from Jews and the consfication of their property. He outlined the Nazi eugenics proposals advocated by Alfred Rosenberg ('who seeks to atone for his Jewish name by exceeding all others in anti-Semitism'). Hitler, Binchy explained, would extend sterilisation policies to those who were either corporally or mentally unfitted to have vigorous offspring.[186] Binchy's scrupulous refutation of anti-Semitism stood out from a degree of implicit anti-

Semitism within a number of contributions to *Studies* during the 1930s. It also differed starkly from the enthusiastic anti-Semitic perspective of Charles Bewley, who headed the Irish legation in Berlin from 1933 to 1939.[187]

'The Nazi Movement in Germany' (1938) also contested Nazi racial theories. The Reverend Denis O'Keeffe, then Professor of Ethics and Politics at UCD, rubbished Rosenberg's book *The Myth of the Twentieth Century*: 'The Nazi assumes that society is an organism of people of the same race; he assumes that mentality follows race; he assumes that an accident of birth is the sole determinant of a man's fitness to be a member of a community.'[188] O'Keeffe was clear that Nazi racial theories were 'pseudo-scientific nonsense'. Their real importance, he implied, was as psychological tools of nation-building:

> It is a natural tendency for nations to seek an escape from the inadequacies of the present in a mythical past. This is a common experience in all countries. But it requires a portentous absence of humour to accept the theory in the form given to it in Nazi literature – in this form it is altogether pathological. A certain minimum of self-esteem is, no doubt, necessary for the nation as for the individual. And unsuccessful peoples, in moments of stress, may have difficulty in reaching it. This is the purpose of mass-propaganda. It aims at restoring self-respect to a defeated people. In moderation racial feeling may be at the worst an amiable weakness, at best a proper pride. The Greek, with much justice, thought himself superior to the barbarian. And in a negative way we have all heard, nearer home, of 'lesser breeds without the law' and of the 'wild hysterics of the Celt'.[189]

If for O'Keeffe extreme racial theories were absurd it was still necessary, if possible, to 'think well of one's nation as one's family'. His meditation on Rosenberg and national identity as it might apply to Ireland brings to mind the fictional responses to Irish Jews in James Joyce's *Ulysses*. For the Jewish character Bloom a nation consisted of the same people living in the same place, a *non sequitur* that allowed the Citizen, the belligerent cultural nationalist, to place him outside the bounds of the Irish one. The principal problem faced by Jews in the Irish case proved be their exclusion from the dominant religious solidarity that defined the Ireland of *Studies*.

What Ireland might or might not do about Nazi anti-Semitism was touched upon in two 1939 articles. The first, 'The Refugee Problem', addressed international norms and options for dealing with refugees. It referred to German and Austrian refugees but not to the fact that many of these were Jewish. It noted that in Ireland the functions of determining which refugees should be admitted and guaranteeing that they did not become a public charge by caring for them while they were in the country were supplied by a private organisation, the Irish Co-ordinating Committee for Refugees in Ireland.[190] First and foremost the Co-ordinating Committee was envisaged as a vehicle for Catholic solidarity. This body was chaired by T.W.T. Dillon, a Professor of Medicine at UCD and author of thirteen contributions to *Studies*. Michael Tierney was also a member.[191] The UCD committee was charged by the Department of Justice with vetting refugee applications, and, more importantly to its members, perhaps, by Cardinal Pacelli, who had recently become Pius XII and had forwarded a donation of £1,000 'to form the nucleus of a Catholic fund ... to help Catholics from Germany'.[192]

Preoccupation with Nazi persecutions of Catholics was unsurprising. A necessarily anonymous 1935 article from inside Germany had described these in trenchant detail.[193] Solidarity with beleaguered Catholics was inevitable. However, Dillon's article sought to justify why the Irish Co-ordinating Committee, with effective control over Irish refugee policy, did not recommend the admittance of Jewish refugees to Ireland.[194] It outlined the rationale for and workings of an Irish State policy which explicitly discriminated against Jewish refugees before, during and after the Holocaust.[195] Dillon advocated a policy of admitting Christian refugees considered as non-Aryan 'hybrids' or *Mischlinge* (those, he explained, with Jewish ancestry who had converted to Christianity) under the Nuremburg Laws, but not unconverted Jews. Dillon argued that the plight of these 'Christian Jews' exceeded that of the unconverted Jews because they could not turn to wealthy Jews in America for assistance.[196] In essence, he argued that only Catholic refugees should be admitted. Dillon's attitude to the Nazi expulsion of the Jews from Germany was, to say the least, ambivalent. The Nazis had, he noted with a degree of admiration, thoroughly cleared out 'modern European culture' even if it left a void that he doubted they would be able to fill.[197] Dillon drew on prevalent anti-Semitic stereotypes in justifying, in effect, why Ireland should not admit Jewish refugees.

Irish anti-Semitism variously portrayed the Jews as enemies of Church and nation though not of the Irish 'race'. By the 1930s, notwithstanding the terminological confusion inherent in the term 'race', cultural understandings of national character had become distinguished from genetic phenotype. Social hygiene in terms of racial eugenics or the control of unfit populations ran clearly against Catholic philosophy.[198] Prevalent conceptions about the undeserving poor, which implied that the undeserving poor were intrinsically disordered and hence unfit, were also challenged. For example, in 1920 Lambert McKenna SJ described living conditions in the city's slums and tenements and their effects: 'the high mortality, the impaired physical vigour, the prevalence of sickness, the temptations to drink, the thriftlessness, the impossibility of parental control over children, the temptations to immoral conduct, the very common neglect of religious duty'.[199] However, McKenna was at pains to distinguish such people from prevalent Victorian liberal stereotypes of the people of the abyss. On the whole, McKenna argued, they were 'wonderfully good – good, thousands of them, to the point of heroism'.[200]

Studies, then, occasionally echoed a prevalent anti-Semitism prominently articulated in some Catholic periodicals such as *The Catholic Bulletin*, *The Irish Mind*, *The Irish Rosary* and *The Cross*.[201] Amongst the Jesuits this was epitomised by Edward Cahill. Cahill often emphasised how many communists were Jews.[202] He expounded a range of anti-Semitic propositions in his 1932 book *A Framework for a Christian State*.[203] McKenna on the other hand had contested such stereotypes noting for instance that in the Munich revolt some Jews had been victims of the Bolsheviks.[204] As far back as 1914 a review of *Jewish Life in Modern Times* depicted Jewish society as having 'wonderful powers of organisation and co-operation' and cultural and scientific achievements of which any nation should be proud.[205]

CONSTITUTIONAL MATTERS

Responses within *Studies* to partition and the Treaty emphasised the advantages of the former and the sad inevitability of the latter. In June 1922 *Studies* published a piece of reportage by a Jesuit on anti-Catholic violence in Belfast: 'A city in which over 400 men, women and children have been murdered and over 1,600 wounded in religious pogroms that have gone on unchecked for almost two years'.[206] The article vividly described the murders of several Catholics and Catholic experiences of widespread intimidation in and around Easter 1922. However, it appeared alongside another, 'Partition in Practice', which counselled a *realpolitik* acceptance of the status quo, not least for the safety of Northern Catholics.[207]

Studies stood squarely behind the Treaty. In one of a several of appreciations of Arthur Griffith published after his death in September 1922, P.S. O'Hegarty argued that President Griffith had 'brought to Ireland a Treaty with England which made Ireland absolute master in her own house, with full economic and cultural freedom and with practically full political freedom'.[208] In 1922 O'Rahilly published a two-part assessment of its constitutional status. In 'Is There Common Citizenship?' he argued that the terms 'subjects of the Crown' and 'British subject' might have had emotional or psychological value but they had no political value. The latter was, he argued, quite innocuous: 'It merely serves to bring home to each individual the formal or symbolic unity of the British Empire ... [and] usefully disguises from the uneducated the absence of political unity.'[209] Citizenship, on the other hand, was defined in terms of the complex of social, civil and political relations to the community of which a person was a member. In such terms there was no common citizenship within the British Empire, especially not within a Dominion with 'the inherent power to legislate *for its own territory*'.[210] Any so-called common citizenship could only be, he argued, the product of joint legislation by independent Parliaments which, he concluded, any Dominion was at any time free to cancel or modify. In a subsequent article he argued that the Crown, to whom the oath of allegiance pertained, had evolved as a separate legal entity from the State. It was, he argued, 'merely a roundabout Anglo-sentimental way of saying that the Dominions, under the ambiguity of the Crown, are the real recipients of effective allegiance'.[211]

In 1933 *Studies* published a symposium on constitutional reform. John Horgan's article outlined options drawn from the very different wells of the Swiss system, which he argued would allow for a model that could incorporate Northern Unionists, and Antonio d'Oliverira Salazar's Portugal. What attracted Horgan in particular to Salazar's model, which 'made no pretence at democratic principles', was the restriction of the franchise to heads of families only. Horgan argued that Irish society was essentially primitive, patriarchal and agricultural and that the family was, and he hoped would remain, the keystone of the structure. Adult suffrage was the fruit of an industrial civilisation, where the family was 'in fact' disintegrating. It was, in his opinion, totally unsuited to and destructive of Irish moral and social life. One option that attracted Horgan was granting votes on the basis of age, one for a person aged between 21 and 30, two votes for those between 30 and 40 and so on. This would restore control to the responsible elements in the nation.[212]

Horgan's proposals were opposed by William T. Cosgrave, the good steward of Free State democracy from 1922 to 1932. Cosgrave professed faith in the 'genius and capacity of our citizens for self-government'. He ranked 'the gradual education of the people by experience of political life and by the inculcation of proper standards of political conduct' above any evaluation of suitability on the basis of age.[213] Senator James Douglas, who had been a member of the 1922 Constitution Committee, was pessimistic that a Swiss model of power rotation could work given the outlooks of the present-day 'Orangeman from Portadown' and 'Catholic Irish-speaker from Dingle'. As for doing away with the party system, he quoted an American friend who held that the Irish knew how to run a party machine better than any other people on earth. Michael Tierney, in his role as Honorary Secretary of the United Ireland Party (renamed Fine Gael), had more sympathy for his fellow party member Horgan, at least on the franchise issue.[214] His personal preference was for restricting it to those over 25 years of age.[215] He was opposed to continuing with proportional representation on the grounds that it brought out the worst in party politics: 'All it has done is to make the ordinary healthy functioning of party government more cumbersome, and thereby to make political contests more bitter, more expensive and more futile.'[216] Collectively the other commentators on Horgan's proposals anticipated Churchill's later maxim that democracy was the worst political system except for all the others.

In 'Ireland and the Reform of Democracy' (1934) Tierney observed that 'democracy is a flower of delicate nature and brief duration ... Like civilisation, democracy is a difficult enterprise, a complex and subtle way of life.' He argued that autocracy had been the historical norm, 'the easiest and safest refuge for humanity when higher and more dangerous forms of government have broken down'. It offered a 'short-cut method of saving civilisation from anarchy' but represented 'a failure of nerve'.[217] Praising Horgan's 'able and stimulating article' he argued that Irish democracy needed its own distinct renovation. By this he meant a Christian-inspired divorce from 'the superficial mysticism of the French Revolution, the visionary mysticism of the English liberal school and the confused and inadequate mechanisms which revolutionaries and radicals have imposed upon older political theories and systems', the defective doctrine of Tom Paine's *The Rights of Man* and *On Liberty* and 'the inverted Hegelian dialectic of Marx'. Paine, for Tierney, represented 'the visionary Jacobin deification of the State which had triumphed over the equally visionary individualism of the English radicals'.[218]

Tierney's preference was for a minimalist state that stripped back the existing administrative and institutional inheritances from 'the cumbersome traditional system of Great Britain'.[219] Tierney criticised the orthodoxy that, through its elected representatives, the democratic state was to be the sole legitimate expression of the will of the people. The Irish state, he argued, should abdicate from 'its exclusive claims to be the unique mouthpiece and controller of social action'. Noting that article 45 of the 1922 Constitution empowered the Oireachtas 'to provide for the establishment of Functional or Vocational Councils representing branches of the social or economic life of the Nation', he advocated the establishment of a Corporate Chamber to replace the existing Senate, representing these in accordance with *Quadragesimo Anno*. This would provide Parliament with 'a new type of trained representative standing for a well-defined group'.[220]

In 'Partition and a Policy of National Unity' (1934) Tierney argued that the cause of reunification would benefit if the Free State now declared a twenty-six county Republic. To sit on the fence without either doing so or actively embracing membership of the Commonwealth merely left the country with the disadvantages of both options.[221] The greatest dangers now facing Ireland, he argued, were sham republicanism and sham dominionism. The first held off declaring the twenty-six counties as a Republic. It kept the so-called ideal of an all-Ireland Republic dangling out of reach and thereby fostered 'a pathology of unrest'. Tierney was opposed to any declaration of a sham (he kept using the word) all-Ireland Republic. The sham dominionist, he argued, appeared to think that the Irish state could stay indefinitely within the British system ('which he dearly desires to do') while knocking away, one by one, 'all of the very light and easily borne chains' that bound it to that system.[222] Tierney argued that the declaration now of a twenty-six county Republic would set the ground for a project of national cohesion.[223] In a context where Ireland could not be reunited by 'any single act of statesmanship', reunification had to take a back seat to achievable nation-building politics. Behind all this Tierney aspired to pre-Reformation Gaelic Christian ideals as filtered through the lens of Catholic social teaching. Civil war politics got in the way of such ideals.

Respondents to Tierney's article ignored his hopes for the restoration of Christendom-in-one-country and focused on his case for declaring a twenty-six county Republic. As one generously put it, Tierney knew his Plato too well to confuse ideal with practical politics.[224] Horgan, in his response, advanced the (in Tierney's view 'sham') argument that the cost of affixing the label 'Republic' to the existing 'Free State' would be the sacrifice of the 'the historic Irish nation'.[225] Daniel Binchy, former diplomat and self-described 'convinced Dominionist', argued that Britain could afford politically to bully an Irish Republic with impunity. Leaving the Commonwealth would, he argued, lower the standard of living and cut off avenues to Irish citizens 'in territories which Irish hands and Irish brains had done much to build up'. However, he accepted Tierney's case that sham republicanism was sapping the foundations of national morale and that no sacrifice would be too heavy if it ended the cynical exploitation of an ideal for party purposes. Much more than Tierney, he was concerned about not sinning further against the cause of Irish unity. Without the glue of Commonwealth status and common institutions, unity would be even more difficult to conceive of than it was at present. The declaration of a Republic now might be to 'commit the most deadly sin', one the next generation would find impossible to commit. The best solution was to hold a plebiscite and let the Irish citizens decide on which side of the fence they wanted to be.[226]

In 'The Constitution and the Senate' (1935) O'Rahilly observed that the Corporate State, something he had long supported, was popular on paper, but that Ireland was as far from being one as it had ever been.[227] He had shifted away, he explained, from supporting the organisation of Irish society on the basis of different guilds, an idea that had since encountered a serious setback. There was no real point to a vocational Senate with, say, one doctor, one professor, a few industrialists, some farmers, shopkeepers and workers, and so on. Dáil Éireann was, as things stood, probably just as diverse. Instead the emphasis had to be on the adoption of a Christian Constitution protecting, as he put it, 'our natural and religious rights and embodying our social aspirations'.[228] The 'our' in question were 'the People to whom God has given political authority'.[229] In a burst of earlier articles, four between 1918 and 1920, O'Rahilly had emphasised a Thomist Aristotelian tradition of democratic thought and natural rights distinct from the 'travesty' of Rousseau and Paine.[230]

In O'Rahilly's scheme the Senate would function as a guardian of the Constitution to prevent unconstitutional legislation 'more effectively and less pedantically than the judiciary'. Who exactly, then, would protect the Christian Constitution? Part of the Senate would be elected by the Dáil; the rest by such existing bodies as 'could be fairly taken to be occupational or representative groups'. These, as identified by O'Rahilly, would include: 'Trade Union Congress, Federation of

Irish Industries, General Council of County Councils, Teachers (Primary, Secondary and University), Lawyers, Medical Practitioners, Engineers, Auditors'; he wished to add farmers but did not know which organisation could represent them.[231] The nation-building conversation pursued within *Studies* inevitably emphasised prevalent Catholic conceptions of the good society framed in accordance with papal teaching. Behind the scenes the Jesuits had a considerable influence upon the wording of de Valera's 1937 Constitution.[232]

Many articles in *Studies* genuflected to the ideal of a united Ireland. What this could and should mean in practical terms was up for continual debate. The anonymous 'Present Position of Catholics in Northern Ireland' (1936) described as absurd 'the myth of papal domination' deployed by Unionists. Propaganda that Catholics were subversive conspirators was deployed to justify systematic discrimination against them.[233] It detailed a lengthy list of attacks on Catholics from early May to 12 July 1935. The '1935 pogrom' resulted in several deaths, seventy-three families burned out of their homes and 514 families displaced.[234] Notwithstanding such occasional accounts, debates about unification were usually abstract.

A 1938 article by Tierney wearing his Senate hat, 'The Problem of Partition', considered three potential solutions including the one routinely preferred by nationalists: 'the spiritual assimilation of the [Northern] people into the nation'.[235] Southern Protestants, he observed with distaste, had yet to become so assimilated. Indeed, the opposite had happened. Hunt Balls filled a cultural vacuum in the upper echelons of the Free State. Petit bourgeois surburbanity, he argued, was effectively puritan or post-puritan. His implicit assertion was that the real spirit of the Irish nation had really more in common with Northern Protestantism than could be admitted by what he described as the 'hasty, superficial and uncertain propagandist creed' of Irish cultural nationalism.[236] That this might provide a basis for future reunification was ignored and would, on all evidence, have horrified Tierney in any case. The South should assimilate the North, not vice versa.

His argued that unless the existing cultural nationalist creed could be replaced by a solid cultural foundation 'the Irish nation-state will neither have the certainty of direction nor power to assimilate or attract elements now separated from it physically and spiritually'.[237] How the Gaelic cultural restoration he advocated would appeal to Northern Protestants was left unexplained. The implication was that the will to power of a so-reconstituted Ireland would find a way to make it so.

Tierney's second option was to redraw the border, place some Catholic areas within the Free State and introduce direct rule from Britain: 'The untransferred territory might be administered as an English county.'[238] With the passage of time, especially in the face of any new European crisis, this rump would be vulnerable to assimilation. A third 'less possible' option of power sharing was also mooted. A key aim here would be to institutionalise arrangements that achieve 'the protection of our fellow-countrymen against violent and notorious persecution'. Otherwise the powers of the Belfast Parliament 'could be left as they stand', although financial and military responsibilities would be shared by the British and Irish governments.[239] Another article in the same issue by an Irish army officer explained that the Irish state was poorly placed to exploit any European crisis. In 'Can Ireland Remain Neutral in War?' (1938) Colonel J.J. O'Connell found vulnerability to invasion on many fronts. He went as far as to suggest indelicately that the 'effective militarily defence of Ireland demands unity of military control', that is, under British control.[240] This was not power sharing as understood by Tierney.

By the early 1930s, as Maurice Manning put it, 'Tierney had acquired a reputation for combining the visionary with the authoritarian.'[241] Amongst contributors to *Studies* he stood out for his engagement with and synthesis of the different nation-building experiments it advocated before the Second World War. Nobody agreed to all that he had to say; his argument for isolationism was a high culture one, his cultural nationalism was an aristocratic one no less 'fake' than the common or garden Gaelic revival he disparaged, the licence with which he evoked imaginary Irelands of his choosing stood in contrast to the vehemence of his constitutionalism. His political compatriot John Horgan was by no means wedded to democracy for its own sake.[242] Horgan's prioritisation of paternalism over democracy stood in opposition to the criticisms of Fascist corporatism elsewhere in *Studies*. Yet, long before Tierney's 1932 proposal to restrict the franchise to persons over 25, a 1915 article, 'Votes for Youth', had seriously advocated extending it to all persons over the school leaving age of 14 years.[243]

ECONOMICS AND ISOLATIONISM

A common theme in the early years of *Studies* was the promotion of Irish economic self-sufficiency. In 1918 Æ argued that the experience of the Great War demonstrated the need to develop self-sufficiency through agricultural co-operatives. These could be used to build up food manufacture and so increase the viability of rural Irish society.[244] Ireland, Alice Stopford Green noted, had supplied almost 30 per cent of the meat supplies imported by England in 1910.[245] Overall agricultural exports of £22.25 million at that time were almost as much as the combined worth of the three other leading industries: ships, linen and porter. The first two of these were located in the north-east. The success of Ulster, she argued, had become an object lesson for the rest of Ireland, where industry had steadily declined during the second half of the nineteenth century.[246] She insisted that political independence would bring some economic benefits. Irish imports and exports could be assessed properly (as profits and losses) rather than be obfuscated by the English Treasury. She also reported concerns from British commentators that the Irish would embrace economic protectionism.[247]

After independence Irish economic policy was anti-protectionist. A punctilious observance of British economic orthodoxies, including the doctrine of free trade, prevailed.[248] This was reflected in *Studies*. 'A New Currency for the Free State' (1923) by Bernard McCartan warned about temptations to devalue Irish scrip to fund state expenditure.[249] The Irish pound could go the way of the German mark. In a Swiftian digression it was suggested that those north of the border would benefit, buy goods and holiday in the Free State and, inevitably, succumb to its charms and hasten reunification. This in turn would bring economic viability and a strong Irish currency. A number of response articles engaged with the specifics of managing a currency pegged to a gold standard or some other form of security. Ireland's gold had been shipped to England during the war. One suggestion was to call in the British Treasury notes still in circulation and use these to underpin an Irish currency of the same nominal value.[250] Against a general consensus in favour of a conservative policy – putting actual and perceived financial stability above all else – the case for using fiscal policy to fund an economic reconstruction was made.[251]

A 1924 article by C.H. Oldham, Professor of National Economics at UCD, lambasted the assumption that protectionist tariffs would foster industrial development.[252] Oldham pointed to the incapacity of the Irish home market to absorb the whole of industrial output. Exports were crucial for the survival of Irish manufacture. Protectionism would be inflationary because imported raw materials were needed. Economic development, he argued, could be sustained only by *laissez-*

faire policies and by resisting a sentimental chauvinism towards Irish goods.[253] Oldham used the analogy that it made no economic sense to give alms to beggars. All this did, he argued, was increase the number of beggars. Irish industry would have to survive on its own merits.

Against this George O'Brien, in an article on the 1925 budget, suggested that a tax on advertisements could be levied so as to give preference to those of home manufacturers, 'thus affording a harmless measure of protection'.[254] O'Brien noted, approvingly, that the Irish budget continued to be modelled on the pre-Treaty British system of taxation. Capital expenditure adhered strictly to the narrowest and most conservative interpretation of orthodox budgetary management principles. The 1923 budget had reduced income tax levels by a shilling in the pound. This equalised rates with Great Britain. Post-independence economic policy was slaved to that of Britain. However, a 1926 article warned that Ireland could ill afford what Tom Kettle had called the 'champagne standard' of the United Kingdom. By this Kettle meant that measures that involved only small charges upon the immense revenues of Great Britain, and which confirmed real benefits upon an industrial country, were forced upon an Ireland that could not afford or benefit from these.[255] Independent Ireland needed to cut its cloth to its own measure.

Debates about economic protectionism overlapped with ones about censorship and the Irish language. In December 1927 *Studies* published a symposium article with replies advocating tariffs on imported newspapers and magazines.[256] At that stage the Report of the Committee on Evil Literature had yet to be translated into a bill. Richard Devane, the Jesuit author of the lead article, argued that imported media, including magazines and papers for children, were undermining efforts to revive the Irish language. He cited evidence from the Catholic Truth Society to the Committee on Evil Literature that estimated sales of the *Daily Mail* in the Free State at between 70,000 and 100,000, alongside sales of 65,000 for other English dailies and combined weekly sales of 352,803 of English Sunday newspapers.[257] To this he added anecdotal evidence of weekly sales of 145 English juvenile papers in a single shop in a Dublin slum. The only Irish competition was the fortnightly *Our Boys*, published by the Christian Brothers. 'Against such propaganda of the English language and English ideas', he argued, 'the present effort at national revival looks very much like an effort to beat back an avalanche with a sweeping-brush. At school the Irish language is drilled into the children; but when they come home they seek relaxation and amusement in

English papers and story books.'[258] Devane advocated that imported printed matter other than scientific, technical, trade, literary and arts journals be subject to a tariff of 25 per cent. Such matters were the business of the Committee on Evil Literature but were also, Devane concluded, a matter for the Tariff Commission.[259]

For the most part Devane's arguments were enthusiastically endorsed. The editor of *The Irish Rosary* agreed 'heartily with every word' but added that a tariff of 100 per cent on imported publications would scarcely break the stranglehold which foreign daily papers had gained over the Irish public.[260] For Senator P.J. Hooper, editor of the *Freeman's Journal* between 1916 and 1924, Father Devane deserved the gratitude of all who had at heart the moral and cultural welfare of the Irish people. According to Professor Tomas O'Rahilly, Devane had 'rightly stressed that mere political freedom is valueless if intellectually we are in chains'.[261] The problem for P.J. Hooper was one of countering the kind of literature and cinema that was '*de-nationalising* and demoralising'. In his view, Devane's proposals did not go far enough. Measures to check the distribution of 'de-nationalising' publications were required.[262] Hooper enthusiastically looked to the Commission on Evil Literature to promote legislation that would 'bar out a great mass of prurient and demoralising publications'.[263]

Tierney's endorsement of this majority position was qualified. A tax on imported newspapers might remove the need for the Irish press to compete with and imitate the mass-produced sensationalism of much of the imported press. However, he argued that 'a good deal of the attacks on the alien press were little removed from hypocrisy' in so far as they let Ireland's equally objectionable press go free. The main difference between Irish exponents of mass-produced anti-intellectual ideas – 'standardised knowledge, peptonised "views", chatty paragraphs about celebrities, elaborately emotional descriptive articles, jingoism in politics' – was that the Irish did it less efficiently.[264] On the other hand, there was, Tierney maintained, nothing to compare for intelligence and real value with *The Observer* and *The Sunday Times*.

Economists writing in *Studies* counselled against the impact of protectionism on Ireland's open economy. In 'Foreign Trade and National Policy' (1927) Busteed advised that tariffs 'were part of a larger complex problem and in themselves produced endlessly complex reactions'. On their own they could not solve the problems of the Irish economy.[265] In 1933, *Studies* published the text of the first Finlay Lecture at UCD, delivered by none other than John Maynard Keynes.[266] Keynes spoke at the invitation of George O'Brien, who had championed his work at UCD.[267] Keynes's theme in 'National Self-Sufficiency' was his own personal shift away from being a doctrinaire liberal free-trader of the nineteenth-century mould. Following an account of the changing nature of transnational economic interdependencies since the nineteenth century he concluded that national self-sufficiency, although it came with costs, was a luxury that nation-states could afford if they wanted to. Ireland, Keynes noted, had 'lifted a lively foot out of its bogs to become a centre for economic experiment'.[268] The world, he observed, was embarking on a variety of politico-economic experiments, and different ones appealed to different national temperaments and national environments. No one could yet foresee which of the new economic systems would prove to be the best. National self-sufficiency, he argued, was not an end in itself but one that enabled other ideals to be pursued. Ireland needed to be as free as possible from economic changes elsewhere, in order to make its own 'favourite experiments towards the ideal social Republic of the future'.[269]

Keynes's suggested ideal Republic was one that would deliberately set out to make Dublin 'a splendid city fully endowed with all the appurtenances of art and civilisation on the highest standards of which its citizens were individually capable'. This, he argued, would be money better spent than on any dole and would make any dole unnecessary. The wealth spent on the dole in England since the war could have made its cities the greatest works of man in the world.[270] Turning to what he understood Irish aspirations to be, he contended that Ireland was by no means obliged to sacrifice rural traditions for purely economic reasons. Agricultural processes, he argued, 'had deep roots, work themselves out slowly, are resistant to change and disobedient to administrative order, and yet are frail and delicate, so that when they have suffered injury they are not easily restored'.[271] Here he referenced the rural 'dislocations' of the Soviet experiment. His preference was for gradual social and economic change.

Keynes argued that Ireland could, within prudent limits, pursue its own national project. He empathised with Irish goals for political and cultural autonomy, stating that if he were Irish he would find much to attract him in 'the economic outlook of ... [the] government towards greater self-sufficiency'. This, O'Brien reported, brought smiles to the faces of many members of de Valera's government in the audience.[272] However, Keynes counselled against economic isolationism. He argued that it would be wise for Ireland 'to retain her traditional British markets'. To do so, in his view, was not threatening to Irish cultural and political autonomy.[273] Prudent economic nationalism (although he did not use that phrase) avoided 'the silliness of the doctrinaire'. There was nothing wrong with the stimulation of wild words in political debate, but when it came to policy there was a need to count the cost of rhetoric. The biggest barrier to success, he maintained, was the stifling of criticism. Here he referred to the violence underpinning politics in Germany, Italy and Russia. Compared to these he would, he concluded, 'prefer his old nineteenth-century ideals'.[274]

Keynes, when later recalling his visit to Dublin, described Cosgrave as very much the nineteenth-century liberal.[275] Tierney, who had been active in Cosgrave's *Cumann na nGaedheal*, advocated erasing the liberalism that Keynes would prefer to fascism and to socialism. But liberalism had not just survived in twentieth-century Ireland as a legacy of the nineteenth. It was integral, Tierney accepted, to the very nation-building that had led to independence. When Tierney advanced his own high culture Gaelic pre-Reformation archetype he was in essence saying that nothing short of this – certainly not the existing sham Gaelic revival – would be intellectually or culturally robust enough to succeed. That is, anything short of his thought experiment in decolonisation was one that would fail. Cultural isolationism was doomed to failure because the unfinished Irish nation-state could not keep out what it had already internalised. Tierney himself, by way of personal example, demurred from economic barriers to foreign publications when it came to his own favourite British broadsheets.

CONSERVATIVE CIRCLES

Studies emerged in 1912 at a time when, as Lee puts it, Sinn Féin was but a mere fringe nationalist faction.[276] Its political hinterland was that of the Irish Party and after independence one that overlapped considerably with Cumann na Gaedheal. Like UCD it represented, or at least addressed, the Catholic bourgeoisie expecting to benefit from Home Rule. Its response to the 1916 Rising depicted the poets of the insurrection as exemplars of Catholic piety and true patriotism, but the journal cautioned against romantic nationalism. Tom Kettle exemplified what *Studies* stood for far better than did Patrick Pearse. Inevitably *Studies* became Treatyite. It went on to reflect the conservative intellectual politics that dominated the new state. The debates examined in this chapter demonstrate connections and cleavages between various strains of Catholic conservatism but also a weaker strain of liberalism that connects the nineteenth century with the second half of the twentieth century, when a liberal modernising nation-building project emerged. Kettle anticipated the ideological approach to economics that flourished in *Studies* after independence, one shaped by nineteenth-century liberalism and Catholic humanism. Its main enemy was socialism.

The first three decades of *Studies* witnessed a preoccupation with the main strands of Western ideological debate. Catholic social thought was mobilised against British and European socialism even in the absence of influential Irish socialist politics. Liberalism had been an important ingredient of pre-independence nation-building but was now being smothered by the conservative cultural and religious politics of the post-independence era. The two now-dominant strands of Irish intellectual politics were those rooted in neo-Thomism and in Catholic cultural nationalism. Both meshed where medievalist or anti-Enlightenment yearnings for an idealised Christendom and an idealist Gaelic civilisation overlapped.

A number of strains of Catholic conservatism vied with one another and intersected with cultural nationalism. Initially, *Studies* had eschewed the anti-modernist or neo-medievalist strain of Thomism associated with Hilaire Belloc. However, anti-modernist rhetoric sat well with the sort of cultural nationalism promoted by Corkery. Both would turn back the clock on the Reformation and on the post-Reformation destruction of Gaelic Catholic culture. Bucolic accounts of the medieval order as the pinnacle of human achievement in accordance with God's natural law co-existed with claims that the bardic 'Hidden Ireland' was the pinnacle of local civilisation. Both were presented together as offering compatible ideals for post-independence nation-building. In 1919 Corcoran had anticipated Corkery's case for cultural isolationism.[277] As late as 1938 Tierney championed a Catholic cultural 'restoration' that would turn back the clock on nineteenth-century utilitarianism and liberalism and other 'great heresies' of the last three hundred years.'[278] Implicit in Tierney's last call for a conservative order was the realisation that the great heresies had prevailed.

Notwithstanding such anti-modernist rhetoric *Studies* was characterised by the search for viable social, economic and political alternatives. Economists cautioned against the impact of protectionism on Ireland's open economy. They also concluded, as did a number of clerical observers of European political experiments, that there was no viable third system alternative to liberalism and socialism. Article after article struggled with the practicalities of alternatives to both. The sole political programme on offer was one inspired by Mussolini, one deemed remote from the principles of natural law. Corporatism offered an off-the-shelf political programme. But the term corporatism had itself become politically tainted by its association with Mussolini.[279] By the time a corporatist state was mooted by General O'Duffy it found little support in *Studies*. Significantly, Tierney, a key intellectual figure in Cumann na nGaedheal and a founder of Fine Gael, wrote nothing in *Studies* that advocated corporatism.[280] In the absence of a viable institutional fix, Catholic social thought was promoted successfully in two important ways. Firstly, it was injected to a degree into the 1937 Constitution. Second, the long debates on education, ranging from the seemingly esoteric proposal by Arthur Little SJ to teach 'philosophy' in schools to schemes adapting the Labour College model for Catholic purposes, bore fruit in the institutional development of Catholic social science. Where Aquinas had failed Ireland as a political scientist he would now come to its rescue as a sociologist.

CHAPTER FOUR

Disenchanted Land: *Christus Rex* and Irish Sociology, 1947–70

The first issue of *Christus Rex: An Irish Quarterly Journal of Sociology* appeared in 1947. That its ethos was Catholic was evident from the title. That its audience was clerical might be supposed from the advertisements that ran on the back cover for finest altar wines and fire insurance for buildings 'devoted to Catholic purposes'. Its subtitle might have raised an eyebrow. *Christus Rex* managed studiously to avoid most of the debates within the academic subject of sociology until its final *glasnost* issue in 1970. The editorial in each issue declared that the contents were to be considered free from doctrinal or moral error.[1] Sociology, as represented within *Christus Rex*, excluded ideas, theories and literature that contested such orthodoxy. Its 'intellectual' battle was one for the preservation of Catholic society and Catholic influence. This was to be achieved by keeping dangerous ideas at bay, partly through the control of sociology itself. The journal was based at St Patrick's College, Maynooth. The founder editors were two Maynooth professors, both clerics, Peter McKevitt (Professor of Catholic Action) and Cornelius Lucey (Professor of Social Ethics). McKevitt's Chair was endowed by the Knights of Saint Columbanus.[2] He was succeeded in turn by two able clerical sociologists, Jeremiah Newman (the dominant figure in the journal) and Liam Ryan (the final editor). The replacement of *Christus Rex* by *Social Studies* in 1971 coincided with the appointment of Damian Hannan as the first lay professor of sociology in the Republic of Ireland.

Christus Rex was primarily a journal of applied Catholic thought. Many of the articles were opinion pieces that reflected anxieties about social change rather than contributions to the study of such change. Yet clerical sociologists advocated empirical research.[3] *Christus Rex* was preoccupied with 'real' sociological questions on the nature and consequences of social change, social cohesion, rural decline, urban alienation and poverty. It represented a distinct vantage point troubled, for sound reasons, by many elements of such change. *Christus Rex* published a handful of pioneering empirical studies of Irish social problems that influenced both social policy and the development of the social sciences in Ireland.

Eamon de Valera's St Patrick's day speech of 1943 had evoked a Catholic, anti-materialist, rural social ideal with comely maidens dancing at the crossroads. But Irish society itself was at a crossroads. As a clerical contributor put it in 1959 to the journal, writers such as O'Casey, O'Faolain and O'Flaherty captured a widespread disillusionment but had also propagated it: 'Much of Irish writing today has blind-alleyed itself into a few hard-pressed themes, like clerical autocracy, obscurantist censorship, matriarchal morality. Much of it gnaws at Ireland from afar. For some time now the writers have been blaming everything on an uncomprehending clergy.'[4] To some extent, the instinct in *Christus Rex* was to shoot the messenger. Its effective censorship of academic sociology made it a last bastion of isolationism. However, the journal also sought to understand and grapple with social problems.

Both kinds of response offered an implicit critique of social change that mirrored much written about modernity in the secular canon of thought it sought to exclude. Empirical research was safe enough. So too was the study of social values if thorny epistemological issues could be avoided. A sociology that grounded itself in eternal truths inevitably found it difficult to engage with secular dissections of religiosity. In *Christus Rex* there was no sociological debate about religion itself. Emile Durkheim, for example, understood religion as part of the structure of human relations as a social fact that could not be discounted in explaining the workings of society, but crucially insisted that it was a human creation. Max Weber also placed religion at the heart of his critique of Western individualism. He argued that the technical and economic conditions of modern life had stripped life of the religious and ethical meanings that gave rise to the modern West in the first place. The growth of rational empirical knowledge resulted in the world becoming disenchanted with social reality.

There was more to this than the dominance of secularism and empiricism. Disenchantment referred to the crowding out of many aspects of human identity or, as Weber put it, spirit. Weber worried about the dominance of empirical knowledge. He argued that belief in the sacred had given way to belief that everything could be subject to rational calculation. The result was a presumption that any argument against rational calculation itself was irrational.[5] However, Weber's epistemology was an explicitly secular one. In a 1909 letter to another sociologist, Ferdinand Tönnies, he affirmed that he was 'religiously unmusical'. He had, he wrote, neither the need nor the ability to erect within himself any 'psychic structures of a religious character'. He just could not bring himself to hold religious beliefs.[6] This, then, was the stumbling block that made accommodation impossible. *Christus Rex* represented doctrinal orthodoxy. But Weber had been discussed in *Studies* as early as 1926.[7] The Episcopal Imprimatur's writ did not apply to the Jesuit journal. Here regular contributors to *Christus Rex* such as Newman could engage intellectually with the very sociology they were required to ignore. For this reason contemporaneous articles from *Studies* on sociology are considered in the final section of this chapter.

If much of the canon of secular sociology was to be kept at bay, social change itself was by no means ignored in *Christus Rex*. Nor was the default position always a conservative one. A 1962 editorial accepted 'the sociological need for Irish education to gear itself to face a new economic future'. It was becoming clear that national material progress depended on technical skills. The principle of subsidiarity, it was emphasised, cut both ways. The state had a duty in making good what private initiative was unable or unwilling to do when the public welfare was at stake.[8] In 'Foundations of Social Justice in Ireland' (1959) the Reverend Robert Prendergast argued against a prevalent anti-statist rhetoric, noting that social ills were complex. The general principles of Catholic social thought were not enough. 'We must not', he argued, 'run the danger of imagining that there is a blue-print social system, neatly parcelled in theological formulae and officially stamped as the Catholic social ideal.' Prendergast was also critical of the dread amongst Irish Catholic thinkers of state interference in the family, arguing that the 'paltry welfare safety nets' of the British welfare state hardly amounted to an omni-competent state.[9] Similarly, a 1967 article argued that while liberals might oppose the welfare state Catholics should not.[10]

Christus Rex also reflected on the changing times. A 1962 review of *Morality and the Homosexual* commended it to priests 'challenged to transfer what had hitherto been regarded as an unnatural vice to the category of permitted human association'.[11] Television, the subject of a 1961 study conference, was portrayed in a mostly positive light in a 1962 issue on the topic. One article took the Thomist view that every gift was from God, whether it be television or alcohol. BBC and ITV programming aimed at children was described as excellent.[12] Another hoped that television would promote mutual understanding between urban and rural areas and combat Irish tendencies towards insularity, political apathy and ignorance about social problems.[13]

A SENSE OF VOCATION

The Christus Rex Society was inaugurated at a meeting of newly ordained priests held in September 1941.[14] Its format was derived from social study circles that many had participated in as students at Maynooth. A draft constitution was drawn up. The objects of the society were (a) to promote amongst Irish diocesan clergy the study of the Church's social teaching, and (b) to encourage and assist priests in all forms of social work. Membership was open to all diocesan priests interested in social work declaring the purpose of the society. Its first Priests' Summer School of social study took place in Galway in August 1946. The theme was 'Justice for the Worker'. More than seventy priests attended, the society's constitution was finalised, and plans were drawn up for further events. The journal of the society was launched in 1947.

The first article in the first issue was 'Why Catholic Priests should Concern Themselves with Social and Economic Questions' by Michael J. Browne, Bishop of Galway.[15] Browne argued that the education of Irish public opinion in the social teaching of the Church was the right and duty of every priest: 'It depends on him whether the Catholic people – men and women of every class – will understand the issues and perform their duty at local and general elections and their political clubs as Catholic citizens.' There were plenty of occasions at sodality meetings and in parish hall gatherings where the people could be told about Church social teaching. However, people who informed national opinion needed more attention. Browne advocated targeting trade unions and employers' organisations. Other early articles advised priests how to run parish study circles. Study groups were directed to organise surveys of local issues, such as unemployment in their communities, aimed at fostering mutual understanding between different social classes. Fact-finding, according to McKevitt, could shake up complacent attitudes towards social problems:

> How often do we hear it said that no man willing to work is unemployed? Yet a little searching out would convince us that there are many who find it hard to get suitable employment.

> Perhaps we might by this method of enquiry get masters and workers to see some of their own deficiencies and acquire a new understanding of the other's point of view.[16]

Diagnosis of the specific problems facing communities was the first step. Understanding of participants then had to be directed. The role of the priest, as director of the study circle, should be to foster rational debate in keeping with Catholic principles.[17] This, McKevitt concluded, should be within the range of any priest who had read a course of social science.

Articles on the findings of study groups offered good-practice guides alongside analyses of social issues. For example, a 1947 article presented the findings of 'a factual survey' of youth clubs undertaken by a Cork study group. Fifteen youth clubs were surveyed, member levels and attendances were tabulated, and the spiritual and secular activities of each were summarised. The clubs aimed 'to keep boys off the streets and bring them under Catholic influences' or 'to supply through pleasurable activity the character training which the girls are not getting at home'. All the clubs listed spiritual activities such as hymns, prayers or rosaries each night. Secular activities for boys leaned towards sports but also included lectures, Irish language classes, drawing, film classes, hikes and summer outings. The girls' clubs favoured indoor games, dancing, knitting, elocution and, in the case of the six Our Lady's Parlours clubs aimed at girls from lower socio-economic groups, hygiene and 'behavioural exercises'. The article that summarised these findings was entirely descriptive. The stated purpose was to provide information to others contemplating the establishment of similar clubs.[18]

Many articles combined some emphasis on social problems with further emphasis on the reproduction of Catholic influence. Material and spiritual welfare were understood to be interdependent. The spiritual welfare of those who would provide services was also emphasised. In 1947, Agnes McGuire, director of social work training at UCD, argued that above all the social worker 'requires to hold tight to her fundamental faith that all men, however weak and wretched, are God's children and that He can bring good out of evil in ways that are "not our ways".'[19] For McGuire the formation of a social worker was, by necessity, a spiritual one:

> The candidate for training dedicates herself to the as yet unknown needs of her future acquaintance, and prepares herself

> to help them to the maximum of her acquired knowledge and experience, making a full use of mutual personalities. The inspiration of charity not only survives the process but must be deliberately renewed and augmented. The social worker, constantly giving of herself, needs not less but greater love. She must often remind herself of St. Paul's famous verses to the Corinthians and in the face of depravity see with faith the shattered image of God, setting out on the great adventure of having some part in restoring the dignity of His Design. However unconscious the Christianity may be, I cannot see proper social work survive as humanitarian, if that means loving one's neighbour for his own sake and for his own limited merits. To attempt that is, to my mind, like trying to pour out water indefinitely out an unreplenished vessel – one's heart, like the vessel is soon empty and dry. Presumably, the confirmed humanitarian hopes to find his reward in a sense of power and in human gratitude, but it is the business of the social worker to help, that no gratitude seems necessary, since increase in confidence makes the client imagine that he has done everything himself. It should be the joy of the social worker to foster that illusion: but it can, in practice, be very exhausting work.[20]

McGuire's spiritual self-therapeutic approach to social work was one that emphasised 'caritas', a Christian ideal of charity.[21] At its core was the understanding, set out by St Augustine in *The City of God*, of how caritas spirituality benefited the giver.[22] For other authors personal spiritually had to be reinforced communally. That emigrants, especially young female ones, were in spiritual danger was emphasised in a 1949 article, 'An open letter to Irish Girls about to emigrate', by a British-based Catholic social worker.[23] The article combined practical advice about employment, accommodation, bank accounts and rationing (clothes were easier to obtain in Ireland) with advice aimed at preserving the religiosity of emigrant girls. It noted that living as a Catholic in England was a different business in so far as the prevalent 'Catholic atmosphere' to be found in Ireland was absent. In the absence of such protections it was necessary be more than a habitual Catholic: 'Each of you coming here is for the Church or against her. There is no middle course.' It cautioned prospective emigrants that when it came to films and libraries they would have to act as their own censors. She advised them to consult a priest or the Index of Books listing those dangerous to Faith and Morals. She warned them not to be misled by books with Irish-sounding titles or written by writers with Irish names: 'Many such books are unwholesome, to say the least of it – and have in fact been banned in your own country, so it would not be right for you to abuse your freedom by reading them here, would it?'

The presence of an open letter to young women in a journal targeted at priests was not incongruous alongside surveys of emigration that interviewed only priests. Shepherds were expected to be responsible for their flocks as social workers or social researchers. A 1949 article on a survey of Waterford described how questionnaires had been distributed to 'a sufficiently representative body of younger clergy'.[24] The study was inevitably concerned with spiritual as well as material welfare. It indicated that most emigrants were men, the vast majority left home because of unemployment, most had been builders' labourers and casual workers and those who were women had been domestic workers or factory hands. The majority of emigrants (both sexes) were between 18 and 25 years of age. The survey noted that those married men who emigrated did so because they felt unable to support their families on the wages available locally. A big problem for many was the insecurity of local employment; men were 'laid off' frequently for several days in the week.

The anonymous authors, local priests, vouched 'from personal knowledge' that girls had left factory work with reasonably good conditions and wages and home residence to go to England 'just because they felt the opportunities or recreation were better there' and elaborated that 'the ambition for "a good match"' was 'not improbably the font from which springs such desires and romantic longings for "change", "glamour" and amusement facilities'. They concluded that the religious and moral state of the vast majority of both male and female emigrants was usually quite satisfactory. When it came to moral lapse it was agreed that much depended on the kind of background from which the emigrant derived, although the environment they found themselves in across the channel could also be a factor: 'Hotel service for girls, in London especially, was held to be dangerous.'

The article recommended that measures be put in place to develop new industries in Waterford City and the towns of the diocese, that new housing be provided, that subsidised accommodation be developed for agricultural labourers, that the agricultural wage be raised and that it should be aimed to reduce the hard and unpalatable nature of farm work where possible. Such recommendations were commonplace. The achievement of the City of God required that earthly social conditions be improved. Another 1949 article, 'The Foundations of Social Justice', identified three problems confronting Irish society, chief of which was the economic one, second the Irish reluctance to marry, too few too late, and third emigration: 'The number of boys and girls, born in Ireland, and now living in England, has not been exactly determined, but no one can seriously quarrel with the figure, 800,000.'[25]

If, for many writers, prosperity was necessary to prevent emigration and spiritual exile, others seemed to argue that austerity was needed for national and spiritual survival: de Valera's argument, in other words. In 1961, in *The Emigration Issue* the Reverend Daniel Duffy depicted emigration as the economic consequence of a desire for higher living standards in Ireland.[26] He argued that economic austerity and generally lower living standards than enjoyed in richer countries had to be accepted if people were not to be displaced by emigration: 'The pursuit of living standards, such as the affluent society demands, can only lead to an indefinite postponement of our economic salvation. It is no dishonour to be poor. It is foolish and contemptible to aim at the incomes and expenditures of those more prosperous than ourselves.'[27] Duffy's paean to the spiritual and communal benefits of austerity was rebutted by Sean Lemass, then Taoiseach.[28] In his article Lemass blamed emigration on 'the insufficiency of our efforts to develop a completely attractive way of life for all elements of the national community, and adequate opportunities of employing individual talents in Ireland to earn livelihoods equivalent to those which emigrants hope to find elsewhere'.[29] Unlike Duffy he did not believe that emigration could be ended by urging people to willingly accept less than could be obtained elsewhere[30] Fatalism, he implied, was part of the problem. If people believed that economic expansion would bring more jobs and opportunities, they might be less likely to emigrate.[31]

DEFENDING AUSTERITY

Prosperity, or even the prospect of it, subsequent articles retorted, brought moral dangers in its wake.[32] One, in 1961, by 'a management consultant lecturing in the Catholic Worker's College in Dublin', echoed both Duffy and McGuire. This author 'believed' in an Irish way of life that was pleasing to the Creator.[33] He viewed Irish approaches to economic development as megalomania: 'we are deliberately setting ourselves targets that are unnecessarily high, that are unrealistic, and that are tantamount to escapism. In deliberately placing ourselves in such an unfavourable contrast with others, we content ourselves with decrying our lot.'[34] In the same issue, in 'Ireland in a Changing World', the Chairman of the Irish Management Institute argued that its principal need was for 'moral resources such as self-reliance, self-confidence and strong loyalty to one another and to the country'. The author, D.A. Hegarty, counselled that 'an easy prosperity is as harmful to a young country as it is to a young man unless both have the wisdom to see it for what it is worth'.[35] However, Hegarty insisted that social change was inevitable. The Church, he argued, needed to adapt to survive. He highlighted the impossibility of censoring information about birth control and previously banned topics in the era of television.

A conservative polemic in the same 1961 issue by Desmond Fennell warned about future perils. Writing about Sweden but thinking about Ireland, Fennell depicted the transition from peasant to urban society as inevitably traumatic, particularly for men. He questioned the 'so called emancipation of women'. Emancipation, he argued, was the wrong word. Women in Sweden went out and fought 'rather fanatically' for their new status. The result, he argued, was a mixed blessing: 'When such an emancipated woman, even at some inconvenience to herself, but for egotistical and pig-headed reasons breaks up a home, the husband can be regarded as a real victim. He loses a home and his children and becomes a refugee.'[36] Fennell spelt out the dangers of losing what other contributors called austerity:

> Advertising, songs, television and the political platforms tell us that each man and woman can here on this earth possess happiness and has a right to. These naïve modern idealisms make refugees who kill themselves rather than live what society tells them are paltry and deprived lives.[37]

The critique of social change offered in *Christus Rex* bore clear similarities to secular sociological accounts of modernity even if its core concepts – such as anomie, alienation and rationalisation – were eschewed. In a nutshell, the thesis was that a spiritual life sustained by individual faith and social habits could be damaged by removal from a society within which religious norms prevailed. Existing Irish society was seen to be economically and socially unsustainable. Materialism threatened to undermine communal solidarities and undermine individual spiritual resilience. Yet social and economic innovation was needed to ensure their survival. All this amounted to a gut rather than intellectual critique of social change.

This was presented in themed issues of the journal. Examples included *Faith and National Revival* (1959) *The Parish, The Challenge of Television* (1962), *The Renewal of Society, Education and the Future* (1963), *Work and Man* (1964) *Renewal and the Church* (1966), *The Vocations Situation* (1967) and *Vocations to the Sisterhood* (1968). In the 1966 issue the sole article not written by a cleric was entitled The *Layman and the Church*.[38] Many articles had a pastoral or doctrinal emphasis and were given over to value statements or expressions of anxiety about faith and fatherland. Not all were pessimistic. Many read like after-dinner speeches and a few actually were so.[39] Some by the laity were demonstrably devotional. Yet sometimes these contained serious sociological analysis.

For example, the summer 1964 issue contained a solitary article on the theology of work alongside several on work and wage patterns and on research about attitudes towards work. One of these 'Psychological and Sociological Aspects of Work', addressed relevant international academic literature.[40] Here, just two of the eight contributors were clerics. Newman's 1966 article on (deteriorating) industrial relations made no reference to Catholic teaching. Instead it sought to study industrial disputes empirically.[41] He examined a number of hypotheses as to why this rise had occurred. Possible factors weighed up included feelings of economic insecurity amongst workers, inadequate labour–management relations (both significant in Newman's view) and the influence of troublemakers (i.e. Marxists) within unions, for which he found little evidence.

In the face of Newman's empiricism it fell to a lay contributor, Charles McCarthy, the General Secretary of the Vocational Teacher's Association and a former President of the Irish Congress of Trade Unions, to profess the devout fidelity of Irish trade unionism to Mother Church. McCarthy made the somewhat unlikely claim that Irish Catholic trade unionist 'frequently found himself unhappy with the socialist trade union philosophy, seeing in it the easy and shallow optimism of humanism and the Pelagian abandonment of the doctrine of Grace'.[42] How frequently was not clarified. According to Pelagius God made humans free. Having been so made, they could choose between good and evil according to their will. The Pelagian affirmation of individual autonomy was taken to challenge the spiritual leadership of the Church. Pelagian bishops were excommunicated from the mainline Church in 418. Pelagius, then, stood against orthodoxy. Incidentally, the central conceit of Anthony Burgess's 1962 very Catholic science fiction novel *The Wanting Seed* was its equation of social liberalism run riot with Pelagianism.[43] The suggestion is not at all that McCarthy had read Burgess, nor that Burgess knew or cared about sociology, but that theological references came more easily than sociological ones.

A small core of university-based clerical sociologists flew the flag of rigorous empiricism. Newman, for instance, published books on conservative political philosophy, but within the confines of *Christus Rex* was devoutly quantitative. In 'Vocations in Ireland' he undertook a comparative analysis of declining vocations in various European countries. At Maynooth ordinations had peaked in 1941 at eighty-six. Irish ordinations overall had peaked in 1961 at 447 and were now falling away. There were 412 in 1965. Further declines, Newman demonstrated, would follow.[44] He posited a number of causal factors. These included increased affluence and urbanisation (mirroring the conditions of other societies that experienced vocational decline), changes in the structure of the education system (resulting in the decline of influence of priests upon young people), developments in lay spirituality that encouraged marriage and the challenge of materialism to the attractions of religious life. The following year saw a similar assessment of falling female vocations.

SOCIAL COHESION, SOCIAL DYNAMITE

A 1947 *Studies* article, 'Catholic Rural Action', had opened with a proposition and a claim: (i) rural communities were of pivotal importance in the social and religious life of the nation; (ii) the Church had the power to influence the life and mould the character of the rural population. Even as rural Catholics became urbanised they bought 'a fresh accession of strength to the Church in the cities'.[45] That said, a perceived decline in rural depopulation was seen as a grave concern. Social activism by priests was needed to arrest this decline. Priests could, it was argued, 'promote parish games and entertainments, everything in fact which goes to make up the full social life of a community'. Rural decline resulted in more people 'growing more eager to escape from a dreary isolated existence'.[46]

Within *Christus Rex* practical advocacy of rural development jostled, to some extent, with the old yearnings for a distinct Catholic social order. Many articles recycled formulaic expositions of social teaching alongside attacks on the evils of statism. These were rarely married to any practical focus on social problems. In the new language doctrinal errors were sociological ones and vice versa.[47] In 'Agriculture in a Vocationalist Order of Society' (1956), the sensibly anonymous 'Feirmeoir' (Farmer) argued that since the army took control of Portugal in 1926 Salazar had given his people: 'many salutary lessons in the art of living, not least of which is the lesson of thrift'. Corporatism had brought about 'a condition of stability and tranquillity previously unknown in that turbulent country'.[48] That Portugal was even poorer than Ireland was neither here nor there. While the practical study groups of The Christus Rex Society worried about actual rural living conditions, for Fermeoir and some others the real dangers were ideological. Statism of any sort (especially that of the Department of Agriculture) was anathema. The 'logical way forward' was a 'vocationalist social order centred territorially on the Parish as the nexus between the social, agricultural and religious aspects of the problem'.[49] The Parish would become the economic as well as spiritual unit of social organisation.[50] As put in another article in the same issue, subsidiarity required an active role by the priest in developing voluntary co-operative activism so as to avoid the need for justifiable action by the state.[51] In 'Co-operation in Rural Ireland' (1956) Lt.-General M.J. Costello, writing as a member of the Executive Committee of the National Co-operative Council, cited developments in the co-operative movements of Scandinavia, Belgium, Holland and Israel. After expressing the need to fight every kind of statism he discussed practical measures to extend rural co-operation through sharing of expensive agricultural machinery, fencing, drainage, local benevolent societies and credit unions.[52] Another article, authored by an economist, traced the development and efficacy of the National Farmers' Association. That its members eschewed 'sanctimonious pronouncement' should not, the author, Louis Smith, argued, be interpreted as indicating a shortage of supernatural motive as far as individual members were concerned: 'The ideal of a more Christian form of society is clearly in the minds of many farmers.'[53] Other articles in the same issue emphasised Church documents on principles for rural life. These argued that rural life had great potential for uncorrupted moral and religious living. The answer, all agreed, lay in rural co-operation.[54]

The sole sociological contribution to this debate came from Newman. The year 1961 saw the publication of a study he had led on the causes and motives of migration from some County Limerick parishes.[55] As a piece of research this had exceeded the scope of anything attempted to date by Catholic sociologists. Analysis of census records of demographic change was accompanied by the analysis of 'hundreds of questionnaires' covering the period 1951–56. Newman had gone to the United States to consult a number of sociologists on the design of the study. The initial plan had been to bring in experts from Holland or America to carry out the survey, but it was subsequently agreed that an Irish graduate would travel to Holland for 'further formation' under the tutelage of a Dutch sociologist who later contributed to its planning and design.

Newman argued that the findings provided 'a sober counterbalance to those critics who would have us believe that lack of adequate marriage opportunity is a primary cause of rural depopulation'. In the parishes surveyed, only twenty-five out of the 117 persons who had migrated between 1951 and 1956 had married by 1959. The fact that so few married after migration was taken to undermine the hypothesis that obstacles to marriage were compelling reasons for migration.'[56] This argument was disputed by Lemass in the same 1961 issue. He argued that the findings suggested that social reasons for migration predominated over economic ones. It was also the case that young men and women from rural areas and smaller towns found it easier to go to Britain for employment than to migrate to other parts of Ireland.[57] Here Newman concurred. In the face of ongoing rural decline the only way to conserve rural population was, 'paradoxical though it may seem', to develop a number of towns in each county with adequate social and cultural facilities. To measure this Newman formulated an index of social provision for towns and villages in County Limerick. This quantified the availability of public utilities, different kinds of commercial activities (the presence of various kinds of shops, banks, etc.), public transport, 'places of assembly' (social facilities such as Churches, libraries, public houses, cinemas) and social organisations. In short Newman's proposal was to concentrate on building up a number of sustainable communities in the country. A 1970 article by a former Limerick County Manager, T.M. O'Connor, discussed the influence of Newman's 'theory of rural centrality' and other influences on regional planning for the county.[58] Another 1970 article by Father Harry Bohan, subsequently an innovator of rural social housing, proposed a synthesis of 'pastoral theology and empirical social sciences' in promoting community activism and community development.[59] All this was in keeping with the original rationale for the study groups.

In the early 1960s the rural bias of *Christus Rex* showed signs of giving way intermittently to articles that focused upon urban social problems. A number of these grappled with the consequences of poor planning, the complexities of urban poverty and welfare paternalism.

In 'The Other Ireland' (1964) John Brady SJ took his title and thesis from Michael Harrington's *The Other America*. This was a survey of American slums, rural and urban poverty and the exclusion of the 'coloured people' that portrayed a culture of poverty originating in a 'mesh of interlocking vicious circles'. These included bad housing, high and long-term unemployment, low educational standards, malnutrition, high incidences of physical and mental illness, breakdown in family life and alcoholism.[60] Brady translated Harrington's thesis about the nature and consequences of poverty to the Irish situation in discussing inadequate responses to 'itinerants' and other 'poverty stricken groups'. Brady argued for more state action.

In 'Social Dynamite: A Study of Early School Leavers' the Reverend Liam Ryan published the findings of a landmark study of Irish urban poverty. Ryan's was the first survey work to be commissioned by *Christus Rex*.[61] The previous year he had published an empirical analysis of access to university education by social class.[62] Other contributors had already focused on the growth of urban Ireland.[63] 'Social Dynamite' was unique in so far as it emphasised the role of educational disadvantage in creating urban inequalities. Its analysis of class inequalities and urban educational inequality offered an equivalent to contemporaneous research in the United Kingdom.

Ryan's article was based on qualitative research undertaken in 1965 and 1966 of a hundred respondents aged between 14 and 16 years, all of whom had either left school or were attending the one-day-a-week schools put in place to allow them to remain (technically) in education until they reached the new statutory school leaving age.[64] Ryan's starting place was that one-third of all school leavers had been condemned, the great majority through no fault of their own, to unskilled labour, unemployment or emigration.[65] Ryan argued that the introduction of free secondary education of itself would not solve their problems. There was, he argued citing British research, 'a complex of social, psychological, economic and educational factors'.[66] These, he argued, demonstrated a need to take into account the 'total situation' of a child's life rather than focus on poverty defined solely in terms of income levels. Here he drew upon the work of an American sociologist W.J. Thomas, who identified three major elements in any social situation. The first of these was the 'objective conditions' under which the individual or society had to act, the second element was the pre-existing attitudes of the individuals or groups who influenced behaviour and the third element was the definition of the situation by the individual himself, influenced by the group.

Ryan's study described the experiences of families now housed in 'Parkland', a social housing estate in Limerick. They had been transplanted, through a process of slum clearance, from old overcrowded Georgian or Victorian buildings or smaller houses in the back-lanes and alleyways:

> It was felt that if you gave each family a house with a little garden they would become clean and respectable. And so they were uprooted, from being ten families in one house, or ten children in one cellar, they moved into beautiful big three-bedroom houses. But they just could not cope with the new situation. They lost many of their roots. Their friends and neighbours of years and years were lost. They had no choice as to where they would go or when they would go; they had no choice as to what street they would live in or as to who would occupy the house next-door or across the street. The policy was to scatter the better families around in the hope that they would set the standard of the locality. Today it is not the best family in the street but rather the worst or the rowdiest who sets the standard.[67]

Ryan identified a fear and hatred amongst residents of officialdom that remained curbed because their lives were too dependent on the goodwill of people in authority: 'All government officials are enemies, the Gardai, rent-collectors, welfare officers – all who have "fine soft jobs".' The same attitude sometimes extended to teachers and priests. Ryan recounted experiences of discrimination and clientelism amongst those seeking housing. He described the difficulties encountered by interviewees in their own frank language. As put by one respondent:

> At present you must have four children to qualify for a house. But how can they have children? They live either with a relative for a while. Then they get thrown out and move into the City Home. He is put on one side, and she on another. Where are they supposed to have sex; is it in the street? These were young married people.

The frankness about 'social factors' that distinguished 'Social Dynamite' from the reports of study groups was, to some extent, the outcome of the qualitative methodologies employed by Ryan. Whilst earlier clerical surveys canvassed the opinions of other priests, Ryan taped interviews with fifty boys and fifty girls. The local clergy, teachers, police, social workers and shopkeepers were also tape-recorded to place these in context. For Ryan it was crucial that the research reflected the world of youth as reported and seen by themselves. His study reflected a new social justice perspective on poverty. This, to some extent, reconstituted the social question to focus on power and paternalism as well as on caritas and the successful reproduction of the Catholic community. There were a few antecedents. An article in 1947 by Agnes McGuire had concluded that the expansion of social work had resulted in 'far too much invasion of the homes of the poor, which certainly destroys their privacy, if it is not positively demoralising'.[68] She emphasised resistance by the urban poor to efforts to manage their lives by social workers and allied trades (she listed ten) whose roles overlapped in their dealings with individual families:

> When you calculate that there may be a Health Visitor, A T.B. Visitor and a School Nurse, you get some idea of the flying squad of good intentions and doubtful results that may chase one another in and out of Housing Estates and tenements. For that reason I am in full sympathy with the harassed mother, hailed by one of her children with the news – 'which nurse from which clinic?' – Never to mention the famous cartoon in Punch, where the irate slum dweller lets go good and proper at some uninvited guest: 'It's a pity you women wot ain't got nothing to do, ain't got something better to do than to come worryin us women wot as'.[69]

Two traditions of 'sociological' engagement with social problems emerged over time in *Christus Rex*. One defined doctrine and natural law as sociology, was preoccupied with ideological dangers and could propose only abstract remedies. A later second tradition could more legitimately claim to be sociological. This was rooted in imported models of Catholic social action and by the 1960s emphasised the empirical study of social problems.

RESTRICTIVE PRACTICES

The project of Catholic sociology was to provide an intellectual platform for Catholic social thought whilst keeping at bay rival theories of social order. Almost to the end *Christus Rex* maintained a firewall against most of the mainstream theorists and texts of Western sociology thanks to its doctrinal *imprimatur*. The sort of international books reviewed closely reflected the preoccupations of the journal; those preferred were, as one reviewer put it, the ones worth a place in every priest's library that could be read and studied by any (Catholic) layman.[70] For example, a 1963 review of a book on agricultural co-operation bemoaned the absence of a chapter on the Irish co-operative movement but praised it as implicitly endorsing Catholic social teaching.[71] Inevitably, some explicit and implicit debates on epistemology ensued.

A number of book reviews by Jeremiah Newman engaged with the relationship between natural law principles and use of empiricist and positivist theory by some Catholic sociologists. One 1959 review of a sociology textbook written by Joseph Fischer, an American Jesuit, noted that the book contained nothing that would indicate that the author was a Catholic.[72] Sociology, according to Fischer, was a purely empirical science that was not aligned with any particular social system:

> [It] studies the pattern of regularities of social behaviour as they exist everywhere in society. As a body of knowledge, it centres around the fact of human sociological relations; and anything that contributes to, or flows from, this human association is sociological. Sociology, then could not be democratic, totalitarian, Christian or Mohammedan. The social scientist, as scientist, avoided judgements about the cultures and societies being studied.

Newman acknowledged that students of what is 'commonly called "Sociology"' in Ireland, that is those taught by him and other contributors to *Christus Rex*, would be very confused by Fischer's definition of the subject. He accepted that there might be a great need for a more empirical sociology in Ireland. There was, he acknowledged, 'much more to the study of society than Social Ethics and without adequate factual knowledge the application of ethical principles is impossible'. Newman ended his review of Fischer by endorsing the positivist proposition that the 'exact and valid knowledge' of society that sociology would allow for intelligent and productive social engineering and social reform.

In a 1961 review Newman noted that a new American textbook contained 'nothing in the way of "Social Ethics" of the kind we have been accustomed – indeed also, too exclusively – to call "Sociology" in Ireland'. The author, he noted, excluded 'Social Ethics' from social science except when it was confined to making comparative studies of norms of social conduct or moral systems. She restricted her definition of sociology to factual examination of the ethics of individual groups and as such excluded the Catholic 'Social Ethics' principles from sociology *per se*.[73] This approach, Newman noted, had been cultivated for a number of years by Catholic sociologists, particularly in America, in an effort to have their work accepted by secular sociologists, 'who would have nothing to do with ethical norms in anything other than a factual capacity'. There then followed a rare naming of secular theorists:

> Of course, there is a big difference between the Catholic writers on 'factual' (positive) Sociology and the followers of Comte and Durkhiem, who did not believe at all in the validity of ethical norms, whether within or without the field of Sociology.[74]

This difference was an ontological one. Newman argued that it was impossible to divorce oneself completely from one's system of philosophy or values. Sociology, however constituted, could never stand apart from beliefs and values. He argued that Catholic sociology should unblushingly stand by the truths about human nature represented by the Christian tradition and to seek to integrate these with factual knowledge of all kinds in an effort to solve social problems. Sociology, the science of society, was inevitably normative as well as empirical.[75]

A growing consensus that Catholic principles were not enough was expressed in a 1961 article by Joseph Foyle, then the economics correspondent of the *Irish Press*: 'Too often it is a matter of memorising moral principles, derived from the textbooks or papal encyclicals, without being equipped to appraise the social situation in which it is hoped to have those principles in operation. Many have begun to see that fatal weakness in Irish sociology.'[76] Foyle praised the 'tentative' introduction of training in social research in courses in sociology in UCD under Father Conor Ward. Ward instigated survey-based social research in UCD in 1960 and established a Social Science Research Centre the following year. This had completed eleven social research studies by 1972.[77]

Newman's 1961 review of Ward's *Priests and People* ('an important contribution to the sociology of religion') attacked the main thrust of American and continental sociological understandings of individualisation. 'Sociological jargon', he argued, 'has it that, in the industrial urban civilisation of our time, society is merely a mass of secondary social aggregates, pluralities of individuals thrown together for various reasons but without any real social unity.'[78] This misrepresented the work of secular sociologists who, after all, were in the business of studying society. Newman was using a kind of rhetorical trick that allowed for attacks on ideas that he did not want to explain. Yet, here, Newman went on to at least mention the kind of social theory he would protect Irish priests and sociologists from. This was the 'anti-religious philosophy of Comte'. Newman argued that the Catholic 'natural science approach to social research' appeared to be losing favour 'in so far as it claims to be the only valid method of studying social life'. Ward's empirical research, he continued, stood apart from the natural law stance of most Catholic sociologists. Ward's work, with its emphasis on the contribution of empirical research to the sociology of religion, revealed social trends that could be accepted, controlled or changed through, as Newman put it, 'the use of human reason, understanding and the grace of God'. As such the priest-sociologist could fruitfully employ the methodologies of secular positivists as long as he combined them, as Ward did in Newman's view, with 'that reverence and understanding of spiritual realities which is only to be expected by a sociologist who is also a priest'.

Sociology so defined was the study (and manipulation) of human norms by those who believed in eternal truths. Socialisation, according to a 1962 article, referred to 'conscious or unconscious, spontaneous or imposed, mutual adaptations of personality and personal action to society and social action'.[79] This, unusually, acknowledged the works of secular sociologists such as Weber, Durkheim and the 'brilliant misfit' Marx, although the reader would be hard pressed to extract any hard information about their work from the article. These were described as pessimistic, one-sided and exaggerated in their analysis of the modern social condition because they 'did not conceive of society working out its destiny in the mystical body of Christ'. The point of healthy socialisation had to be the sustenance of the human person and his supernatural destiny.

Irish priest sociologists identified two courses of action. One was to study social change. Here Professors Newman, Ward and Ryan made significant academic contributions even if they were motivated by religious faith. Ryan's 1970 article 'Social Factors in Irish Education' exhibited many typical preoccupations. Both opportunities for social mobility – and consequential anxieties about social status – and the decline of traditional communal solidarities were identified as risks.

Education tended to reflect rather than challenge societal preoccupations with materialism, for instance in the curricular pressures it imposed on students. Yet social inequality, as reflected in the education system, was now also understood as a problem.

Second, clerical dominance of Irish sociology facilitated censorship long after literary censorship and other forms of cultural isolationism became unfeasible. The requirement for doctrinal orthodoxy discouraged intellectual engagement with the sociological imagination. However, through empiricism, as practised by Newman and Ward, was safe enough. Ryan seemed to implicitly draw on theorists such as Durkheim and Ferdinand Tönnies whilst cleaving to the general *Christus Rex* convention of not mentioning the names of secular social theorists. *Christus Rex* functioned like Albania under Hoxha whilst life around it changed. Newman, as editor of *Christus Rex*, was patently unwilling to open the Pandora's Box of thinking about social change to be found in Western sociology. By the 1960s a flood of international popular sociology was now available to Irish readers.[80] The subject could no longer be a clerical fiefdom.

Newman's 1970 swansong, an article on the urban social crises, explicitly referenced a torrent of previously unmentioned theorists ranging from the Marxist Frankfurt School (he cited Herbert Marcuse's *One Dimensional Man*), Ferdinand Tönnies, John Kenneth Galbraith, Desmond Morris (*The Naked Ape*), Thorstein Veblen (*Theory of the Leisure Class*), Lloyd White (*The Living City*), Marshall McLuhan (*The Medium and the Message*) to Richard Hoggarth (*The Uses of Literacy*).[81] Newman even quoted the lyrics of a Beatles song (*She's Leaving Home*), the Parisian graffiti of *les jours de Mai 1968*, referred to Jack Kerouac's *On the Road* and drew parallels between some hippies and early Christian hermits. This cornucopia of sociological and pop-cultural references represented, on all evidence, an unwilling glasnost. More correctly, it revealed the breaking that comes after insufficient bending.

SOCIOLOGY UNFROCKED

Of course *Christus Rex* did not have a monopoly on sociology in Ireland. In 1952 and 1953 Newman published a two-part extensive survey of contemporary British thought – philosophy not sociology but concerned with issues of epistemology relevant to sociological theory – in *Studies*.[82] There was arguably more discussion of the main currents of sociology in the Summer 1963 issue of *Studies* alone than in the entire run of *Christus Rex*, if Newman's article in the final issue were exempted. Within *Studies* seminal sociological analyses of Irish society such as Conrad Arensberg's *The Irish Countryman* (1937) and *New Dubliners* (1955) by A.J. Humphries SJ were located in an international literature about modernisation and urbanisation.[83] The latter, for example was compared with Michael Young and Peter Willmott's *Family and Kinship in East London*.[84]

In 1963, in 'Bettering Our World: The Contribution of Sociology', T.S. Simey, then the Charles Booth Professor of Social Science at the University of Liverpool, defined the subject using terms that might have perplexed many readers of *Christus Rex*. Booth's achievement, Simey maintained, was to abandon moral explanations and social justification for the existence of the poor. Poverty became a problem to be studied scientifically 'as a function of a given form of social structure'.[85] Gunnar Myrdal was cited as defining the task of the social theorist as 'to clarify, by a study of the social facts, how by social policy men and society can be improved'.[86] This, with its implication that human nature was malleable, seemed to contradict claims about the eternal truths of Natural Law. Yet most of the concepts Simey commended to readers of *Studies* were, as he put it, 'old-fashioned' ones within sociology. His core argument was that emphasis on structural factors within society needed to be balanced by one on factors that could influence human agency. Social reality was, he argued, a process of continual creation. Such an assertion would have been impossible within *Christus Rex*.

Writers in *Studies* were more emphatic about the social scientific shortcomings of social ethics.[87] In 'Seeking a National Purpose' (1965) Garret FitzGerald included a section titled 'Inadequacies of Catholic Social Teaching in Ireland'. Natural law, he implied, could not be taught as fixed doctrine. Nor could it be presented as sociology while deliberately excluding efforts to research and understand the social world. As he put it with some diplomacy: 'the over-theoretical approach of many clerical sociologists has diverted their attention from actual social situations in the light of the unique insight into man's role in society that they have available to them through the traditional Christian teaching in regard to the natural law'.[88] In effect he criticised a conservative unwillingness to study real society in case this might contradict Catholic social thought. This in some cases was unfair, particularly in the case of Newman's Limerick study. FitzGerald's argument was that Catholic thinkers should trust their own vantage point as a theoretical basis for thinking about Ireland and face facts as they find them.[89]

In 1964 David Thornley castigated the intellectual isolationism of clerical sociology. He suggested that upheavals within Irish society must have much in common with those examined by sociologists in other countries, such as Michael Young in Britain and C. Wright Mills in the United States.[90] The view that examination of developments abroad could shine light on Irish social change found expression in the response in *Studies* to the upheavals of 1968. In 'The University, Revolution and Freedom' (1969) James Schall outlined the goals of the Socialist German Student Movement and discussed American groups influenced by the German concepts and the influence of thinkers such as Herbert Marcuse. Schall emphasised the broader context of runaway social change that underpinned student dissent:

> The university students of the western world, by any comparative standards, are undoubtedly amongst the most privileged classes ever to have existed. The *elite* of tomorrow are not to be capitalists or bureaucrats, but information gathers and knowledge manipulators. Already, it is estimated that over half the new occupations and professions in modern society are created by communications and information systems.[91]

Yet, Schall argued, the student protest movements were both nihilistically anti-technological and anti-historical. These neglects, he argued, could not but lead to a future loss of freedom. Revolution against the past brought into question whether intelligence 'can continue to find a home in the university'. The sanctification of current fads worked to undermine scholarship at a time when the state, the army and corporations were all establishing their own research and knowledge facilities independent of the university.[92] Against this, E.F. O'Doherty's 'Psychological Aspects of Student Revolt' (1969) sympathised with student alienation from a 'desert of academic aridity'. Many students within the expanded university systems of the West were, he argued, culturally displaced. When tertiary education was a rare privilege it was highly valued. Not so now. Nurture within the *alma mater* had been replaced by processing within a mass further education. Students, with considerable cause, viewed the university system as an over-restrictive and over-demanding machine. Student protestors influenced by Daniel Cohn-Bendit were, as such, neo-Luddites.[93]

Studies drew on foreign correspondents such as Schall to prompt debate about Irish social change. Critics of the sociological status quo at home tended to come from outside the field. FitzGerald was an economist, Thornley a political scientist. In 'Reflections on Sociology' (1972) the Reverend James Kavanagh depicted the subject as being endangered from without and within. He described having regularly to defend it in conversations with sceptical academic colleagues from other disciplines who considered it flaky ('If I had had long hair and a beard, the picture would have been complete'[94]). He professed to agree with much of this whilst ignoring Irish criticism of clerical sociology. The sociology department he controlled in UCD would, he argued with autocratic certainty, regard a completely theoretical approach to the subject as defective.[95] By way of example (but without any explanation) he referred to the 'infantile' and 'arid pessimism of Marcuse'. Irish supporters of such 'destructive radicalism' were pithily disparaged as 'sea-green incorruptible Robespierres'.[96] He was adamant that the subject needed to remain empirical, scientific and modest in its claims about offering understandings of society.[97] Radical social theory, whatever that meant, was a Pandora's Box that should not be opened in the Irish case.

Irish sociology, in any case, followed trends. It did not make them. It reflected, and reflected on, growing secularisation and disenchantment. The Church, as Tom Inglis put it in his classic account, had lost its moral monopoly.[98] The rural Ireland that *Christus Rex* sought to repair had, it was argued, become deeply sexually and psychologically dysfunctional. A 1981 review in *Studies* endorsed the typically devastating analysis of a dying rural community in Nancy Scheper-Hughes's *Saints, Scholars and Schizophrenics: Mental Illness in Rural Ireland*. The community 'Ballybran' had a tiny birth rate pitifully unable to balance the loss due to death and emigration. It was full of ageing and lonely people living on unviable small-holdings. Young women, reluctant to marry even the landowners and the abler young men, left, never to return. The less able young men who stayed were maintained in an immature role by ageing parents. Too often these failed to marry and formed alliances with spinster sisters characterised by scarcely concealed mutual hostility. This was the society the study groups could not stick together with God's glue. These were the social factors that Newman argued were less important than economic ones. Within the new critique, the Irish version of Catholicism, with its Jansenistic repressive morality, carried the seeds of its own destruction.[99] But as Tom Inglis observed, Jansenism imprecisely described the rigid moral regulation that followed in the wake of the Famine and the Catholic emancipation that allowed the Church to rebuild and exercise considerable influence within society.[100] Its unravelling wrote much of what *Christus Rex* stood for out of history.

CHAPTER FIVE

Liberal Agendas: Catholic and Liberal Alliances, *Studies*, 1940–68

The period covered by this chapter roughly coincides with the reign of John Charles McQuaid as Archbishop of Dublin. For three decades McQuaid was the inelastic face of Catholic power in Ireland whilst all around him society changed. *Studies* found itself at the crossroads of various conflicts. British plans for a welfare state were explained and widely discussed. Yet, in 1951, at the time of Noel Browne's Mother and Child Scheme, *Studies* determinedly opposed state interventionism. McQuaid by no means acted alone. In *Studies* liberal economists and clerics borrowed each other's clothes to argue against the spectre of the welfare state. Roadblocks across what F.A. Hayek labelled 'the road to serfdom' were fashioned from an admixture of both. In the case of Bishop William Philbin it could sometimes appear that the twentieth-century Catholic Church was the nineteenth-century Liberal Party at prayer. However, *Studies* also championed and prepared the ground for T.K. Whitaker's *Economic Development*. It gave a platform to Patrick Lynch to argue for Keynesian planning and offer reassurances about growing state activism. *Studies* published a number of seminal articles advocating an economic developmental role for the state. By the 1950s the compact against the state between Catholic and liberal thought was reformed to promote a new state-led nation-building developmental project. Here it was no longer the case that an enemy's enemy was a friend but that Keynesian thinking about economic planning debated in *Studies* for two decades had finally become intellectually institutionalised.

The short of it was that different positions and arguments were articulated in different domains. Conservative ones prevailed with respect of the pastoral kingdom of family welfare services. Here, subsidiarity was presented as inviolable. The perceived battleground was for moral influence within Irish homes. On one hand the Church sought to reproduce religiosity through denominational education. On the other the state, notably through the 1965 joint OECD/Irish government report *Investment in Education*, promoted human capital goals for education.[1]

Yet Catholic dominance in education found no shortage of champions, including senior civil servants. The need for secondary schooling had exceeded the capacity of clerical providers. The need to build human capital challenged an existing predominant emphasis on religious formation. Both stood to undermine the reproduction of religious identity from one generation to the next. Debates on education within *Studies* from the 1940s to the 1960s exemplified a broader recalibration of post-independence nation-building. The burden of institutionalising the Irish language within Irish society had been placed on the shoulders of teachers to the detriment of both education and the language. But the education system had not delivered an Irish language revival. The language debate was increasingly viewed as a sideshow.

The old Thomist vocabulary of Catholic social thought was gradually retired. In 'Ireland: The End of an Era' (1964) David Thornley argued that its influence on future social policy would be negligible. The state, he argued, would have to develop welfare services to the same extent as other countries in the European Economic Community that Ireland was on the road to joining.[2] Under the editorship of Roland Burke-Savage SJ (from 1950 to 1968) natural law rhetoric was superseded by new borrowings from socialist and liberal thought. In his landmark 'Seeking a National Purpose' (1964) Garret FitzGerald, a recent convert to social liberalism, outlined a social justice agenda that was to be shared by many contributors to *Studies* over the next two decades.[3] Like Burke-Savage he advocated borrowing some socialist ideas. FitzGerald also savaged Catholic sociology. *Studies* came to encapsulate a range of tensions within Irish society. Catholic power was declining. In 1965, with authoritarian Catholicism now on the ropes, *Studies* rallied around McQuaid even though it had, on occasion, rebuffed his interference. During McQuaid's reign *Studies* became a forum for a new guard who would come to lead Irish society. It reflected an era where the key documents against which Irish social change was to be interrogated were government policy reports rather than papal encyclicals.

REPRODUCTIVE FAILURES

In 1941 the then editor of *Studies*, Patrick Connolly S.J, commissioned an article from Michael Tierney that was subsequently spiked. Since 1922 Tierney had contributed thirty-five articles to the journal. A 1937 *Irish Independent* piece by Tierney celebrating the silver jubilee of *Studies* described it as a mirror of Irish thought watched over by the Jesuit Fathers and its devoted editor. He described the journal as 'one of the finest things Ireland has produced in our time'.[4] The commission Tierney received in 1941 was to examine the need for a review of the 1909 Act that established the National University of Ireland. The article he submitted mooted the amalgamation of University College Dublin with Trinity College. What transpired sheds some light on Church politics just before the appointment of McQuaid. It also reveals something about the precarious ground that progressive Jesuits occupied.

Tierney's article was initially supported by all members of the editorial board except Timothy Corcoran SJ, UCD Professor of Education, who 'single-handedly' blocked the publication at the last moment. A briefing letter to the Jesuit Provincial outlined why most of the board felt it should be published:

> The article raised so many controversial issues, and made some statements which reflected unfavourably on the position in UCD from a Catholic point of view so obviously, that the Fathers of the Editorial Board rejected his article last March, much to Fr. Connolly's grief. However, it was made plain to him that the article could be used as a peg for comments by other Professors, and might thus serve a useful purpose for the next [June] issue. Incidentally we knew that Dr Conway, the new President of U.C.D., had read the article, and favoured publication as a means of calling the attention of the Government to the great financial needs of the College.
>
> He [Corcoran] objects to any discussion of the TCD plan and holds that discussion must be limited to possible improvements in the present College. Actually, four of the five university commentators refuse to consider the proposal of amalgamation as possible politics (myself included). That is why the majority of the Fathers hold that the discussion makes it plain that Tierney's scheme is impracticable, and throws useful light on the present

> needs of the College. But Fr. C. is not satisfied, and ended the discussion by stating that he would write to your reverence (as I had indeed suggested to him), and also to His Grace. He holds strongly that publication of this article might mislead or embarrass the new Archbishop, who is undoubtedly interested in the University.[5]

Corcoran had been on the editorial board from the outset in 1912. He had had played a major part in securing the election of de Valera as Chancellor of the National University.[6] He also contributed to the luridly anti-Protestant and anti-Semitic *Catholic Bulletin*.[7] Corcoran had been an influential mentor to McQuaid who had studied under him at UCD from 1918 to 1920. In particular, McQuaid was influenced by Corcoran's views on education.[8] If *Studies* represented a continuum of Catholic opinion, Corcoran inhabited the illiberal wing that came to be dominated by his one-time protégé.

The Jesuits who supported publication found themselves in an invidious position. Their Provincial concluded that the new Archbishop would have to be informally consulted.[9] McQuaid indeed proved interested in UCD and subsequently worked to increase clerical academic influence, especially in the social sciences.[10] Corcoran's argument against publication of Tierney's article shared the rationale behind McQuaid's subsequent 1944 edict preventing Catholics from attending Trinity College. In 1941 Corcoran represented the battle for the hearts and minds of the next generation of educated Catholics in explicitly sectarian terms:

> 1. Prof. Tierney proposes to either:
> (a) Inject into the National University or some other newly-named university, about 1000 Protestant and nondescript students and their staff;
> Or:
> (b) Inject into University College Dublin in a quite *undesirable* and even *repulsive* way 1000 such persons, who are not wanted in any combination whatever.
>
> 2. To do so, he seeks to disrupt our very homogenous and consistently Catholic University population (98 to 99 per cent Catholic both as to students and to staff, in our four University Colleges, so as to force our 99 per cent Catholic students and staff, at U.C. Dublin, into the most unasked-for coupling with an

> English College in Dublin; of some 2,500 Catholic students with about 900 Protestant students.[11]

The debate stymied by Corcoran was resurrected a quarter of a century later by the then Education Minister Donagh O'Malley, who pushed for a merger of Trinity and UCD.[12] In an article published in *Studies* O'Malley emphasised the cost benefits of the merger he sought. Both, for instance, had small Veterinary Faculties. UCD had about 900 science students and 900 more who took the subject in their first year only. Trinity had only 300 science students. O'Malley argued that it would be more economical for all of them to be educated 'under the one roof'. What made economic sense would also make educational sense. Collaboration could not but raise standards. O'Malley stated that the proposed new university would be multi-denominational, with provision for Catholic and Protestant Schools of Divinity and Theology.[13] The lack of these at UCD had always been a sore point for advocates of a Catholic university system.

The 1967 public debate in *Studies* was a very different one from the one prosecuted behind the scenes by Corcoran in 1940 and publicly by McQuaid in 1944. Broadly speaking UCD, the larger institution, advocated a full merger whilst Trinity sought a federal system that preserved its autonomy. An overall lack of anxiety amongst Catholic commentators, so different from the mood of the 1940s, suggested that much had changed in the politics of education. Yet the core concern about protecting Catholic ethos remained to the fore. One respondent to O'Malley's article argued that it would be necessary that provision be made in subjects like philosophy and history 'for a full education for Catholics' and that the Catholic hierarchy would need to be represented on the governing body.[14]

On the Trinity side concerns were voiced that the 'religious and racial minority' be assured of sufficient representation. Otherwise Southern and Northern Protestants, according to a Trinity classicist, 'would have to send their sons abroad for a university education'.[15] Basil Chubb, then Professor of Political Science at Trinity, observed that the majority of the college were opposed to what many understood as a 'takeover bid'. There was a small hard-core *laager* culture of extreme opposition alongside a broader unease that a distinctive academic community would be maimed by the merger.[16] Chubb argued that the problem for UCD was a different one of preserving academic standards in the face of rapid projected expansion.[17]

An article by J.P. McHale, the UCD Bursar, emphasised that both universities were under-resourced. There could be no question of saving millions. In 1965–66 staff student ratios were 1:16 in Trinity and 1:22 in UCD compared with 1:8 on average for British universities. Trinity's annual income per student stood at £250 compared to £190 at UCD, whilst most British universities 'enjoyed' about £800 per student.[18] He predicted that a merger would almost certainly diminish the current bloc of 741 Northern (Protestant) students.[19] McHale termed the decision of UCD to support the merger as the 'Great Acceptance' by way of contrast with the 'Great Refusal' of Trinity in 1908 to join a scheme for a Dublin university.[20] *Studies*, long and closely entwined with UCD, reflected this position.[21] A sense of majority-cultural confidence contrasted with the isolationist sectarianism promoted by Corcoran in the 1940s and McQuaid in the 1960s. That the merger did not come to pass had much to do with the death of O'Malley in 1968.

The debate about university education was something of a sideshow compared to the one precipitated by the need to expand secondary education. To do so beyond the capacity of clerical resources implied a greater role for the state. However, the view that educational formation was the business of the Church was one shared by many civil servants. A 1949 article by Joseph O'Neill, who had been Secretary of the Department of Education from 1923 to 1944, presented the case for a minimal role for the state in the control of education.[22] Mass education in Ireland, he argued, had preceded any state involvement. In 1812, a quarter of a century before the establishment of the National Board, a Government Commission of Enquiry reported that there were 4,600 schools in Ireland, with an attendance of nearly a quarter-million pupils. Further surveys from 1824 to 1826 put the number of schools at 12,000 with an enrolment of over half a million. Two-thirds of these were Parish Schools under the management of local clergy.[23] What emerged, by necessity, and continued after independence, was a necessarily elastic co-operation between state and Church.

O'Neill the civil servant warned against opposed state-dominated education, citing the French primary schools as hotbeds of unrest and communism.[24] The state, he insisted, should not usurp the natural role of the Church and community (no distinction was drawn between either) in education:

> Here in Ireland the Church, the State, the teachers and the parents combine harmoniously to form an organism with the

> flexibility and the power of adjustment of an organic growth. Behind the Iron Curtain, gangs of men who have seized the machines of State are forcing a mechanical system on nations whose Churches, teachers and people detest and resist it by every means in their power.[25]

For O'Neill, the main purpose of education was social reproduction of religious humanism rather than human capital understood in terms of skills and qualifications for employment:

> From our point of view it is incredible that such a machine-made "Education" could last. Apart altogether from the fact that an Education system which has not religious conviction at the heart of it is still-born, a mechanical system of Education is a contradiction in terms. Educational systems must be organic; they must have the vitality and growth and adjusting power of life.[26]

In 1954 Sean O'Cathain SJ, who later succeeded Corcoran as UCD Professor of Education, argued that compulsory secondary education would destabilise the then existing system of clerical control. There was, he warned, no guarantee that the 'unique and happy system' of a free primary education system able to resist undue state interference could be replicated in an expanded secondary sector.[27]

O'Cathain's 1954 article contrasted the apparent success of education in reproducing Catholicism with its failure to revive Gaelic. Compulsory Irish was a compulsion that remained meaningless to most Irish people.[28] 'People', he wrote, 'do not like to be pushed around too much.' Teachers were unrealistically expected to shoulder sole responsibility for reviving the language. Children, according to available evidence, disliked learning Irish in schools. Ordinary people found it hard to see why a postman must pass an examination in oral Irish, but a Minister of Posts need not. Implicit in his argument was that the Church was better at religious formation than the state had proved at promoting the Irish language.

The language revival had been a key element of pre-independence nation-building. The revival of Gaelic, begun by Protestants in the mid-nineteenth century, had spread within the mass movement politics of the predominantly Catholic Gaelic League. Gaelic was central to the claims of national distinctiveness advanced before independence. It proved less important to post-independence nation-building not least because its role as proof of ethnic distinctiveness in a predominantly

Catholic-nation state had evaporated. You did not have to speak Irish to prove yourself to be Irish. Catholicism remained central to post-independence nation-building not least because it dominated education and permeated other elements of social and cultural reproduction. *Studies* had, in its early years, dedicated considerable space to debates on the future of Irish. However, the emphasis of these was on the failure of linguistic revival outside the schools. Article after article had suggested in vain that one more push was needed. The notion that schools should shoulder the burden of linguistic revival met with resentment. The centrality of the Irish language to curricular ideology was sniped at on an ongoing basis in *Studies*.

In 'The Curriculum of the Secondary School' (1962) Patrick McCann described the language debate as part of a wider malaise. Societies were unhealthy where 'there is a gross discrepancy between what is commonly thought and what is publicly said'. Educational debates about the Irish language were but one example of such gross discrepancy.[29] The inability to have a real dialogue about the Irish language revival exemplified this. Official policy forty years after independence still insisted that Irish was to replace English as the vernacular of the country. That this had not occurred was patently obvious. Any theory or practice of education, McCann tautologically argued, built upon the denial of such obvious truth was one built on illusion.[30] The revival, he concluded, could not be imposed by diktat:

> In the early days of our freedom, when national cohesion and unity were not assured, it was only natural that our people, and particularly those in authority, should fear rather than welcome genuine dialogue; for differences might lead to extremes of action, and the stability of society be thus imperilled. An imposed unity was preferable to chaos. Yet in the long run the unity of a society will not be something imposed from above.[31]

After independence, *Studies* had published many articles on the development of second-and third-level curricula. A short-lived preoccupation with science and technical education amongst educationalists such as Corcoran had evaporated. Within the Catholic-dominated secondary sector the preoccupation with religious formation persisted. A 1938 symposium in *Studies* had vainly sought to advance the introduction of scholastic philosophy into the curriculum.[32] By the 1960s the language question had become a sideshow. The battle for hearts and minds refocused on control of the expanding secondary system. The most crucial debate about the relationship between educational ethos and religious social reproduction came from the hugely influential *Investment in Education.* It was commissioned in 1962 by Patrick Hillery, Minister for Education, as a joint report with the Organisation for Economic Co-operation and Development (OECD).[33] The main author, Patrick Lynch, was a former Department of Finance ally of Whitaker who had moved to UCD. In essence, *Investment in Education* proposed to shift the emphasis of education from being primarily concerned with the cultural and religious reproduction of Irish society towards a focus on human capital for economic growth.

A 1965 article by Garret FitzGerald had detailed its findings without addressing the politics of reforming secondary education.[34] Peter Troddyn's editorial in a 1968 issue on the reorganisation of Irish education emphasised that the stakes were high. Hitherto, the system was run at zero capital cost to the state. In effect the Churches owned as well as controlled the secondary education system. If, as Troddyn put it, the state had 'wisely underplayed' its entry into the field of secondary education, so too was his own approach a calculatedly diplomatic one: 'We hold that, at least on balance, the religious-run schools of this country have had a valuable formative influence on their pupils.'[35] Troddyn insisted that there was no need to import the pluralist (understood as 'usually meaning agnostic') educational norms of America or 'materialistic Northern Europe'.[36]

Troddyn solicited a flagship article from Sean O'Connor, then Assistant Secretary in the Department of Education. The aim here was to tease out the implications of a rapid expansion of the secondary system. However, immediately prior to publication O'Connor's Minister, Brian Lenihan, sought to spike the article. Permission had been revoked when O'Connor indicated that he would be expressing his own personal views.[37] This was not the only obstacle that Troddyn overcame. McQuaid had obtained a draft of O'Connor's article and asked the Jesuit Provincial Cecil McGarry to stop its publication.[38] McGarry refused the Archbishop as well as the Minister. A frank, seminal debate about secondary education ensued.

O'Connor strongly criticised plans to bring about compulsory secondary education without measures to address the needs of those (one-third of all pupils) now required to remain on until 15 years of age. Many of them would 'linger on at the back ends of primary classes until the day of release comes'.[39] As for 'the problem of Church/State relations', O'Connor let the figures speak for themselves.

In 1966 the 485 Catholic secondary schools had a pupil population of 103,558. There were now 2,728 lay teachers, out of a total of 4,871, with 1,986 additional unfilled posts. Most of these were vacant 'because the religious authorities were not able to staff them with their own people'. Schools could not afford to pay the full salaries they would have to give to lay teachers. Vocations for the priesthood and teaching orders also seemed to be shrinking. There was another side to it. O'Connor complained that the lay teacher remained always a hireling: 'never part of the decision-making. If he wants authority so that he may innovate, experiment, he must go elsewhere.'[40] O'Connor argued that something had to give:

> I lay stress on these things because I believe a change must be made; otherwise there will be an explosion, maybe sooner than later. No one wants to push the religious out of education; that would be disastrous, in my opinion. But I want them in it as partners, not always as masters.[41]

Some reacted to O'Connor by wanting to shoot the messenger. For example, the Christian Brothers accused him of seeking to drive a wedge between clerical and lay teachers by implying without evidence that some of the latter were dissatisfied with the status quo.[42] O'Connor was seen to exemplify 'nationalisation by stealth, whereby property is not taken over, but management is'.[43]

A decline in clerical intellectual influence within education debates had been evident for some time. Whilst Corcoran enjoyed considerable influence O'Cathain had little or none. O'Cathain's essays on secondary education in *Studies* were published in book form in 1958 but attracted little attention from education policy-makers.[44] O'Connor in his 1986 memoir described some of them as missives from Cloud-Cuckoo Land.[45] The new ideas proposed by *Investment in Education*, about shifting the focus of education from religious reproduction to human capital formation, from humanism to technocracy, were ones that had already gathered much impetus during the 1950s. O'Cathain saw the writing on the wall but could only rail against change in vain. In lectures at UCD throughout the remainder of his career he mourned the 'wrong turn' represented by *Investment in Education*.[46] However, *Investment in Education* and the new developmental ethos that emerged as the dominant nation-building project of the second half of the twentieth century owed much to the alliances between Catholicism and liberalism that had been nurtured in *Studies*.

LIBERAL ALLIANCES

From the 1940s Catholic writers in *Studies* struggled to come to terms with shifting Western economic and social policy norms. The Beveridge Report was widely read by Irish civil servants, clerics and academics. The theories of Keynes were promoted in *Studies* more than a decade before these became orthodox within the Department of Finance. In 1942 Michael Tierney was wide of the mark in commenting that: 'We are quite probably on the threshold of a new age which will be marked by a universal distrust of State intervention in any but a carefully delineated group of activities.'[47] However, many contributors to *Studies* shared Tierney's distaste for the welfare state.

In 'Catholic Political Theory' (1941) the Reverend Denis O'Keeffe (Professor of Ethics and Politics at UCD) combined the standard Catholic objections to utilitarianism with F.A. Hayek's attack on the concept of the greater good. Hayek was subsequently championed by a number of contributors, including George O'Brien. O'Keeffe's starting point was the standard one. An abiding wisdom and body of sound principles had been inherited from Plato, Aristotle, Cicero, St Augustine and St Thomas Aquinas.[48] These principles, he insisted, were not necessarily opposed to a role for the state. Catholic political and social theories had evolved over time in response to new problems and issues. No form of state organisation that respected natural rights and endeavoured to realise the common good could be declared unlawful.[49] O'Keefe distinguished the conception of natural rights developed by John Locke from God-given (hence his use of the upper-case) Natural Rights emanating from natural law. Lockean natural rights were merely the result of legal positivism. Rights to welfare as conceded by the state were merely the product of the circumstances of some particular time and place. These were, in effect, rules that could be changed.[50]

O'Keeffe's attack on utilitarian conceptions of the greater good used essentially the same argument as Hayek. Because it was 'in practice impossible to work out what does or does not bring the greater good to the greater number, the theory affords no guarantee against tyranny'.[51] Hayek counselled individual autonomy against the state. O'Keeffe maintained that it had been the task of the Church in times of anarchy to uphold legitimate authority and, when authority had been overstretched, to stand up for the rights of the individual and the family.[52] There was, then, a degree of common ground between natural law understandings of subsidiarity and Hayek's case for individual autonomy.

In 1944, O'Brien published three influential articles. The first, 'Capitalism in Transition', observed that a 'more socialised society' was nigh. A second explained and criticised the Beveridge Report outlining the plan for the British Welfare State. The third promoted Hayek's *The Road to Serfdom* as an antidote to its likely excesses. 'Capitalism in Transition' argued that the great age of capitalism had passed. Reform had won out over revolution. This new society would be more egalitarian than the old, with less poverty and no pauperism. Variants of the Beveridge scheme would conquer want.[53] O'Brien's acknowledgement of a new mood of social democratic optimism stood in contrast to other wartime analyses in *Studies*. So too did his apparent lack of anxiety about the new order he believed it would produce:

> People will be less forward-looking. Social security will provide against the risks and hazards of life ... The falling birth-rate and the gradual ageing of the population will reduce the importance of the family as a unit in the social structure. Saving, the typical Victorian virtue, will cease to arouse applause. The accumulation of a fortune, the dearest Victorian ambition, will no longer command respect.[54]

In his second article O'Brien examined the White Paper produced by the British government in response to Beveridge Plan's aspiration for full employment. Beveridge's *Full Employment in a Free Society* had been commended by Sean Lemass to members of the Dáil in 1944 as a useful guide to dealing with Irish conditions.[55] O'Brien did not oppose public expenditure on public works to promote employment so long as these expanded goods or services. However, his support for interventionism came with clear limits, as can be seen from his closing sentence: 'Whilst unemployment is admittedly an evil, employment is not an end in itself. Wealth, not work, is the end of economic activity.'[56] A third article marked out the common ground between Catholic anti-statism and that advocated by Hayek:

> *The Road to Serfdom* is more than a mere reaffirmation of the principles of political liberalism. It is a restatement of fundamental Christian truths that are in danger of being denied or forgotten in the modern world – that man is master of his own fate, that he must shoulder the moral responsibility for all his deeds and misdeeds, and that the State exists for man, not man

> for the State. The argument of the book is capable of being condensed into a single sentence of Hilaire Belloc's – 'The effects of socialist doctrine on capitalist society is to produce a third thing different from either of its begetters – to wit the Servile State.'[57]

Here, O'Brien echoed a 1943 polemic, 'Mr. Belloc's Servile State and the Beveridge Plan'. Hilaire Belloc, in *The Servile State* (1911), had railed against the introduction of limited old age pensions and unemployment insurance by the Liberals, equating these with slavery.[58] O'Brien's attempt to Catholicise Hayek suggested a profound ambivalence towards social democracy, even if he was convinced of the economic benefits of a stronger state role. In 'New Views on Unemployment' (1945) O'Brien summarised the thesis of Keynes's *General Theory of Employment* (1936), the theory underpinning the Beveridge Report. O'Brien had long championed Keynes. The *General Theory* argued, amongst other things, that free trade could no longer be trusted to maximise the volume of production. There was, then, a *prima facie* case for state intervention in the economy. The state, Keynes argued and Beveridge accepted, could alleviate chronic unemployment by stimulating demand through state expenditure. That is, it could break past cycles where high unemployment and high saving co-existed. By spending more than its current revenue, it could add to the total expenditure of the community. It could add directly to consumption, that is, stimulate economic demand by subsidising goods through schemes of public investment or by redistributing income from the rich to the poor.[59] O'Brien endorsed the validity of Keynes's paradigm and Beveridge's proposals based upon it.[60]

The political problems arising from these policies were, he argued, the crucial issue. Beveridge, he emphasised, accepted that essential British liberties were more precious than full employment. Hayek's insistence that freedom could not be reconciled with the supremacy of any one single aim to which society much be subordinated (except in the case of war, where a temporary sacrifice of freedom could be seen to make it more secure in the longer term) was endorsed by O'Brien.[61] The problem was how to introduce the necessary central controls without a sacrifice of political liberty and with an absolute minimum interference with personal liberty and initiative. In 'Socialist Myth and Russian Reality' (1945) O'Brien championed Arthur Koestler's critique of Soviet totalitarianism to hammer home again the same point.[62] Koestler, Hayek and Belloc each served to qualify O'Brien's endorsement of Keynesian economics. O'Brien remained a dedicated communicator of liberal objections to collectivism, not least in his obituary of Keynes in 1946, where he depicted him as a liberal in the Whig tradition. He explained that Keynes' objection to socialism was political. Liberty was best pursued in an individualist society purged of its abuses.[63]

The British wartime proposals for a welfare state had stimulated widespread debate in Ireland amongst academics, civil servants and clerics. In 'The Beveridge Report and Eire' (1943) the Reverend Cornelius Lucey explained its emergence as resulting from shifting social norms. Today no civilised country left the poor to their own resources or the care of private charity.[64] Again, Lucey's argument drew on liberal as well as Catholic ideals; for instance, in how he distinguished between the deserving and undeserving poor:

> The proposal is to secure citizens against all unmerited poverty. Intemperance, idleness, gambling, thriftlessness, etc, all help and help very considerably, to swell the ranks of the needy. However, to secure people against intemperance and the like would be to secure them against the consequences of their own failings and destroy in them all sense of personal responsibility. Hence the Report, wisely presupposing the traditional distinction between the 'deserving' and the 'undeserving' to furnish security only against the causes that result in poverty through no fault on the part of the victim himself.[65]

In principle, Lucey endorsed the use of expanded social insurance to protect the deserving poor from the risks of poverty. However, when it came to the Irish case he introduced a number of objections to any endorsement of welfare universalism. Lucey argued that the majority of Irish people were property owners rather than wage earners and that most were in a position to provide for their own families. As such, they did not need to be secured from poverty through compulsory social state insurance. Most, he argued, were smallholders and some might be bankrupted by having to make compulsory insurance payments. He argued for the reform of means-tested social assistance – which he noted many found degrading – rather than the introduction of universal entitlements in the Irish case. He further maintained that it was premature for Ireland to convene a commission to discuss the development of social security and allied services. His concluding argument (from *Rerum Novarum*) emphasised the need to tackle unemployment and the lack for many of a living wage. In other words, work not welfare. Many of the poor, he argued, would perceive a state system of security as a ready instrument of tyranny.[66]

In 'Tuberculosis: A Social Problem' (1943) T.W.T. Dillon described the effects of TB and urban poverty in graphic detail yet portrayed state activism as a greater potential evil: 'Family life, that central pivot of Society, begins to disintegrate; the State acquires an ever increasing power over the family; and we find ourselves caught in the meshes of bureaucratic totalitarianism.'[67] Again, in 'Public Health Planning' (1944), Dillon emphasised the relationship between poverty and chronic disease. He bemoaned reluctance to acknowledge it amongst experts and institutions. The result of this past neglect was that public health now threatened 'to become the storm centre of antagonistic social and political doctrines – all equipped with detailed blueprints for an expensive and radiant hygienic future'.[68] This planning fever, incubated in Moscow, but which had now swept across the world, might, Dillon argued, prove to be a benign pandemic as long as limits 'set by the inexorable laws of human liberty' were imposed.

Dillon saw the proposed British National Health Service as an enviable model, at least in terms of the resources (envisaged at £170 million per annum) it would involve. The problem was that the ratio of the Irish national income to the British equivalent was 1:45 whilst the population ratio was 1:15. Eire would have to spend much more per head of population to realise the levels of provision envisaged in Britain.[69] Ideology aside, this was a key argument. The 'big bang' reforms envisaged in the United Kingdom could be realised only gradually in the Irish case. Even the Irish proposals advocated by Bishop Dignan in his role as Chairman of the National Health Insurance Society could, in Dillon's view, only be realised gradually.[70]

Dillon's 1945 article on slum clearance noted that the number living in one-room tenements was 3,000 higher in 1938 than in 1911.[71] Unlike Lucey, Dillon rejected liberal stereotypes of an undeserving poor. The dignity, courage and patience of the families who lived in the 'sordid rat-holes' of Dublin slums were emphasised even if he portrayed the worst off of them – a 'class of social pariahs' – as a potentially dangerous underclass.[72] Dillon cited examples of unemployed workers forced to move from corporation housing because of 'lunatic' administrative practices. The rent allowance subsidy system compelled families to rent the worst (cheapest) accommodation from slum landlords. Dillon's article detailed how the Corporation condoned a system of ruthless exploitation of tenants by placing people in the power of exploitative landlords.[73] In 'The Social Services in Eire' (1945) Dillon presented a vivid account of Irish poverty. It was, he argued, concentrated amongst two categories: large families and an unemployable proletariat. This time he focused on the former, arguing that present policies retained most of the disadvantages of the old poor law with the addition of administrative waste and inefficiency. The main defect was stigma: 'people were made to feel that poverty was a sinful thing and the poor had lost their rights as human beings'.[74] He could not warm to the liberal presumptions of the Beveridge Plan because it placed a liberal conception of equality (same wages for the same work) instead of earnings adjusted according to family need (the family wage).[75] He argued for the replacement of poor law institutions by voluntary ones working in co-operation with the clergy. The clergy were, by office, intimately concerned with the relief of distress. He implied that such a faith-based welfare system would not reproduce the stigma of the existing system based on the Poor Law.[76]

It was no surprise, then, in the face of such opposition to state welfare, that *Studies* trenchantly opposed Noel Browne's 'Mother and Child Scheme'. The summer 1951 issue of the journal included three polemics attacking the Scheme. A Jesuit contributor, Edward Coyne, emphasised the right of the hierarchy to give moral leadership, then gave it chapter and verse, citing papal encyclicals to argue against the universal provision of free services.[77] A UCD Professor of Obstetrics and Gynaecology opposed 'free-for-all' services and argued that the scheme would be a waste of money.[78] A lawyer, again writing outside his specific expertise, argued that the country could not afford it.[79] Coyne lambasted Browne's proposals as a 'ready-made instrument for future totalitarian aggression'.[80] He offered vivid propaganda to evoke the dangers of giving the state a limited role in social work and public health policy:

> It is a very serious thing when a County Council official has the power by law to walk into any Irishman's home, whether once, twice or oftener in the year, against the will of the parents. It is a very serious thing that this County official should have the legal right to order the children of the family to be brought before him, make these children, boys and girls of 12, 13, 14, 15 and 16, undress and submit to a most intimate medical inspection. It is a very serious thing when such an official has the right to inspect such domestic arrangements as he thinks would militate against the safeguarding of the health of the children: a right to give

> instructions as to food, exercise and the sleeping arrangements and possibly to bring the habits and directions of the parents in these matters into contempt with the children and so shake all parental authority.[81]

Coyne's opening claim was shrill hyperbole, given the emphasis on family rights in the 1937 Constitution.[82] It was typical of a broad clerical hostility to the 'Mother and Child Scheme'. In 1951 *Studies* and the Church played hardball. Browne was removed and the Inter-Party Government fell. Two years later Coyne 'sincerely' welcomed the broadly similar Fianna Fáil Health Bill. On this occasion he offered what he called 'reasonable and conciliatory, constructive criticism'.[83] There was, Coyne insisted, 'something sacred and primary and personally intimate and holy and inviolate in the privileges and duties of paternity: a married man is more than a man, when he shoulders, alone, the proud burden of responsibility for wife, mother and child'. The state, with its 'necessarily clumsy, almost sacrilegious methods' should not interfere in this sphere of life.[84]

THE SPIRIT OF DEVELOPMENT

A 1958 article, 'Government by the People' by William Philbin, Bishop of Clonfert, at once emphasised the importance of political participation, the requirement of citizens to obey the rightful authority of the state, the need to resist state absolutism *and* the need to de-emphasise individual liberty; in other words, responsibility to community rather than individual rights. 'Democracy', Philbin noted, 'was an industry with a large labour content. Its plant, far from possessing the properties of automation, needs much control and servicing in order to avoid getting out of order.' The Bishop called for widespread participation in democratic politics through active citizenship and civil society.[85] There was, he insisted, a moral obligation to give allegiance to the authority that the community had established. Philbin distinguished a necessary loyalty to such concrete institutions from 'a vague devotion to abstract nationhood.'[86] This, again, was a democratic theory purged of John Locke, Tom Paine and the Enlightenment. The sole temporal authority countenanced was Edmund Burke.[87] 'Citizens', Philbin insisted, 'should cherish something higher than the state.' They should place the City of God above Plato's Republic. Philbin seemed to epitomise clerical orthodoxy but was destined to become something of a prophet and apostle of developmental nation-building. It had been an inspiration, T.K. Whitaker wrote in the introduction to *Economic Development*, to read what Philbin had written a year earlier in 'A City on the Hill' (1957) about the need to combine enterprise in spiritual fields with greater initiative in agriculture, industry and commerce. His own report, Whitaker claimed, was a contribution, in the spirit advocated by the Bishop of Clonfert, towards the working out of the national good in the economic sphere.[88]

In 1953 *Studies* had published a symposium on economics and public policy with a lead article by Patrick Lynch. Lynch had been close to Whitaker in the Department of Finance. As an economist at UCD he became a key public intellectual advocate of state-fostered economic planning. In 'The Economist and Public Policy' (1953) Lynch, argued for realistic debate, stripped of polemic, about the need for some state activism. Many critics of state interventionism sheltered behind 'the lingering shadows of economic liberalism to deny positive economic functions to a government'. Their views were, he argued, based on an incorrect reading of classical economics and on a convenient disregard of economic history:

> To circumscribe the economic role of the state by invoking Jeremy Bentham and John Stuart Mill is to do less than historical justice to either of these men. Mill's doctrine prepared the way for the modern British welfare state, and Bentham's pointed, if somewhat equivocally, towards George Orwell's *1984*; as economists, both are significant not so much because of their advocacy of unlimited individual rights against the encroachment of the state as their powerful promulgation of concepts which have the opposite effect.[89]

Economic arguments were one thing – these depended on time and place – and ideology was another. Lynch quoted Keynes: 'Practical men who believe themselves to be quite exempt from any intellectual influences, are usually the slaves of some defunct economist.'[90] Specifically, Lynch argued that economic liberalism had been intellectually bankrupt since the Great Depression. He emphasised the impracticality of *laissez-faire* ideology ('the only untried utopia' because it had never naturally occurred in the world).[91] Both overt and implicit dependence on ideology stood in the way of deciding what could and should be done to promote economic development and social welfare in society. The role of economics was to contribute to a realistic public policy debate. Much criticism of state social policies could be avoided if the advocates of these were more modest in their claims. Using 1952 figures he noted that the British 'welfare state', which accounted for no more than five and a half per cent of personal incomes, hardly amounted to state absolutism.[92]

In 'Escape from Stagnation' (1963) Lynch was still beating the same drum: '*Laissez-Faire* was always more an unrealised Utopia than a fact; in fact it was little more than a slogan.'[93] Citing Gunnar Mrydal, he argued that it was by accident that planning became associated with Marxism. Lynch's definition of economic planning was 'the conscious management, to the extent consistent with democratic political freedom and individual liberty, of the course in which the national economy should be directed, if the agreed economic and social objectives are to be attained'.[94] His emphasis on management through agreement anticipated the later of the Irish social partnership model. Here, Lynch promoted a co-ordinating role for the National Economic Development Council, forerunner of the later National Social and Economic Council.[95] Lynch described his preferred approach as 'non-doctrinal state activity'.

Coyne took Lynch to task for discounting (that is, not mentioning) Catholic alternatives to economic liberalism.[96] But, for most writers on economy and society in *Studies*, vocationalism was now dead. Arguments against the state were increasingly ones grounded on liberal premises; the debate had shifted. As put by another Jesuit respondent to Lynch: 'We are all planners today' ... Here in Ireland, as almost in every other country of the world, men have come to accept greater state direction of participation in economic life.' The question now was about protecting the liberty citizens from the newfound power of the state.[97] In 1963, in 'Ireland 1963–1973', Burke-Savage stressed the consensus between Church (he meant Bishop Philbin[98]) and state (T.K. Whitaker and Sean Lemass) about economic development. Economics was represented as a means to an end. The one advocated was a meritocracy where, as Burke-Savage put it: 'opportunity will be open to all according to their ability irrespective of whether they have the means or not'.[99]

In 'Seeking a National Purpose' (1964) Garret FitzGerald set out the manifesto for much of his own subsequent political agenda.[100] FitzGerald epitomised a new social liberalism within *Studies*. As he later explained, the conservatism and clericalism of his youth had given way to 'a more liberal and progressive outlook'.[101] After acknowledging (at some considerable length) the profound influence of fifteen centuries of Christian tradition FitzGerald emphasised the importance of other 'streams of thought' with Irish society, a republican one, the Irish language movement, the Protestant Anglo-Irish tradition, English liberal ideas and socialist thought. FitzGerald's thesis was that ideas of 'the good' within the last two of these owed 'a very large part of their inspiration to the mainstream of Christian thought'.[102]

However, this mainstream should not, he insisted, in a section on 'Inadequacies of Catholic Social Thought in Ireland', be beyond criticism. The Church viewed the state 'partly for philosophical reasons, but partly also for institutional ones' as a rival claimant on man's allegiance, but was in error in doing so. This misconception rested, he insisted, on a common misunderstanding of natural law. The essence of his argument was that if natural laws were to be understood through the use of reason then the available facts about Irish society could not be ignored. He then argued that sociological studies revealed the nature of society and man's relationship with his fellow man in society. If one presumed that there was such a thing as natural law then one must accept that social research added to understandings of it. Natural law, he implied, could not be taught as fixed doctrine, and presented as sociology, while deliberately excluding efforts to research and understand the social world.[103] In effect he criticised a conservative unwillingness to study real society in case this might contradict Catholic social thought. FitzGerald argued that Catholic thinkers should trust their own vantage point as a theoretical basis for thinking about Ireland and face facts as they find them.

Less diplomatic attacks on Catholic conservatism emerged in *Studies* during the 1960s. A scathing 1962 review of Jeremiah Newman's *Studies in Political Morality* noted sarcastically that once again 'Godless liberalism is slain and contrasted with the sounder tradition of Burke, Acton, Clinton Rossiter and Russell Kirk'. The reviewer advised that when it came to being critical of religious intolerance (Newman in his book emphasised John Locke's refusal in the *Letters Concerning Toleration* to advocate toleration for Catholics): 'the only wise policy for Catholic writers on such topics is to lean over backwards to be absolutely candid about all that is dark in Catholic history'.[104]

Philbin's contribution to the new developmental spirit was his insistence on an improved work ethic. In 'The Irish and the New Europe' (1962) he argued that the Irish had going against them a, not in his view unjust, reputation for being apathetic, irresponsible and individualistic, not good at co-ordinated effort, possessing a faculty of imagination that was 'as much a hindrance as an asset' and as lacking in self-discipline. Sayings such as 'the man who made time made plenty of it', he continued, carried disconcerting hints of the *mañana* philosophy and banana republics.[105] That these were Catholic countries (colonised by southern Europeans) went without comment. Against this, he argued, Irish emigrants in America had worked hard and thrived. He put this down to partly to competition and partly to influences that emigrants came under that were absent in Ireland. The Common Market, he hoped, would be just the thing to jostle Irish people out of their complacency and lethargy: 'If we can see', he proposed, 'our entry into the new community as a national emergency, with implications of opposition and conflict in which we shall be individually involved – and these features are not difficult to find – we may realise the necessity of something in the nature of character training for it.'[106]

Philbin's formula of moral communitarianism and individual responsibility proffered a recipe to replace the loss of 'austerity' bemoaned by conservatives in *Christus Rex*. His remedy for the moral challenge of prosperity owed much to what Max Weber described as the Protestant Ethic. Prior to the Reformation work was predominantly portrayed by theologians as unavoidable but tedious. For instance, Aquinas viewed it as spiritually valuable but by no means noble, rewarding or satisfying. Its very tedium and endlessness made it spiritually valuable. The emergence of the Protestant work ethic, the idea that one's work was one's calling, led to an emphasis on the capacity of work to provide intrinsic satisfactions. This modern ethic made work an essential prerequisite of personal and social advancement, of prestige, of virtue and of self-fulfilment. Notwithstanding its potential tedium, the spiritual rewards of modern work were emphasised by Philbin. 'We should', he insisted, 'come to realise that work, and co-operative and industrial work especially, may have enormous value in schooling our variety of wayward human nature and bringing our characters to full maturity.'[107]

The final part of Philbin's article sought to reconcile the subordination of society to economy with Catholic social thought. Economic development, he argued, was clearly a Christian objective, in so far as it bought a diffusion of benefits to society. 'We must not be defeatist', he insisted, 'in regard to material things. God has put us in a material world and made us part of it. We shall have to make the best of it, and making the best of it means turning its contents into instruments of spiritual good.'[108] What then followed might well have been inspired by Calvin's *Institutes of Religion*:

> We must appreciate that our secular work is significant in working out our supernatural destiny. The tastes and therefore the vocation of most men lie in the manipulation of material things in one way or another and unless they see their work as a way of honouring and obeying God the bulk of their time will, from the highest point of view, be wasted.[109]

The Irish were enjoined to work as if their salvation depended on it, to understand that time was money, to strive for economic growth in a spirit of national Christian corporatist co-operation and to respond competitively to the European Community as if jolted by national crises. The New Europe, as perceived somewhat presciently by Bishop Philbin, was not to be Christendom reborn but would be a vehicle for economic competition. Here, FitzGerald argued, was an opportunity for Ireland to box politically and economically above its weight.[110]

THE THIN BLACK LINE

During the 1960s *Studies* offered a forum for progressive debate. The new mood found expression within the editorials and articles of Burke-Savage. In the forward-looking 'Ireland: 1963–1973' he called for a new openness to the disparate intellectual traditions that had shaped Irish society:

> The best of the Protestant Anglo-Irish tradition has much to offer us in its concern for civic responsibilities, for virtues of truthfulness and hard work, and for its concern for the appreciation and cultivation of arts and letters. Our national ideal would be a poor one without these qualities. Thinking in Ireland has been much influenced by English Welfare liberals and socialists. Again many of their ideas must find a place in our national ideal, ideas which often find a firmer foundation and a stronger motive-power in the authentic Christian tradition than in the premises from which their formulators derived them.[111]

Burke-Savage promoted a new social reformism. Socialist ideas, he implied, could be claimed for Christian social justice.[112] These ran counter to the old Poor Law liberalism exemplified by Philbin which extolled the virtues of individual effort but also, contrary to the mainstream of Catholic social thought, understood poverty as a moral problem of individual failure. Catholic social action, Burke-Savage argued, should draw intellectually on socialism. He introduced the author of a 1965 article as 'an important thinker of what can be broadly described as the French Catholic Left'.[113] In 'Reflections of a Left-Wing Catholic' Claude Tremontant, a Professor of Philosophy at the Sorbonne, distinguished between a Christian 'left' that practised a theology that could accept both faith and reason in an era of scientific knowledge, and a 'right' which had an evangelical heart but not a theological head.[114]

If Burke-Savage seemed an editor for his times he also was required to hold the thinning black line against mounting criticism of the Church within Irish society. In winter 1965 he published a 16,000-word-long apologia for the episcopate of John Charles McQuaid. The context was one of now-open criticism of Church authoritarianism. Burke-Savage took issue with a 1965 series of articles about Irish society by the journalist Peter Lennon that had been published in *The Guardian* under the general title 'Censorship in Ireland'. The series was to form the basis for Lennon's subsequent documentary film *The Rocky Road to Dublin* which, incidentally, opened with an interview with Sean O'Faolain. Lennon exemplified a new and confident anti-clericalism. His 1965 article that criticised McQuaid's actions over the 'Mother and Child Scheme' was sub-titled 'Grey Eminence'. Disparagement of the all-powerful Archbishop was surely a sign of changing times.

Burke-Savage's article on McQuaid ran several times the usual length.[115] It broke with protocol in that all previously published appreciations of senior Church figures had been posthumous. *Studies* published an accompanying full-page photograph of McQuaid, something it had never done before even for popes. This depicted the Archbishop, as the caption had it, 'completely at his ease in the Clongowes Boys' Club'.[116] It showed him looking downward, but by no means sternly, at a boy kneeling to kiss his ring. Criticism of McQuaid, Burke-Savage argued, tended to be personal and (by implication) unfair. In the role of defending barrister he dismissed the accusation that the Archbishop was aloof: 'Unless you are relaxed before a camera you just can't be photogenic: the secret of the slightly sinister figure with the cloak and dagger air is as simple as that. So we haven't a Hollywood-style Archbishop, and are we really the worse for that?'[117] This was disingenuous, not least because the Archbishop had a reputation for being vain.[118] Although the intent was to sidestep substantive criticisms it nevertheless, in a roundabout way, grappled with the unpopularity of McQuaid's leadership.

Burke-Savage emphasised McQuaid's many achievements. These included the building of thirty-four new churches, the establishment of twenty-six new parishes as the city expanded, the promotion of social housing, the building of twenty new schools in 1964 alone, the founding of sixty-seven secondary schools between 1940 and 1965 and the development of Catholic social services. His legacy, Burke-Savage argued, would be a great and important one notwithstanding 'un-informed, destructive, and in some instances, blatantly unjust' personal attacks on him.[119]

Lennon accused the Jesuit of attacking him with sulphuric prose.[120] The spat between Burke-Savage and Lennon suggested that, although *Studies* promoted reformism, the nuances of internal Church debates were lost to outside critics. The defence of McQuaid in *Studies* anticipated the extent to which the Archbishop was becoming a focal point for criticism of the Church in Ireland. As summarised by Tom Garvin: 'McQuaid was an odd mixture of the progressive, the reactionary, the creative and the authoritarian.'[121] Burke-Savage rightly praised him on the first and third counts. He was perhaps occupationally myopic on counts two and four. McQuaid, in Garvin's later summary, had become 'a kind of ecclesiastical dictator' who dominated Dublin's civic as well as religious life, 'whose word was law in large sections of the Catholic Church, parts of the Civil Service, Dublin Corporation, the university colleges, and, of course the primary and secondary school systems'.[122] The standard case against McQuaid focused considerably on his role in bringing down the Inter-Party Government over the 'Mother and Child Scheme' in 1951. Within the public domain, Noel Browne's account of events had become an anti-clerical equivalent of Emile Zola's *J'accuse*.[123] The Mother and Child Scheme controversy became arguably the most picked-over event in the history of the state. Burke-Savage's defence was an initial attempt at rehabilitation in the face of recent folk history. The case for the defence, as developed by Father James Kavanagh, attributed much of the controversy to Browne's political ineptitude.[124] According to Conor Cruise O'Brien, Browne was fatally undermined by his own ('anti-socialist') party leader, Sean MacBride.[125]

In *Studies*, during the decade leading up to the controversy, doctrinal hostility to the ideal of the welfare state was augmented by liberal antipathy. The developmental liberals who came to prominence in *Studies* did so with assurances that a state role in economic development would not undermine subsidiarity. Whitaker had to carefully bide his time for eleven years until 1956 before being able to advocate Keynesian economic policies on behalf of the Department of Finance. The genesis of *Economic Development* lay in 1945 papers both wrote that mirrored those in *Studies* at the time.[126] In the years that followed Lynch wrote to reassure that state planning would not place Ireland on the road to serfdom. By the time of FitzGerald's 'Seeking a National Purpose' (1964) the contours of a new nation-building project had been outlined. That same year in 'Ireland: The End of an Era' David Thornley argued that Catholicism had lost its intellectual influence.[127] In *Studies* these debates prompted an editorial emphasis on social relevance.

CHAPTER SIX

Faithful Departures: Culture and Conflict, *Studies*, 1951–86

This chapter addresses three strands of debate that developed within *Studies* from the 1950s to the 1980s. Each saw intellectual breaks with the past. It first considers belated efforts to foster Irish literature and constitute a cultural mission for it now that censorship had lost its grip. During the 1960s literary censorship became trenchantly opposed in *Studies*, even if it still found endorsement amongst the hierarchy.[1] This belated literary turn constituted a revisionist departure. The second strand examines debates about Irish nationalism and Northern Ireland. *Studies* criticised the role of Irish state propaganda in precipitating the 1956 'Border War'. From 1966 it published influential critiques of the legacy of the 1916 Rising. It then became an important forum for debate about the Northern crisis. *Studies* hammered away against violent nationalism. Overall its critique of the Northern problem – built up since the 1950s – faulted mainstream Catholic ethnic nationalism. A strong emphasis on the dangers of religious sectarianism also emerged. The need for ecumenism and pluralism in the North fuelled the case for reform down South. Here criticism emerged of the very constitutional provisions successfully promoted by the the Jesuits of *Studies* in 1937. A 1985 editorial argued that the State should not prohibit divorce, a dramatic break with the traditional Catholic stance. The third strand in this chapter addresses the radical critique, by Irish standards, of social inequality that emerged in *Studies* from the 1970s. This owed something to the influence of the liberation theology that emerged in South America after Vatican II. Catholic social action had become partially reconstituted as a leftist Catholic social justice movement.

These shifts owed much to the editorship of Roland Burke-Savage SJ, from 1951. His predecessor, Patrick Connelly SJ, had held on since 1916. In a 1968 article about the editors of *Studies* James Meenan described both as men in tune with the very different moods of their times.[2] Burke-Savage depicted post-independence nationalism as 'responsible for a series of miscalculations' including past isolationism and unrealistic claims upon the Six Counties.[3] He was a strong opponent of censorship and was more comfortable engaging with liberal ideas than in defending Church authoritarianism.[4] The baton subsequently passed to Peter Troydyn SJ (editor 1968–73), Patrick O'Connell SJ (1974–83) and Brian Lennon SJ (1984–89). None of these sought to turn back the clock. Lennon argued that pluralism necessitated accommodation by the government (if not the Church) on issues such as divorce.[5]

Studies under Burke-Savage proved open to international debates about racism and civil rights. These arguably fostered more complex sociological understandings of social inequalities in the Irish case. In 1951, in *The Negro In America*, Daniel Lyons SJ had sought to explain the workings of racism in the United States and the scale of political, economic and social injustices faced by what are now called African-Americans. He explained the prejudice they encountered ('a whole framework of theories against the Negro' that allowed them to be treated as inferior) as efforts to rationalise the consequence of these injustices. They were stereotyped as criminal but 'their paltry thievery reflects mainly on the white society that subjects them to severe economic discrimination'.[6] Another review commended Gordon Allport's classic *The Nature of Prejudice* to readers of *Studies*.[7] The Year 1974 saw a pioneering assessment of the Itinerant Settlement Movement that emerged in the wake of the *Report of the Commission on Itinerancy* (1963). Using quotes from interviews with Travellers the authors described discrimination against Traveller children placed in 'special schools' but denied the same education as other children.[8] In a number of articles from the 1970s poorer socio-economic groups were portrayed as no less denigrated and discriminated against. Class inequalities were discussed frankly.

Increasingly, theology and Church history became relegated to the book review pages. The editorial vantage point remained a religious one notwithstanding increased reliance on lay contributors. Inevitably, *Studies* grappled with the decline of religiosity within Irish society. In 'Towards a Pastoral Theology of Indifference' (1979) Michael Paul Gallagher SJ mourned the death of anguished atheism. Religious indifference was, he argued, the most radical form of atheism even though it was rarely militant or aggressive. Nietzsche's dictum that God was dead at least allowed discussion of the possibility of knowing God. Religious indifference denoted a complete lack of interest in the possibility of faith.[9] Whilst Gallagher was upbeat about what could be done through pastoral work, his conclusion that Catholicism was failing to reproduce itself was telling.[10] By 1985 *Studies* faced the reality of Dublin working-class parishes where less than 10 per cent attended Sunday mass regularly.[11] A review article by Tom Inglis put it as follows:

> The Church is no longer able to pull the people away from the gloss and glitter of modern consumer society back towards a more simplistic family and community life. For many Irish Catholics engagement in public rituals has become an empty shell which has no yolk to sustain itself against the forces of materialism. The teachings of the Church are having less and less relevance to their everyday lives, and religious practice has become compartmentalised into Sunday mornings and special occasions.[12]

Inglis's definition of secularisation emphasised 'the decline of traditional religious practices that produce a shared meaning and consciousness amongst members of society'.[13] In other words, what had become stripped away was a collective religiosity that mediated the relationship between individual Catholics. A companion article by Michael Paul Gallagher SJ argued that 'under the open conditions of Irish modernity' faith could no longer be imposed. The decline of traditional authority meant that it could not be accepted passively. It became, like many other things, a matter of individual choice.[14]

In this context *Studies* promoted anti-authoritarian solidarity rather than a return to obedience. Themed issues such as spring 1983's *Upstairs Downstairs* emphasised the need to challenge social inequality.[15] Autumn 1983's *'Private' Property* emphasised 'the ever widening gap between the managerial class and the Irish worker'.[16] Spring 1984's *A Solution to Homelessness* outlined the history of vagrancy laws and their current use against homeless people who had been denied social housing.[17] If from the late 1950s the consensus that *Studies* promoted about the need to prioritise economic development had helped produce a secular national faith, now it preached a social justice sermon.

CULTURAL POLITICS

In 'Fifty Years of Irish Writing' (1962), Sean O'Faolain sought to explain the huge difficulty of building a post-independence national literature in a cultural climate of censorship.[18] For O'Faolain it was not censorship itself that was the substantive problem, but the mentality behind it. Twentieth-century Irish writing, he argued, fell into two parts: a period of growth from 1900 and one of decline that began to operate immediately after the Free State was founded in 1921. At that stage the general mood was romantic, nationalist, fervid, critical of others, especially one's opponents, whether native or foreign, but not very self-critical.[19] The effects of decline were, O'Faolain argued, held at bay for a time by the continuing momentum, exemplified by Sean O'Casey, of nationalist excitement persisting after the revolution. *Juno and the Paycock* in 1924 and *The Plough and the Stars* in 1926 both dealt with an evolutionary period that was finished and done with, but the excitement around these recalled the old days of *The Playboy of the Western World*. After independence, the theatre suffered in the face of 'hyper-patriotic' criticism.[20]

Independence, O'Faolain argued, was accompanied by 'a nervy sensitive, touchy, defensive-aggressive, on-guard mentality'. This mood, he insisted, was fairly typical of post-colonial politics. It involved no special criticism of Irish character. The resultant censorship was a 'blending of the moral and the patriotic: the desire to protect from corruption this infant nation born out of so much hardship'.[21] One of the striking effects of this was the comparative failure of the modern Irish novel: 'If one were to exclude Joyce – which is like saying if one were to exclude Everest – and Liam O'Flaherty how little was left!'[22] What held for the theatre also applied to the novel. Most of O'Flaherty's contemporary novels, like O'Casey's plays, were set in the revolutionary period. Just one, *The Puritan*, 'a study of the new Irish rigorism', was set after independence. His subsequent novels were mostly historical ones. O'Faolain's view was that the bulk of acclaimed contemporary novels, including his own, would not stand up as first rate. With the exception of the short story, which thrived, it had proved difficult to write realistically about the present and get published. Within *Studies*, this argument about the poverty of post-independence Irish literature met little dissent. James Stephens found a champion in Augustine Martin, who would place him in 'the thin second rank' for his 1912 novel *The Crock of Gold*, but Stephens was hardly a post-independence writer.[23] A 1966 appraisal of theatre since independence described it as 'active but not vital', arguing that no theatre was vital that was not contemporary.[24]

The contribution of *Studies* to the morbidity of post-independence literature had been two-fold. It offered a forum for those who championed literary censorship during the 1920s and 1930s. It broke no ground in championing new Irish literature until the 1960s. In 'Irish Writing Today' (1955) John Sheridan argued that a 'truly representative Irish literature' would be one that was 'Catholic in tone'. However, since independence, indeed since Canon Sheehan, Ireland had not produced one Catholic apologist of real stature. 'It is to be deplored', Sheridan complained, 'that whilst we have devised machinery to keep out the wrong sort of book we have done very little towards producing the right sort.'[25]

In *Studies*, as earlier in *The Bell*, articles on foreign Catholic writers found favour.[26] A 1963 example, 'Evelyn Waugh: Sanity and Catholicism', offered the reassuring conclusion that Catholicism in his novels 'emerges as a coherent philosophy whose claims, however shattering, are based on truth and therefore acceptable to the intellect'.[27] The distinction here between Catholic writer and Catholic apologist was crucial. Sean O'Faolain was the former, but not the latter. Nevertheless, he was not mentioned in Father Stephen Brown's 1940 bibliography, *Novels and Tales by Catholic Writers*, although his books were included (if disparaged) in equivalent American guides. [28] Brown's 1944 article 'The Role of the Library in an Intellectual Revival' made no reference to censorship but presumed throughout that reading should be edifying and not to the 'religious and moral detriment' of readers.[29]

Defences of censorship became increasingly rare, but anxieties about Western popular culture persisted. A 1944 symposium on the social influence of American cinema kicked off with a polemic, by a female lecturer in education at UCC, against mass culture. Here, B.G. MacCarthy emphasised the disjuncture between Irish society and the images portrayed by Hollywood and the power of the latter over the former:

> ... consider the average farm labourer, walking five or six miles into Bruff (let us say) to go the pictures, and that long way home again in our Irish rain. What has he seen that has the slightest relation to life as he knows it? He has seen night-club queens covered by a few spangles, Chicago gangsters talking a peculiar argot, society playboys babbling airily of Reno divorce. He has seen crooning cowboys, coal-black mammies, typists clad in Schiaparelli models living in luxurious flats and millionaires living in Babylonian palaces. He is going home to fall into his bed in the loft, to rise next morning to feed the pigs. What does he

> make of it all? And what will they make of it – those city children who queue up outside the cinemas, who even beg from passers-by the money to buy admission, and who return to the slum room which is all the State can afford to give them?[30]

The cinema, she acknowledged, was a place of physical comfort for such people, a universal haven and a universal aspirin. But Hollywood films, she protested, did not express Irish national life: 'they are mass produced films we share with the sweating coolie of Shanghai, the Canadian trapper, the people of Brazil, of London, of Japan'. Was it not too much, she pleaded rhetorically and in vain, to hope that 'weary of the fetid breath of a sick world we may find in our own culture our true inspiration?'[31] A companion article worried about the effects of such cinema on uneducated minds and argued that frequent exposure to the cinema impeded mental development.[32] Another, by a former inspector of secondary schools, praised MacCarthy's eloquence (her 'Schiaparelli-clad typists' was regarded a deft touch) yet maintained that her argument was alarmist.[33]

Even the chairman of the Censorship Board described much of what she had to say as exaggerated and myopic.[34] The cinema that she objected to had already been filtered through the Irish censorship board and, at an earlier stage, through the Hays Code that American Catholics had lobbied for. Hollywood's influence upon the Irish national *Kultur* was, he accepted, a denationalising one, but the measures MacCarthy advocated to achieve freedom from its influence were Hitleresque. Irish society, he argued, needed entertainment as well as education.[35]

The early 1960s saw advocacy of non-Catholic foreign writers such as Boris Pasternak and Lawrence Durrell. It was nigh impossible to write about Pasternak's Nobel Prize without discussing censorship. A 1959 article, 'Reflections on Dr Zhivago', argued that Pasternak was a moralist in the tradition of Dostoevsky. In the book Zhivago was presented as a deeply Christian sinner exemplifying an enduring humanity. Representations of his passion for the married Lara (of the sort an Irish writer could not yet get away with) were considered valid.[36] The book aside, David Lean's 1963 film *Doctor Zhivago* had a degree of cultural impact. *Zhivago's* also proved to be a popular name for Irish nightclubs.[37]

A 1963 review of a published extract of John McGahern's first book by Augustine Martin found the evocation of rural Leitrim so well done that 'one gets from it a suspicion of genius'.[38] In 'Inherited

Dissent: The Dilemma of the Irish Writer' (1965) Augustine Martin argued that relations between artists and society were complex ones in the Irish case. Whilst relations between the Irish artist and his society continued to be strained, the clichéd notion of the artist as pariah at odds with his smug, philistine society hardly bore scrutiny.[39] This was how Joyce was understood, but there was a danger that this image had become moribund and that it fostered literary and critical complacency. The key question, for Martin, was the willingness of writers to grapple with and reflect actual changes within Irish society. Those who did so tended to be rural ones. The danger was that they would be enslaved by established literary tradition: 'Literary history is strewn with the corpses of talented writers who allowed an inherited mode or sensibility to blind them to the realities of their own age and place.'[40] Belated homage to Yeats and Joyce, while admirable in terms of piety, had served to intensify their influence on an emerging generation. Joyce in particular had become deified and central to an emerging industry of 'literary palesmanship'. The problem, in part, was that neither Joyce nor Yeats typified Irish writing: 'both were philosophical eccentrics', Joyce in particular, seeing Dublin as a 'centre of paralysis'. Joyce offered a fiercely personal vision, whose influence now was to impair the relationships between the present generation of artists and their environment.[41] The influence of the previous generation of writers, one that also included Frank O'Connor and Austin Clarke, was an equally hardening cliché of didactic dissent that now served as a straitjacket. As such: 'The young writer had his position in society defined, stated, ramified and laid down for him.'[42] Martin's example was the response of British critics to John McGahern's 'brilliant first novel', *The Barracks*. The erroneous presumption that McGahern's perspective was hostile to rural Irish life was grounded in a now powerful and relentless cliché:

> Ireland is a backward, unsanitary, inert, despairing country; a people priest-ridden and superstitious, which despises its artists and intellectuals, treats its autocratic, avaricious and crafty clergy with a sanctimonious servility; a people soaked in dreams and booze, fixated backwards on the events of Easter Week, 1916, blind to the meaning of the present and the future, without economic hope, helpless in the face of emigration, ignorant of the facts of life, overcome with a Jansenistic fear of sex and the body, bemused by the opium of past splendors – yet in spite of it all, a people friendly, poetic, with a certain gentle unreliable charm.

> This set of traits cannot be ascribed to the pages of any one writer; they are the cumulative end-product of half a century of writing which was by turns hostile, embittered and penetrating. Whatever the contemporary social veracity of these portrayals, I do not think that any observer of provincial Ireland over the past ten years would claim that the picture holds good today.[43]

Martin's thesis, then, was that the generation of dissenters who had stood against the hidden Ireland of the early post-colonial era were now a dead hand that obscured the present. Summed up in a ditty by John Montague:

> Puritan Ireland's dead and gone,
> a myth of O'Connor and O'Faolain.[44]

Provincial life, Martin insisted, was now in a ferment of change and development. The new 'great ugly dancehalls' disputed the charge of Jansenism. There was an excitement in rural life that he found totally unknown to Dubliners – and, in particular, literary Dubliners. Narrow-mindedness, philistinism and autocracy survived but were being challenged by a new cultural openness (exemplified by the younger clergy and their promotion of local drama and arts) and by huge advances in education levels. None of this was being reflected in Irish fiction.[45] He instanced Austin Clarke as hugely influential, but argued that Clarke's 'scorching sincerity' expressed a singular vision that had no genuine relevance to the younger generation.[46] To a considerable extent Martin's gripe was with 'literature drawing its strength from literature' being hostile or indifferent to life outside the confines of the ivory tower or literary pub. It was also one with the tyranny of the past ('Even at the moment Mr Thomas Kinsella is calmly engaged in yet another prose telling of the Tain'). What he sought instead was an Irish equivalent to Kingsley Amis, John Wain, Philip Larkin or Muriel Spark, a poet of middle-Ireland who would immortalise present-day Mullingar or Roscrea.[47] Certainly, from anecdotes about him, it would be easy to contemplate Gus Martin as a character in an Amis-type novel.[48]

Martin's thesis that out-of-touch Irish writers were still fighting the wars of yesteryear warrants scrutiny. It was born out of a sense of optimism about the future and a sense of defensive loyalty to the provincial Catholic culture that *Christus Rex* made its mission to renew. In 'Inherited Dissent' he praised the younger clergy as energetic champions of cultural advance.[49] Later that year he singled out Austin Clarke as a particularly misguided critic of Irish society. Martin's 'The Rediscovery of Austin Clarke' (1965) portrayed Ireland's 'leading poet' as a relic of the Celtic Twilight: 'it was his tragedy that he embraced its enthusiasms when the movement was on the point of flickering out'.[50] Martin depicted Clarke's formation, and hence his anti-clericalism, as aberrant and therefore his judgement as ill-informed.[51] Not since Voltaire, he argued, had there been such a pungent and obsessive anti-clericalist. Martin cited as an example of Clarke's unfairness his accusations against the nuns who devoted their lives to the care of unmarried mothers in 'voluntary Magdalene Homes'.[52] This example, in retrospect, offered scant endorsement of his case.[53] Martin's effort to disassociate Catholic institutions from the criticisms voiced by 'anti-clerics' was a bridge too soon. His article appeared alongside an apologia for John Charles McQuaid by Burke-Savage. Both articles, prickly defensiveness notwithstanding, suggested that dissent, inherited or otherwise, could not be dismissed.

From the late 1960s debates about literature in *Studies* became politicised anew. Gone was the pining for Catholic apologias. Now the worry was about moral responsibility in reading and writing the past under the shadow of renascent political violence. Here *Studies* proved influential and established a critique that *The Crane Bag* responded to a decade later. It placed past religious authoritarianism as well as past political violence in the dock. In 1969 the insidious damage of the former was summed up in an article entitled 'Censorship in Ireland':

> No one growing up in the nineteen-thirties and forties in Ireland could fail to be struck by the absence of communication between the Church and the educated Catholic. At a time when university education was increasing rapidly the aim of the schools appeared to be to produce a safe man who led a good life and asked no questions; a sort of Catholic 'yes-man'. A premium was put on the man who 'never thought of thinking for himself at all'. As a result, many young men became estranged from the Church; and a further result was the bitterness and frightening lack of charity displayed towards those who held unorthodox views.[54]

Within this new revisionism past articles in *Studies* that promoted literary censorship, such as 1942's 'Art, Morality and Censorship' (unsure about the first, enthusiastic about the second and third) could be themselves be criticised.[55] Writers deliberately ignored during their lifetime, such as Liam O'Flaherty and Frank O'Connor, could now be safely championed. O'Flaherty's *Famine* (1937) could be appraised (as distinct from reappraised) in 1974 as a masterpiece.[56] A 1969 article claimed Samuel Becket for the Irish canon.[57] When it came to previously censored and neglected writers the past was no longer a foreign country.

During the 1970s the relevance of living poets, especially Northern ones such as John Montague and Seamus Heaney, was emphasised.[58] A 1977 review of Paul Durcan's second volume of poems, *Teresa's Bar*, likened some of it to work by Philip Larkin. The cast assembled in *Teresa's Bar* were, the reviewer complained, a parade of stereotypes: suicidal seminarians, neglected housewives and the eighteen-hole bourgeoisie. These were presented in the main with compassion but one poem, 'A Day in the Life of Immanuel Kant', was held up as 'a bitter attack on middle-class values':

> The boy grew up to be a manly Christian lad,
> A powerful hurler and petrified of women,
> And became like his father, an auctioneer,
> A respectable member of the criminal classes,
> A zealous anti-Semite and a decent Catholic,
> And now in middle age is enjoying the fruits of his labours.
>
> His little 'wifey' brings him up breakfast in bed each morning
> After which he herds the brood to school
> In the deluxe saloon.[59]

This was hardly the celebratory turn that Martin had sought twelve years earlier. But it sat easily with the now regular 'Film Report' by Michael Paul Gallagher SJ. Here Gallagher commended cinematic studies of American alienation, such as Bob Rafelson's *Five Easy Pieces*, and praised Brian de Palma's *Carrie* as 'escapism that would be hard to improve on'.[60]

By the 1970s many contributions to *Studies* on literature were indistinguishably part of the now flourishing field of Irish Studies. As the number of scholastic and scholarly priests declined, their place in *Studies* was partly taken by the secular ones of academic literary criticism.[61] Richard Kearney, who replaced Gallagher as film critic, also contributed a number of articles whose style and content differed little from those in *The Crane Bag*.[62] A 1975 article by Brian Donnelly, 'The Big House in the Recent Novel', had exemplified the mixture of recovery and reappraisal of the Irish cultural past. Here, within an account of writers from Maria Edgeworth to Elizabeth Bowen to John Banville, Donnelly revisited Daniel Corkery's thesis about the Big House novel. Corkery had emphasised how the genre reflected insular Ascendancy preoccupations about its own decay, decline and fall.[63] Donnelly's argument was that the genre allowed for comedy and tragedy and, as developed after independence by Bowen, J.G. Farrell and Jennifer Johnson, examination of the failure of the two nations of Ireland to integrate successfully. Another article in the same issue on one of Maria Edgeworth's minor novels (*Belinda*) exemplified the run-of-the-mill literary criticism of the time. This came complete with the ubiquitous introductory rationale for addressing 'this hitherto much neglected topic'.[64]

NORTHERN QUESTIONS

In 'The Irish Economy: North and South' (1956) Garret FitzGerald's theme was the now overwhelming lack of understanding of Northern Ireland. The Republic's newspapers ignored the North except to report sectarian disturbances or some 'dust up' within the Unionist Party. In what passes for a joke amongst economists, he maintained that the fact that Northerners spent twice as much on amusements as people in the Republic suggested that they were less dour than was generally assumed.[65] More seriously, he partly attributed higher rates of female emigration in the Republic to fewer industrial employment opportunities for women. In 1957 *Studies* published two articles challenging nationalist presumptions about the possibility of a united Ireland. The context was the 'Border War', a series of raids launched by the IRA from the South. Conor Cruise O'Brien's 'A Sample of Loyalties' analysed 'the ideas and feelings contained in a batch of essays written towards the end of 1953 by a class of twenty-six boys, aged 13 to 14 years attending a large Protestant secondary school in the Six Counties'. The set topic of the essay was 'Ireland'.[66] Donal Barrington's 'United Ireland' offered scathing criticism of the capacity of Irish nationalism to transcend religious sectarianism. What he had to say prefigured much that O'Brien later wrote on the subject.[67]

O'Brien was uncharacteristically modest in describing this contribution to the understanding of patterns of loyalties within Northern Irish society. The value of the exercise for O'Brien was 'an unguarded candour and clarity' unlikely from 'older or more intellectual members of that community'.[68] Twenty of the essays expressed various degrees of positive feeling towards Ireland as homeland. Many were attached to some sense of Irishness. As put by one boy who professed to like the poetry of Yeats: 'I am sort of a way attracted to its music, its famousness and its green fields. We should be proud of it.' Another wrote: 'Ireland is a good country in spite of their overcrowded towns and their slums and the Roman Catholic inhabitants.'[69] Nine of the twenty-six boys stated a preference for unification. Just one of the boys came out unequivocally against it. Only four went into any specifics about what they meant by reunification. One concluded that it would be good if Northern Ireland and 'Eire' were brought together under the Queen's rule. The second maintained that reunification should be under the British flag. The third suggested that Ireland should be a separate nation with a king. For the fourth, it required forgetting the seventeenth century.[70] These responses were far removed from Nationalist understandings of what was meant by the unification of Ireland. A degree of religious sectarianism was identifiable, but O'Brien cautioned against reading too much into some of the misconceptions the boys demonstrated about Catholicism. A similar exercise conducted amongst Southern Catholic schoolboys would produce similar howlers. That said, O'Brien left the teacher to whom he owed his article anonymous lest, in the grim words of one of his essayists, he be 'silently disposed of '.[71]

Barrington, writing as a nationalist, argued that prevalent nationalist thinking was impoverished. It blamed partition on British rule and claimed that what Britain had done it must undo. It must take home its money, its men and its influence, liberate the six occupied counties and re-unite Ireland. The paradox was that nationalists ultimately relied on the British army to coerce all Irishmen to live together. Partition, he argued, was not forced on Ireland by Britain but necessitated by the conflicting demands of the two parties of Irishmen. It was Ireland's crime against itself rather than England's crime against Ireland.[72] Barrington was fiercely critical of the inability of Irish politicians and diplomats to foster what de Valera once called a unity of wills in support of a United Ireland. Rather than endeavour to 'convert' Unionists to a belief in a United Ireland, Eamon de Valera, John A. Costello and particularly Sean MacBride had tried to lever international opinion in favour of Southern claims. This, Barrington implied, restated the old demand that the British should impose Irish unity. The scale of Southern misunderstanding of the North was huge. Southern efforts (the 'ill-fated Mansion House Committee') sought to fund the campaigns of anti-partition candidates. This met with a backlash in the 1949 general election. It gave the Unionist Party its biggest victory to date and 'wiped out' the Northern Ireland Labour Party. For the first time the latter then came out against partition.[73] Barrington blamed the 'armed raids' of 1956 on the ill-considered propaganda efforts of de Valera and Costello:

> When the attempt failed, as it was bound to fail, some of our young men took the matter into their own hands. Anyone who thought at all about the history of Ireland could have expected no other result ... This propaganda has always employed emotionally charged phrases such as 'occupied Ireland', and 'the British army of occupation' with a view to isolating Britain as the party solely responsible for creating and maintaining Partition.[74]

In his *Memoir*, O'Brien recalled life as a Foreign Affairs civil servant under MacBride, who, in 1951, took responsibility for anti-partition propaganda; 'at that time', according to O'Brien, 'the hottest political property in town'. O'Brien's work for MacBride was the making of his Civil Service career.[75] As part of his duties he was tasked to establish an Irish News Agency to put out stories comparing the British 'occupation' of the North with Soviet occupation of Eastern Europe. O'Brien recalled a pamphlet designed for Irish-American consumption, supposedly authored by the American League for an Undivided Ireland but ghost-written by MacBride.[76] MacBride's successor, Frank Aiken, deemed this policy of 'brandishing the sore thumb all over the world' to be unproductive.[77]

Barrington argued that propaganda that the North was 'unfree or enslaved' did little to address the real discrimination and system of 'apartheid' experienced by Catholics in the North. He detailed the workings of gerrymandering which effectively disenfranchised Catholics in some areas, discrimination in the allocation of council houses and discrimination in appointments in the public service. Unionists had largely themselves to blame for 'the revolutionary situation' that was to be found within the Six Counties. However, Barrington insisted, this was not the whole story. Unionist bigotry had also been stoked by the Southern coercive approach to unification. So long as such threats persisted, reactionary Orangemen would continue to control the Unionist policy and 'ordinary Protestants' would tolerate discrimination against Catholics in ways that would be impossible were such fears absent. The constant threat from the South had kept alive sectarian bitterness in the North, had prevented the emergence there of a Liberal or Labour party and had defeated the ambitions of liberals within Unionism. Barrington proposed a remedy:

> The best way for us to us to prove that we would respect the wishes of the Northern Protestants inside a United Ireland is by respecting their wishes as long as they wish to remain outside it. Formally guarantee the territorial integrity of Northern Ireland in return for effective guarantees, including electoral reform, to protect Northern nationalists against the discrimination they now experienced. Unilaterally renounce coercionism. Discourage specifically Catholic organisations, such as the Ancient Order of Hibernians, from mobilising in Northern politics. Foster cross-border co-operation in areas such as economic policy, university education and sport.[78]

The irony was that the main commerce between North and South was the smuggling that had been disrupted by heavy frontier patrols. The South did not even have a trade council in the North. Many Unionists studied in Dublin, but only at Trinity. Northern nationalists came in similar numbers, but only to UCD. Barrington also argued that the 'reprehensible' GAA ban on foreign games also fostered *apartheid*.[79]

Prevalent cultural nationalism was, he argued, 'exclusive and narrow, designed to cut Ireland in two'. A new form of broad nationalism – one inspired by Thomas Davis – was needed. There was a rich 'English-speaking' cultural history to draw on. Potential shared foreign policy concerns were identifiable – Irish diplomats could explore avenues of European unity and work for international peace and justice – but Partition should not even be mentioned in international assemblies. Contemplate re-entering the Commonwealth. Tolerance, restraint, moderation, perseverance and above all else charity were what was needed and, even then, it was necessary to accept that these might not lead to unity. The only thing to be certain about was that there was no other road.[80]

Burke-Savage's *Studies* was, at times, vehemently critical of nationalism. The 1966 issue that marked the fiftieth anniversary of the 1916 Rising saw more than a few digs at sacred cows. Fifty years, Burke-Savage wrote, was 'long enough to produce the full-grown myth, the myth which can make or undo a man'. History had certainly done some queer things to the men of 1916. His editorial was a defence of patriotism of Eoin MacNeill, who had opposed the Rising at the last moment.[81] History itself was present in Sean Lemass's modest eyewitness account 'I Remember 1916'. He recalled meeting Professor MacNeill on Easter Monday. MacNeill 'seemed agitated and depressed' and 'very clearly unhappy about the whole situation'.[82] David Thornley's article on Patrick Pearse emphasised his preoccupation with the idea of blood sacrifice. Pearse was quoted from December 1915 as writing about the European war:

> The last sixteen months have been the most glorious in the history of Europe. Heroism has come back to Earth ... The old heart of the earth needed to be warmed with the red wine of the battlefields. Such august homage was never before offered to God as this, the homage of millions of lives given gladly for love of country.[83]

A strong regard for MacNeill's disquiet was evident in Augustine Martin's reflection on the poetry of 1916. Martin emphasised the terrifying rhetorical power of Pearse's advocacy of blood sacrifice and bloodshed. With Yeats's connivance, the Rising had acquired the aura of Christ-like sacrifice. But what Pearse had in mind was not necessarily self-sacrifice. Martin quoted Pearse from *The Coming Revolution*:

> We may make mistakes in the beginning and shoot the wrong people; but bloodshed is a cleansing and a sanctifying thing, and the nation which regards it as the final horror has lost its manhood. There are many things more horrible than bloodshed; and slavery is one of them.[84]

Subsequent elegies by Irish poets 'to the Rising and its ruthless aftermath' worked with ready-made symbolic themes. Martin's article was much cited and subsequently influenced the critique of nationalist violence developed in *The Crane Bag* during the late 1970s.

However, perhaps the most trenchant criticisms of the myth of 1916 published in *Studies* in 1966 came from Garret FitzGerald. If he was politic about 'well-meaning' admiration for the leaders of the Rising he was adamant that they hardly warranted admiration as thinkers:

> This almost medieval respect for the letter of what had been written or spoken between 1913 and 1916 by the leaders of the Rising is misconceived. Even if these men had been political or social thinkers of world standing, their thoughts on the Ireland

> they knew could not have stood up to such prolonged and unthinking veneration, but they did not regard themselves – nor were they in fact great thinkers.[85]

They had, FitzGerald argued, few clear-cut ideas of political or social philosophy. He acknowledged deep differences between Pearse and Connolly over the 1913 strike. However, he insisted that neither went into the GPO with a coherent intellectual, political or social programme: political freedom was an end in itself.[86] FitzGerald argued that to treat the Proclamation of 1916 as a great source of political or social doctrines was to misunderstand what it meant to those who wrote it. Granted, it contained noble ideals, the wish to secure political freedom expressed in an enduring language, but no clear ideas. It was a mistake for Irish people half a century later to ask themselves what they might do or say on any issue: 'Their views on modern Ireland would be no more valuable than many of their colleagues still alive, and probably less valuable than many of our contemporaries.'[87] FitzGerald's argument was that Ireland could not be administered on a day-to-day basis by the dead.

Notwithstanding such criticisms of national shibboleths *Studies* still pulled some punches. An article by Francis Shaw SJ, was spiked by Burke-Savage as 'untimely and even inappropriate' for what was intended as a commemorative special issue. It was subsequently published in 1972 and described in an accompanying editorial by Peter Troydyn as a 'tract for the present troubled time'.[88] Shaw's 'The Canon of Irish History: A Challenge' presented a synthesis of the arguments made in 1966 by Burke-Savage, Thornley, Martin and FitzGerald but did so in a powerfully direct and therefore presumably unpalatable manner. When it came to commemoration, Shaw argued, 'Sentiment is a poor substitute for intellectual honesty and sincerity.'[89] What made him too hot to handle in 1966 might be gleaned from quotes such as: 'In 1916 half-a-dozen men decided what the nation should want' and 'In fact, the Rising could only begin by bringing men out to fight who had no way of knowing to what they were summoned; and this had to be done in violation of the constitution of both the Irish Republican Brotherhood and of the Irish Volunteers.'[90]

Shaw offered an analysis of the religious symbolism emphasised by Thornley (the holiness of blood sacrifice) and Martin (its Christ-like character). Pearse had claimed that nationalism and holiness were one and the same. Shaw insisted that this 'false equation of the patriot with Christ' was in conflict with the whole Christian tradition:

> In the Judea of his day, Christ was set down in a situation comparable to that in Ireland in 1916. Christ made it unmistakably plain that he was not a national saviour, and his words to his disciples on the day of the Ascension expressed his sorrow that those who knew him and loved him could continue so long in error.[91]

Shaw marshalled his own religious imagery in attacking the canon of nationalist history sanctified by Pearse by likening him to a prophet of its New Testament.[92] The Old Testament, now to be written out of existence, included everything in the real Irish past that could not be yoked to revolutionary nationalism. Pearse, unlike Eoin McNeill, referred little to the Old Testament. O'Neill, Shaw observed, had never tired of pointing out that the old Irish did not have a clear concept of Ireland as a geographical and cultural unit. Irish nationality was a New Testament abstraction.[93]

In the New Testament 'gospel of Irish nationalism', Shaw observed, the 'four evangelists' were Wolfe Tone, Thomas Davis, Fintan Lalor and John Mitchel. Tone, because of his separatism, was, by a long way, the most prominent even if he placed no emphasis on a Gaelic Ireland. As put by Pearse in *The Separatist Idea*: 'God spoke to Ireland through Tone.'[94] What made Shaw really shudder was how Pearse 'lost all restraint' in idolising the idea of nation over the people who comprised it. As put by Pearse in *The Coming Revolution*:

> The people will perhaps itself be its own Messiah, the people labouring, scourged, crowned with thorns, agonizing and dying, to rise again immortal and impassable. For peoples are divine ...'[95]

Here the worshipped dead Irish were destined to rule the living. During the 1970s the remaining building blocks of Richard Kearney's thesis about atavistic nationalist violence fell into place. In 'The Tradition of Blood Sacrifice to the Goddess Eire' (1974) G.F. Dalton, somewhat fancifully, located Pearse's obsessions within centuries-old mythic tales and bardic poetry. What stalked through the Post Office also ranged over the Hill of Tara:

> The tradition of the blood sacrifice has existed so long and operated so powerfully that it is now, perhaps, a permanent part of the national character. It has inspired some magnificent poetry

> and some heroic actions. But it is based on primitive barbaric ideas which are clearly false. Moreover, it is morally ambiguous. The element of *voluntary* sacrifice is no part of the original scheme; the only essential is the shedding of blood. The tradition may animate a man to feel that he has a sacred duty to die for Ireland; equally it may teach him that it is a sacred duty to kill for Ireland.[96]

In 'Patrick Patrick Pearse and the "Noble Lie" of Irish Nationalism' (1983) John Coakley revisited themes addressed by Francis Shaw, specifically Pearse's mobilisation of the four prophets to forge a 'one-nation' nationalism. The 'Noble Lie' took the form of intellectual self-deception. Tone's argument, overlooked by Pearse, was that no United Ireland sense of a nation capable of superseding religious denomination actually existed. Tone's 'pan-Irish' object was to create one.[97] Pearse chose to believe that it already existed. He showed little awareness of, or interest in, Protestant Ulster. Pearse's widely accepted proof of its existence was, Coakley demonstrated, merely proof by assertion. For Pearse, nationality referred to 'the sum of the facts, spiritual and intellectual, which mark off one nation from another'. This defined nation as collective soul manifested in a characteristic language, literature, culture and institutions. Here, Coakley suggested, the unconscious intellectual influence was the romantic idealism of J.G. Herder. For Herder, a nation was more than its constituent parts. The national soul, as manifested in culture, language and literature, pre-dated the lives of the individuals who composed it.[98] The one-nation version of it pronounced by Pearse – his synthesis of Tone, Davis, Lalor and Mitchel – had achieved an unquestioned posthumous orthodoxy through both informal socialisation and a deliberate policy of political education promoted by the Department of Education.[99] Coakley concluded his article by contrasting Pearse with his contemporary Thomas Masaryk, the Czech nationalist leader. Masaryk debunked as forgeries 'ancient' Czech manuscripts 'discovered' in 1817 and subsequently used to fill the vacuum of national self-esteem. This was something one could not easily imagine a leader such as Pearse being able to do.[100]

During the 1980s *Studies* engaged with mythic nationalism in a fashion somewhat different than of *The Crane Bag*. In the latter the premises advanced by Herder were taken as givens. *Studies*, through articles such as Coakley's, engaged empirically with the claims of nationalist ideology. It gave prominence to attitudinal studies by political scientists that indicated high levels of support for Republican violence amongst Southerners.[101] Earlier, with Shaw, this revisionist engagement had been a predominantly hermeneutic one. A 1983 article, 'The Theology of the IRA', which appeared alongside Coakley's combined both methodologies. This drew on a content analysis on coverage in *An Phoblacht* of writing about religion. The findings here were of pronounced hostility to the Catholic hierarchy ('theological thugs', 'the shoneen bishops' 'anti-Irish') yet not to ordinary priests or Catholics. It was also characterised by efforts to demonstrate an absence of anti-Protestantism. Working-class Protestants were depicted as natural allies of their Catholic equivalents. This extended to, at times, praising Protestant leaders such as the Reverend Ian Paisley. The IRA campaign was represented as a Republican one but not a sectarian one. Even Oliver Cromwell was described as a Republican.[102] The article concluded that there was a gap between this non-sectarian theology and the opposition, in practice, to integrated schools together with the reality of sectarian violence.

A third article in the same issue by Henry Grant SJ came closer to The *Crane Bag* diagnosis. Grant viewed the dynamics of the conflict in terms of two sets of 'closed historico-mythic consciousnesses' that interpreted events differently yet in such a way as to reinforce existing self-perceptions and perceptions of the other. Grant argued that each group in times of crisis selected those elements from the narratives of its origins and history that seemed to sanction the group's current collective behaviour. Each had versions of the chosen people *motif*. Closed mentalities were transferred from one generation to the next. Rich heritages became simplified and the more open, liberal and universal cultural, religious and social elements in each tradition became subordinated to collective amnesia.[103] Grant described a tit-for-tat tightening spiral of violence (complete with diagrams) whereby group A selects certain selected features of a public event – often an atrocity attributed to group B – according to the precedents of its own historico-mythic consciousness. Its subsequent action against B is lent passion by all the feelings, beliefs, presuppositions and assumptions encapsulated by its own group consciousness. B then interprets this response in an equivalent manner and retaliates. Each group is reinforced in its own thought and action regarding the other, is further distanced from the other and is so sensitised that it is ready to go even further when the next potentially divisive event occurs.[104]

The cycle had become a difficult one to break. It was reinforced by the partisan media of both groups. Political leaders had an uncanny instinct for choosing the symbols, words and phrases that instantly reinforced the closed positions of their followers. Outsiders, such as the British army, who intervened without understanding its dynamics became enmeshed. Even peace movements became perceived as partisan. Grant argued that, in so far as the cycle was fuelled by segregation, any work that helped people meet across the divide was worthwhile.

Grant's understanding of group consciousness differed ontologically from Kearney's. Notwithstanding a shared fondness for terms such as 'historico-mythic consciousness' Grant presumed that groups had specific dynamics that could be researched.[105] Grant, like Kearney, found others to engage with his approach. In 1985, in 'History Lessons' Edward O'Donnell SJ gave examples of biased history and one-sided educational curricula. It was not well known amongst Protestants that the Pope took the side of William of Orange at the Battle of the Boyne. Belfast Protestants subscribed £1,800 to the construction of St Patrick's (RC) church in 1815. O'Donnell's suggestion was that historical narratives, on which groups hung their identity, could be opened up. Partisan histories should be replaced in school curricula North and South. Irish Protestants and Catholics shared a history but, as things stood, one or the other owned events such as 1690 or 1916. He outlined teaching methodologies aimed at encouraging students to step back from the particular histories they inherited. A focus on world history and the study of conflict resolution elsewhere was advocated alongside one on local histories. The latter, O'Donnell argued, could challenge the claims of national history through a focus on the real complexity of the lives of earlier generations.[106]

Grant's doctoral thesis had been on the relative ineffectiveness of moderate leaders in Northern Ireland. He emphasised the empirical study of group behaviour patterns, the observation of concrete facts and the crucial importance of standing back from partisan positions.[107] Grant identified six major conflicts, not one. These were distinct political, economic, social, cultural, religious and ethnic conflicts. Some of these (cultural, religious, ethnic) did not translate into quantifiable reality. Politicians frequently confused these with conflicts of interest. Some of the conflicts overlapped significantly: Unionists faced nationalists in a political conflict, opposition between Protestants and Catholics constituted a religious one, but they were different conflicts requiring different remedies. In some cases, such as religious belief, the solution was to agree to differ. This, he implied, was what ecumenism boiled down to.[108] When it came to political conflicts the aim had to be to challenge the domination of one group by the other. John Whyte, the political scientist who was in effect driven from UCD by clerics influenced by McQuaid for writing *Church and State in Modern Ireland*, fleshed out what this might mean in a summary of his submission to the New Ireland Forum published in *Studies* in 1985.[109] This outlined measures aimed at safeguarding minorities within the Republic. Whilst access to divorce and contraception were obvious issues, a Pandora's Box of wider debates had now opened. These included the decriminalisation of homosexuality.[110]

In 'Constitutional Aspects of Pluralism' (1977) Mary Redmond observed that it was relatively easy to single out various phrases and provisions that might be said to offend against a pluralist society. Her list included the Preamble, where the people of Eire were proclaimed in effect to be a Catholic nationalist people, Articles 2 and 3, which claimed the North, Article 8, which proclaimed a Gaelic ethos in addition to the nationalist one and, of course, Articles 41 to 44, which reflected Catholic teaching. Her remedy included gradual change by referendum.[111] In an accompanying article, 'Cultural Pluralism', Liam de Paor argued that time would solve many of the problems rooted in the different origins of the two main communities on the island. English at the end of the day was the common language, the Republic had abandoned the culturally isolationist preoccupations of the post-colonial era and even in the North there was ample common cultural ground.[112]

In 1978 John Brady SJ argued that citizens of the Republic must emphasise that they did not wish to govern Northern Ireland against the wishes of the majority. He argued that there was a need to modify those aspects of law and public administration that may seem to give the state a markedly Catholic character. These included issues such as divorce and contraception. A carefully framed divorce law would, he argued, be for the common good. The Irish prohibition on the sale of contraceptives in the wake of the 1973 McGee ruling was described as 'bizarre'. Brady argued that to abstain completely from all efforts to influence the decisions of mixed marriages – the abandonment of *Ne Temere* – would be 'an appropriate gesture'. Inter-denominational schooling was needed in the North. Children could be taken to separate classes for religious education, but there was a case for pilot work on the ecumenical teaching of religion using the same textbooks for Protestant and Catholics which would explain divergences in understanding and the existence of a common Christian heritage.[113] In his winter 1985 editorial, Brian Lennon SJ advanced a pluralist utilitarian equation to the effect that 'individual needs have to be balanced against the good of society in a way that allows the maximum possible freedom and diversity that is compatible with the common good'. This formula required that divorce be not prohibited by the state.[114]

SOUTHERN DILEMMAS

The winter 1982 editorial had proclaimed a 'radical shift' in future editorial policy. 'We aim' it began, 'to be non-academic in future, reacting more to the problems of the day, while maintaining the traditional interest of *Studies* in general Irish culture.' The view from the late 1970s was that *Studies* had misplaced its *raison d'être*.[115] The new search for relevance was sketched out in an admixture of editorial statements and questions:

> The breakdown of Christian values in Irish society particularly where the poor and 'marginalized' were concerned; This is a matter of justice which challenges the reality of the faith professed by the majority of our people.
>
> The cultural impoverishment which goes hand in hand with economic poverty, and which is reflected in our system of education.
>
> To what extent may the Irish families of today be described as Christian? What is the atmosphere of most of our homes – Christian or post-Christian?
>
> Is our *democracy* working to further depress the under-privileged? Does an 'order of the Minister' represent the will of our people? Are we on the 'Road to Serfdom?'[116]

The new emphasis was to be upon the perceived dislocations resulting from social injustices, secularisation and loss of political legitimacy. These were understood as being somehow intertwined with the problem of declining Catholic influence in the Republic but also with conflicts in the North. The focus on poverty and inequality was then, to some extent, about reacquiring moral capital. But the new radical emphasis on social justice was also heartfelt. Galvanised by Third

World liberation theology, Gerry O'Hanlon SJ criticised the preoccupation of Northern clergy with doctrinal orthodoxy at the expense of secular welfare. He argued that social justice was a burning issue for Northern Catholics whilst the sermons of their clergy tended to focus on matters of personal piety.[117] Down South relevance was equated with radical commitment to addressing social inequalities. With neo-liberalism in the ascendant, Hayek's *The Road to Serfdom* had many new admirers in the West, but none in *Studies*.

The proposed editorial shift indeed jarred with the then predominant focus. The Northern question aside, *Studies* had become 'overtly absorbed' in academic contributions to art history and literary criticism.[118] Richard Kearney contributed a number of articles on aesthetics to *Studies* from 1981 onwards. These were cut from the same cloth as his writings in *The Crane Bag*. His review of the 1981 Dublin Theatre Festival approvingly quoted Deane's 'courageous if cryptic' manifesto for the Field Day theatre collective that presented it as creating a new liberating consciousness.[119] The 1982 issue that advertised the planned new direction opened with an appreciation of Augustus John's portrait of Kuno Meyer, a former Chair of Celtic Philology and continued with 'Violence, Disintegration and New Vision in O'Casey's Plays' and an appreciation of the paintings of Hubert van Eyck. This emphasis on aesthetics persisted in the remaining articles, 'From History to Episode – An Irish Intermezzo in Eighteenth-Century Bohemia', '*Rambles in Eirinn* by William Bulfin' and 'Under Ben Bulben: Art as Looking Glass'.[120] Kearney's 'Poetry, Language and Identity: A Note on Seamus Heaney' (1986) sketched connections between Heaney's *oeuvre* and that of Seamus Deane.[121] Another Kearney article rounded off the special 300th issue of *Studies*. Its overall theme and title, *Towards a New Irish Identity*, owed much to the influence of *The Crane Bag*.

The new social justice direction promoted in 1982 built to a considerable extent on now longstanding sociological examinations of inequality. During the 1960s *Studies* had provided an outlet for sociological debates not permitted within *Christus Rex*, even if it too favoured a blend of Catholic social action and empirical research over theoretical debates. During the 1970s it published a number of sociological accounts of poverty in Ireland that owed much to leftist critiques of structural inequality.[122] The unmentioned rhinoceros in the corner of Irish Catholic sociology had been its neglect of the issue of power. This failing was hardwired by the consensual models of social order presumed by Catholic social thought and its ideological rejection of conflict models such as were derived from Marx. Partially influenced by revolution theology (in turn influenced by Marxism) a new focus on social justice came to the fore.

In 'Power and its Victims in Ireland' (1972) Seamus O'Cinneide challenged the 'illusion' that Irish society was egalitarian. In Ireland, he argued, there may be a vague humanistic or Christian commitment towards one's neighbour or a diffuse support for human rights and egalitarianism, but this did not count for much.[123] Poverty was seen to confer powerlessness in a number of ways. Politically, the poor were least likely to benefit from patronage or to be protected and supported by the law. When it came to social or medical services they were expected to be subservient. In short, they were more likely to experience injustices. Poverty, he explained, was a social condition expressed through social institutions. Some forty to fifty thousand Irish people were physically institutionalised, some under penal conditions.[124] In getting his argument across O'Cinneide invoked the spirit of Vatican II alongside British literature promoting rights-based approaches to welfare.[125]

In 'Unemployment and Public Policy' (1976) Desmond Norton, an economist, outlined a pessimistic future of ongoing and rising unemployment, economic recession and inflation. If these were left unchecked, he argued, social and political stability would be severely threatened. Unemployment was now higher than in the 1950s, but the unemployed were better educated and less likely in his view to want to emigrate. Full employment, through state-sponsored industrial development, was not achievable as things stood. The state, he argued, should soak up some of the pool of unemployed by setting them to work on community development programmes, road improvements and other public works.[126] A reply article by John Brady, 'The Public Purpose in the Irish Economy'(1976), made the case for pragmatic socialism.[127] The state had a legitimate but finite role within the mixed economy. Here he invoked Patrick Lynch's advocacy of economic planning in 1963. It was now time for a further instalment of public effort.[128] Brady argued that the state should fund employment as an alternative to paying unemployment benefits. Rather than the community employment schemes advocated by Norton this should be part of an 'all-out effort' to build the infrastructure that would be needed in the 1980s. It should be regulated in such a way as to avoid unfair competition with existing private sector employers. Brady also advocated planned temporary emigration:

> The facts should be faced. Even the most vigorous drive to expand employment cannot cope with the problem of unemployment over the next few years and planned temporary emigration is a necessary part of a total response. Some of the European countries, such as the Federal Republic of Germany, are already moving out of the world recession, and there will be increased job opportunities in them. These opportunities should be availed of in a planned manner, with a view to giving young people training and experience in industrial skills which they could use on returning to Ireland after four or five years.[129]

AnCo (the state employment training agency) could negotiate with German firms to train and transport workers they needed, and periodic charter flights could be arranged 'so that contact with the Irish scene and with families could be maintained'.[130] Planned and purposeful emigration, Brady argued, would be better for those affected than the haphazard emigration of the past. It would lead to an injection of fresh thinking and new methods into the Irish economy.

Studies reflected a new language of analysis that distinguished between cores and peripheries, development and underdevelopment. A 1978 article on Irish economic dependency likened targets for farm modernisation and rural depopulation to the scale of social and economic desolation wrought by the Famine.[131] It quoted the blunt conclusion of the National Economic and Social Council that if the foreign investment needed to provide new jobs was discouraged, Irish people would still have to work for foreign capital, but would be doing so outside of Ireland rather than at home.[132] A 1984 review article on T.K. Whitaker's writings looked back despondently to the now bygone days of Keynesian orthodoxy.

Whitaker's innovation, according to Raymond Crotty, had been to introduce sustained public sector deficit financing in 1948. This had come unstuck by the mid-1950s, with a balance of payments deficit that, relative to national income, remained unequalled until the late 1970s. Whitaker's policy of state-supported economic development and capital formation aimed to increase exports but did so at the sacrifice of houses, schools and hospitals.[133] Crotty's thesis was that capital formation had historically brought little benefit to Irish society:

> Yet the whole Irish experience for the last 160 years throws doubt on the assumed relationship between capital formation and social well-being. Capital formation was more rapid in

> nineteenth-century Ireland than in other countries, but its social consequences were disastrous. Irish capital formation, in flocks and herds, like automation now, made people 'redundant' and caused the starvation of millions.[134]

From the early nineteenth century, he argued, when cattle and sheep became more profitable than people, little more than half the latter succeeded in getting a livelihood in Ireland. The rest had to emigrate or starve. Civil servants such as Whitaker could not be expected to have the necessary imaginative empathy: 'insulated as these are from emigration, the inflation that is not offset by index linked salaries and pensions, and from the redundancies and unemployment that are the common lot of the plain people of Ireland'.[135] Etatism aside, Whitaker in his various roles (first Secretary of the Department of Finance, then Governor of the Central Bank) was, Crotty argued, unwitting handmaiden to the current economic crisis:

> The cost of servicing a public debt, which was negligible when Whitaker became Secretary of the Department of Finance, had become of much greater significance when he left to become Governor of the Central Bank. The continued need for public sector deficit financing together with compound interest have thereafter ensured that the accelerating growth of the cost of servicing debt. Irish producers respond to the high taxes that go to servicing debt rather than to provide current services by raising their prices – a procedure that was facilitated by Dr Whitaker in his role as Governor of the Central Bank. These higher prices, triggered off by the taxes to service public debt and made possible by monetary expansion, reduce Irish competitiveness and result in larger balance of payments deficits. These require for their financing more borrowing, especially of foreign currency. There has been a very close correlation between debt service costs and balance of payments deficits throughout the past 30 years. The rising cost of servicing public debt and the resulting balance of payments deficits, which now are the cause of the disarray in the Irish public finances were implicit in the policies of *Economic Development*, of 'Capital Formation, Savings and Economic Progress', and other papers of an economic character in *Interests*'.[136]

In Crotty's twenty–twenty hindsight, Keynesian economics did not work in an open economy. Capital formation did not benefit Irish people because it was expropriated. In a 1980 article, Frank Sammon SJ outlined what he termed a structural paradigm of poverty. This understood poverty within Irish society as resulting from inequality of power and resources, as a problem that could not be solved just by economic growth. Economic development, he argued, had created two Irelands: one comfortable, educated, well-housed and employed, and the other deprived, poorly educated, poorly housed and unemployed.[137] Sammon's analysis drew on the work of the 1971 Kilkenny Conference of the Council of Social Welfare, an influential gathering of Catholic and left anti-poverty activists. This, in turn, had built conceptually on that of Peter Townsend of the persistence of poverty within the British Welfare State.[138] The resultant analysis was one to the left of mainstream Irish opinion. This, according to a 1977 EEC survey, was that 56 per cent of Irish respondents did not think there were any poor people or did not know any, while 55 per cent of respondents imagined that poverty was caused by either personal misfortune or laziness.[139] The new radical Catholic mood was exemplified by Sr Stanislaus Kennedy's *One Million Poor? The Challenge of Irish Inequality*.[140]

'Upstairs, Downstairs: The Challenge of Social Inequality' (1983), by John Sweeney SJ, opened with a parable (the resemblance to reality was 'strictly intentional') that contrasted the lives of bored, frustrated, unemployed young men living in Ballymun with those of smug and complacent bureaucrats and businessmen on an aircraft above on their way to Brussels. Its themes were social inequality, segregation and the justifiable anger of dispossessed youth. In the story Jerry and his friends identify with the H-Block campaign while middle-class Dublin becomes aghast at their rowdy support for the hunger strikers. It ends by citing a 1975 description of such estates by the Irish bishops as 'social time-bombs with slow-burning fuses' and by drawing parallels with the Toxteth riots: 'The same images of cars burning and shop windows crumbling that enter the nightmares of the passengers to Brussels, are part of the day-dreams of Jerry and his friends.'[141]

Sweeney argued that economic successes that followed *Economic Development* in 1958 had created an Irish society that was more relatively unequal than before. Work, he emphasised, was the key to Jerry's problems. However, Sweeney concluded that: 'Surrendering to the market ... such fundamental decisions as how many work, in what and how, was a recipe for social disaster.' Sweeney's argument was backed by an editorial that condemned Irish capitalists ('those who preyed on us then and now are our own people') and the conservatism of political leaders ('When Bernadette Devlin in her heyday described our former Taoiseach, Mr Jack Lynch, as "a green Tory", she said something profound about Irish society').[142]

Similarly in 1985 Kieran Kennedy argued that the market was a good servant but a poor master. The state should not allow the market to dominate when it produced socially unacceptable results. He argued that the current ideological anti-interventionism was vacuous. It failed to confront real social problems.[143] Also, in 'The Church and Justice' (1985), Senator Brendan Ryan portrayed the Church as victim of the new right consensus with its emphasis on freedom from social responsibility. The patron saint of this new right was identified as the broadcaster Gay Byrne: 'liberal on personal freedom, reactionary on the real issues like distribution of wealth, income and power'.[144] Here, and in many other social justice articles, the Church was urged to position itself to the left of the political mainstream.[145] Now market forces rather than the state were the enemies of social cohesion. A 1985 editorial offered revisionist criticism of Church responses to socialism.[146] An accompanying article regretted that Irish socialism had been stillborn. It concluded that the current Irish labour movement had 'produced the most opportunistically conservative Labour Party anywhere in the known world'.[147] This victory of Catholic thought was now to be regretted.

By the 1970s the natural law card, the intellectual trump of so many articles in *Studies* since its inception, was rarely played. Articles about rights were more likely to invoke common law. Articles on industrial relations were more likely to invoke OECD reports than to cite papal encyclicals.[148] A 1980 reviewer carped that Basil Chubb's seminal *The Constitution and Constitutional Change in Ireland* neglected to mention that a judge (who used to write for *Studies*) had quoted an encyclical in a landmark ruling described in the book. Nor were readers informed that the ruling in the 1973 McGee case identifying a right to marital privacy (i.e.; contraception) 'was arrived at from traditional Thomist assumptions'.[149] A 1977 article in *Studies* concluded that the McGee judgment vindicated the rights of a particular married citizen whose case had cried out for justice.[150] The woman in question had four children in three years (two were twins) after difficult life-threatening pregnancies. The family lived in a cramped mobile home. Yet it was argued that for many women the victory was at best symbolic. It was still illegal to sell contraceptives. Those who would most likely benefit from the ruling were the well-off and the articulate, who generally had no real difficulty before McGee anyway.

The great defining political event of the early 1980s, the 1983 Constitutional Referendum on the Right to Life of the Child, vindicated the influence of Catholic conceptions of human rights, even if religious observance had gone into decline. Aquinas scarcely endorsed the 1869 doctrine that human life begins at conception. His view was that the embryo lived an animal life until, quickened, it received it rational soul from God. Intellectual defences of constitutional protection for the unborn in *Studies* were framed for an audience indifferent to Scholasticism. '*Studies*, a 1983 editorial in the journal thundered, 'regards abortion as murder' and illegal under the English Common Law that the Republic had inherited.[151] A 1981 article, 'Pessimistic Origins of the Anti-Life Movement', speculated that the prevalence of abortion in wealthy capitalist society was an existential response to materialism born out of secular despair.[152] However, much of the despair in evidence was arguably of the economic kind.

CHAPTER SEVEN

Fables of the Reconstruction: *Administration* and Development, 1953–86

This chapter examines debates about economic development and technocratic modernisation articulated in *Administration* since its establishment as the intellectual house journal of the Irish public sector in 1953. It centres on the contributions of three pivotal figures: T.K. Whitaker, Patrick Lynch and Tom Barrington.[1] *Administration* began life as a forum for publishing papers read to a discussion group formed by some higher civil servants. The initial intent was to restrict access to readers within the public service. The nervousness of the founders was reflected in the fact that the editor, Barrington, was not named.[2] The first three issues carried a secrecy notice to the effect that 'no public reference to its existence could be made'. The intended audience was an internal one. Subsequently a more public remit emerged tied into the Institute of Public Administration (IPA) of which Barrington was the first director. The IPA, each issue of the journal stated, was founded to promote the study and improve the standard of public administration, and to foster mutual understanding between the public and public servants. The journal emerged alongside, and reflected, a distinct state technocratic project of modernisation. This was formally instigated by The First Programme for Economic Expansion in 1958 but had been honed by Whitaker's influential study *Economic Development*, published in the same year.

The task of setting up *Administration* fell initially to Lynch, who did much to shape its intellectual contours in a series of influential articles beginning with 'The Economist and Public Policy' in 1953. However, this appeared in *Studies*. As *Administration* took shape the anticipated relationship between the journal and its Civil Service constituency mirrored that of the doctrinally orthodox *Christus Rex* and the clergy that were its principal target audience. The equivalents in *Administration* to the repetitive invocation of natural law principles (and struggles to apply these) were recurring articles about administrative and planning processes. *Administration* acquired its own doctrinal text in *Economic Development*.

Civil servants no less than priests had to negotiate gingerly institutional controls, questions of doctrine and expectations of surrender to authority. They were normatively prevented from publishing under their own names outside their own formal expertise, and when writing as civil servants arguably faced greater doctrinal constraints than priests. An invisible college of writers and intellectuals existed within the Civil Service. Conor Cruise O'Brien published the series of essays on Catholic writers in *The Bell* that would become his first book, *Maria Cross* (1954), under a pseudonym. This, he recalled in his *Memoir*, was 'prudential on his part'. A Department of Finance colleague, John O'Donovan, told O'Brien of 'a chilling experience' he had with a book on the cattle trade that he published under his own name. A superior told him that the book would be a millstone around his neck for the rest of his career.[3] O'Donovan left the Civil Service soon afterwards. In another example John Garvin, who wrote about local government in *Administration* under his own name, wrote about James Joyce as Andrew Cass.[4] Brian O'Nolan, who answered to the Gaelic form of Brian O'Nualainn at the Department of Local Government, employed two literary pseudonyms, Flann O'Brien and Myles na Gopaleen, but, indifferent to many rules, also wrote as Brian O'Nolan.[5]

Just before the first issue was published Lynch was pushed aside. Having left the Civil Service for academia he could no longer serve the journal's function 'as a medium for the exposition of official thinking on matters of policy'.[6] He stayed on to run the books section with Basil Chubb and contributed a series of influential articles that promoted and subsequently reassessed critically the developmental project over the next quarter-century. By the time the first issue appeared Barrington was editor. His first editorial proclaimed that *Administration* had no axe to grind: 'we are concerned, not with ends, which is politics, but with means, which is administration. We are concerned not with why a service is provided, but with *how* it is provided. We believe that a dispassionate (but we hope not dull) study of the hows of the many public services will be of interest and value.'[7] Yet, as *Administration* developed, the relationship between ends and means became one of crucial importance. The ends in question were initially heralded in Lynch's 1953 article. However, the crucial document was Whitaker's subsequent *Economic Development*. This

1958 report, along with a number of articles by Whitaker, Lynch and Barrington, mapped out the agenda pursued by *Administration*.[8]

Crucially, it lacked the historical baggage of default opposition to state activism that characterised the Irish Catholic journals.[9] Yet the public sector it sought to energise was one with little apparent faith in itself. A 1977 account of the founding of *Administration* recalled a prevailing 'sense of studied disenchantment' that had been distilled into a spirit of biting cynicism.[10] The response to this was a navel-gazing focus on institutional disabilities that, combined with a technocratic ethos, did not lend itself to broad social debates. There were occasional exceptions, notably the 1967 special issue on television that, like single-themed issues of *Christus Rex* and *Studies*, examined specific topics.[11] Articles published in the first two decades addressed topics such as the use of statistical data, ombudsman systems in other countries, the strengths and weakness of scientific management, industrial relations, spatial planning and the administration of research programmes alongside articles on particular functional policy areas. *Administration* functioned as a forum of professional debate as well as an instrument of top-down institutional reform. Initially most articles were written by civil servants. The proportion produced by academics rose over time, to one-third by the mid-1960s rising to almost two-thirds by the mid-1980s.[12] *Administration* enthusiastically supported the European project advanced by Jean Monnet with, inevitably, a strong focus on calculating the Irish interest as the EEC expanded.[13] When it came to policy development at an Irish level *Administration* was also characterised by ongoing insider criticism of Civil Service culture and policy failure.

PRINT THE LEGEND

What amounted to a generational revolution had elevated Whitaker to the apex of the Department of Finance around the same time that Sean Lemass, the youngest of the 1916 gerontocracy, succeeded Eamon de Valera as Taoiseach. A logjam had burst that allowed for institutional recognition of what were now long-established orthodoxies in other Western countries. *Economic Development* became venerated as one of the great classics of Irish economic writing. However, most of the ideas it presented as a new national project had been percolating for over a decade in *Studies* and elsewhere. For example, back in 1942, in 'Economic Visions and Revisions', George O'Brien argued that *laissez-faire* was a thing of the past. Ireland, like other small nations, would, he accepted, have to develop a planned economy.[14] James Meenan's 1943 'Irish Industrial Policy 1921–1943' prefigured *Economic Development* as a sector-by-sector economic stocktaking exercise.[15] Meenan's second 1943 article, 'Irish Industry and Post-War Problems', offered few answers in the face of an uncertain post-war future but, again, offered a prototype for *Economic Development* in its analysis of past policy shortcomings and in the degree of emphasis it gave to agriculture.[16] A 1951 article by Roy Geary set out an extensive survey of Irish economic development since the Treaty. Geary, like Whitaker, later addressed the economic and social consequences of emigration.[17] Within the Civil Service the key architects of the new official climate were Whitaker and Lynch. Their double-act began with their participation as junior finance officials in a debate on full employment at the Statistical and Social Inquiry Society (SSIS) in April 1945.[18] Within the Department of Finance Lynch instigated the first capital budget in 1950. His 1953 *Studies* article 'The Economist and Public Policy' had contested the arguments of F.A. Hayek, the economist of choice for Catholic anti-statists. This made a specific case for state-directed economic planning in the Irish case and, crucially, had emphasised the new skills needed in the public sector to direct such planning, thus establishing the *raison d'être* of the IPA.

Whitaker had entered the Civil Service with a secondary education but later obtained a degree in economics from the University of London. Twelve years after the SSIS debate, now head of the Department with a new sympathetic Taoiseach onside and in a prevailing climate of economic despair, he got his way. The old sacred cows of economic nationalism could finally be slaughtered.[19] Whitaker had not only authored *Economic Development*, he had pushed it through Cabinet and secured permission for it be published under his own name. More than that, *Economic Development* included as an appendix his December 1957 memorandum to the cabinet proposing the new policy direction.[20] In effect the government had not only permitted a civil servant to determine policy but went on to publish the fact to help market that policy to the public.[21] Whitaker's 'coup' captured the imagination. The resultant First Programme for Economic Expansion, in Whitaker's later summary, 'changed the direction of policy, co-ordinated the development process and gave a fillip to confidence which, supported by buoyant world conditions, generated an outstanding economic performance in the 1960s'.[22]

Whitaker's own version of the *Economic Development* foundation narrative subsequently dominated *Administration* in its efforts to promote a change of culture within the Irish public sector.[23] There was, he argued, a sound psychological reason for having an integrated development programme. It would counter the 'the all-too-prevalent mood of despondency about the country's future'.[24] As put in *Economic Development*:

> A general resurgence of will may be helped by setting up targets of national endeavour which seems reasonably attainable and mutually consistent. This is an aspect of good leadership. But there is nothing to be gained by setting fanciful targets. Failure to reach such targets would merely produce disillusionment and renew the mood of national despondency.[25]

Whitaker argued that there was a pragmatic need to foster a new national ideology:

> No programme of development can be effective unless it generates increased effort, enterprise and saving on the part of a multitude of individuals. Its eventual success or failure will depend primarily on the individual reactions of the Irish people. If they do not have the will to develop, even the best possible programme is useless.[26]

Here was pragmatism as the American philosopher who coined the term understood it. Charles Sanders Pierce in 1878 had proposed that beliefs were important as rules for action rather than as attempts to represent reality.[27] In the Irish case beliefs suited to the task of development were needed. Whitaker's argument that the essence of the problem was that 'an attitude of mind amongst all groups was inimical to growth' owed a lot to the writings of Bishop William Philbin in *Studies*. Philbin's 1957 article had been cited in the introduction to *Economic Development*.[28] Lynch described the Bishop as 'a distinguished source of Mr Whitaker's inspiration'.[29] In *Studies* in 1964 Garret FitzGerald argued that that *Economic Development* and subsequent attempts at planning 'more than anything' provided 'a psychological basis for economic recovery' in so far as it helped to change radically the unconscious attitude of many influential people and to make Ireland a growth-orientated community.[30] There is a sense throughout such claims that psychology was a proxy for ideology, belief and even faith in a new Irish manifest destiny. As put by Whitaker in 1961:

> ... the psychological factor which, in my view is, and for long will remain, the most important factor of production in Ireland. This means that it is vital to sustain an atmosphere of enterprise and progress. In such an atmosphere we shall not allow ourselves to be over-awed by future difficulties or to fall into despondency by reason of temporary reverses and setbacks. If enterprise is welled to realism we can advance.[31]

The first issue of *Administration* – a symposium on efficiency in the Civil Service – contained a review essay by Lynch on Edwin Chadwick under the heading 'A Great Public Servant'. Chadwick, Lynch noted, was hardly apolitical in his advocacy of public health:

> In blue-book after blue-book he assailed the waste that followed from supporting at public expense the victims of fevers while the community tolerated the conditions that inevitably produced those epidemics. No expenditure, he argued, could be more profitable than that which removed the causes of preventable ill-health. He shocked the public conscience with his tactless and inconvenient exposures of horrors that vested interests and prejudice would have liked to suppress. But there was no resisting his heroic strength and indefatigable energy.[32]

In Whitaker the Irish Civil Service found its hero. *Economic Development* was repeatedly invoked in dozens of articles in a manner that recalled how an earlier generation ritualistically referred to the encyclicals that set out Catholic social thought. Around Whitaker and *Economic Development* a new nation-building renaissance myth was propagated, one less glamorous, perhaps, than the 1916 Rising – yet one that partially supplanted it – with public servants rather than poets in the driving seat. Whitaker's argument that a cultural change was a precondition of economic development evolved into the mantra that a cultural change had precipitated the sixties boom and a new modern Irish history that dated progress from 1958. As put by the newspaper editor in John Ford's 1962 revisionist Western *The Man Who Shot Liberty Valance*: 'when the legend becomes fact, print the legend'.

As a post-independence cultural event the nativity of *Economic Development* was rivalled in the telling only by the story of the conflict surrounding the 'Mother and Child Scheme' in 1951. Calls for psychological change and retrospective emphasis on its importance warrant some scepticism. A 1976 review article by Michael Fogarty entitled 'Age of Miracles' emphasised that *Economic Development* did not emerge in isolation from the trials and errors of a whole generation of previous effort. What was missing from Irish valorisations of Whitaker's 'flash of inspiration' was any theory of the learning process at organisational or societal levels.[33] In 1959 C.F. Carter, one of Whitaker's key economic advisers, had written that the problems of human nature, 'in Irish nature more than most', were ultimately administrative ones. 'Since it is a slow job improving human nature,' Carter wrote, 'our first efforts should be devoted to improving this machinery; and since the "machines" are in fact the minds of men, a great deal of the future of Ireland may depend on the quality and training of those found for key positions.'[34] The developmental narrative was primarily an ideological one, crucially important in constituting an economic nation-building project of modernisation. But its rhetoric, Fogarty implied, had obscured administrative problems and sidestepped real difficulties. The project of *Administration* was to address such difficulties.

PUBLIC ENTERPRISE AND THE PURSUIT OF GROWTH

When Lynch told Dr Michael Browne, Bishop of Galway, that he was considering a career in academia Browne expressed surprise that he would consider surrendering the influence he held in the Civil Service and added, ominously: 'I hear you have Marxist leanings.' Before Lynch could reply Dr Browne thundered: 'Well at least you are not a Benthamite like most Dublin economists.'[35] Lynch knew his Marx but was hardly a Marxist. Seven years earlier, in 1946, he had written on nineteenth-century Irish contributions to socialist thought in *The Bell*. In 'William Thompson of Cork' Lynch described Thompson's contributions to the co-operative movement and his achievements as 'the first systematic writer on industrial communities' more than four decades before the publication of Marx's *Das Kapital*.[36] Thompson had dismissed the utilitarian concept of 'the greatest happiness of the greatest number' as a mirage under the system of individual competition which, even in its freest and best form, was so arranged as to enable one man to deprive another of the produce of his labour.[37] Lynch praised Thompson as a practically minded critic of capitalism. Thompson's proposals for co-operatism on his Cork estate were, Lynch argued, more pragmatic than those of Robert Owen. Thompson was a socialist in so far as he was preoccupied with the equitable distribution of surplus value.[38] However, he wrote as an economist whereas Marx, as Lynch put it, 'was more concerned with making socialism predatory than making it scientific'.[39] Overall Thompson was depicted as a pioneer of the kind of pragmatic yet idealistic approach to progress that Lynch later promoted in the Irish case.

Lynch's own critique of Irish capitalism – and the case for state planning he advanced during the 1950s – was summarised in what became his most widely read essay, 'The Economics of Independence: Some Unsettled Questions of Irish Economics'. Initially published in 1959 as an *Administration* article, it was reprinted as one half of a pamphlet by *Tuarim* and then serialised in the *Irish Times*.[40] After bluntly rehearsing the now standard argument against economic protectionism – the 'Sinn Féin myth' that Irish political independence implied economic independence[41] – Lynch argued that public enterprise, using foreign capital, needed to make up for a failure of private enterprise. Specifically, he argued that integration with the British economy should be pursued. Britain, heavily reliant on food imports, would benefit from aiding the development of Irish agriculture through capital investment and grant aid.[42] Irish tax incentives for export should induce British firms to establish plants in Ireland and to take advance of the Irish labour supply, thereby reducing the number of Irish workers who migrated. When it came to foreign capital investment, Britain was the logical first port of call. Closer economic association with Britain, he insisted, was entirely compatible with an intelligent conception of Irish nationhood and pragmatic because of emigration and Irish expectations of British living standards. 'Rightly or wrongly, the Irish people demand the standard of living to which they might be entitled if all Ireland were still part of the United Kingdom.' The result had been emigration and, for those who did not have to emigrate, a higher standard of living than could be afforded if the Irish state were obliged to cater for everyone born there since independence.[43] Unless the political obstacles to economic co-operation with Britain could be overcome, Ireland would inevitably turn towards the European Common Market for the external support it needed to pursue economic growth.

However, capital was but one factor of production. When it came to enterprise Lynch considered that the Irish private sector had more drones than pioneers. In Ireland, as elsewhere, he enthused, 'the modern counterpart of the pioneering businessman of nineteenth-century capitalism is the professional manager. He is largely the reincarnation of the old entrepreneur's spirit.'[44] But in 1954, in 'Some Problems with Public Enterprise', Lynch had argued that while public authorities in Ireland were already responsible for the nation's capital assets these were poorly co-ordinated. In 1950 their share represented 65 per cent of net capital formation. This far exceeded the norm in many European countries and was more than double that in the UK under an avowedly socialist government.[45] By default rather than by ideological design the Irish government had assumed considerable responsibility for investment, risk-taking and regulation. Moreover, the size of state companies, such as Coras Iompair Éireann (CIÉ, the national railway and road transport company) or the Electricity Supply Board (ESB), dwarfed private commercial firms, two-thirds of which employed fewer than twenty workers. Just 400 out of a total of 4,500 had more than a hundred employees.

The vista described by Lynch within the state sector was hardly conducive to strategic co-ordination. State companies used their monopoly status to ward off competition from other State companies as well as from the private sector. CIE, for instance, in 1952 had proposed legislation that would limit the operation of all road vehicles of more than two tonnes, other than its own, to a radius of twenty miles. Other State companies had pursued similar forms of restrictive protectionism within the Irish market. These were often targeted at other State companies.[46] The public interest, he argued, with considerable understatement, required improved regulation and co-ordination.

Similarly, within the Civil Service, the spirit of enterprise seemed elusive. In 1956, in 'Administrative Theory and the Civil Service', Lynch offered trenchant criticism of Civil Service culture:

> A great part of the intellectual ability of the country is employed in the Civil Service. Can we contrive to empower that service to use this ability effectively? Are we sure that no part of that ability is presently under-employed? An unconstructive attitude will not help. Where negation is elevated to a virtue, the pinnacle of efficiency must surely be achieved by doing nothing.[47]

Lynch argued that bureaucratic organisational forms were slow to adapt and were unwieldy.[48] Innovation in such a context was no easy thing. There was a need to distinguish between the bureaucratic approach ('a form of institutional degeneracy') and the administrative one. The difference, he explained, was chiefly one of degrees of rigidity or flexibility. Rigidities tended to be justified as procedurally necessary to ensure parliamentary accountability. Scrutiny of expenditure was necessary but not, he argued, the proliferation of excessive and perfectionist 'bureaucratic' controls. Semi-State companies as public corporations had been freed from such strictures. The Civil Service that created them had, however, so far failed to establish a satisfactory relationship between these bodies and Parliament. The public corporation seemed destined to flourish in the absence of any better public sector alternatives to Civil Service inflexibility.[49]

Lynch was scathing of the 'fictional relationship between official advice and policy-making' promoted by civil servants. It was, he argued, 'hopelessly naïve and positively misleading and fostered bureaucratic inflexibility'.[50] It set up a false dichotomy – the civil servant offering impartial advice, the minister making policy – that misrepresented the workings of policy-making processes. These, he emphasised, were incremental. To appreciate Anuerin Bevan's role in developing the British Welfare State, one needed to understand it as the culmination of a process for extending and unifying social services that dated back to 1601.[51] Generally civil servants left ministers without any freedom of choice or ability to test the correctness of their advice. Ministers were dependent on the goodwill of officials who were protected from accountability because of their anonymity. The problem with this fiction was that it impeded honest self-appraisal.[52] Self-delusion and bureaucratic inflexibility reinforced one another and produced the 'studied disenchantment and low morale' that defined the Civil Service culture he had left for academia. Here then, perhaps, was the answer to Bishop Browne's question. Lynch recalled that a great number of civil servants were too intelligent and educated too highly for the jobs they were given. A common criticism was that not enough effort was made to match levels of responsibility with levels of ability:

> When an organisation is so unwieldy that it is overcome with Byzantine immobility, it destroys the enthusiasms and feeds the frustrations of its members who would wish it to move with reasonable agility. Satisfactory social relationships cannot be established, much less managed, in an organisation which is being eroded by indifference and strangled by frustration.[53]

The solution would be an administrative culture that encouraged the delegation of responsibility, established and analysed standards of performance for all jobs and offered intelligent co-ordination and organisation. However, Lynch was adamant that specific structural reforms to the Civil Service would not solve what was, principally, a problem of organisational culture. What was needed was effective personnel management. In so far as the problem was one of organisational culture it was essentially an intellectual one that could be remedied only through debate and education. In this spirit five articles – and an introductory literature review by Basil Chubb – on management and administrative theory appeared alongside the one by Lynch.[54]

Lynch was not the only 'outside' critic of public servitude. For example, in 'Creativity in the Public Sector' (1971) Brendan O'Regan, public entrepreneur *par excellence*, referred to the popular belief that men of ability and ambition could find themselves in Civil Service jobs with little scope or responsibility.[55] Such assessments challenged the prevalent notion that the senior Civil Service constituted an intellectual elite. Lemass in his 1961 article had claimed that 'the Civil Service has tended to attract the best brains of the nation and is still doing so'.[56] A decade later the policy unit of the IPA formally begged to differ. The appropriately titled 'The Idea of a Profession' (1971) noted that just five out of the ninety-nine higher civil servants appointed in 1968–69 had degrees when they joined. Thirty-five had gone on to take degrees whilst serving as civil servants.[57] It concluded that the Civil Service had lost much of its power to attract the top flight of school leavers and had little ability to attract graduates. The administrative pyramid was in some cases still based wholly on clerical recruitment.[58] Barrington's IPA research unit made the case, quoting Chubb, for developing a school of administration to produce graduates for the Civil Service. As put by Chubb:

> The advance of the social sciences and of accounting and statistical techniques to the point where they are essential tools for policy making and management have made it vital for public services everywhere to be peopled by a more professional race than has usually been found in the higher administrative ranks of British-style Civil Services. Increasing numbers of senior officers have to be capable of observing, appreciating, and using large amounts of systematic economic and social data in order to elucidate problems and to formulate adequate plans to place before their ministers. If, as in Ireland, the vast majority of senior officials are recruited at secondary school level, formidable education and training problems are posed, embracing the appropriate social sciences including management, not to be solved by programmes measured – as most have been in the past – in days or weeks but demanding months and years.[59]

A professional Civil Service, it was concluded, required the establishment of a public sector college by the IPA. Here the curriculum would draw on the debates promoted within *Administration*.

ADMINISTRATIVE PURPOSE

Failures to manage effective planning were blamed on an inability to rise to the ideal of professionalism promoted by the IPA. Lynch's arguments about weak accountability became central to an ongoing debate promoted by Barrington. During the 1960s he had been preoccupied with developing an equivalent to the debate about national purpose in *Studies* to which his brother Donal Barrington contributed.[60] His 'Administrative Purpose' (1965) emphasised the limits of ruthless pragmatism as well as mistakes made in the shadows of past ideologies.[61] The ends central to 'administrative purpose' as outlined by Barrington reflected what he understood to be the broader societal values of (all in upper case) Christianity, Nationalism and Democracy.

However, the first two elements of Barrington's trinity were rarely manifested in *Administration*. His 1965 article and a couple of nods to the very atypical Bishop Philbin aside, Catholicism hardly got a look in. Debates about nationalism were also sidelined. *Administration*'s commemoration of the fiftieth anniversary of the 1916 Rising made no mention of the ghosts of the GPO. The sole historical figure celebrated was Sir Horace Plunkett for his contributions to pre-independence agricultural development and social policy administration.[62] It included a survey of Irish political change through the lens of foreign policy shifts up to and including the decision to join the European Economic Community. This was no less revisionism than concurrent challenges to the legacy of 1916 in *Studies*.[63] The closest the issue came to a philosophical engagement with the Rising was an extended book review addressing understandings of the common good. The book in question was Richard Flathman's *The Public Interest: An Essay Concerning Normative Discourse of Politics*. Desmond Roche, a civil servant, noted an occupational tendency to reject idealist conceptions of the common good alongside one towards elitism. If 'pious formulas about the will of the people' warranted scepticism, so too did the elitist claims of modern administrators to represent the public interest when it came to understanding complex issues. Flathman's remedy – one described rather than endorsed by Roche –

was an infusion of Kantian ethics into public administration. Roche drew no analogy between the 1916 revolutionaries and the officials who now stalked the corridors of power. However, he set out grounds for scepticism about the kinds of claims that might be made by from either an idealist or an elitist standpoint.[64]

Barrington argued that the relationship between means and ends was one best served by democratic accountability: the third element of his trinity. The equation he repeatedly emphasised was one between administrative and democratic efficiency. His grail search for administrative purpose was one framed by ongoing debates in *Administration* about accountability. In this vein a 1960 article by Max Abrahamson argued that the best defence against the routine injustices perpetrated by the State was an ombudsman system of administrative tribunals. As things stood the courts were unable to ensure Civil Service accountability.[65] A decade later, in an issue dedicated to local government and regionalism, Barrington portrayed centralised technocratic services as poorly placed to address the human needs of Irish society. He insisted that complex problems of individuals, families and communities often did not fit within the tidy functional divisions of administrative agencies.[66] His own personal crusade was for the reform of local government.[67]

In a 1974 paper to officials of the European Commission, Barrington explained that Irish administrators had tended to be the children of small farmers, small shopkeepers and petit bourgeois, not drawn from some hereditary or economic elite. They were the product of an education system whose authoritarian bias had 'discouraged the speculative and reinforced the natural bent towards the practical, the unintellectual, the non-speculative'. This, he suggested, found expression in a realistic and pragmatic enthusiasm towards the European Community. Irish pragmatism, however, tended to be *ad hoc*, near-sighted and anti-intellectual:

> The pragmatic, short-term view of change, where it was necessary, led to a number of ad-hoc solutions, and the system of centralisation devised these solutions in ways that seemed sensible from the centre. But viewed from the periphery, from the viewpoint of the ordinary citizen, the aggregate of these solutions seemed to result in fragmentation and incomprehensibility. Again, the practical men had little time for introduction, for a review of the effectiveness of their services, for a lively recognition of the value of feedback from the puzzled, and

> increasingly distrustful citizen. One might have expected that the universities would have provided an antidote to these ills; but they themselves were almost equally infected.[68]

There was something patrician rather than anything self-loathing about this. Barrington, the son of a senior and supposedly independent minded Finance official, was an exception to his own rule and something of an outsider to the culture he disparaged.[69]

He argued that the authoritarian culture within the Civil Service 'tended to silence those who might otherwise have criticised it and to lead others to overlook the need for re-thinking of the whole system, its continued fitness for its overall propose in a changing world. In this the public service was only too representative of the society from which it came, and which it served.'[70] Yet he expressed a 'wary optimism' that Irish intellectual failings were being transcended.[71] He hoped that the rise of research and a new mood of scientific analysis would lead to 'some system of orderly development'.[72] But the old problems of both political and administrative culture remained; the people distrusted their administrators and administrators evidenced 'a defensive and distrustful attitude to the people'.[73] Hence the stress on accountability as a necessary corrective to what increasingly looked like a narrow unreflective project of technocratic modernisation.

Whitaker, on the other hand, kept faith with the planners' dream. In 'Planning Irish Development' (1977) he argued that planning in a democratically governed country should be 'a complete and internally-consistent statement by government of the policies and actions to be followed in order to achieve specified objectives of an economic and social character'; in short the supreme policy document of the Government in power. Questions of ends were political ones. Politics, no less than economics, involved choices between alternatives. These would be understood better if placed before the public and discussed by the 'social partners'. Development, Whitaker emphasised, required the mobilisation of consensus. Without consultation the objectives of social and economic policy could not be realistically resolved. Planning so understood, he argued, 'through its combination of realism, idealism, equity and purpose', could be a strong community-binding force and a generator of the confidence and co-operation needed to achieve difficult goals. The Irish experience, he reiterated, 'shows that the psychological factor can, at times, be the most powerful factor of production'.[74]

The nascent corporatism described by Whitaker, one that developed into social partnership, offered a developmental model different from the top-down one initially proposed. During the 1970s *Administration* focused increasingly on academic debates about interest groups. Articles depicted government as an 'all-inclusive mediating agency' which held the balance between competing pressures in society.[75] These viewed administration as inseparable from politics.[76] In 1977 Tony McNamara, a future editor of *Administration*, argued that the challenge in the face of proliferating interest groups was to offer courageous advice that allowed decisions between demands based on clear judgements. This could only work, he argued, if there was more and better public disclosure of official information so that judgement on the relative importance of demands might win out over the strength of lobbies.[77]

In 'Can Administrative Science Aid the Administrative Profession?' (1979) Barrington emphasised the failure, as he saw it, of the 1969 Devlin Commission on pubic service reorganisation. Devlin had defined the problem as 'the need to restructure an extraordinarily disorderly system so that the government would have a more responsive and creative instrument' to hand. A Department of Public Service was established to do the job. This was precisely the approach Lynch had warned against in 1959. Barrington argued that the Civil Service could not be reformed through generic managerial restructurings (his interpretation of why Devlin had failed) that ignored organisational history and culture. Much of Irish public administration, he continued, even the state-sponsored sector, was still based on mid-nineteenth-century thinking.[78] A number of central government services were derived from nineteenth-century entities; for example, the Department of Agriculture from the activities of the Land League and the work of Sir Horace Plunkett. The Department of the Environment was rooted in the Benthamite ferment of the mid-nineteenth century. The local government system derived mainly from the ideas of Joseph Chamberlain. The ideas behind the departments of Health and Social Welfare owed much to those of Beveridge. Each had their own turf to protect, their own hinterland of specific ideas and their own reasons for resisting change or encroachment.

Many countries had now attempted organisational reforms along the lines of Devlin with disappointing results. These he attributed to the narrow framing of debates akin to the dominance of logical positivism within philosophy, the result being that much that was important became marginalised.[79] Administrative science, he argued, needed to incorporate a broader focus on the ideas and intellectual influences shaping the administrative system.[80] A range of intellectual disciples could be seen to influence the administrative system, including politics, sociology, management theory, organisational theory, law, economics, psychology and geography. It was, as such, difficult to agree upon one intellectual map for administrative science. In this context, Irish public administration as a profession was suffering an identity crisis, 'having enormously extending its periphery without attaining or creating a unifying centre'.[81] Difficulties in achieving institutional reform, a 1979 article by a Department of Public Service official concluded, were legion.[82]

As put bluntly by one academic writing in the same issue, the battle for hearts and minds still seemed unwinnable given 'in-built conservatism within the system, general hostility towards change'.[83] Another rubbished the psychological argument that poor economic performance was largely the result of entrepreneurial pessimism.[84] John Bristow doubted whether Irish economic programmes had of themselves any direct positive impact on the decisions of entrepreneurs. The idea that top-down planning could create micro-economic certainty was, he argued, a delusion. Although plans could be seen to shape the targets set by public bodies and state companies this had more to do with the politics of corporatism than with planning.[85]

In 'Whither Science Policy?' (1979) Lynch sought to inject a new reflexivity into the Irish developmental project. More than a decade earlier his *Investment in Education* had promoted a human capital focus that challenged the dominant emphasis on religious reproduction within Irish schools. Yet Lynch remained critical of narrow utilitarianism, quoting Jacques Maritain's argument that the trouble with utilitarian education was that it was not utilitarian enough.[86] Lynch argued that the humanities had not adjusted successfully to the industrial age. Technological change advanced (here he quoted Bertrand Russell) like an army of tanks that had lost their drivers, blindly and ruthlessly, without goal or purpose. This was because men and women of scholarship and imagination were still living in a pre-industrial world. The exponents of classicism had failed to show how technological advance could be humanised. It now fell, Lynch argued, to the universities to humanise science and technology as the inter-relationships between third-level institutions and industry in Ireland developed. Lynch specifically advocated the development of an Irish university-based multi-disciplinary centre for science innovation, and the extension of Irish science policy generally.[87]

'Whither Science Policy?' gave the readers of *Administration* a rare taste of thinkers such as Arnold Toynbee, Ralph Dahrendorf and Karl

Popper, of debates about epistemology and of critiques of the intellectual premises that sustained administrative rationality. Modern societies, Lynch claimed, 'glibly substitute verification for truth and embrace narrow forms of rationality which leave no room for value criteria to govern choices'.[88] If the primary focus of his paper was on the development of science policy – promoting research and policy debate about the social implications of technology – he offered, in parallel, reflections on the epistemological shortcomings of economics.

Irish economists, he argued, had often worked from narrow but also incomplete statistical data. The importance of economists to policy-making, he argued, had often been overemphasised in the Irish case. That of other disciplines such as sociology, social history and public administration also needed to be emphasised.[89] Lynch's solution in the case of both science and economics emphasised the need for interdisciplinarity and the preservation of independent critical thinking:

> Specialists whose disciplines contribute to policy-making must be drawn from independent, autonomous institutions, from universities, the regional colleges, the Economic and Social Research Unit, the Institute of Public Administration and other research institutions. It is an excellent tradition that, under responsible direction, workers in research institutes should publish their own work freely under their own names, and that they, and not their institutions should be responsible for the results of their research. Research must be translated into the written and published word before the task of the research work is complete.[90]

Whitaker and Barrington had emphasised the need for planning to be rooted in democratic politics yet sufficiently informed by empirical data to win over the demands of interest groups. Here the emphasis seemed to be upon securing the legitimacy of effectively top-down policy goals. Lynch emphasised the need for intellectual pluralism and defined policy as a broad process that might counter technical rationality and narrow pragmatism.

However, when it came to broader social debates *Administration* tended to follow rather than lead. The policy and academic debates about poverty that emerged in the wake of the Kilkenny Conference in 1971 (see Chapter Six) were not reflected until 1985, when these were acknowledged in the then national plan Building on Reality.[91] This mirrored the slow wake-up to gender inequality within the Civil Service. In 'Women in the Civil Service' (1956), the first article by one such person, Neans de Paor, had criticised pay inequalities.[92] It took nineteen more years before the topic was addressed again. The main article of the 1975 special issue on the status of women, two years after the ban on the employment of married women within its ranks was lifted, was a progress report by the 'chairman' of the Commission, Thekla Beere.[93] *Administration* remained normatively focused on means rather than ends and retained a tin ear for social issues not yet formally constituted as policy goals.

UNEQUAL ACHIEVEMENT

Yet, by the early 1980s, social discontents proved difficult to ignore. In 1982 a special issue of *Administration*, entitled *Unequal Achievement: The Irish Experience 1952–82*, assessed the achievements and failures of the three decades that followed the launch of the journal. As noted by its editor, Frank Litton, the economy was now in recession. Unemployment was rising and the social problems that followed from economic stagnation were growing. Current problems were portrayed as recalling the crisis of the 1950s. Litton's diagnosis and proposed cure echoed that put forward by Whitaker in 1958:

> Despondency seems to be on the increase, as though the intractability of our problems had at last sapped our will to solve them. It is difficult to avoid recalling the grim fifties, the last severe economic depression. We survived the fifties to enjoy the boom of the sixties. What was accomplished once can presumably be accomplished again. External circumstances undoubtedly played a part in our recovery then; equally conditions in the world economy set limits in the chances of success today. But the important lesson of the fifties is not about our dependence on the world economy. Things improved then because the administrative and political leadership searched out and responded to the opportunities which the improving world conditions brought. This responsiveness reflected not only a will to win: joined with it was a clear perception of reality and an understanding of the means required to transform it.[94]

Unequal Achievement came at a time when Keynesian economic orthodoxies had unravelled. An article by Moore McDowell portrayed the Irish state as Hobbes's *Leviathan*, depicting uncontrolled public expenditure as an expression of the State's coercive power at odds with the common good.[95] *Unequal Achievement* was also published at the near zenith of 1980s emigration. Contributors such as Tom Garvin and J.J. Lee wrote critically about social change and economic stagnation yet contested in their writings a then prevalent intellectual fatalism centred on post-colonialist thought, Marxist perspectives on underdevelopment and Catholic liberation theology; in other words the critique of Irish society that found expression in *Studies* at the time. Here a key figure was the agricultural economist Raymond Crotty. His 1966 economic history *Irish Agricultural Production: Its Volume and Structure* had been reviewed disparagingly ('a one-dimensional view of history[96]). His core argument was that agricultural output had remained static from 1840 notwithstanding the Famine, the abolition of landlordism, independence, the economic war, the World Wars and the first and second Programmes for Economic Expansion. His diagnosis was that peasant landholders not required to pay a rent had no impetus to maximise their use of their holdings. In 1986, in *Ireland in Crisis: A Study in Capitalist Colonial Development*, Crotty depicted civil servants ('in pensionable and often unproductive jobs') as a similarly insulated interest group. He portrayed Irish society overall as more willing to displace surplus people than to create surplus value:

> People made unemployed by trade unions forcing wage rates above the level at which people would be willing to work rather than remain unemployed, have not remained in Ireland. Neither have those made unemployed by the substitution of livestock for people. Emigration has given to Ireland, for over a century, conditions approximating to 'full employment' with no large pool of unemployed labour to form a source of competing non-unionised labour, working either as self-employed persons or for non-union firms. These virtually 'full employment' conditions bought about by mass emigration, have been fundamentally different from the normal conditions of massive, growing labour surpluses in the former capitalist colonies.[97]

Garvin's review of *Ireland in Crisis* found merit in Crotty's argument as an ethical rather than empirical one, an exercise in the now unfashionable subject of political economy as distinct from economics. It was also, he argued, a maddening book. Here Garvin referred to Crotty's proposed solution of removing historical privileges that protected capital and displaced surplus labour, penalising inefficient use of agricultural land, downsizing the civil servants and repudiating the national debt.[98] Crotty's advocacy of an agricultural year zero aside, his arguments about how privileged interest groups blocked development found a degree of favour in *Administration* – which had been wrestling with bureaucratic intransigence for a quarter of a century. For example, Garvin wrote that the system as a whole exported surplus labour and tried to shore up its incompetent and inefficient political economy through a mixture of clientelist politics and borrowing.[99]

Four years earlier, in *Unequal Achievement* in 'The Changing Social Structure', David Rottman and Philip O'Connell offered essentially the same analysis that employment security and high wages for some without the necessity of economic growth became possible through an acceptance of emigration.[100] The society produced by thirty years of economic development was, in their analysis, a highly unequal one. Now, in the early 1980s, 'in contrast to the late 1950s', there was no confidence in Ireland's ability to control its future. Nor could the experts inject any.[101] *Unequal Achievement* also reflected the critique of planning failure that had been developed by Barrington. In 'Change and the Political System' Garvin argued that planning – in vogue during the 1950s, conjuring up images of rational 'scientific' and 'Swedish' styles of social management – now appeared as irrelevant to Irish political life as the 1930s concept of intellectual censorship that had died in the 1950s. Political culture had remained largely unchanged, and backbench politics rather than scientific government dominated much of its behaviour.[102]

The key difference between Crotty's underdevelopment thesis and the essentially liberal critique of the post-1958 era that dominated *Administration* was one between the relative presumed importance of social structure and individual agency. Crotty, an economic determinist, stressed the former. Farmers and civil servants resisted change not for psychological reasons but because it was in their material interests. Unless the structure of social relations was changed, little else would.

Lee, on the other hand, within *Unequal Achievement* and in the more extensive essay on Irish economic modernisation that concluded his monumental *Ireland: 1912–1985*, drew heavily on the narratives offered by Whitaker, Lynch and Barrington.[103] Lee identified heavily with the arguments of all three. Although his 1982 article was entitled 'Society and Culture' the focus was very much upon the Civil Service. He opened by defining culture as 'the set of meanings and values that informs a way of life'. In such terms, he argued, Whitaker's *Economic Development* loomed as a landmark on the mid-twentieth-century landscape. The maturity of a culture, he argued, was reflected in the urge to search for, and the capacity to confront, the truth about itself: '*Economic Development* extended an invitation to Irish society to embark on a search for self-knowledge and not flinch from the findings.'[104] Here too were shades of Sean O'Faolain with his exhortation to see clearly and his opposition to national self-delusion. Here also was the implication that the Irish people and their public servants had broken faith with the promise of progress inscribed on the tablet of *Economic Development*:

> That an official should put his name to a virtual manifesto dismayed those who power lay partly in their ability to stifle dissent behind the amiable façade of 'ministerial responsibility.' By venturing to publish, Whitaker showed he had come to accept the view of Patrick Lynch that public confidence in the quality of the official mind was itself an important prerequisite for national progress. That this attitude has failed to permeate the Civil Service may contribute to what seems to be a growing lack of public confidence in the calibre of the official mind.[105]

The work of Barrington too at the IPA also seemed to be in vain. Lee concluded that quality of decision-making elites remained extraordinarily uneven. The Civil Service, he argued, had proved woefully unwilling to become a meritocracy.[106] It remained hostile to the publication of information not because of cost or difficulties but out of fear that public knowledge would limit its freedom of action.[107] An apparent overall unwillingness to reform stood in contrast with the flood of articles debating reform in *Administration*.[108]

The critique of post-1958 Ireland set out in *Ireland 1912–1985* was a synthesis of Lynch, Whitaker and Barrington: 'If a small open society must live largely on its wits, if its main weapon in improving the quality of its life is the calibre of its own mind, then sustained analysis of the quality of decision-making, and actions based on that analysis, are crucial to the overall performance of the society.'[109] The achievement of the likes of the IPA and *Administration*, Lee suggested, was to move policy-making and analysis some way towards a quantifiable rational basis, but not far enough. Ireland entered a period of rapid economic change with little grasp of the criteria by which it might access and guide its own performance.[110] It was still the case that policy-orientated research seemed to have little or no direct impact on policy.[111] The result for Lee was an uncritical modernity. A 'poverty of perspective had been peculiarly unfortunate at a time when the cult of technological determinism became increasingly fashionable'.[112] Here he drew on Lynch's 'Whither Science Policy?' Lynch's argument was that the Irish outpost of Western humanism needed to rise to the challenges of modernity and not abandon scientific, technical or economic questions affecting society to narrow expertise.[113]

However, Lee, in *Ireland 1912–1985*, writing at the bottom of the well of an economic crisis that viscerally recalled the early 1950s, de-emphasised such caveats. What Whitaker referred to as psychology and what Barrington had described in 1974 as a partly peasant bureaucracy both emerged as central to Lee's diagnosis. Lee offered a culturally deterministic equivalent of Crotty's economic determinism. Post-Famine Ireland, he argued, had witnessed the emergence of a 'zero sum' mindset whereby people saw the advancement of others as possible only at their own expense: 'The size of the cake was more or less fixed in more or less stagnating communities and in small institutions. In a stunted society, one man's gain did tend to be another man's loss. Winners could only flourish at the expense of losers. Status depended not only on rising oneself but on preventing others from rising. For many, keeping the other fellow down offered the surest defence of their own position.' Lee argued that such begrudgery severely hampered the emergence of meritocracy and of an 'enterprise culture'. His cure for prosperity-blocking fatalism was a liberal mindset adept at enterprise; in other words the power of positive thinking promoted by Whitaker. But the times had changed. Neo-liberalism had superseded the Keynesian liberalism that warmed to public enterprise. The pursuit of growth as national religion persisted and seemed indifferent to what a number of contributors to *Administration* variously as a ruthless, narrow, *ad hoc*, anti-intellectual pragmatism.

IN THE COMING TIMES

Whitaker and Lynch both seemed to stand for different wings of the developmental project, even if their respective roles and intellectual contributions overlapped. The contents of the Festschrifts published in honour of both – *The Clash of Ideas* for Lynch in 1988 and *Ireland in the Coming Times* for Whitaker in 1997 – suggested an intellectual cleavage between idealist and pragmatist developmental approaches. Here the former included challenges to unequal distribution of the fruits of growth as well as critiques of Irish modernity in the tradition of 'Whither Science Policy?'[114] The latter unreservedly prioritised the pursuit of economic growth. But the schism between the two books was hardly an absolute one. For example, Miriam Hederman contributed an article to the book celebrating Whitaker about tax policy.[115] She also edited *The Clash of Ideas*. She had been the general secretary of Tuairim when it had promoted a civil society debate on Lynch's 'The Economics of Independence' in 1959. From this she opened *The Clash of Ideas* with the following quotation, presented as a developmental desideratum in the following layout:

> An essential condition of progress is
> the desire for change,
> a resentment of stagnation,
> a willingness to depart from obsolete ideas,
> leadership with a consistent sense of direction
> a healthy, courageous and constructive public opinion;
> above all, concern for the preservation or reform where necessary,
> of every institution which the community has established as
> an instrument of achieving national and economic advance.
> Ireland has unused human and material resources, but there must be a change of attitudes towards using them. More than anything else, new ideas count in the long run – provided they are the right ones.

In 1959 Lynch had observed that Irish political economy had tended to be more political than economic. It was misleading to pretend that goals chosen for political or ideological purposes had inherent economic significance. Lynch concluded that economic development was too important to be left in the hands of economists.[116] This was essentially the same point he subsequently emphasised in 1979 in 'Whither Science Policy?'

In *The Clash of Ideas* John Maguire argued that progress since 1958 ('bourgeois modernisation') had poorly served the interests of most.[117] In 'The Case of a New Social Order' he argued that the 'rhetoric of Irish modernisation' had been shot through with references to the betterment of 'our' situation and prescriptions as to what 'we' should do to achieve this.[118] Post-1958 modernisation, Maguire maintained, was the project of an elite and it was unsurprising that admissions of its shortcomings were inadequate.[119] Yet *Administration* published copious insider criticism of the public sector. Nor did *Unequal Achievement* mince words. It became a landmark text (it was republished as a book) that set in train further critiques of inequality and policy failure in areas such as health. The IPA developed into a significant academic publisher of Irish social science texts and lived up to Barrington's aspiration for broadly based administrative scholarship.[120]

'Whither Science Policy?' struck a chord both with administrators and with academics schooled in sociological critiques of rationality and modernity. Maguire recalled the 'breezy technicism' of the June 1963 cover of *Time* that marked President Kennedy's Irish visit: 'The new and shining Ireland of brightly burnished high-technology factories: the metal fist in the shamrock glove that promised replacement of the myths of tradition with the truths of science'.[121] If this seemed to draw on Lynch it must be remembered that what Lynch sought was an engagement with science. His criticism was that the academic humanists were incapable of this except at a rhetorical level. There was no point in hurling on the ditch. Rather it was *Ireland in the Coming Times* that contained an article on the role of science and innovation which was closer to Lynch's intent in terms of historical focus, emphasis on the challenges facing universities and highlighting challenges for policy-makers.[122]

Richard Kearney's contribution to *The Clash of Ideas* called for a post-modern Irish project that would circumvent the antagonism he perceived between the traditionalist project of national revival and the modern one of consumer individualism. What was needed, he argued, was 'a hermeneutic of pluralism; a pluralist communicative ethic in contrast to the atomic individualism of liberal pluralism'.[123] A book edited by Kearney the same year, *Across the Frontiers: Ireland in the 1980s*, opened with a chapter by Barrington called 'Frontiers of the Mind'. Although its title recalled *The Crane Bag* Barrington's subject, the malaise of centralised government overloaded beyond the capacity of politicians and officials, remained true to the critique of Irish statism he championed in *Administration*. His call for regional devolution was but a hermeneutic of pluralism expressed in plain terms.

The foreword to *The Clash of Ideas* by John Kenneth Galbraith described Lynch as 'the opposite pole from the careful scholar who commutes from passive domesticity to equally passive mathematical models'; a contrast in other words with the econometric empiricism that predominated within *Ireland in the Coming Times*.[124] Whitaker's *Festschrift* focused on the policy challenges of ongoing change and future prospects for economic development. A mood of technocratic business like determination prevailed, upbeat about globalisation ('Adapt and prosper: procrastinate and decline'), the individualisation of society ('the pursuit of independence of actions and ideas') and the benefits of applying market forces to institutions. *Ireland in the Coming Times* emphasised a politics of consensus where possible but not at a cost to growth ('the optimal and ultimately the only sustainable course').[125]

In *Unequal Achievement* Rottman and O'Connell had observed that the State increasingly performed a mediating role in the market between organised interests. Top-down planning, they implied, was being superseded by a State corporatism managed through State-created institutions. A public enterprise elite was called for, but when it came to 'top-down' leadership the Civil Service was found wanting. What transpired was something more diffuse. Planning found a degree of expression through corporatist negotiation.[126] A 1999 article in *Administration* described the resultant developmental ideology of social partnership as hegemonic.[127] However, social partnership was also the fruit of the Catholic thought experiments that sought alternatives to class conflict.

Pragmatism seemed to have won out within the Irish clash of ideas about economic development. The post-1958 development project became institutionalised without many of the caveats emphasised by Lynch or Barrington. However, a number of crucial developments took place off-stage. The *Economic Development* narrative de-emphasised the broader social change and wider intellectual debates to be found in the long interplay of liberal and Catholic thought expressed in *Studies*. The liberal agendas considered in Chapter Five concerned not just questions of economics but ones about social, religious and economic reproduction through education. Here the focus was on human capital rather than public enterprise. Here the crucial secular encyclical was *Investment in Education*. This sought to shift the focus of education from cultural and religious social reproduction towards the development of human capital for economic nation-building. Here, again, Lynch was a key actor.

CHAPTER EIGHT

Thinking Inside Boxes: Main Currents, Institutional Contexts

The preceding chapters presented a series of documentaries about distinctive and influential domains of intellectual debate. This final chapter locates these main currents of Irish thought within some broader institutional and societal hinterlands. Those who wrote for *Christus Rex*, *Administration* and *Studies* were generally clerics, academics and civil servants. These long-lived journals became institutions in their own right. *The Bell* was the exception, a cottage industry sustained by sometimes censored writers. As Irish journals went it was a big success, with sales of up to 3,000 copies per issue. By 1944 academics counted for less than one per cent of its contents.[1] *The Bell* spawned a strand of subsequent journals including *The Envoy*, but these were generally short-lived.[2] To some extent *The Crane Bag* reflected the template of earlier literary academic journals such as Atlantis. Whilst in comparative terms it was a success, sales were still in the order of about 2,000 copies per issue.[3] Unlike *The Bell* and *The Crane Bag* most Irish literary journals did not find an audience outside small like-minded cliques.[4] Both journals had an immediate public intellectual impact and became canonical in retrospect. Their own writings aside, the contributions of Sean O'Faolain and Richard Kearney as local intellectual entrepreneurs loom large on the post-independence landscape. However, much that proved influential in the intellectual politics of Irish nation-building found expression in institutionally affiliated journals. *Christus Rex, Studies* and *Administration* with their ties to the Church, university and the Civil Service defined the contours of many influential debates about political, social and economic development.

In the previous chapter some parallels were drawn between the hurdles and constraints that clerics and civil servants faced in contributing to debates. The contributions of academics also depended on institutional factors. Inevitably these were circumscribed by peer norms within disciplines. Nowhere was this more the case than in sociology where, in *Christus Rex* and in the universities, a successful clerical project of institutional control emerged. With its demise Irish social science was stranded between a narrow empiricism and a vista of secular social theory that had not previously been central to Irish scholarship. With the social sciences in intellectual poor repair literary criticism became central to Irish intellectual life, bringing with it its own theoretical orthodoxies. 'Irish Studies', as distinct from studies of Irish society, flourished.

The lack of influence of social science was particularly evident in *The Crane Bag's* conception of the 'Irish Mind'. To a considerable extent this was a hangover from the core ideas of the pre-independence phase of Irish nation-building politics.[5] Articles by Stephen Brown SJ in *Studies* in 1913 on Irish nationality and national identity contested then prevalent ideological claims about the characteristics of the Irish 'race'.[6] In the language of the time the term 'race' was equated with national characteristics whereby the 'true' Briton, German or Gael could be distinguished from other groups. This was different from the other usage of 'race' to presume intrinsic attributes based on presumptions about skin colour or biological phenotype. But the core presumption was the same. Ideological nation-building was to be fostered by the presentation of ideological archetypes governing rules of national belonging. The sort of claims interrogated by Brown included the kind outlined, for example, in *The Gaelic Annual* (1907–8), which insisted that: 'The ideal Gael is a matchless athlete, sober, pure in mind, speech and deed, self possessed, self-reliant, self-respecting, loving his religion and his country with a deep and restless love, earnest in thought and effective in action.'[7]

Almost three-quarters of a century later *The Crane Bag* still inhabited the same imagined nation as *The Gaelic Annual* and the 'Irish-Ireland' nation-building project that it had exemplified. The archetypes of belonging articulated in *The Crane Bag* emphasised earnest Irish thought rather than Irish physical prowess as a means of refuting colonialist legacies.[8] In a retrospective retelling of the 'Irish Mind' debate Kearney argued that part of what he sought to contest was a colonial racist refutation of very idea that the Irish could think. Here, he identified a common cause with Deane's critique of Matthew Arnold's depictions of the fanciful Irish around the time of the 1886 Home Rule Bill. As such, the archetypes of the 'Irish Mind' deployed in *The Crane Bag* were explicitly bound up with claims of racial distinctiveness advanced by the cultural nationalists of the late nineteenth and early twentieth centuries. In *The Crane Bag* Kearney's Jungian 'Irish Mind' presented the felt sense of belonging to nation as something far beyond mere attitudes. The ties that held imagined communities together were presented as innate, psychic, mythic and mystic. From this vantage point Mark Patrick Hederman argued that because Conor Cruise O'Brien was 'deracinated' he was not to be taken seriously as a critic of the pathologies of the 'Irish Mind'.[9] Kearney's own taxonomy of Irish intellectual history was one that emphasised a number of rival hermeneutic models or 'readings' of the Irish past.[10] Amongst these, *The Crane Bag* strongly identified with the one he later described as a nationalist/republican hermeneutic and stood opposed to what he referred to as the Anglo-Irish one.

The gulf between ideological nationalism and its Irish critics resembled nothing so much as the one between atheism and religiosity. The atheist might disparage religious fervour but could not wish it out of existence. With this analogy in mind it is perhaps ironic that much of what was written by Catholic clergy about romantic nationalism in *Studies* was atheistic. Priests were disinclined to believe in a national *Geist*. The writings of Stephen Brown SJ in *Studies* in emerged as an empirical critique of then prevalent claims of romantic nationalism but were no less relevant in examining those advanced in *The Crane Bag* more than six decades later. Brown admitted the notion of a collective consciousness but insisted that there was nothing mystic about the patrimony of shared communal memories.[11] Although revolutionary nationalism often equated Irishness with Catholicism it also invested spirituality in the nation. *Kultur*, as Alfred O'Rahilly put it a year before the 1916 Rising with German militarism, Hegel and Fichte in mind, was a state product manufactured in school and camp.[12] Catholic thought emphasised keeping the state at bay from such institutions. In 1966 Francis Shaw SJ challenged what he characterised as the 'new testament' gospel of Irish nationalism. This as presented by Patrick Pearse was, he insisted, a distortion of what its 'old testament' prophets had advocated and a misrepresentation of the actual Irish past.[13]

Catholic doctrinal opposition to romantic nationalism was by no means the same as the opposition grounded in what Jeffery Prager calls the Enlightenment tradition of Irish nationalism, one he sees as rooted in Wolfe Tone and the Irish Ascendancy. Within Prager's typology the Irish-Enlightenment objective was to construct a social order characterised by autonomous individuals and independent spheres of social life in which Irish citizens could rationally influence the course of Irish affairs. This was O'Faolain's liberal project in a nutshell. This Prager contrasted with a second Gaelic-romantic archetype. Its aim was to promote a 'solidarity nation without conflict or disharmony, imbued with a vivid sense of the past in the functioning of the present'.[14] This is a fair summary of the kind of nation-building aspirations outlined by Michael Tierney in *Studies* in 1938. It captures the appeal of cultural nationalism to Catholic social thinkers and the common ground between the ideological *Gemeinschaft* of Corkery's *The Hidden Ireland* and that of the Catholic 'sociology' later promoted by *Christus Rex*.

Yet the sort of neat ideological demarcations that academic typologies propose were rarely so clear-cut on the ground. In a 1945 essay Tierney described the opening section of Corkery's *The Hidden Ireland* as almost worthy of the pen of J.G. Herder himself. But Tierney was trenchantly critical of Herder's influential belief in the nation as a kind of intermediary between God and the individual.[15] He likened the doctrine of nationalism to a powerful intoxicant, harmless and even stimulating in small doses but dangerous and addictive in large quantities.[16] There was, he argued, nothing sacred about nationalism and nothing logical in the idea of a 'national culture'. Tierney's preference was a minimalist state, one that kept its hands off culture, religion and language, in which subsidiarity prevailed. He argued that if a limited view of state power could be made to prevail then there would be ample room within its framework for 'a wide cultural, religious, linguistic and racial variety'. The sort of subsidiarity Tierney envisaged here was something akin to what would now be described as multiculturalism, albeit one that emphasised the rights of the dominant cultural group. Tierney professed an allegiance to what would now be called an ethnic identity, one he referred to as '*Kulturation*', the shared common traditions of a cultural group or community. This was different from the *Kultur* promoted by the state. The specific ethnicity he identified with was an ethno-Catholic one. In a 1954 article Tierney observed that the prohibition on a theological faculty at UCD under the 1908 University Act had helped stem conflicts with the laity and, in the context of a dominant Catholic culture, proved no barrier to Catholic intellectual influence.[17] Irish Catholic culture, he implied, had not needed the authority of the state to prevail. It had benefited from being the dominant culture within Irish society and from not being co-opted by the state.

When planning this book I conducted a straw poll of about thirty Irish social scientists, historians and academics from the humanities. I asked them who in their view had been the pre-eminent Irish public intellectual since independence. Conor Cruise O'Brien's name always came to the fore, even when those responding were not admirers. The charge in *The Crane Bag* was that he was an iconoclastic cosmopolitan detached (or deracinated) from the main currents of Irish thought. Yet O'Brien was the product of many of the influences that shaped twentieth-century Irish intellectual politics. *The Bell* published the series of articles on Catholic writers that became his first book, *Maria Cross*. O'Faolain was clearly an intellectual influence, as was Frank O'Connor. O'Brien derived much of his critique of Yeats's fascism in his 1965 essay 'Passion and Cunning' from O'Connor's 1941 one in *The Bell*.[18] However, most elements of O'Brien's cultural intellectual formation were represented within *Studies*, from the Irish Party political tradition to the affinity with Edmund Burke expressed by some clerics. In his various autobiographical writings O'Brien locates himself within the Catholic elite favouring Home Rule that *Studies* identified with. Tom Kettle was his aunt's husband.[19] O'Brien came to champion the critique of the United Ireland ideal outlined by Donal Barrington in *Studies* in 1957.[20] Barrington blamed the ill-considered nationalist propaganda produced by Seán MacBride (and cooked up by O'Brien, who then worked for him) in precipitating the 1956 IRA 'border campaign'. A decade later the critiques of Yeats by Augustine Martin, published in *Studies* to mark the fiftieth anniversary of the 1916 Rising, attacked the same targets as O'Brien's *Passion and Cunning*.

Maurice Goldring recounts a conversation in the late 1960s between Sean McEntee, the last surviving poet of the 1916 Rising, and his son-in-law O'Brien. McEntee, provoked by O'Brien's assertion that '1916 was a mistake', replied that maybe it was, but he was glad to have been a part of it, it had got him, the son of a publican, where he was today. He would never have become a minister, and been able to afford a fine house and the best schools for his children, without 1916. He reminded O'Brien that his grandfather had been a member of the Irish Parliamentary Party and that O'Brien had sprung from the old elite. 'Exactly,' O'Brien ruefully replied, 'your people pushed my people aside.'[21] This political displacement began with the rise of revolutionary nationalism after 1912. The economist and *Studies* stalwart George O'Brien recalled the shattered expectations of the Catholic bourgeois to which he had belonged. They, the members of the UCD debating society, had groomed themselves for political careers in a Home Rule parliament. The College, he recalled had many connections with the Irish Party that was expected to dominate a Home Rule Parliament sited on College Green:

> We all confidently expected in a short time we would be exercising our oratory, not in the dingy precincts of the old Physics Theatre in 86 [Earlsfort Terrace], but in the 'Old House in College Green'. It was because of this hope that we took our debates so seriously. We had heard that future prime ministers were picked because of their performances at the Oxford Union, and we believed that, when the chair of the 'L.&H.' was taken by distinguished visitors, such as John Dillon, some future Irish Prime Minister might attract influential attention if his oratory aroused sufficient admiration.'[22]

Studies formed part of the milieu that produced this putative Catholic Establishment. Catholic bourgeois conservative political instincts were amplified by the Civil War, after which Cumann na nGaedhal conservatism formed alliances with various strains of Catholic conservatism.

Catholicism affected intellectual politics in at least two distinct ways. The first concerns religiosity as a social fact and the Church as an institution. Here, as earlier chapters have suggested, there is a need to avoid the sort of reductionism that would portray Catholic conservatism as merely engaged in blocking debate. Catholic institutions constituted an intellectual field in their own right and a prism through which other social and political ideas were refracted. The second concerns the dominance of an ethno-Catholic conception of national identity, the *Kulturnation* referred to by Tierney. For many Catholic commentators, most of those considered in this book, nationalisms and their discontents provided *the* second alternative prism through which all other ideas were interrogated.

After independence the politics of ethno-Catholicism as well as Catholic ethics found expression in legislation on divorce, contraception, adoption and censorship. The Church itself possessed a 'non-decisional' form of power. As good Catholics, legislators and voters were deeply committed to expressing their faith in the laws and institutions of the country.[23] So also in Catholic-dominated UCD the dominance of Catholic thought was unsurprising. Writing in 1971, in *Church and State in Modern Ireland*, John Whyte observed that the extent of the hierarchy's influence in Irish politics was by no means easy to define. A theocratic-state model one hand, and the Church-as-just-another-interest-group model on the other, could both be ruled out as over-simplified.[24] There was therefore a need to distinguish between the Church as an interest group and Catholicism as a broader cultural and intellectual prism through which a range of ideas were refracted.

Tony Fahey offers a nuanced analysis of why the principles of Catholic social thought failed to transfer into a coherent political programme in the Irish case. Catholic social thought, as he puts it, was handed down from the Olympian heights of Rome. This remoteness was particularly notable in the Irish case:

> The central thrust of papal social teaching, which strove to find a middle way between what the Vatican saw as the extremes of *laissez-faire* capitalism and state socialism, had only limited relevance to social conditions in Ireland. Outside of the industrialised north-east of the island, capitalism had failed to take off in Ireland and the socialist movement scarcely developed beyond the embryonic stage. The main targets of attack for Catholic social teaching were thus either weak or largely absent in Ireland – or were present primarily as external conditioning circumstances.[25]

This does much to explain why the specific institutional recipe that was advanced in Europe – a vocationalist 'third-way' alternative to socialism and liberal democracy – was never a serious runner in the Irish case. However, to some extent, as debates in *Studies* suggest, Irish clerical dismissal of the vocational model had to do with distaste for the fascism that accompanied its establishment elsewhere. Arguably, the political implosion of the Blueshirts ended the possibility of a vocational state. The ambivalence towards liberal democracy expressed in *Studies* by John Horgan and Michael Tierney was typical of many right-wing European Catholic intellectuals.[26] In *Studies*, it proved not to have an enduring appeal.

The main institutional success of Catholic social thought lay with the insertion of natural law principles into the sections of the 1937 Constitution on family.[27] A key actor here was the Jesuit Edward Cahill. His 1932 book *The Framework of a Christian State* qualified him as a Catholic social theorist.[28] If anyone was well placed to advance such a theory, it was Cahill. His submission to de Valera in 1936 proposed a basic law 'which would make a definite break with the Liberal and non-Christian types of state'. de Valera was receptive to this as rhetoric. He invited Cahill to have a go at writing the preamble to the new Constitution.[29] But the break with liberal democracy that Cahill proposed did not happen. The institutional possibilities for developing Ireland in accordance with the principles of natural law had become exhausted. Increasingly, the emphasis shifted towards education. Thomism was presented as sociology, the science of society that held the answers to social problems. When it came to meeting the challenges of modernity the focus was on the development of intellectual software.

Vocationalism withered on the vine but the natural law principle of subsidiarity flourished. It was presented in various papal encyclicals as a strategy to ameliorate the worst features of capitalism while resisting state interference in civil society. This held that the state should not usurp the relationship between Catholic institutions and the family. These included Catholic schools, hospitals and welfare services. The collectivisation of such services by the state was opposed. Such institutions provided a means of transferring the faith from one generation to the next. They were also infrastructure owned and controlled by the Church. As explained by Michel Peillon: 'In defending the family unit and independence of voluntary organisations, the Church was seeking to consolidate its own authority and influence.'[30] In theory, subsidiarity meant the devolution of responsibility for welfare to the family. In practice, it was used to defend the Church's position as moral guardian from state interference. Subsidiarity, as such, was a watchword for potential demarcation disputes between Church and State but usually in areas potentially to do with religious reproduction. Conflicts were pretty much restricted to the areas of education and health. As debates in *Studies* and even *Christus Rex* illustrate, opposition to State activism in areas such as social insurance and planning was by no means absolute.

Yet liberalism also became an intrinsic component of the ideological, social and institutional processes of Irish nation-building.[31] What comes across from the analysis of the contents of *Studies* is the extent to which Catholic institutions served as conduits for liberal thought. Here, early on, Kettle represented the Catholic liberal tradition of the Irish Party. This influenced his student George O'Brien and a subsequent third generation of influential economists. Partly due to their influence a developmental project that fused an emphasis on individual social capital and state planning became *the* core Irish nation-building project from the late 1950s onward. But the flipside of liberal ideology, whereby social problems were attributed to the failings of individuals, also proved to have enduring influence.[32]

The Irish mixed economy of welfare, to paraphrase Patrick Lynch, continues to reflect the emergence during the nineteenth century of two demarcated state and religious voluntary spheres of provision.

Liberal prescriptions dominated the institutions of the former while Catholic ones presided over the latter. The pre-independence institutions of the State from the 1838 Poor Law Relief Act onwards were defined by liberal presumptions about self-reliance. After independence State systems of social insurance remained residual. In the post-Second World War era these were still pretty much defined by legislation ushered in by Lloyd George.[33] For the most part these two spheres co-existed without conflict. The political conflict in 1951 about what became known as the 'Mother and Child Scheme' was the most notable exception. In other domains and on other issues liberalism could be engaged with. To a considerable extent the demarcation evident in the welfare economy also existed in the mostly Catholic-dominated universities. Philosophy, sociology and education, each pre-occupied with the social reproduction of Catholicism, were bastions of Catholic orthodoxy. Economics was the longstanding exception. But this too preached against unwarranted interventions by the state.

Lynch's influential argument was that when it came to state planning and development there was no conflict of interests between Church and State. However, the new developmental nation-building project incubated in *Studies* and hosted by *Administration* undermined the predominant Catholic humanist focus of Irish education. Developmentalism, as promoted by T.K. Whitaker, was an ideology masquerading as psychology. When Whitaker referred to psychological factors inhibiting economic performance he meant a prevalent sense of national despondency that he had detected. Whitaker implied that planning, even if it accomplished nothing else, might engender a sense of optimism and a shift in social attitudes. If what Whitaker claimed was vague, at least attitudes could be measured. The verdict in *Administration* during the 1980s was that the psychological shift proclaimed by Whitaker had not transpired. J.J. Lee drew on Whitaker's psychological rationale for planning as a national placebo in his diagnosis. This identified a spirit-blocking fatalism allied to a prevalent 'zero sum' conception of welfare. Here was a hypothesis that understandings of social conditions affected behaviour and that a cognitive or ideological shift towards an individualist sense of agency was needed to create the conditions for economic growth, whether amongst civil servants or in Irish society as a whole.

Developmentalism fostered the expansion of education beyond the capacity of clerical control and a shift from religious reproduction towards technocracy. This was the battleground emphasised by Garvin in *Preventing the Future*. But, as debates within *Studies* emphasise, institutional Catholicism was by no means monolithic. Catholic and liberal intellectual ideas intertwined and found ideological expression in subsequent institutional developments. The technocratic planning advocated in *Administration* evolved into a system of social partnership that realised some of the prescriptions of *Quadragessimo Anno*. The developmental project became politically institutionalised as competitive corporatism.[34] The pursuit of economic growth became the defining nation-building one.

Notes

INTRODUCTION: THINKING FOR IRELAND, 1912–86

1. Denis Donoghue, 'Songs the Sirens Sing', *Studies*, 1961, 50, 403–15, p.409.
2. John M. Regan, *The Irish Counter Revolution 1921–1936* (Dublin: Gill and Macmillan, 1999) p.xvi; J.J. Lee, *Ireland: 1912–1985* (Cambridge: Cambridge University Press, 1989), p.8.
3. Eric Hobsbawm, *Age of Extremes: The Short Twentieth Century 1914–1991* (London: Michael Joseph, 1994).
4. John Whyte, *Church and State in Modern Ireland* (Dublin: Gill and Macmillan, 1971); Tom Garvin, *Preventing the Future: Why was Ireland so Poor for so Long?* (Dublin: Gill and Macmillan, 2004).
5. Maurice Goldring, *Pleasant the Scholar's Life: Irish Intellectuals and the Construction of the Nation State* (London: Serif, 1993), p.11.
6. For a reference to priests as intelligentsia (in Poland) see Liam O'Dowd, 'Intellectuals and Intelligentsia: A Sociological Introduction', in Liam O'Dowd (ed.), *On Intellectuals and Intellectual Life in Ireland: International, Comparative and Historical Contexts* (Dublin: Royal Irish Academy, 1996), p.23.
7. Stefan Collini, *Absent Minds: Intellectuals in Britain* (Oxford: Oxford University Press, 2006), p.4.
8. See John Wilson Foster, 'Strains in Irish Intellectual Life', in O'Dowd (ed.), *Intellectual Life in Ireland,* p.78.
9. Thomas Duddy, *A History of Irish Thought* (London: Routledge, 2002).
10. For an account of *The Bell* that emphasises the role of O'Donnell see Lawrence William White, 'Peadar O'Donnell, "Real Republicanism" and *The Bell*', *The Republic*, vol. 4, June 2005, pp.80–99.
11. See Richard Kearney, *Dialogues with Contemporary Continental Thinkers: Paul Ricoeur, Emmanuel Levinas, Herbert Marcuse, Stanislas Breton and Jacques Derrida: The Phenomenological Heritage* (Manchester: Manchester University Press, 1984).
12. Hederman studied in Paris with Levinas and did a Master's degree thesis on 'The Philosophical Integrity of Emmanuel Levinas' followed by a doctorate on 'The Phenomenology of Education' from the National University of Ireland.
13. L.P. Curtis, 'The Greening of Irish History' in *Eire-Ireland*, 26.2 (1994), pp.23–5.
14. D. George Boyce and Alan O'Day, '"Revisionism" and "Revisionist Controversy"', in D. George Boyce and Alan O'Day (eds), *The Making of Modern Irish History: Revisionism and the Revisionist Controversy* (London: Routledge, 1996), pp.3–4.
15. For an overview see Ciaran Brady (ed.), *Interpreting Irish History* (Dublin: Irish Academic Press, 1994).
16. Richard Kearney, *Navigations: Collected Irish Essays 1976–2006* (Dublin: Lilliput Press, 2006), p.21.
17. *Catholic Bulletin*, June 1925, cited in Roy Foster, 'History and the Irish Question', in Brady (ed.), *Interpreting Irish History*, 112–45, p.139.
18. John Wilson Foster, 'Strains in Irish Intellectual Life', p.139.
19. G.I. Smyth, *Decolonisation and Criticism: The Construction of Irish Literature* (London: Pluto, 1998).

20. Brendan Bradshaw, 'Nationalism and Historical Scholarship in Modern Ireland', in Brady (ed.), pp 191–211, p.205.
21. Stephen Howe, *Ireland and Empire: Colonial Legacies in Irish History and Culture* (Oxford: Oxford University Press, 2000), p.107.
22. James Meenan, *George O'Brien: A Biographical Memoir* (Dublin, Gill and Macmillan, 1980), p.23.
23. Cited ibid., p.163.
24. Garvin, *Preventing the Future*.
25. John Murray, 'Christian Parties in Europe', *Studies*, 1961, 50, 190–205, p.205.
26. Eileen Kane, 'The power of paradigms: social science and intellectual contributions to public discourse in Ireland', in O'Dowd (ed.), *On Intellectuals and Intellectual Life in Ireland*, 132–55, p.129.
27. Ernest Gellner, *Nations and Nationalism* (Oxford: Blackwell, 1983), p.57.
28. David Kennedy, 'Whither Northern Nationalism', *Christus Rex*, 1959, xiii.4, pp.269–83.
29. Benedict Anderson, *Imagined Communities: Reflections on the Origins and Spread of Nationalism* (London: Verso, 1983), p.15.
30. Most Rev. William Philbin, Bishop of Clonfert, 'Patriotism and Faith: Landmarks and Horizons', *Christus Rex*, 1959, xiii.4, pp.231–42.

CHAPTER ONE

TAKING THE FIFTH: THE CRANE BAG, 1977–84

1. Walentina Witoszeck and Patrick F. Sheeran, 'Irish Culture: The Desire for Transcendence', in *Cultural Contexts and Literary Idioms in Contemporary Literature,* ed. Michael Kenneally (Gerrards Cross: Colin Smythe, 1988), p.76
2. Volumes 1 to 5 were republished as a collection: page numbers in the following references are as appears in Richard Kearney (ed.), *The Crane Bag Book of Irish Studies 1977–1981* (Dublin: Blackwater Press Dublin, 1982). References from Volumes 6 to 8 include original page numbers. The complete listing of the journal is as follows:

   The Crane Bag: Art and Politics, vol. 1.1 (1977) edited by Richard Kearney
   The Crane Bag: A Sense of Nation, vol. 1.2 (1977) edited by Richard Kearney
   The Crane Bag: Mythology, vol. 2.1–2.2 (1978) edited by Richard Kearney
   The Crane Bag: The Idea of Tradition, vol. 3.1 (1979) edited by Seamus Deane
   The Crane Bag: Anglo-Irish Literature: Perspectives, vol. 3.2 (1979) edited by Seamus Deane
   The Crane Bag: Images of the Irish Woman, vol. 4.1 (1980) edited by Christine Nulty
   The Crane Bag: The Northern Issue, vol. 4.2 (1980) edited by Barre Fitzpatrick
   The Crane Bag: Minorities in Ireland (and the Church and State Debate), vol. 5.1 (1981) edited by Timothy Kearney
   The Crane Bag: Irish Language and Culture, vol. 5.2 (1981) edited by Declan Kiberd
   The Crane Bag: Joyce and the Arts in Ireland, vol. 6.1 (1981) edited by Richard Kearney
   The Crane Bag: Latin American Issue, vol. 6.2 (1982) edited by Ronan Sheehan
   The Crane Bag: Socialism and Culture, vol. 7.1 (1983) edited by Richard Kearney
   The Crane Bag: The Forum Issue, vol. 7.2 (1983) edited by Mark Patrick Hederman and Richard Kearney
   The Crane Bag: Ireland: Dependence and Independence, vol. 8.1 (1984) edited by Mark Patrick Hederman and Richard Kearney
   The Crane Bag: The Media and Popular Culture, vol. 8.2 (1984) edited by Mark Patrick Hederman and Richard Kearney

3. Tom Paulin, *Ireland and the English Crisis* (London: Bloodaxe, 1984), p.17.
4. Richard Kearney, 'Editorial', *The Crane Bag: Beyond Art and Politics*, 1.1, p.10.
5. Kearney, '*Editorial*', 1.1, p.11.
6. Richard Kearney, 'Beyond Art and Politics', 1.1, p.13.
7. Ibid., p.14.
8. Conor Cruise O'Brien 'An Unhealthy Intersection', *Irish Times*, 21 August 1975, cited in Kearney, 'Beyond Art and Politics', p.14. O'Brien's argument was more completely expounded in 'Passion and Cunning: An Essay on the Politics of W.B. Yeats' in A. Norman Jeffares and K.G.W. Cross (eds), *Excited Reverie: A Centenary Tribute to William Butler Yeats, 1965–1939* (London: Macmillan, 1965).
9. Kearney, 'Beyond Art and Politics', p.19.
10. Ibid., p.15.
11. Ibid., p.18.
12. Cyril Farrell, 'A Sense of Image (Analysis of Cinema)', 1.1, p.36.
13. Farrell, 'A Sense of Image', pp.40–1.
14. Bruce Merry, 'A Sense of Humour', 1.1, p.49.
15. Ibid., p.45.
16. Peter Mew, 'A Marxist View of Art and Politics', 1.1. p.57.
17. Mark Patrick Hederman, 'The Playboy Versus the Western World: Synge's Political Role as Artist', 1.1, p.62.
18. William Butler Yeats, *The Cutting of an Agate*, cited ibid., p.62.
19. Preface, J.M Synge, *Four Plays and the Aran Islands (*Oxford University Press, 1962) cited ibid., p.59.
20. Hederman, *Playboy Versus The Western World*, pp.63–4.
21. Seamus Deane, 'Unhappy at Home: Interview with Seamus Heaney by Seamus Deane', 1.1, p.66.
22. Ibid., p.66.
23. Ibid., p.67.
24. Ibid., p.68.
25. Ibid., p.69.
26. Ibid., p.69.
27. Ibid., p.71.
28. Francis Stuart, 'Literature and Politics', 1.1, p.78.
29. Ibid.
30. Peter Sheridan, 'The Theatre and Politics', 1.1, p.76.
31. Ibid., 1.1, p.76.
32. Richard Kearney, 'Editorial', 1.2, p.93.
33. Ibid., p.94.
34. Bryan Fanning, *Racism and Social Change in the Republic of Ireland* (Manchester: Manchester University Press), p.79.
35. Conor Cruise O'Brien 'Nationalism and the Reconquest of Ireland', 1.2, p.98.
36. Ibid., p.99.
37. Mark Patrick Hederman, 'Interview with Seamus Twomey', 1.2, p.107.
38. Ibid., p.108.
39. Ibid., p.111.
40. Mark Patrick Hederman, 'Far-off, most secret, and inviolate Rose', 1.2, p.115.
41. Ibid., p.117.
42. Ibid., p.119.
43. John Hill, 'An Archetype of the Irish Soul', 1.2, p.138.
44. Seamus Deane, 'Yeats, Ireland and Revolution', 1.2, p.147.
45. Ibid., p.139.
46. Ibid., p.140.
47. Ibid., p.140.

48. Ibid., p.144.
49. Ibid., p.146.
50. S. J. Connolly, 'Culture, Identity and Tradition', in B. Graham (ed.), *In Search of Ireland: A Cultural Geography* (London: Routledge, 1997), p.59.
51. Ibid., p.56.
52. P.J. Duffy, 'Writing Ireland: Literature in the Representation of Irish Place', in B Graham (ed.), *In Search of Ireland: A Cultural Geography* (London: Routledge, 1997), p.68.
53. Harry Levin, *The Essential James Joyce* (Penguin, 1963) quoted by Mark Patrick Hederman, 'The Dead Revisited', p.178.
54. A quotation from T.S. Eliot, Hederman, 'The Dead Revisited', p.178.
55. Augustine Martin, 'Who Stalked through the Post Office?' Reply to Seamus Deane, *Crane Bag*, 2.1, p.313.
56. Yeats's 1939 essay 'On the Boiler' was influenced by his keen interest in eugenics. Yeats had joined the Eugenics Society in London in 1936. For his biographer Terence Brown the essay was 'a gross piece of truculence'. Terence Brown, *The Life of W.B. Yeats* (London: Blackwell, 1999), p.366.
57. *The Letters of W.B. Yeats* edited by Allan Wade, London 1954, pp.850–1.
58. Richard Kearney, 'Myth and Terror', 2.2, p.273.
59. Ibid., p.273.
60. Ibid., p.275.
61. Cited ibid, p.281.
62. Richard Kearney, 'Myth as the Bearer of Possible Worlds: Interview with Paul Ricoeur', 2.2, p.260. The interview concerned Ricoeur's book *The Symbolism of Evil* (Boston: Beacon Press, 1969).
63. Ibid., p.261.
64. Ibid., p.265.
65. Ibid., pp.265–6.
66. Mark Patrick Hederman, 'The "Dead" Revisited', 2.2, p.178.
67. Seamus Deane, 'Editorial', 3.1 p.340.
68. Declan Kilberd, 'Writers in Quarantine? The Case for Irish Studies', 3.1 p.353.
69. W.C. McCormack, 'Yeats and the New Tradition', p.362.
70. Seamus Deane, 'An Example of Tradition', 3.1, p.377.
71. Ibid., p.378.
72. Joseph Stephen O'Leary, 'The Riddle of Sacrifice', 3.1, p.417.
73. Ibid., p.418.
74. Seamus Deane, 'Postscript', 3.2, p.512.
75. Ibid., p.512.
76. Ibid., p.513.
77. Ibid., p.513.
78. Ibid., p.514.
79. See the interviews with both in Stephen J. Costello's *The Irish Soul in Dialogue* (Dublin: Liffey Press, 2001).
80. During the 1970s following the Commission on the Status of Women, legislation addressed many of the lesser rights and entitlements of women. For example, following the Employment of Married Women Act (1973), married women could be employed in the Civil Service.
81. Percy Allum, 'The Irish Question', 4.2, p.643.
82. The emergence of a nationalist school of Irish history was an important component in the building of the 'Irish nation'. The 'greening of Irish history' placed heavy emphasis upon the struggle against British imperialism and landlordism, upon the dignifying of Irish Gaelic culture, and upon the positive and often heroic representation of the key figures of Irish nationalism and of

nationalist struggle in general. It served to contest anglocentric and pejorative representations of Ireland and thus foster national self-respect. Against this an alternative school of historigraphy, described by the former as revisionst, has contested many of these interpretations of the Irish past. L.P. Curtis, 'The Greening of Irish History', in *Eire-Ireland*, 26.2 (1994), pp.23–5, J. Hutchinson (1996), 'Irish Nationalism', in George D. Boyce and A. O'Day (eds), *The Making of Modern Irish History: Revisionism and the Revisionist Controversy* (London: Routledge, 1996), p.114.

83. Richard Kearney, 'The IRA's Strategy of Failure', 4.2, p.700.
84. Mark Patrick Hederman, '"*The Crane Bag*" And The North of Ireland', 4.2, p.731.
85. Cited in ibid., p.735.
86. Letter to Conor Cruise O'Brien, 20 June 1977, cited ibid., pp.735–6.
87. Ibid., p.735.
88. Ibid., p.738.
89. Mark Patrick Hederman, '"The Dead" Revisited', 2.1, pp.178–86.
90. Mark Patrick Hederman, 'Seamus Heaney: The Reluctant Poet,' 3.2, pp.481–90.
91. Hederman referred to Martin Heidegger, *Poetry, Language and Thought* (New York: 1971), p.96.
92. Conor Cruise O'Brien, 'The Protestant Minority: Within and Without', 5.1, p.788.
93. Garret FitzGerald interviewed by Barre Fitzgerald, 'The Politics of Pluralism', 5.1, p.789.
94. Deane, *Postscipt*, 3.2, p.512.
95. Gerald Goldberg, *Ireland is the Only Country ... Joyce and the Jewish Dimension*, Vol.7.1, p.7.
96. Deane, *Postscript*, 3.2, p.513.
97. See Richard Kearney, *Postnationalist Ireland: Politics, Culture and Philosophy* (London: Routledge, 1997).
98. Marie Keenan, 'Child Sexual Abuse: The Heart of the Matter', *The Furrow*, 2003, pp.597–605.
99. Olivia O'Leary and Helen Burke, *Mary Robinson: The Authorised Biography* (London: Hodder and Stoughton, 1998), p.139.
100. Lorna Siggins, *Mary Robinson: The Woman Who Took Power in the Park* (London: Mainstream, 1977), p.149.
101. For example, much of Deane's critique of Arnold and Yeats echoed writings from the 1930s. See Francis Shaw SJ 'The Celtic Twilight and W.B. Yeats', *Studies*, 1934, 23.260–69, p.265.

CHAPTER TWO

OUT OF THE MIST: *THE BELL*, 1940–45

1. Richard Bonaccorso, *Sean O'Faolain's Irish Vision* (New York: State of New York Academic Press, 1987), p.71.
2. Sean O'Faolain, 'For the Future', *The Bell*, 1940, 1.2, pp.5–6.
3. O'Faolain, 'Answer to a Criticism', *The Bell*, 1940, 1.3, pp.5–6.
4. O'Faolain, 'Attitudes', *The Bell*, 1941, 1.3, pp.5–13.
5. O'Faolain, *The Irish* (London: Penguin, 1969), p.141.
6. O'Faolain, 'On Editing a Magazine', *The Bell*, 1944, 9.2, pp.93–101.
7. O'Faolain, 'Why We Don't We See It', *The Bell*, 1942, 5.3, pp.161–4.
8. O'Faolain, 'A Challenge', *The Bell*, 1941, 1.5, pp.5–7.
9. Ibid.

10. Ibid.
11. O'Faolain, 'On Editing a Magazine', pp.93–101.
12. O'Faolain, 'Attitudes', pp.5–13.
13. Ibid.
14. O'Faolain, *King of the Beggars: A Life of Daniel O'Connell, the Irish Liberator, in a Study in the Rise of the Modern Irish Democracy 1775–1847* (Dublin: Poolbeg, 1980), p.39.
15. O'Faolain, *The Irish*, pp.101–2.
16. Ibid., p.103.
17. O'Faolain, 'Attitudes', pp.5–13.
18. Edward Fahy, 'The Boy Criminal', *The Bell*, 1940, 1.3, 41–51, p.47.
19. A Secondary Teacher, 'The Decline of English', *The Bell*, 1941, 1.4 , pp.23–32.
20. Peadar O'Donnell cited by Flann O'Brien, 'The Dance Halls', *The Bell*, 1941, 1.5, pp.44–53.
21. O'Faolain, 'The Gaelic League', *The Bell*, 1942, 4.2, pp.77–86.
22. O'Donnell, 'The Irish in Britain', *The Bell*, 1943, 6.5, pp.361–70.
23. Probationer, 'I Wanted to be a Nurse', *The Bell*, 1944, 4.2, pp.213–25.
24. O'Faolain, 'Silent Ireland', *The Bell*, 1943, 3.6, pp.457–66.
25. Recorded, 'I Live in a Slum', *The Bell*, 1940, 1.2, pp.46–9.
26. Unemployed, 'Neutral Night', *The Bell*, 1942, 4.1, 37–9.
27. O'Faolain, 'The Craft of the Short Story', *The Bell*, 1944, 7.4, pp.337–43.
28. Bill Kirwin,'The Social Policy of *The Bell*', *Administration*, 1989, 37.2, pp.99–118.
29. Robert Collis, 'The Delicacy', *The Bell*, 1941, 1.5, pp.33–9.
30. Charles Woodlock, 'Two Years in a Sanitorium', 1941, 1.5, pp.40–2.
31. Collis, ibid., p.36.
32. James Deeny, *To Cure and To Care* (Dublin: Glendale Press, 1989), p.96.
33. Unemployed. 'Off the Dole', *The Bell*, June 1941, 1.2, pp.44–6.
34. M.P.R.H, 'Illegitimate', *The Bell*, 1941, 2.3, pp.78–87.
35. O'Faolain, 'Attitudes', pp.5–13.
36. Compiled, 'Other People's Income', *The Bell*, 1943, 6.4, pp.290–8.
37. Compiled 'Other People's Incomes – 2: How to Live on £400 a year', 1943, 6.6, pp.467–72.
38. Compiled, 'Other People's Incomes – 3 A. How to Live on £300 a Year, B. How To Live on £100 A Year', 1943, 7.1, pp.55–62.
39. Taken Down, 'Slum pennies', *The Bell*, 1941, 1.4, pp.75–7.
40. Recorded, 'I Live in a Slum', *The Bell*, 1940, 1.2, pp.46–7.
41. Charles Booth, *Life and Work of the People of London* (London: Macmillan, 1902).
42. John O'Connor, *The Workhouses of Ireland: The Fate of Ireland's Poor* (Dublin: Anvil, 1995), p.52.
43. *Report of Select Committee, House of Lords, on the State of Ireland 1825*, HC 1823 (561).
44. O'Faolain, 'Silent Ireland', September 1943, 6.6, pp.457–66.
45. Maurice Harmon, *Sean O'Faolain: A Life* (London: Constable, 1994), p.66.
46. *Irish Statesman*, 5 September 1925.
47. Boanaccorso, *O'Faolain's Irish Vision*, p.51.
48. O'Faolain, *King of the Beggars*, p.23.
49. Daniel Corkery, *The Hidden Ireland: A Study of Gaelic Munster in the Eighteenth Century* (Dublin: Gill and Macmillan, 1970), p.10.
50. Ibid., pp.25–7.
51. Ibid., p.29.
52. Ibid., p.36.
53. Ibid., p.67.

54. Ibid., p.80.
55. O'Faolain, *The Great O'Neill*, p.25.
56. O'Faolain, *King of the Beggars*, p.25.
57. Ibid., p.26.
58. Ibid., p.27.
59. Ibid., p.25.
60. Ibid., p.139.
61. Corkery, *The Hidden Ireland*, p.242.
62. Ibid., p110.
63. O'Faolain, *King of the Beggars*, p.36.
64. O'Faolain, *The Irish*, pp.138–9.
65. Corkery, *The Hidden Ireland*, p.229.
66. Ibid., p.239.
67. Ibid., p.238.
68. J.N. Fahey, *The Midnight Court* (trans., 1998), www.uhb.fr/langues/CEI/midcrt.htm.
69. Frank O'Connor, 'Preface' to Brian Merriman, *The Midnight Court* (Dublin: O'Brien Press, 2000), p.13.
70. Ibid., pp.12–13.
71. Ibid., p.14.
72. Merriman, *The Midnight Court*, trans. Frank O'Connor, p.49.
73. Harmon, *O'Faolain*, pp.163–4.
74. O'Faolain 'Attitudes', pp.5–13.
75. Ibid.
76. Ibid.
77. C.B. Murphy, 'Sex, Censorship and the Church', *The Bell*, 1941, 2.2, pp.65–75.
78. Sean O'Faolain, 'The Mart of Ideas', *The Bell*, 1943, 4.3, pp.153–7.
79. Frank O'Connor, 'The Old Age of a Poet', *The Bell*, February, 1.5, pp.7–9.
80. Ibid. Also see Conor Cruise O'Brien, 'Passion and Cunning: An Essay on the Politics of W.B. Yeats', in A. Norman Jeffares and K.G.W. Cross (eds), *Excited Reverie: A Centenary Tribute to William Butler Yeats, 1965–1939* (London: Macmillan, 1965).
81. O'Connor, 'The Old Age of A Poet', pp.7–9.
82. Karl Popper, *The Open Society and its Enemies* (London: Routledge, 2002).
83. Ibid.
84. O'Faolain, 'Ireland and the Modern World', *The Bell*, 1943, 5.6, pp.423–7.
85. Peadar O'Donnell, 'Cry Jew', *The Bell*, 1943, 5.5, pp.343–6.
86. O'Faolain, 'The Stuffed Shirts', *The Bell*, 1943, 6.3, pp.181–92.
87. Ben Rogers, *A.J. Ayer: A Life* (London: Vintage 2002), p.87.
88. Ayer, A.J. 'Logical Positivism and its Legacy', in B. Magee *Men of Ideas: Dialogues with Fifteen Leading Philosophers* (Oxford: Oxford University Press, 1978), p.97.
89. Rogers, *A.J. Ayer*, p.88.
90. Rudolph Carnap, 'The Elimination Of Metaphysics Through Logical Analysis Of Language', in *Logical Positivism*, edited by A.J. Ayer (Westport, CT Greenwood, 1959), pp.60–61.
91. O'Faolain, 'Why we don't we see it', *The Bell*, 1942, 5.3, pp.161–5.
92. Ibid.
93. Harmon, *O'Faolain*, p.181.
94. Ibid., p.166.
95. Ibid., pp.198–9.
96. O'Faolain, *The Vanishing Hero* (Boston: Little, Brown, 1957).
97. Harmon, *O'Faolain*, pp.190–2.
98. Bryan Fanning, *Evil, God, the Greater Good and Rights: The Philosophical Origins of Social Problems* (New York: Edwin Mellen, 2007), pp.18–20.
99. O'Faolain, 'Shadow and Substance', *The Bell*, 6.4, 1943, pp.273–9.

100. Paul E. Sigmund, *St Thomas Aquinas on Politics and Ethics* (New York: Norton, 1988).
101. Jacques Maritain, *The Rights of Man and Natural Law* (London, Centenary Press, 1944), p.26.
102. Ibid., p.100.
103. O'Faolain, 'To What Possible Future', *The Bell*, 1942, 4.1, pp.4–9.
104. O'Faolain, 'On State Control', April 1943, 6.1, pp.1–5.
105. Harmon, *O'Faolain*, p.42.
106. Richard Kearney, 'Myth and Terror', *Crane Bag*, 2.2, p.284.
107. O'Faolain, *Viva Moi*, cited ibid.
108. Sean O'Faolain, 'A Portrait of the Artist as an Old Man', *Irish University Review*, 1976, 6.1, p.11.
109. Bonaccorso, *O'Faolain's Irish Vision*, p.16.
110. Harmon, p.114.
111. O'Faolain, 'On State Control', pp.1–5.
112. Harmon, p.209.

CHAPTER THREE

UNFINISHED REVOLUTION: NATION-BUILDING, *STUDIES*, 1912–39

1. 'Foreword: Higher Studies in Ireland', *Studies*, 1912, 1, pp.3–4.
2. James Meenan, *George O'Brien; A Biographical Memoir* (Dublin: Gill and Macmillan, 1980), p.135.
3. The *Catholic Bulletin*, an 'anti-Cosgrave journal pulsating with confessional prejudices', kept alive 'largely on anti-Masonic propaganda'. Louis McRedmond, *To the Greater Glory: A History of the Irish Jesuits* (Dublin: Gill and Macmillan, 1991), pp.236–7.
4. Joseph O'Neill, 'The Educationist', *Studies*, 1943, 32.157–160, p.158.
5. Michael Tierney, 'The Revival of the Irish Language' (symp. Gen. Richard Mulcahy, T.D., Rev. Prof. Patrick Browne, Prof. Osborn Bergin, Prof. Liam O'Briain), *Studies*, 1925, 16.1–22, p.8.
6. 'It is called a review of philosophy, letter and science but there was practically no science and very little literature. The articles are largely historical.' From a confidential editorial memorandum (1913 or 1914) which included a heading 'Why *Studies* failed', Irish Jesuit Archives, CM/Lees. D.87.
7. Edmund Power, 'Tradition in Islam', *Studies*, 1912, 1.80–86; J.M Murphy, 'Athenian Imperialism', *Studies*, 1912, 1.97–112.
8. Joseph MacMahon OFM, 'Catholic Clergy and the Social Question in Ireland 1891–1916', *Studies*, 1981, 70. 263–88, p.283.
9. Ibid., p.274.
10. Leo XIII (1891), *Rerum Novarum: On Capital and Labour*, http://www.vatican.va.
11. Aquinas, 'Expositio super Librum Boethii de Trinitate', in Timothy McDermott (ed.), *Thomas Aquinas: Selected Philosophical Writings* (Oxford: Oxford University Press, 1993), p.16.
12. Aristolte, *Metaphysics*, 15.1039b20–4.
13. Aquinas, 'de Trinitate', in McDermott, *Aquinas: Selected Philosophical Writings*, p.17.
14. Quoted from 'The Catholic Social League', *Irish Monthly*, XLV, p.191. See MacMahon, *Catholic Clergy and the Social Question in Ireland*, p.284.
15. Peter Finlay SJ, 'Divorce in the Irish Free State', *Studies*, 1924, 13.49, 352–362, p.353.

16. J.J. Lee, *Ireland 1912–1985: Politics and Society* (Cambridge: Cambridge University Press, 1989), p.158.
17. Matt, xix.4, cited ibid., p.354.
18. Ibid., p.361.
19. Archbishop Byrne of Dublin in 1923. See Lee, *Ireland 1912–1985*, pp.158–9.
20. John J. Horgan, 'Prohibition in Practice', *Studies*, 1925, 14.545–558.
21. Gabriel Daly, Foreword to George Tyrell, *Medievalism* (Tunbridge Wells: Burns and Oates, 1994), pp.7–19.
22. Tyrell, *Medievalism*, p.45.
23. Ibid., p.108.
24. Letter to Alfred Loisy 12 July 1903, cited in Nicholas Sagovesky, *Between Two Worlds: George Tyrell's Relationship to the Thought of Matthew Arnold* (Cambridge: Cambridge University Press, 1983), p.47.
25. George Tyrell, *Christianity at the Crossroads*, p.xv, cited by Sagovesky, p.51.
26. A.J. O'Rahilly, 'The Meaning of Evolution', *Studies*, 1912, 1, 32–51.
27. Ibid., p.32.
28. Ibid., p.51.
29. O'Rahilly, 'The Gospel of the Superman', *Studies*, 1914, 3.381–403.
30. Ibid., pp.384–5.
31. Ibid., pp.389.
32. Ibid., p.390.
33. A. O'Rahilly, 'The Influence of German Philosophy', *Studies*, 1915, 4, 563–77, p.475.
34. Ibid., p.577.
35. As summarised by Professor Cleary: 'At his death he left behind him one two original works that had attained to hard covers – *The Open Secret of Ireland*, a brilliant pot-boiler and that collection of supremely good essays, *The Day's Burden*, in which, with one exception, the best of him is to be found. A.E. Cleary, 'Thomas Kettle', *Studies*, 1916, 5, 76–83, p.504.
36. Ibid., p.505.
37. Ibid., p.507.
38. Tom Kettle, 'The Future of Private Property', *Studies*, 1912, 1.2, p.147.
39. Ibid., pp.148–9.
40. Ibid., pp.147–8.
41. Henry Somerville, 'The Variations of Socialism', *Studies*, 1912, 2, 369–83.
42. Ibid., pp. 382–3.
43. Somerville, 'Socialism and the War', *Studies*, 1914, 3, 419–36.
44. Ibid., p.427.
45. Somerville, 'Labour Disorders in War Time', *Studies*, 1915, 4, 589–600, p.595.
46. Ibid., p.598.
47. C.F. Henry, Review of C. Day SJ, *Catholic Democracy, Individualism and Socialism* (London: Health, Cranton and Ouesley, 1914), *Studies*, 1914, 3.12, p.543.
48. Rev. J. Kelleher, 'Priests and Social Action in Ireland' *Studies*, 4, 69–183.
49. Somerville, 'Labour Disorders in Time of War', *Studies, 1915*, 4, 589–600, p.593.
50. Peter Finlay SJ, 'Socialism and Catholic Teaching', *Studies*, 1919, 8, 352–66.
51. Somerville, 'The Economics of Nationalisation', *Studies*, 1920, 9, 20–9, p.25.
52. Lambert McKenna SJ, 'Character and Development of Post-War Socialism', *Studies*, 1920, 9, 177–94.
53. McKenna, 'The Bolsheviks', *Studies*, 1921, 10, 218–39.
54. Ibid., 238.
55. Violet Connolly, 'Two Months in Soviet Russia', *Studies*, 1926, 17, 637–48.
56. Somerville, 'Reflections After Visiting Russia', *Studies,* 1929, 18.72, 556–68, p.561.
57. John Busteed, 'Soviet Russia', *Studies,* 1932, 21, 531–48.

58. Ibid., p.557.
59. Ibid., pp.566–7.
60. Somerville, 'An Alternative to Capitalism' (symp.-comments by Belloc, Canavan, Kelleher, O'Brien, Ryan), *Studies*, 1925, 13, 521–9, p.523.
61. Ibid., p.523.
62. For instance, a 1920 article proposed profits haring schemes and co-operative ownership as the most effective obstacle to socialism. See John A. Ryan, 'The Democratic Transformation of Industry', *Studies*, 1920, 9, 383–97, p.393.
63. Ryan, symposium comment on Somerville, *An Alternative to Capitalism*, pp.532–3.
64. George O'Brien, ibid., pp.540–2.
65. Rev. J. Kelleher, ibid., pp.538–9.
66. Hilaire Belloc, ibid. pp.533–4.
67. George O'Brien, 'Religion and Capitalism', *Studies*, 15, 217–30, p.220–2.
68. Ibid., p.229.
69. Somerville, 'The '*Rerum Novarum*' after Forty Years', *Studies*, 1931 20.70, 1–12, pp.11–12.
70. John Busteed, World Economic Crisis and '*Rerum Novarum*', *Studies*, 1931, 20.70, 13–23, p.21.
71. Ibid., p.23.
72. Busteed, 'Soviet Russia', *Studies*, 1932, 21, 531–48, p.541.
73. Ibid., p.451.
74. Ibid., p.649.
75. C.L. Ronayne, 'Italian Catholics and the Economic Problem' *Studies*, 1923, 12, 106–19.
76. Virginia M. Crawford, 'The Rise of Fascism and What it Stands For', *Studies*, 1923, 12, 539–52, p.547.
77. Corcoran, 'Newman's Ideals and Irish Realities', *Studies*, 1912, 1, 114–29.
78. Ibid., p.122.
79. Ibid., p.123.
80. Corcoran, 'Social Work and Irish Universities', *Studies*, 1912, 1, 534–47.
81. Ibid., p.534.
82. Ibid., p.555.
83. The certainties of Catholic social thought grounded in conceptions of natural law, Corcoran argued, stood upon firmer ground and, as such, had more to offer applied social science. As he put it: 'Security in fixed norms of action gives immense leverage in moving the mountainous difficulties of applied sociology: it would be foolish to set it aside', p.545.
84. Ibid., p.545.
85. Ibid., p.548.
86. Henry Somerville, 'A Catholic Labour College', *Studies*, 1921, 10.39, pp.391–400.
87. Ibid., 397–400.
88. Ibid., p.391.
89. Ibid., p.391.
90. T.W. Adorno, E. Frenkel-Brunswick. D.J. Levinson and R.H. Sanforo, *The Authoritarian Personality* (New York: Harper and Row, 1950); Herbert Marcuse, *One-Dimensional Man* (London: Abacus, 1964).
91. William E. Kellicott, *The Social Direction of Human Evolution*, cited in Somerville, 'A Catholic Labour College', p.392.
92. For example, Corcoran quoted Pius IX from 1863 on the ultimate subordination of physics to metaphysics and of reason to faith: 'Trustworthy development of the Sciences, their exposition, their utilisation, their verification, cannot be secured if the limited light of human reason ... were not to hold in very great reference (as is fitting) the unerring and uncreated light of Divine Intelligence.'

He also quoted a 1854 letter from Pius IX to Irish bishops on the occasion of the foundation of the Catholic University of Ireland: 'Let the most watchful care be exerted in providing that our Divine Religion shall be the soul of the entire academic education.' Corcoran also quoted Leo XIII from 1878 urging educators to 'bring into full conformity with the Catholic faith all that is taught in literature, in sciences and above all in philosophy'. Cited in Timothy Corcoran SJ, 'The Catholic Philosophy of Education', *Studies*, 1930, 19, 200–210.

93. Arthur Little SJ, 'The Present Crisis of Intelligence', *Studies*, 1937, 26, 89–100, pp.89–107.
94. Ibid., p.105.
95. Little, 'The Case for Philosophy in Secondary Education (symp.– comment by Browne, Dillon, Leen, O'Mahoney, O'Rahilly, Tierney)', *Studies*, 1938, 27, 529–55.
96. Ibid., pp.542–43.
97. Ibid., p.545.
98. Tierney, 'The Revival', p.549.
99. Corcoran, 'Industrial Education – American or German', *Studies*, 1919, 8, 268–78, p.278.
100. Dun Carirn, 'The Argument from Irish History', *Studies*, 1918, 7, 31, 545–51, p.551.
101. Æ (George Russell), 'Lessons of Revolution', *Studies*, 1923, 12, 1–6.
102. Gustav Lehmacher SJ, 'Some thoughts on an Irish Literary language (symp. comment by Bergin, O'Connell, O'Maille, O'Rahilly, Sheehan), *Studies*, 1923, 12, 26–44.
103. Lehmacher, 'Some Thoughts', pp.28–9.
104. Sheehan, response to Lehmacher, ibid., p.23.
105. Bergin, response to Lehmacher, ibid., p.35.
106. O'Rahilly, response to Lehmacher, p.39.
107. O'Donnell, response to Lehmacher, ibid., p.36.
108. Michael Tierney, 'The Revival of the Irish Language (symp. Gen. Richard Mulcahy, TD Rev. Prof. Patrick Browne, Prof. Osborn Bergin, Prof. Liam O'Brian), *Studies,* 1927, 16, 1–22, p.1.
109. Ibid., p.1.
110. Mulcahy, p.20.
111. Bergin, p.11.
112. Mulcahy, p.13.
113. Mulcahy p.15.
114. Ibid., p.13.
115. Tierney, 'Politics and Culture: Daniel O'Connell and the Gaelic Past (symp.– comment by Binchy, Murphy, O'Faolain, Ryan)', *Studies*, 1938, 27.107, 353–81, p.353.
116. Ibid., p.354.
117. Ibid., p.355.
118. Ibid., p.357.
119. Ibid., p.358.
120. Ibid., p.361.
121. Ibid., p.359.
122. Ibid., p.361.
123. Ibid., p.368.
124. Ibid., p.368.
125. Ibid., pp.370–1.
126. Ibid., p.373.
127. Ibid., p.379.

128. William Boyle, 'Some Types of Irish Character', *Studies*, 1912, 1, 221–35, p.235.
129. Francis Shaw SJ 'The Celtic Twilight and W.B Yeats', *Studies*, 1934, 23, 260–9, p.265.
130. In 1934 the Censorship of Publications Board described O'Faolain's novel *A Bird Alone* as 'an immoral and dangerous book, the more so because there was some good writing in it'. See Peter Martin, *Censorship in the Two Irelands: 1922–1939* (Dublin: Irish Academic Press, 2006), pp.203–5.
131. P.A. Pearse, 'Some Aspects of Irish Literature', *Studies*, 1913, 2, 810–22.
132. Ibid., p.818.
133. X.Z, 'Poets of the Insurrection I: Thomas MacDonagh', *Studies*, 1916, 5, 179–86. p.182.
134. Peter McBrien, 'Poets of the Insurrection III: Joseph Plunkett', *Studies*, 1916, 5.536–47.
135. Padric Gregory, 'Poets of the Insurrection IV: John F. MacEntee, *Studies*, 1917, 6, 70–9.
136. Ibid., p.343.
137. Ibid., p.346.
138. Cleary, *Thomas Kettle*, p.515.
139. Henry V. Gill SJ, 'The Fate of the Irish Flag at Ypres', *Studies*, 1919, 8, 119–28.
140. John Ryan, 'The Cinema Peril', *Studies*, 1918, 7, 112–26.
141. Ibid., p.112.
142. Ibid., p.119.
143. Ibid., p.116.
144. Named for former Postmaster General Will H. Hays. He organised a Committee of Public Organisations influenced heavily by Catholic groups. Charles A. McMahon, 'The American Public and the Motion Picture', *Studies*, 1926, 15, 47–65.
145. Stephen Brown SJ' Irish Fiction for Boys,' *Studies*, 1918, 7, 665–70.
146. Ibid., p.666.
147. Ibid., p.665.
148. Brown, 'What is a Nation', *Studies*, 1913, 1, 496–510, Stephen. J. Brown SJ, 'The Question of Irish Nationality', *Studies*, 1913, 1, 634–55.
149. Tom Kettle, *The Open Secret of Ireland* (Ham-Smith, 1912), p.170, cited in Brown, 'What is a Nation', p.496.
150. Original italics, Brown, 'What is a Nation', p.499.
151. Ibid., p.498.
152. Bryan Fanning, *Racism and Social Change in the Republic of Ireland* (Manchester: Manchester University Press, 2002), p.10.
153. Brown, 'What is a Nation', p.503.
154. Ibid., p.503.
155. Sir John Seeley, *The Expansion of England*, p.261, cited ibid., p.504.
156. Ibid., p.505.
157. L. Legrand, *L'Idée de Patri*, p.58, cited in Brown, 'What is a Nation', p.505.
158. Ibid., p.505.
159. Brown, 'What is a Nation', p.509.
160. C.H. O'Hehir, 'The Problem of Nationality', *Studies*, 1913, 2, 175–84.
161. Ibid., p.177.
162. Ibid., p.178.
163. Ibid., p.181.
164. C.J. O'Hehir, 'Class and Nationality', *Studies*, 1914, 3, 677–84.
165. Ibid., p.679.
166. Brown, 'Recent Studies in Nationality', *Studies*, 1920, 9, 20–464.
167. Ibid., pp.458–9.

168. Ibid., p.463.
169. See p.226, John J. Horgan, 'Precepts and Practices: 1914–1919', *Studies*, 1918, 7, 220–6.
170. M.F. Fagan, SJ, 'Kultur and Our Need of It', *Studies*, 1915, 4, 169–84.
171. Ibid., p.214.
172. A considerable number of the then Irish Jesuits had studied with German members of the order in The Netherlands. Fergus O'Donoghue SJ to author.
173. Hugh Ryan, 'German High Grade Industries: A Lesson for Ireland', *Studies*, 1915, 4, 333–48.
174. O'Rahilly, 'The Influence of German Philosophy', *Studies*, 1915, 4, 563–77.
175. Ibid., p.567.
176. Cited ibid., p.568.
177. Ibid., p.568.
178. O' Rahilly, 'Ideals at Stake', *Studies*, 1915, 4, 16–33, p.26.
179. Corcoran, 'State Monopoly in French Education', *Studies*, 1915, 4, 33–48.
180. Brown,, 'An International Enquiry concerning Nationalism', *Studies*, 1923, 12, 306–13, p.313.
181. Minister of Education 1926–32; see Garvin, *Preventing the Future*, p.134.
182. John. M. O'Sullivan, 'Nationality as a Claim to Sovereignty', *Studies*, 14, 633–47, p.634.
183. Prof. Daniel A. Binchy, 'Adolf Hitler', *Studies*, 1933, 22, 29–47.
184. Ibid., pp.37–8.
185. Ibid., p.39.
186. Ibid., p.41.
187. Bewley enthused about the Nazi project and used his position to discriminate against Jews, to the extent of refusing to pass visas to Ireland, approved by his own government, to a Jewish family in Berlin during *Kristallnacht*. Dermot Keogh, *Jews in Twentieth Century Ireland* (Cork: Cork University Press, 1998) p.139.
188. Rev. Prof. Denis O'Keefe, 'The Nazi Movement in Germany', *Studies*, 1938, 27, 1–12, p.5.
189. Ibid., p.6.
190. R.W. Ditchburn, 'The Refugee Problem', *Studies*, 1939, 28, 274–92, pp.290–2.
191. Martin Tierney (ed.), *A Classicist's Outlook: Michael Tierney 1894–1975, A Life and Essays* (Dublin: Martin Tierney, 2002), p.18.
192. T.W.T. Dillon, 'The Refugee Problem and Ireland', *Studies*, 1939, 28, 402–14, p.405.
193. Germanus, 'The Present Position of Catholics in Germany', *Studies*, 1935, 24, 189–204, pp.197–8.
194. Dillon, 'The Refugee Problem', pp.402–14.
195. Fanning, *Racism and Social Change*, pp.76–9.
196. Dillon, 'The Refugee Problem', pp.409–410.
197. Ibid., p.405.
198. For example, in Britain G.K. Chesterton mobilised Catholic opposition against eugenics. Michael Burleigh, *The Third Reich: A New History* (London: Pan, 2000), p.347.
199. Lambert McKenna SJ 'The Housing Problem in Dublin', *Studies*, 1919, 8, 279–95, p.281.
200. Ibid., p.282.
201. Keogh, *Jews in Twentieth Century Ireland*, p.92.
202. Edward Cahill SJ, *Framework of a Christian State* (Dublin: Gill & Son, 1932), p.195; McKenna 'The Bolshevik in Munich', *Studies*, 1923, 12, 361–77.
203. Cahill, *Framework*, pp.205–6.

204. McKenna, 'The Bolshevik Revolution in Munich', *Studies*, 12, 360–77, p.363.
205. A.D.M., 'Review of I. Cohen, *Jewish Life in Modern Times* (London: Methuen, 1914)' *Studies*, 1914, 3, 555–6.
206. Patrick J. Gannon SJ, 'In the Catacombs of Belfast' *Studies*, 1922, 11, 279–95, p.280.
207. James Winder Good, 'Partition in Practice', *Studies*, 1922, 11, 249–78.
208. P.S. O'Hegarty, 'Arthur Griffith: His Politics', *Studies*, 1922, 11, 349–87, p.335.
209. O'Rahilly, 'Is the Common Citizenship?' *Studies*, 1922, 11, 1–12, pp.2–3.
210. Original italics, ibid., p.7.
211. O'Rahilly, 'Allegiance and the Crown', *Studies*, 1922, 11, 168–85, p.169.
212. John J. Horgan, 'The problem of Government',(sypm.- comment by Comyn, Cosgrave, Douglas, Tierney), *Studies*, 1933, 22, 537–60, p.545.
213. Ibid., p.552.
214. The United Ireland Party formed in 1932 out of a merger of Cumann na nGeadheal and the Centre Party under General Eoin O'Duffy, leader of the Blueshirts. Tierney had been a Cumann na nGeadheal TD and was subsequently one of the founders of Fine Gael. Tierney resigned his position on the party executive in 1933 at the apex of O'Duffy's rhetorical fascism. See Maurice Manning, *James Dillon: A Biography* (Dublin: Wolfhound, 2000), pp.95–7.
215. Tierney, 'The Problem of Government (symp.comment), p.558.
216. Horgan, 'The Problem of Government', p.559.
217. Tierney, 'Ireland and the Reform of Democracy', *Studies,* 1934, 23.369–382, p.369
218. Ibid., pp.372–4
219. Ibid., p.374
220. Ibid., pp.380–1
221. Michael Tierney, 'Partition and a Policy of National Unity' *Studies*, 1935, 24, 1–12, p.5
222. Ibid., p.7
223. Ibid., p.13
224. Response by Rev Arthur H. Ryan from Queens University Belfast, a self-described 'northern nationalist.' Ibid, p.14
225. Ibid., p.20
226. Ibid., pp.22–24
227. O'Rahilly, 'The Constitution and the Senate' *Studies,* 1936, 25, 1–19, p.8
228. Ibid., pp.7–8
229. Ibid., p.4
230. Ibid., p.16
231. Ibid., pp.10–12
232. The Jesuits made a submission in October 1936 when the new Constitution was being drawn up. It came about at the instigation of Edward Cahill SJ who 'on his own initiative decided to offer the President some thoughts on a basic law 'which would make a definite break with the Liberal and non-Christian types of state' which had been 'forced on us by a foreign power'. de Valera encouraged Cahill to submit such ideas and in particular have a go at a phrasing a preamble. See Finola Kennedy, 'The Priests, the family and the Irish Constitution', *Studies,* 1998, 87, 353–64
233. Northman, 'Present position of Catholics in Northern Ireland, *Studies* 1936, 25,581–596, p.584
234. Ibid., 589–593
235. Tierney, 'The Problem of Partition', *Studies*, 1938, 28. 637–646
236. Ibid., p.641
237. Ibid., p.641

238. Ibid., p.643
239. Ibid., pp.645–646.
240. Colonel J.J. O'Connell, 'Can Ireland Remain Neutral in War?' *Studies*, 1938, 28.647–655, p.655. See also O'Connell, 'The Vulnerability of Ireland in War', *Studies* 1938,27. 125–135
241. Manning, *Dillon*, p.83
242. Horgan was a fellow founding member of Fine Gael. Ibid, p.83
243. 'Votes for Youth' began by noting that there were three stages of response to any reform; ridicule, indignation, and acquiescence, noting that the third of these stages had only been recently reached in the cases of women's suffrage and Home Rule' Arthur E. Cleary, 'Votes for Youth', *Studies*, 1915, 4.279–285, p.279
244. George Russell (Æ), 'The self-supporting community', *Studies*, 1918, 7.301–30
245. Alice Stopford Green, 'Thoughts on Irish Industries', *Studies*, 1918, 7.385–399
246. Ibid., p.397
247. Cited ibid., p.397
248. Dara McCormack, 'Policy Making in a Small Open Economy' in J.W. Hagan (ed.) *The Economy of Ireland: Policy and Performance* (Dublin: Irish Management Institute, 1984), p.17
249. Bernard McCartan, 'A New Currency for the Free State' (symp. comment by Bastable, Findlay, Leet, Smith-Gordon) *Studies*, 12.177–201
250. Lionel Smith-Gordon, ibid., p.195
251. F.L. Leet, ibid., p.198
252. C.H. Oldham, 'After the Fiscal Inquiry Report', *Studies*, 1924, 13.1–13, p.1
253. Ibid., p.6
254. George O'Brien, 'The Budget', *Studies*, 1925, 14, 117–191, p.188
255. Denis Gwynn, 'The Wastefulness of French Thrift', *Studies*, 1926, 15, 65–77, p.66
256. Richard S. Devane SJ, 'Suggested Tariff on Imported Newspapers and Magazines (symp. McInerney, Tierney, Hooper, Tomas F. O'Rahilly) *Studies*, 1927, 16, 545–563
257. Ibid., p.546
258. Ibid., p.552
259. Ibid., p.554
260. Ibid., pp.553–6
261. Ibid., p.561
262. Ibid., pp558–9
263. Ibid., p.556.
264. Ibid., p.557.
265. John Busteed, 'Foreign Trade and National Policy', *Studies*, 1927, 16, 69–85, p.85.
266. Robert Skidelsky, *John Maynard Keynes: The Economist as Saviour 1920–1937* (London: Macmillan, 1992), p.479.
267. For example, O'Brien lectured on Keynes's *General Theory* in its year of publication. See Meenan, *George O'Brien*, p.167.
268. John Maynard Keynes, 'National Self-Sufficiency', *Studies*, 1933, 22, 176–88, p.183.
269. Ibid., p.186.
270. Ibid., p.187.
271. Ibid., p.190.
272. Skidelsky, *Economist as Saviour*, p.479.
273. Keynes, *National Self-Sufficiency*, p.189.
274. Ibid., p.193.
275. Skidelsky, *Economist as Saviour*, p.479.
276. Lee, *Ireland 1912–1985*, p.8.

277. Corcoran, '*Industrial Education – American or German*, p.278.
278. Tierney, *Politics and Culture*, p.379.
279. Finin O'Driscoll, 'Social Catholicism and the Social Question in Independent Ireland: The Challenge to the Fiscal System', in Mike Cronin and John M. Regan, *Ireland: The Politics of Independence 1922–49* (London: Macmillan, 2000), p.130.
280. Tierney's 43rd contribution to *Studies* in 1944 was his first to address Thomist ideas. It had nothing to say on corporatism or vocationalism. 'M. Maritain on Education', *Studies*, 1944, 33, 21–30.

CHAPTER FOUR

DISENCHANTED LAND: *CHRISTUS REX* AND IRISH SOCIOLOGY, 1947–70

1. In the following wording: 'The *Nihil Obstat* and *Imprimatur* are a declaration that a book or periodical is considered to be free from doctrinal or moral error. This declaration does not imply approval of, or agreement with the contents, opinions or statements expressed.'
2. Brian Conway, 'Foreigners, Faith and Fatherland: The Historical Origins, Development and Present Status of Irish Sociology', *Sociological Origins*, 5.1.3, 2006, 5–36, p.13.
3. Monsignor J.M. Sullivan, 'Jeremiah Newman – A Tribute', *Christus Rex*, 1970, xxvi.1, p.3. Also see Perry Share and Hilary Tovey, *A Sociology of Ireland* (Dublin: Gill and Macmillan, 2000), p.29.
4. Rev. Robert Prendergast, 'Foundations of Social Justice in Ireland', *Christus Rex*, 1959, xiii.4, 243–59.
5. Max Weber, 'Science as A Vocation', in *Max Weber: Essays in Sociology*, ed. H.H. Gerth and C. Wright Mills (London Routledge, 1948).
6. Weber cited by Lawrence Scaff, *Fleeing the Iron Cage: Culture, Politics and Modernity in the Thought of Max Weber* (Berkeley: University of California Press, 1989), pp.225–6.
7. George O'Brien, 'Religion and Capitalism', *Studies*, 1926, 15, 217–30.
8. Editorial, *Christus Rex*, 1963, xvii.1, 1–11.
9. Rev. Robert Prendergast, 'Foundations of Social Justice in Ireland', *Christus Rex*, 1959, xiii.4, 243–59, p.255.
10. C. McCarthy, 'The Christian and the Welfare State', *Christus Rex*, 1967, xxxi.3, 224–9.
11. Anonymous, Review of Rev. M.J. Buckley, *Morality and the Homosexual* (London: Sands and Co.), *Christus Rex*, xv.2, 150–2.
12. Rev. D. O'Connell, 'The responsibility of the Viewer', *Christus Rex*, 1962, xvi.2, 89–95.
13. See 'The Opinions of the Citizen as Recorded by Ita Mangan', *Christus Rex*, xvi.2, 1962, 16.2, 96–111.
14. Rev. C.B. Daly, 'Christus Rex Society', *Christus Rex*, 1947, i.1, 27–33.
15. Micheal J. Browne, 'Why Catholic Priests should Concern Themselves with Social and Economic Questions', *Christus Rex*, 1947, i.1, 3–9.
16. Rev. P. McKevitt, 'The Study Circle', *Christus Rex*, 1947, i. 2, 34–9, p.36.
17. Ibid.
18. Cork City Deanery Group of Christus Rex Society, 'Youth Clubs in Cork City: Spring 1947', *Christus Rex*, i.1, p.37.
19. Noreen Kearney, 'Social Work Training: Its Origins and Growth', in Noreen Kearney and Caroline Skehill (eds), *Social Work in Ireland: Historical Perspectives* (Dublin: Institute of Public Administration, 2005), p.27.

20. Agnes McGuire, 'Some Careers in Social Work', *Christus Rex*, 1948, ii.iii, 33–45, p.33.
21. For an account of contemporaneous Catholic social work, as developed by Mother Cabrini in the United States, see Richard Sennett, *Respect: The Formation of Character in an Age of Inequality* (London: Penguin, 2003), p.139.
22. Augustine, *City of God*, xix.14.
23. Olive Mary Garrigan, 'So you are Going to England: An Open Letter to Irish Girls About to Emigrate', *Christus Rex*, 1949, iii.3, 47–57, p.50.
24. The survey of priests sought to calculate the numbers of emigrants from the locality, their age and sex, their motives for emigrating, the type of employment they abandoned, if any, the type of employment they secured after emigration and the suitability of their accommodation. It also sought information on their 'religious and moral stability'. Waterford and Lismore Branch of Christus Rex Society, 'Report on Emigration', *Christus Rex*, 1949, iii.1, 33–49.
25. Rev. Robert Prendergast, 'Foundations of Social Justice in Ireland', *Christus Rex*, 1959, xiii.4, 243–59, p.246.
26. Rev. Daniel Duffy, 'The Emigration Issue', *Christus Rex*, 1961, xv.1, 7–15.
27. Ibid., p.15.
28. From a speech given on 25 October 1960 to the Dublin Chamber of Commerce. Sean F. Lemass, 'Social Factors and Emigration', *Christus Rex*, 1961, xv.1, 16–19.
29. Ibid., p.16.
30. Ibid., p.18.
31. Ibid., p.20.
32. Rev. Terence Cosgrave, 'Retrospect of Thirty Years of Irish Freedom', *Christus Rex*, 1958, xiii.4, 259–68, p.267.
33. Eoin McCarthy, 'Some Changes We Need', *Christus Rex*, 1961, xv.2, 126–37, p.136.
34. Ibid., p.137.
35. D.A. Hegarty, 'Ireland in a Changing World', *Christus Rex*, 1961, xv.2, 117–25.
36. Desmond Fennell, 'Refugees From Society', *Christus Rex*, 1961, xv.2, 103–16, p.108.
37. Ibid., p.109.
38. T. Honey, 'The Layman in the Church', *Christus Rex*, 1966, 20.1, 52–70.
39. For example, D.A. Hegarty, 'Ireland in a Changing World', *Christus Rex*, 1961, 15.2, 117–25.
40. M.J. Flanagan, Psychological and Sociological Aspects of Work', *Christus Rex*, 1964, 17.2, 114–20.
41. Rev. Jeremiah Newman, 'Industrial Relations in Ireland', *Christus Rex*, 1966, 20.3, 173–94.
42. C. McCarthy, 'Trade Unions and Christianity, *Christus Rex*, 1966, 20.3, 194–7.
43. Anthony Burgess, *The Wanting Seed* (London Heinemann, 1962).
44. Jeremiah Newman, 'Vocations in Ireland: 1966', *Christus Rex*, 1967, xxi.2, 105–22.
45. Rev. John Kelleher, 'Catholic Rural Action', *Studies*, 1947, i.4, 421–36, p.421.
46. Ibid., pp.431–2.
47. Feirmeoir, 'Agriculture in a Vocationalist Order of Society', *Christus Rex*, 1956, xi.1, 46–62, p.60.
48. Ibid., p.47.
48. Ibid., p.49.
49. Ibid., p.47.
50. Ibid., p.57.
51. Rev. D Duffy, 'Rural Organisation and the Priest', *Christus Rex*, 1956, x.1, 9–24.

52. Lt.-General M.J. Costello, 'Co-operation in Rural Ireland', *Christus Rex*, 1956, x.1, 3–13.
53. Louis Smith, 'The National Farmers Association', *Christus Rex*, 1956, x.1, 14–19.
54. The issue contained a digest of social documents setting out Catholic principles for rural life. This included an extract from an Address of Pope Pius XII to the Italian League of Farmers, November 1946, as translated and set out in the *Muintir na Tire Official Handbook*, 1947.
55. Rev. Jeremiah Newman, 'Report on Limerick Rural Survey', *Christus Rex*, 1961, xv.1, 20–2.
56. Ibid., p.19.
57. Sean F. Lemass, 'Social Factors and Emigration', *Christus Rex*, 1961, xv.1, 16–19.
58. T.M. O'Connor Diversifying Employment and Social Opportunities in Rural Areas,' *Christus Rex*, 1970, xxiii.1, 49–65.
59. Fr. Harry Bohan, 'The Social and Religious Aspects of Industrialisation', *Christus Rex*, 1970, xxiv.4, p.243.
60. John Brady SJ, 'The Other Ireland', *Christus Rex*, 1970, xxiv.4, 235–42.
61. Rev. Liam Ryan, 'Social Dynamite: A Study of Early School Leavers', *Christus Rex*, 1967, xxi.1, 7–44.
62. Ryan, 'University Education and Social Class in Ireland', *Christus Rex*, 1966, xxii.2, 118–24.
63. P. O hUiginn and N. Meagher, 'Urbanism in Ireland', *Christus Rex*, 1966, xx.2, 150–9.
64. As explained by Ryan, these schools, which operated in Cork, Limerick and Waterford, provided a continuation course for the children who would otherwise finish their formal education at primary level. The children were required to attend one day a week up to the age of 16.
65. Quoted from *Irish Times,* 12 September 1966.
66. Cited from *Early Leaving: Report of the Central Advisory Council for Education* (United Kingdom, 1954), p.56.
67. Ryan, *Social Dynamite*, p.40.
68. She ended her article with a list of ten accredited social work institutions from the National Society, such as the Society for the Prevention of Cruelty to Children to Public Heath Visitors, whose roles overlapped in their dealings with individual families.
69. McGuire, *Some Careers in Social Work*, p.44.
70. W.F. Phillips, Review of *Work* by Stefan Cardinal Wyszynski (Dublin: Sceptre, 1962), *Christus Rex*, 1962, xv.3, p.222.
71. P.M. Quinlan, Review of L.P. Smith, *The Evolution of Agricultural Co-operation* (Oxford: Basil Blackwell), *Christus Rex*, 1963, xvii.1, 85–6.
72. Rev. Jeremiah Newman, Review of Joseph H. Fischer, *Sociology* (Chicago: University of Chicago Press, 1958), *Christus Rex*, 1959, xiii.3, 220–1.
73. Rev. Jeremiah Newman, Review of Eva J. Ross, *Basic Sociology* (Milwaukee, WI: Bruce Publishing Company, 1960), *Christus Rex*, 1961, xv.1, 73–7, p.75.
74. Ibid., p.77.
75. Ibid., p.77.
76. Joseph Foyle, 'Some Thoughts on Irish Sociology', *Christus Rex*, 1961, xv.1, 23–7, p.26.
77. Fr. Conor Ward, 'The Social Science Research Centre'. Paper presented at Royal Irish Academy, 2006, unpublished.
78. Newman, Review of Conor K. Ward, 'Priests and People', Liverpool University Press, 1961, *Christus Rex*, 1961, xv.4, 323–7.
79. Rev. E. Dougan, 'Socialization: The Principles', *Christus Rex*, 1963, xvii.2, 136–50.

80. David Thornley, 'Ireland: The End of an Era', *Studies*, 1964, 52.1–17, p.2.
81. Newman, 'Progress and Planning', *Christus Rex*, 1977, xxiii.3, 173–86.
82. Rev. Jeremiah Newman, 'Contemporary British Philosophy', *Studies*, 1952, 41.162, 196–208; 'The Ethics of Logical Analysis', *Studies*, 1953, 42, 303–20.
83. Conrad M. Arensberg, *The Irish Countryman* (London, 1937). *New Dubliners*, cited here as a doctoral thesis, was subsequently published. See Francis D'Arcy, 'Mumford and the Sociologists', *Studies*, 1963, 52, 269–82, pp.278–9.
84. Michael Young and Peter Willmott, *Family and Kinship in East London*, (London: Pelican, 1962).
85. T.S. Simey, 'Bettering Our World: The Contribution of Sociology', *Studies*, 1963, 52, 164–71, p.165.
86. Ibid.
87. R.A.B. Leaper, 'The Idea of Community in Town and Country', *Studies*, 1963, 51, 373–83, p.374.
88. Ibid., p.343.
89. Garret FitzGerald, 'Seeking a National Purpose', *Studies*, 1965, 54, 337–51, p.227.
90. Thornley, 'End of an Era', p.3.
91. James V. Schall, 'The University Revolution and Freedom', *Studies*, 1969, 58, 115–26, p.125.
92. Ibid., p.120.
93. E.F. O'Doherty, 'Psychological Aspects of Student Revolt', *Studies*, 1969, 58, 127–34, pp.128–33.
94. James Kavanagh, 'Reflections on Sociology', *Studies*, 1972, 61, 175–86, p.176.
95. Ibid., p.178.
96. Ibid., p.183.
97. Ibid., 185.
98. Tom Inglis, *Moral Monopoly: The Catholic Church in Modern Irish Society* (Dublin: Gill and Macmillan, 1987).
99. Nancy Scheper-Hughes, *Saints, Scholars and Schizophrenics: Mental illness in Rural Ireland* (Berkeley: University of California Press, 1979). P.J. Cullen, 'Review', *Studies*, 1981, 80, 103–4.
100. Inglis, *Moral Monopoly*, pp.136–9.

CHAPTER FIVE

LIBERAL AGENDAS: CATHOLICS AND LIBERAL ALLIANCES, *STUDIES*, 1940–68

1. Bryan Fanning and Tina McVeigh, 'Developmental Welfare Once Again: Growth, Human Capital and the New Welfare Economy', in Katy Hayward and Muris McCartaigh (eds), *Recycling the State: The Politics of Adaptation in the Republic of Ireland* (Dublin: Irish Academic Press, 2007).
2. David Thornley, 'Ireland: The End of an Era', *Studies*, 1964, 52, 1–17, p.10.
3. Garret FitzGerald, 'Seeking a National Purpose', *Studies*, 1964, 53, 337–51, p.337.
4. Michael Tierney, 'A Great Irish Quarterly', *Irish Independent*, 19 January 1937.
5. Irish Jesuit Archives, CM/ Lees/102 (1), 23 May 1941.
6. Louis Redmond, *To the Greater Glory: A History of the Irish Jesuits* (Dublin: Gill and Macmillan, 1991) p.278.
7. 'An anti-Cosgrave journal pulsating with confessional prejudices', kept alive 'largely on anti-Masonic prejudices'. Here the main Jesuit contributor was Edward Cahill. Redmond, *To the Greater Glory: A History of the Irish Jesuits*, p.278. On anti-Protestantism in the *Catholic Bulletin* see Jack White, *Minority*

Report, The Protestant Community in the Irish Republic (Dublin: Gill and Macmillan, 1975), p.116.

8. Whilst studying for a Higher Diploma in Education. See John Cooney, *John Charles McQuaid: Ruler of Catholic Ireland* (Dublin: O'Brien, 1999), p.43.
9. As Connolly put it in a letter to the Provincial: 'the matter was to be kicked up to the Archbishop informally ... We should have really no strict right to publish matter of this kind without procuring a previous approbation of the ecclesiastical authorities, as it seems to come under the extension of Canon 1935, para 1. no.2 ... Hence were it published without previous reference to the diocesan authorities he could come down upon us from the point of view of Canon law.' Irish Jesuit Archives, CM/Lees/102 (5).
10. McQuaid effectively controlled five professorships at UCD (held by priests) in the areas of metaphysics, sociology, logic and psychology, ethics and politics. Tom Garvin, 'The Strange Death of Clerical Politics in UCD', *Irish University Review*, 1998, 28.2, pp.308–14.
11. Letter from Corcoran, Irish Jesuit Archives, Cm/Lees/102 (7).
12. The context was the publication in 1967 of the report of the Commission on Higher Education, which had been established in 1960.
13. Donagh O'Malley, 'University Education in Dublin', *Studies*, 1967, 56, 113–21, pp.116–17.
14. Lt.-General Michael J. Costello, 'Comment on the Foregoing', *Studies*, 1967, 55, 147–55, p.153.
15. W.B. Stanford, 'Comment on the Foregoing', *Studies*, 1967, 55, 186–90, p.189.
16. Basil Chubb, 'The University Merger', *Studies*, 1967, 55, 130–9 pp.133–7.
17. Projections then were for an expansion from under 7,000 students in 1965–6 to 20,000 by 1980. Ibid., pp.135–8.
18. Figures for 1965–66. J.P. MacHale, 'The University Merger', *Studies*, 1967, 55, 122–9, p.127.
19. Ibid., 126.
20. McHale, ibid., p.122.
21. As put by the editor: '*Studies* since its foundation, not long after the National University, has been so closely connected with University College Dublin, we make no excuse, even apart from the element of time, for confining ourselves to a viewpoint from that College.' Peter Troddyn SJ, 'Editorial', *Studies*, 1968, 57, 225–9, p.225.
22. Joseph O'Neill, 'Departments of Education: Church and State', *Studies*, 1949, 38, 419–29.
23. Ibid., p.427.
24. Ibid., pp.426–7.
25. Ibid., 429.
26. Ibid., 429.
27. Sean O'Cathain SJ, 'The Report of the Council of Education', *Studies*, 1954, 41, 361–74, p.355.
28. Ibid., p.374.
29. Patrick McCann, 'The Curriculum of the Secondary School: Monologue or Dialogue; Reflections on the Report of the Commission of Inquiry', *Studies*, 1962, 61, 471–86, p.471.
30. Ibid., p.472.
31. Ibid., pp.471–2.
32. Arthur Little SJ, 'The Present Crisis of Intelligence', *Studies*, 1937, 26, 89–100, pp.89–107.
33. Patrick Lynch et al., *Investment in Education: Report of a Survey Team Appointed by the Minister for Education in Conjunction with the* OECD (2 vols, Dublin 1965, 1966).

34. Garret FitzGerald, 'Investment in Education', *Studies*, 1965, 54, 361–74.
35. Ibid., p.226.
36. Ibid., p.227.
37. O'Connor had discussed the article with his Minister (Brian Lenihan), who suggested he might write a preface to it. O'Connor advised him not to as 'the article would consist in part on his own *personal* views on certain matters'. On 7 August 1967, when the proofs were done, O'Connor telephoned Fr. Troddyn saying he wished to withdraw the article since the Minister had withdrawn his permission for publication (at the intervention of the Secretary of the Department, Dr O'Raifteraigh). Permission would only be given to printing a much-amended form of the article, which Mr O'Connor was unwilling to sign. Troddyn discussed it with legal representatives. The Senior Counsel retained wrote a letter to O'Connor stating 'we had no option but to publish the material already supplied'. Memorandum, Irish Jesuit Archives, Om/Lees/337(19–22).
38. Troddyn was backed by Cecil McGarry, the Jesuit Provincial. When McGarry was summoned to Drumcondra by McQuaid the Archbishop asked if *Studies* intended to publish O'Connor's article. McGarry replied 'Yes' and gave his reasons: 'The Archbishop then courteously sent the Provincial on his way. The end of an era was in sight.' Quoted from Noel Barber SJ, 'His Grace is not pleased', *Studies*, 1998, 87, 400–1.
39. Sean O'Connor, 'Post Primary Education: Now and in the Future', *Studies*, 1968, 57, 233–50, p.241.
40. Ibid., 248.
41. Ibid., 249.
42. The Executive of the Teaching Brothers Association 'Teaching Brothers', *Studies*, 1968, 57, 274–83, p.278.
43. Ibid., p.283.
44. In *Studies* these included O'Cathain, 'Secondary Education in Ireland, 1955', 43, 50–62 and 'Secondary Education in Ireland: Choosing the Curriculum', 1955, 385–98. These and others were collected in O'Cathain, *Secondary Education in Ireland* (Dublin: Talbot Press, 1958).
45. Sean O'Connor, *A Troubled Sky: Reflections on the Irish Scene 1957–1968* (Dublin: Education Research Centre, 1986), p.19.
46. Professor Patrick Clancy in conversation with author.
47. Tierney, 'The Nursing Profession and its Needs (symp. -reply to Moore)' *Studies*, 1942, 31, 273–95, p.279.
48. Rev. Prof. Denis O'Keeffe, 'Catholic Political Theory', *Studies*, 1941, 30, 481–88, p.481.
49. Ibid., p.484.
50. Ibid., p.485.
51. Ibid., p.486.
52. Ibid., p.487.
53. George O'Brien, 'Capitalism in Transition', *Studies*, 1944, 33, 37–44, p.38.
54. Ibid., p.44.
55. O'Brien, 'Stability of Employment: Its Possibility as a Post-war Aim', *Studies*, 33, 304–15, p.312.
56. Ibid., p.315.
57. George O'Brien, 'A Challenge to the Planners', *Studies*, 1945, 33, 210–218, p.218.
58. In the book from which Hollis took his cue Belloc had referred to the liberal welfare reforms that had introduced limited social insurance and state pensions in Britain and Ireland before the Great War. This at the time equated compulsory state social insurance with slavery and prophesised that such legislation would be resisted in Ireland ('the Irish nation would prevent the coming of slavery to

Europe'). Hollis's 1943 article equated unchecked bureaucracy with fascism and freedom with self-reliance and the absence of any dependency on the state. Christopher Hollis, 'Mr. Belloc's Servile State and the Beveridge Plan', *Studies*, 1943, 32, 479–86, pp.485–6.
59. George O'Brien, 'New Views on Unemployment', *Studies*, 1945, 34, 52–64, pp.57–8.
60. Ibid., p.60.
61. Ibid., p.64.
62. George O'Brien, 'Socialist Myth and Russian Reality', *Studies*, 1945, 34, 347–52, p.346.
63. O'Brien, 'John Maynard Keynes', *Studies*, 1946, 35, 189–98, p.198.
64. Rev. Prof. Cornelius Lucey, 'The Beveridge Report and Eire', *Studies*, 32, 36–44, p.38.
65. Ibid., p.38.
66. Ibid., p.44.
67. T.W.T. Dillon, 'Tuberculosis: A Social Problem', *Studies*, 1943, 32.129, 163–74, p.168.
68. Prof. T.W.T. Dillon, 'Public Health Planning', *Studies*, 33, 135, 433–9.
69. Ibid., p.436.
70. Bishop John Dignan, *Social Security: Outlines of a Scheme of National Health Insurance* (Sligo, 1945). See Susannah Riordan, '"A Political Blackthorn": Sean MacEntee, the Dignan Plan and the Principle of Ministerial Responsibility', *Irish Economic and Social History*, XXVII, 2000, 44–62.
71. Some 49,776 lived in one-room tenements in 1938. T.W.T. Dillon, 'Slum Clearance: Past and Future', *Studies*, 1945, 34.133, 13–20, p.12.
72. Ibid., p.15.
73. Ibid., p.16.
74. T.W.T. Dillon, 'The Social Services in Eire', *Studies*, 34.134, 323–36, p.330.
75. Ibid., p.334.
76. Ibid., p.334.
77. Edward J. Coyne SJ, 'The Mother and Child Service', *Studies*, 1951, 49, 128–49, pp.128–38.
78. John F. Cunningham, 'Mother and Child Service: The Medical Problem', 1951, 49, 149–53.
79. Alexis FitzGerald, 'Mother and Child Scheme: The Problem of Finance', *Studies*, 1951, 49. 154–157.
80. Coyne, *Mother and Child Service*, p.139.
81. Ibid., p.140.
82. A half a century later the Children's Act (1991) was introduced to meet Irish obligations as signatory of the UN Convention of the Rights of the Child (1989). Because the Irish Constitution (Articles 41–44) described family rights but not rights for children, the Act had proved ineffective and a Referendum was proposed in 2007.
83. Coyne, 'Health Bill 1952', *Studies*, 1953, 42, 1–22.
84. Ibid., p.6.
85. William J. Philbin, Bishop of Clonfert, 'Government by the People', *Studies*, 1958, 47, 233–46, p.239.
86. Ibid., p.243.
87. Ibid., p.240.
88. William J. Philbin, Bishop of Clonfert, 'A City on the Hill', *Studies*, 1957, 46, 167–259, cited in T.K. Whitaker, *Economic Development* (Dublin: Stationery Office, 1958), p.9.
89. Patrick Lynch, 'The Economist and Public Policy (symp.-comment by Coyne, King, O'Donovan, Quinn), *Studies*, 1953, 42, 241–73, p.243.

90. From the concluding note to Keynes' *General Theory*, p.260.
91. Ibid., p.243, p.247.
92. Ibid., p.253.
93. Patrick Lynch, 'Escape from Stagnation', *Studies*, 1963, 52, 206, 136–63, p.136.
94. Ibid., p.138.
95. Ibid., p.147.
96. Ibid., p.263.
97. Ibid., pp.272–4.
98. Although by then Philbin had been transferred to Belfast.
99. Ronald Burke-Savage SJ, 'Ireland: 1963–1973', *Studies*, 1963, 52, 115–24.
100. Garret FitzGerald, 'Seeking a National Purpose', *Studies*, 1964, 53, 337–51, p.337.
101. FitzGerald, *All in a Life: An Autobiography* (Dublin: Gill and Macmillan, 1991), p.65.
102. Ibid., p.338.
103. Ibid., p.343.
104. Rev. Jeremiah Newman, *Studies in Political Morality,* (Dublin: Scepter, 1962), J.M Cameron, 'Book Review', *Studies*, 1963, 62, 97–101.
105. William J. Philbin, 'The Irish and the New Europe', *Studies*, 1962, 51, 27–43, p.31.
106. Ibid., p.31.
107. T. Watson, *Sociology of Work and Industry* (London: Routledge, 1987), pp. 114–15.
108. Ibid.
109. Philbin, *The Irish and the New* Europe, p.41.
110. Garret FitzGerald, 'Political Implications of Irish Membership of the EEC', *Studies*, 1962, 51, 44–81, p.81.
111. Burke-Savage, 'Ireland: 1963–1973', *Studies*, 1963, 52, 117–18.
112. Such associations had been longstanding in the United Kingdom, for example, in the case of Non-Conformism and Methodism.
113. Editor's preface to Claude Tresmontant, 'Reflections of a Left Wing Catholic', *Studies*, 1965, 54, 385–407, p.385.
114. Ibid., p.407.
115. Burke-Savage, 'The Church in Dublin: A Study of the Episcopate of Most Reverend John Charles McQuaid', *Studies*, 1965, 54, 297–335.
116. Photograph and caption, *Studies*, 1965, 54, 216, p.17.
117. Ibid., p.321.
118. Cooney, *McQuaid*, p.377.
119. Burke-Savage, *The Church in Dublin*, p.299.
120. Peter Lennon, *Sunday Press*, 20 February 1966.
121. See Tom Garvin, *Preventing the Future: Why was Ireland so poor for so long?* (Dublin: Gill and Macmillan, 2004), pp.56–70.
122. Ibid., p.56.
123. Noel Browne, *Against the Tide* (Dublin: Gill and Mcmillan, 1986).
124. Kavanagh's persuasive argument was that de Valera, though a fervent Catholic, always managed to keep a firm independence of Episcopal control, as when shepherding through the 1953 Health Act. Browne, by contrast, was politically naïve. James Kavanagh, 'Social Policy in the Republic of Ireland', *Administration*, 1978, 66, 318–30, p.323.
125. O'Brien worked for MacBride at the time. Conor Cruise O'Brien, *Memoir: My Life and Themes* (London: Profile, 1998), p.153.
126. *Whitaker* and Lynch at the Statistical and Social Inquiry Society of Ireland, 27 April 1945. *T.K. Whitaker, Interests* (Dublin: Institute of Public Administration, 1983), pp.82–3.
127. David Thornley, 'Ireland: The End of an Era', *Studies*, 1964, 52, 1–17, p.10.

CHAPTER SIX

FAITHFUL DEPARTURES: CULTURE AND CONFLICT, *STUDIES*, 1951–86

1. Andrew F. Comyn, 'Censorship in Ireland', *Studies*, 1969, 58, 42–50, p.42.
2. James Meenan, 'The Editor of Studies', *Studies*, 1968, 56, 1–4, p.1.
3. Ronald Burke-Savage SJ, 'Ireland: 1963–1973', *Studies*, 1963, 52, 115–24, p.119.
4. Andrew F. Comyn, 'Censorship in Ireland', *Studies*, 1969, 58, 42–50, p.42.
5. Brian Lennon SJ, 'Editorial: Church and State', *Studies*, 1985, 74, 369–72, pp.369–70.
6. Daniel Lyons SJ, 'The Negro in America', *Studies*, 1951, 40, 69–80, pp.70–7.
7. Gordon Allport, *The Nature of Prejudice* (Cambridge, Ma: Addison-Wesley, 1954). Discussed in Edward J. Brennan, 'Race Prejudice', *Studies*, 1969, 58, 361–62.
8. George Gmelch and Sharon B. Gmelch, 'The Itinerant Settlement Movement', *Studies*, 1974, 63, 1–16, p.11.
9. Michael Paul Gallagher SJ, 'Towards a Pastoral Theology of Indifference', *Studies*, 1979, 68, 249–58, pp.249–51.
10. Ibid., p.257.
11. Brian Lennon SJ, 'Editorial: Secularisation and Irish Society', *Studies*, 1985, 74, 293, 9–11, p.9.
12. Tom Inglis, 'Sacred and Secular in Catholic Ireland: A Review Article of *Irish Values and Attitudes: The Irish Report of the European Value Systems* Study by Micheal Fogarty, Liam Ryan and Joseph Lee (Dublin: Dominican Publications, 1984) *Studies*, 1984, 73, 293, 38–46, pp.40–41.
13. Ibid., p.40.
14. Michael Paul Gallagher SJ 'Secularisation and New Forms of Faith', *Studies*, 1985, 74, 9–25, pp.16–17.
15. John Sweeney, 'Upstairs, Downstairs – The Challenge of Social Inequality', *Studies*, 1983, 72, 6–19.
16. P. O'Connell, 'Private' Property', *Studies*, 1983, 72, 207–9, p.207.
17. Brian Harvey, 'A Solution to Homelessness', *Studies*, 1984, 74, 1–11, p.5.
18. Sean O'Faolain, 'Fifty Years of Irish Writing', *Studies*, 1962, 51, 91–105, p.103.
19. Ibid., p.94.
20. Ibid., p.99.
21. Ibid., p.96.
22. Ibid., p.102.
23. Augustine Martin, 'James Stephens', *Studies*, 1963, 52, 107–8.
24. Leslie Faughnan, 'The Future of the Abbey Theatre', *Studies*, 1966, 55, 236–46, p.237.
25. John D. Sheridan, 'Irish Writing Today', *Studies*, 1955, 43, 80–5, p.84.
26. For example, the articles by Conor Cruise O'Brien that were later collected in his first book. The sole Irish inclusion was a chapter on O'Faolain. Conor Cruise O'Brien, *Maria Cross: Imaginative Patterns in a Group of Modern Catholic Writers* (London: Burns and Oates, 1954).
27. Patricia Corr, 'Evelyn Waugh: Sanity and Catholicism', *Studies*, 1963, 52, 388–99.
28. O'Brien, *Maria Cross*, p.32.
29. Stephen Brown SJ, 'The Role of the Library in an Intellectual Revival', *Studies*, 1944, 33, 218–28, p.228.
30. Ibid., p.46.
31. Ibid., p.52.
32. Ibid., p.54.
33. Ibid., p.63.

34. Ibid., pp.55–6.
35. Ibid., pp.57–8.
36. Ibid., p.63.
37. For example, Zhivago's Nite Club at the Queen's Hotel, Ennis, County Clare, a venue once owned (fictionally) by Leopold Bloom's father in James Joyce's *Ulysses*. A Dublin Zhivago's (on Lower Baggot St.) was advertised as 'where love stories begin'.
38. Augustine Martin, 'Review', *Studies*, 1963, 52, 222–3.
39. Augustine Martin, 'Inherited Dissent: The Dilemma of the Irish Writer', *Studies*, 1965, 54, 1–20, p.1.
40. Ibid., p.3.
41. Ibid., p.4.
42. Ibid., p.13.
43. Ibid., p.10.
44. Cited ibid., p.10.
45. Ibid., p.12.
46. Ibid., p.12.
47. Ibid., p.17.
48. Based on several recollections by the now older generation of academics who drank in his orbit in the UCD Common Room. Martin claimed that his younger self was the model for Pearse McGarrigle, the Catholic ingénue protagonist of David Lodge's novel *Small World*.
49. Martin, 'Inherited Dissent', p.10.
50. Augustine Martin, 'The Discovery of Austin Clarke', *Studies*, 1965, 54, 408–35, p.409.
51. As put by Martin: 'It is fair to state that what the young Austin Clarke received and rejected was not a Catholic education, but an unusually pestilent mixture of Victorian and Jansenist prejudice, reinforced by contemporary, pseudo-medical superstitions about its dangers – especially to sanity – of self abuse', p.420.
52. Ibid., p.431.
53. See for instance Mary Raftery and Eoin O'Sullivan, *Suffer Little Children* (Dublin: New Ireland, 1999), pp.160–2.
54. Andrew F. Comyn, 'Censorship in Ireland', *Studies*, 1969, 58, 42–50, p.42.
55. P.J. Gannon SJ, 'Art, Morality and Censorship', *Studies*, 1942, 31, 409–23, p.43.
56. On both O'Connor and O'Flaherty see Brian Donnelly, 'A Nation Gone Wrong: Liam O'Flaherty's Vision of Modern Ireland', *Studies*, 1974, 63, 71–81.
57. Patrick Murray, 'Irish Echoes', *Studies*, 1969, 58, 166–78.
58. On Montague and Heaney see Thomas D. Redshaw, 'John Montague's The Rough Field: Topos and Text', *Studies*, 1974, 63, 31–46.
59. Paul Durcan, *The Life and Death of Immanuel Kant*, cited in Aiden Mathews, Review, *Studies*, 1977, 66, 83–6.
60. Michael Paul Gallagher SJ, 'Network and Others: Film Report', *Studies*, 1977, 66, 261, 77–82, p.79.
61. For example, Maurice Harmon, 'The Poetry of Thomas Kinsella 1872–1983', *Studies*, 1983, 72, 57–66.
62. For example, Richard Kearney, 'Language Play: Brian Friel and Ireland's Verbal Theatre', *Studies*, 1983, 72, 20–86.
63. Daniel Corkery, *Synge and Anglo-Irish Literature*, cited in Brian Donnelly, 'The Big House in the Recent Novel', *Studies*, 1975, 64, 113–42, p.133.
64. Mark Hawthorne, 'Maria Edgeworth's Unpleasant Lesson: The Shaping of Character', *Studies*, 1975, 64, 167–77, p.167.
65. Garret FitzGerald, 'The Irish Economy – North and South', *Studies*, 1956, 45, 373–88, p.883.

66. Conor Cruise O'Brien, 'A Sample of Loyalties', *Studies*, 1957, 46, 403–10, p.403.
67. Donal Barrington, 'United Ireland', *Studies*, 1957, 46, 379–402.
68. O'Brien, 'A Sample of Loyalties', p.402.
69. Ibid., p.404.
70. Ibid., pp.406–8.
71. Ibid., p.410.
72. Barrington, pp.381–2.
73. Ibid., p.387.
74. Ibid., p.390.
75. Conor Cruise O'Brien, *Memoir: My Life and Themes* (London: Profile, 1998), p.160.
76. Ibid., pp.146–8.
77. Donald Akenson portrayed him as a shrewd and ambitious civil servant with the wit to recognise that the right-to-unity campaign was going nowhere. Donald Harman Akenson, *Conor: A Biography of Conor Cruise O'Brien* (New York: Cornell University Press, 1994) pp.146–7.
78. Barrington, 'United Ireland', pp.395–7.
79. Ibid., p.398.
80. Ibid., pp.400–2.
81. Ronald Savage Burke SJ, 'Current Comment', *Studies*, 1966, 55, 1–6.
82. Sean Lemass, 'I Remember 1916', *Studies*, 1966, 55, 217, 7–9, p.7.
83. Patrick Pearse, *Peace and the Gael*, December 1915, cited in David Thornley, 'Patrick Pearse', *Studies*, 1966, 55.10–28.
84. Ibid., p.40.
85. Garret FitzGerald, 'The Significance of 1916', *Studies*, 1966, 55, 29–37.
86. Ibid., p.32.
87. Ibid., p.33.
88. Peter M. Troddyn SJ, 'Editorial', *Studies*, 1972, 61, 113–14, p.114.
89. Francis Shaw SJ, 'The Canon of Irish History: A Challenge', *Studies*, 1972, 61, 117–53, p.119.
90. Ibid., p.119.
91. Ibid., p.123.
92. Patrick Pearse, *The Separatist Idea*, p. 293, cited ibid., p.124.
93. Ibid., pp.138–139.
94. Patrick Pearse, *The Separatist Idea*, p.293, cited ibid., p.124.
95. Patrick Pearse, *The Coming Revolution*, pp.91–2, cited ibid., p.125.
96. G.F. Dalton, '*The Tradition of Blood Sacrifice to the Goddess Eire*', *Studies*, 1974, 63, 252, 343–54, p.354, p.49.
97. John Coakley, 'Patrick Pearse and the "Noble Lie" of Irish Nationalism', *Studies*, 1983, 72, 119–36.
98. Ibid., pp.123–4.
99. Ruth Dudley Edwards, *Patrick Pearse: The Triumph of Failure* (London: Victor Gollancz, 1977), pp.339–41 cited ibid., p.120.
100. Coakley quoted Masaryk as follows: 'To me the question of the manuscripts was first and foremost a moral question: if they were forgeries we must confess it before the whole world. Our pride, our culture, must not be based on a lie. Besides, we could not truly get to know our own real history while we were obsessed by a fancied past. The case seemed perfectly obvious to me.' Karl Capek, *President Masaryk tells his Story* (New York: G.P. Putman, 1935), pp.154–5, cited ibid., p.134.
101. E.E. Davis and Richard Sinnott, 'The Controversy Concerning Attitudes in the Republic to the Northern Ireland Problem', *Studies*, 1980, 69, 181–96, p.189.
102. David Berman, Stephen Lalor and Brian Torode, 'The Theology of the IRA', *Studies*, 1983, 72, 137–44, p.140.

103. Henry Grant SJ, 'Understanding the Northern Irish Troubles: A Preliminary to Action', *Studies*, 1983, 72, 145–55, p.148.
104. Ibid., pp.151–2.
105. Grant drew on the work of Herbert Blumer, notably *Symbolic Interactionism: Perspectives and Method* (Englewood Cliffs, NJ: Prentice Hall, 1969) and 'Race Prejudice as a Sense of Group Position', *Pacific Sociological Review*, 1.1, 1958, pp.3–7.
106. Edward O'Donnell SJ, 'History Lessons', *Studies*, 1984, 73, 265–71, pp.268–70.
107. Henry Grant SJ, 'The Complex Dynamics of the Northern Troubles', *Studies*, 1984, 76, 272–80, pp.272–3.
108. Ibid., p.277.
109. On Whyte's resignation from UCD in 1966 as 'the unintended result of an extraordinary piece of clerical bullying and interference' see Garvin, *Preventing the Future*, p.73.
110. John Whyte, 'Church and State: Implications of Change', *Studies*, 1985, 74, 296, 411–31, p.422.
111. Mary Redmond, 'Constitutional Aspects of Pluralism', *Studies*, 1978, 67, 265/266, 39–59.
112. Liam de Paor, 'Cultural Pluralism', *Studies*, 1978, 67, 77–87, p.86.
113. John Brady SJ, 'Pluralism and Northern Ireland', *Studies*, 1978, 67, 88–99 pp.92–5.
114. Brian Lennon SJ, 'Editorial: Church and State', *Studies*, 1985, 74, 369–72, pp.369–70.
115. Brian P. Kennedy, 'Seventy-Five Years of *Studies*', *Studies*, 1986, 75.361–374, p.369.
116. Advertisement in *Studies*, 1982, 71, 294.
117. Gerry O'Hanlon SJ, Images of God: Northern Ireland and Theology', *Studies*, 1984, 73, 291–9, p.292.
118. Kennedy, 'Seventy-Five Years of *Studies*', p.369.
119. Richard Kearney, 'Dublin Theatre Festival', *Studies*, 1981, 70, 341–5.
120. Sean O'Luing, '*Kuno Meyer* by Augustus John: A Brief History of a Famous Portrait; T.O. McLaughlin, 'Violence, Disntegration and the New Vision in O'Casey's Plays; Brian Fallon, 'Van Eyck'; H. Walzlawick, 'From History to Episode – an Irish Intermezzo in Eighteenth-Century Bohemia'; P. Callan, 'Rambles in Éireann by William Bulfin'; S. Hirschberg, 'Under Ben Bulben: Art as Looking Glass', *Studies*, 1982, 71, 294, pp.325–404.
121. Richard Kearney, 'Poetry, Language and Identity: A Note on the Poetry of Seamus Heaney', *Studies*, 1986, 75, 552–62.
122. Explanations of poverty as resulting from structural inequalities in Irish society found expression in *Social Studies* (the successor journal to *Christus Rex)* as well as in *Studies*. For example Seamus O'Cinneide, 'The Extent of Poverty in Ireland', *Social Studies*, 1.4, 1972.
123. Seamus O'Cinneide, 'Power and Victims in Ireland', *Studies*, 1972, 6, 335–72, p.335.
124. Ibid., p.337.
125. Walter M. Abbott (ed.) *The Documents of Vatican II* (London: Chapman, 1967) and, for example, Toney Lynes, *Welfare Rights* (London: Fabian Society, 1969) cited ibid., p.372.
126. Desmond Norton 'Unemployment and Public Policy', *Studies*, 1976, 65, 1–16, p.15.
127. John Brady, 'The Public Purpose in the Irish Economy', *Studies*, 1976, 65, 277–78, p.273.
128. Ibid., p.277.
129. Ibid., pp.275–6.
130. Ibid., p.276.

131. Kurt Jacobsen, 'Changing Utterly? Irish Development and the Problem of Dependence', *Studies*, 1979, 68, 276–91, p.285.
132. *NESC Report No. 26: Prelude to Planning* (Dublin Stationery Office, 1976), p.20, cited ibid., p.276.
133. *T.K. Whitaker, Interests* (Dublin: Gill and Macmillan, 1984) reviewed by Raymond Crotty, *Studies*, 1984, 73, 233–7.
134. Ibid., p.234.
135. Ibid., p.235.
136. Ibid., p.236.
137. Frank Sammon SJ, 'The Problem of Poverty in Ireland', *Studies*, 1982, 71, 1–13, p.3.
138. Peter Townsend, *Poverty in the United Kingdom* (London: Penguin, 1979), cited ibid., p.12.
139. *The Perception of Poverty in Europe* (Brussels: EEC Commission, 1977) cited ibid., p.9.
140. Sr Stanislaus Kennedy (ed.) *One Million Poor?- The Challenge of Irish Inequality* (Dublin: Turoe Press, 1981) cited ibid., p.13.
141. John Sweeney SJ, 'Upstairs, Downstairs: The Challenge of Social Inequality', *Studies*, 1983, 72, 6–18, p.7.
142. P. O'Connell SJ, 'The Great Immorality', *Studies*, 1983, 72, 1–6, p.3.
143. Kieran A. Kennedy, 'The Role of the State in Economic Affairs', *Studies*, 1985, 74, 130–44, p.142.
144. Brendan Ryan, 'The Church and Social Justice', *Studies*, 1985, 74, 411–31, p.339.
145. Brian Lennon SJ, 'Editorial: Church and State', *Studies*, 1985, 74, 369–72, pp.369–70.
146. Brian Lennon SJ, 'Editorial: Secularisation and Irish Society', *Studies*, 1985, 74, 9–11, p.11.
147. Emmet Larkin, 'Socialism and Catholicism in Ireland 1910–1914', *Studies*, 1985, 74, 66–92, p.88.
148. For example, see Charles McCarthy, 'Personal rights in the Field of Industrial relations', *Studies*, 1980, 273, 24–44.
149. In McGee (1974) Mr Justice Walsh stated: 'The natural law as a theological concept is the law of God promulgated by reason and is the ultimate governor of the rights of men.' See Edmond Grace SJ, 'Review', *Studies*, 1980, 69, 165–7.
150. See James O'Brien, 'Marital Privacy and Family Law', *Studies*, 1977, 65, 261, 8–24, p.16.
151. Patrick O'Connell SJ, 'The Great Immorality', *Studies*, 1983, 72, 1–5, p.1.
152. Raymond Dennehy, 'The Pessimistic Origins of the Anti-Life Movement', *Studies*, 1981, 70, 1–16, p.15.

CHAPTER SEVEN

FABLES OF THE RECONSTRUCTION: *ADMINISTRATION* AND DEVELOPMENT, 1953–86

1. For a collection of their key writings see Basil Chubb and Patrick Lynch (eds), *Economic Development and Planning* (Dublin: Institute of Public Administration, 1969).
2. Tony McNamara, 'Foreword', Bryan Fanning and Tony McNamara (eds), *Ireland Develops: Administration and Social Policy 1953–2003* (Dublin: Institute of Public Administration, 2003), p.vii.
3. Conor Cruise O'Brien, *Memoir, My Life and Themes* (London: Profile Books, 1998), p.116.
4. John Garvin's pseudonym, Andrew Cass, was a play on Cassandra.

5. Brian O'Nolan, 'Another Bash in the Tunnel', *Envoy*, 1951, 1.1.
6. By 'the mysterious forces ruling the Civil Service' see Desmond Roche, 'The Early Years', *Administration*, 1977, 25.4, 453–62, p.456.
7. T.J. Barrington, 'Editorial', *Administration*, 1953, 1.1, 5–6, p.5.
8. These were collected in Basil Chubb and Patrick Lynch, *Economic Development and Planning: Readings in Irish Public Administration Volume One* (Dublin: Institute of Public Administration, 1969).
9. Basil Chubb, 'Janus in the Jungle', *Administration*, 1954–5, 2.4, 111–17, p.117.
10. Desmond Roche, 'The Early Years', *Administration*, 1977, 25.4, 453–62, p.455.
11. Notably, J.M. Kelly, 'The Constitutional Position of RTE', and David Thornley, 'Television and Politics', *Administration*, 1967,15.3, 205–16, 217–25.
12. Garret FitzGerald, 'Four Decades of Administration', *Administration: Cumulative Index 1953–1992*, 1994, ix–xvii, p.xv.
13. See T.J. Barrington, 'Jean Monet: Mr Europe Plain', *Administration*, 1978, 26.4, 520–4; Patrick Keatinge, 'Ireland and the Enlargement of the European Community', *Administration*, 1979, 27.1, 71–84.
14. George O'Brien, 'Economic Visions and Revisions', *Studies*, 1942, 31.122, 211–20, p.220.
15. James Meenan, 'Irish Industry and Industrial Policy 1921–1943', *Studies*, 1943, 32, 209–30, p.208.
16. James Meenan, 'Irish Industry and Post-War Problems', *Studies*, 1943, 32, 131, 361–8, p.364.
17. R.C. Geary, 'Irish Economic Development Since the Treaty', *Studies*, *1951*, 50, 160, 398–418, pp.403–07.
18. *T.K. Whitaker, Interests* (Dublin: Institute of Public Administration, 1983), p.82.
19. J.J. Lee, *Ireland: 1912–1985*, p.341.
20. *T.K. Whitaker, 'Economic Development* (Dublin: Stationery Office, 1958), pp.227–9.
21. Stepher Lalor, 'Planning and the Civil Service 1945–70' *Administration*, 1996, 43.4, 57–75, p.68.
22. See p.8.
23. See for example John Bristow, 'Aspects of Economic Planning', *Administration*, 1979, 27.2, 192–200, p.193.
24. *Economic Development*, p.4.
25. Ibid., p.5.
26. Ibid., p.5.
27. Charles Sanders Pierce, *Writings of Charles S. Pierce: A Chronological Edition, Vol. III 1872–1878*, edited by the Pierce Edition Project (Bloomington: Indiana University Press, 1993).
28. *Whitaker, Economic Development*, p.9.
29. Patrick Lynch, 'Some Unsettled Questions in Irish Economics', *Administration*, 1959, 7.2, 91–108.
30. Garret FitzGerald, 'Second Programme for Economic Expansion: Reflections', *Studies*, 1964, 53.211, 233–52, p.250.
31. *T.K. Whitaker*, 'The Civil Service and Development', *Administration*, 1961, 9.2, 83–7, p.86.
32. Patrick Lynch, 'A Great Public Servant: Edwin Chadwick and the Public Health Movement', *Administration*, 1953, 1.1, 89–90, p.91.
33. A review of Kieran A. Kennedy and Brendan Dowling, *Economic Growth in Ireland: The Experience Since 1947* (Dublin: Gill and Macmillan, 1975). See Michael Fogarty, 'Age of Miracles', *Administration*, 1976, 24.1, 107–11, p.110.
34. Carter held the Chair in Political Economy at the University of Manchester. He had served on the Department of Finance Capital Investment Advisory Committee. *Whitaker* recommended that he be appointed, along with Lynch, to

the body set up to implement *Economic Development. Whitaker, Economic Development*, p.226; C.F. Carter, 'A Problem of Economic Development', *Administration*, 1959, 7.2, 109–17, p.117.

35. Desmond Roche, 'The Early Years', *Administration*, 1977, 25.4, 453–62, p.455.
36. Patrick Lynch, 'William Thompson of Cork', *The Bell*, 1946, 6.1, 34–46, p.35.
37. The system of voluntary equality referred to here was the one proposed by Robert Owen. William Thompson, *An Inquiry into the Principles of Distribution of Wealth Most Conductive to Human Happiness; Applied to the Newly Proposed System of Voluntary Equality of Wealth*, cited ibid., p.41.
38. Lynch argued that Thompson was an unacknowledged influence on Marx's theory of surplus value. Ibid., p.42.
39. Ibid., p.42.
40. Tuairim (Opinion) was a society with branches in Dublin, Cork, Limerick and later London. It organised public lectures and printed pamphlets on topical issues. Lynch read his paper at a Tuairim study weekend in April 1959. It was published as one half of the fifth Tuairim pamphlet alongside another *Administration* article: C.F. Carter, 'A Problem of Economic Development'. See Patrick Lynch and C.F. Carter, *Planning For Economic Development* (Dublin: Mount Salus Press, 1959). It was then republished in the *Irish Times* in three parts, May 25–27, 1959. As cited here *Administration*, 1959, 7.2, 91–108.
41. Ibid., p.94.
42. At the time the British Exchequer was spending over £200 million a year to subsidise agricultural prices. Lynch's argument was to seek some of this for Irish farmers. Here, he anticipated the subsequent benefits of Common Agricultural Policy (CAP) funding from Europe. Ibid., p.94.
43. Ibid., p.108.
44. Ibid., p.102.
45. See p.11
46. Patrick Lynch, 'Some Problems of Public Enterprise: Public Enterprise in a Free Economy', *Administration*, 1954, 2.1, 11–20, p.18.
47. Lynch, 'Administrative Theory and the Civil Service, *Administration*, 1956, 4.4, 97–116.
48. Ibid., p.101.
49. Ibid., pp.102–3.
50. Ibid., pp.106–7.
51. Ibid., p.106.
52. Ibid., p.108.
53. Ibid., p.109.
54. These were D. Richardson, 'Three Pioneers of Scientific Management', T.J. Barrington, 'Management From the Top: Henri Fayol', A. Scannell, 'The Psychological Approach: Mary Follett', Basil Chubb, 'Administration a Process: Barnard and Simon', Basil Chubb, 'Some Notes on Further Reading', *Administration*, 1956, 4.4.
55. O'Regan was originally a hotelier. He became the architect of the Shannon Free Airport Development Company. The initiatives of SFADCO included the development of regional tourist facilities to boost traffic into Shannon and the establishment of a tax-free enterprise zone to attract industry to the airport. Brendan O'Regan, 'Creativity in the Public Sector', *Administration*, 1971, 19.1, 3–11 pp.8–9.
56. Sean F. Lemass, 'The Organisation behind the Economic Programme', *Adminstration*, 1961, 9.1, 3–10, p.4.
57. IPA Research Unit, 'The Idea of a Profession', *Administration*, 1971, 19.1, 50–60, p.51.

58. Ibid., pp.52–3.
59. Basil Chubb, *The Government and Politics of Ireland*, cited ibid., p.60.
60. Barrington cited three articles from *Studies:* Ronald Burke Savage SJ 'Ireland: 1963–1973', Summer, 1963; Garret FitzGerald: 'Seeking a National Purpose', Winter, 1964; Patrick Lynch: 'The Sociologist in a Planned Economy', Spring, 1965. See Chapter 6. T.K. Barrington, 'Administrative Purpose', *Administration*, 1965 13.3, 176–91.
61. Ibid., p.177.
62. P.J. Meghan, 'Sir Horace Plunkett as an Administrator', *Administration*, 1966, 14.3, 226–45.
63. T.D. Williams, 'Public Affairs 1916–1966: 1. – The Political Scene', *Administration*, 1966, 14.3, 191–8.
64. D. Roche, 'Review of *The Public Interest: An Essay Concerning Normative Discourse of Politics: Richard E. Flathman*, (New York: John Wiley, 1966)', *Administration*', 1966, 14.3, 264–76.
65. Ibid., p.241.
66. T.J. Barrington, 'Regionalism 5: Some Problems with Institutional Development', *Administration*, 1970, 18.3, 247–55, pp.248–51.
67. T.J. Barrington, *From Big Government to Local Government: The Road to Decentralisation* (Dublin: Institute of Public Administration, 1975).
68. Barrington, 'Some Characteristics of Irish Public Administration', *Administration*, 1975, 22.3, 221–33, p.227.
69. Barrington described relations with his father, who had been Civil Service secretary to the 1923 Fiscal Inquiry, as strained, but took considerable pleasure in George O'Brien's description of him as having an independent mind on economic issues. See Barrington, 'Review of James Meenan, *George O'Brien: A Biographical Memoir* (Dublin, Gill and Macmillan, 1980)', *Administration*, 1982, 29.1, 102–4.
70. Ibid., p.227.
71. Ibid., p.233.
72. Ibid., p.227.
73. Ibid., p.233.
74. *Whitaker,* 'Planning Irish Development', *Administration*, 1977, 25.3, 288–307, p.289.
75. Tony McNamara, 'Pressure Groups and the Public Service', *Administration*, 1977, 25.3, 365–80, p.375.
76. Maria Maguire, 'Pressure Groups in Ireland', *Administration*, 1977, 25.3, 349–64, p.359.
77. McNamara, *Pressure Groups*, pp. 376–8.
78. Here he stuck by similarities with what was described in Sir Robert Kane's 1844 *The Industrial Resources of Ireland*. Barrington, 'Can Administrative Science Aid the Administrative Profession?, *Administration*, 1979, 415–27, p.416.
79. Ibid., p.419.
80. Ibid., p.419.
81. Ibid., p.421.
82. Des Kelly, 'The Public Sector Reform Programme', *Administration*, 1979, 27.4, 339–407, p.403.
83. Richard Roche, 'The Role of the Department of the Public Service', *Administration*, 1979, 27.4, 408–14, p.414.
84. John Bristow, 'Aspects of Economic Planning', *Administration*, 1979, 27.2, 192–200, p.193.
85. Ibid., p.196.
86. Lynch, 'Whither Science Policy?', *Administration*, 1979, 27.3, 255–81, p.257.

87. Ibid., p.261.
88. Ibid., p.280.
89. Ibid., p.268.
90. Ibid., p.268.
91. Seamus O'Cinneide, 'Poverty and Policy: North and South', *Administration*, 1985, 33.3, 378–417, p.379.
92. Neans de Paor, 'Women in the Civil Service', *Administration*, 3.2/3, 141–7, reprinted in Fanning and McNamara (eds) *Ireland Develops*, pp.233–9.
93. Dr Thekla Beere, 'Commission on the Status of Women: Progress Report', *Administration*, 1975, 23.1, 31–46, reprinted in Fanning and McNamara (eds), pp.240–56.
94. Frank Litton, 'Editorial', *Administration: Unequal Achievement*, 1982, 30.2/3, p.ix.
95. Moore McDowell, 'Public Expenditure', *Unequal Achievement*, 1982, 30.2/3, 183–200 p.198.
96. Seamus Sheedy, 'Review of Raymond Crotty', *Irish Agricultural Production: Its Volume and Structure* (Cork University Press, 1966), *Administration*, 1967, 15.2, 163–5.
97. Raymond Crotty, *Ireland in Crisis* (Dingle: Brandon, 1986), p.84.
98. Tom Garvin, 'Review of *Ireland in Crisis*', *Administration*, 1986, 34.4, 533–55.
99. Ibid., p.303.
100. Rottman and O'Connell, *The Changing Social Structure*, p.76.
101. Ibid., p.56.
102. Tom Garvin, 'Change and the Political System', *Administration: Unequal Achievement*, 1982, 30.2/3, 21–41, p.37.
103. J.J. Lee, '*Ireland 1912–1985* (Cambridge: Cambridge University Press, 1989).
104. Ibid., pp1–2.
105. J.J. Lee, 'Society and Culture,' *Administration: Unequal Achievement*, 1982, 30.2/3, pp.1–18, pp.1–3.
106. Lee argued that when it came to rewarding initiative and public entrepreneurship it would be a simple matter to distinguish the thrusters from the sleepers as well as 'the not inconsiderable class of dozers' but that the culture of the Irish public sector impeded such necessary distinctions. Ibid., pp.8–9.
107. Ibid., p.4.
108. Lee, *Ireland, 1912–1985*, pp.547–51.
109. Lee, p.7.
110. See p.5.
111. Ibid., p.15.
112. see p.5.
113. Lee, '*Society and Culture*', p.6.
114. Miriam Hederman, *The Clash of Ideas: Essays in Honour of Patrick Lynch* (Dublin: Gill and Macmillan, 1988).
115. Miriam Hederman O'Brien, 'The Organic Role of Taxation', in Fionan O'Muircheartaigh (ed.), *Ireland in the Coming Years: Essays to Celebrate* T.K. Whitaker's *80 Years* (Dublin: Institute of Public Administration, 1997), pp.100–17.
116. Lynch, *The Economics of Independence*, p. 95.
117. John Maguire, 'The Case for a New Social Order,' in Hederman (ed.), *The Clash of Ideas*, pp.61–88.
118. Ibid., p.78.
119. Ibid., p.64.
120. For example, IPA publications included Ruth Barrington's *Health, Medicine and Politics in Ireland*, (1974); Patrick Clancy, Sheelagh Drudy, Kathleen Lynch and Liam O'Dowd (eds), *Ireland: A Sociological Profile* (1992).
121. Ibid., p.79.

122. T.P. Hardiman and E.P. O'Neill, 'The Role of Science and Innovation', in Fionan O'Muircheartaigh (ed.), *Ireland in the Coming Years: Essays to Celebrate* T.K. Whitaker*'s 80 Years* (Dublin: Institute of Public Administration, 1997), pp.253–83.
123. Richard Kearney, 'Post-modern Ireland', in Hederman (ed.), *The Clash of Ideas*, pp.112–41.
124. J.K. Galbraith, 'Foreword', in Hederman (ed.), *Clash of Ideas*, p.x.
125. Fionan O'Muircheartaigh', Editorial, *Ireland in the Coming Times*, pp.xv–xxi.
126. In 1982 Rottman and O'Connell, *The Changing Social Structure*, p.84.
127. Bryan Fanning and Tina McVeigh, 'Developmental Welfare Once Again: Growth and Human Capital', in Katy Hayward and Muris McCarthaigh (eds), *Recycling the Irish State: The Politics of Adaptation in Ireland* (Dublin: Irish Academic Press, 2007), pp.128–9.

CHAPTER EIGHT

THINKING INSIDE BOXES: MAIN CURRENTS, INSTITUTIONAL CONTEXTS

1. William McCormack, *The Battle of the Books* (Mullingar: Lilliput, 1986).
2. For a broad overview of twentieth-century Irish literary periodicals see Gerry Smyth, *Decolonisation and Criticism: The Construction of Irish Literature* (London: Pluto, 1998), pp.101–3.
3. *The Crane Bag* depended on funding from the Northern Ireland Arts Council. On the struggle to produce and distribute *The Crane Bag* see interview with Mark Patrick Hederman in Stephen J. Costello: *The Irish Soul* in *Dialogue* (Dublin: Liffey Press, 2001), p.129.
4. Yet the circulation of these was but a fraction of other kinds of Irish periodical. For example, the small sales of intellectual journals stood in stark contrast with Catholic missionary publications with sales in post-independence Ireland of up to 130,000 copies per issue. E. Hogan, *The Irish Missionary Movement: A Historical Survey 1830–1980* (Dublin: Gill and Macmillan, 1992), p.146.
5. Perhaps the closest Kearney comes to acknowledging the presence of social sciences in Irish intellectual life is his inclusion of the socio-economic or materialist hermeneutic in his taxonomy of Irish intellectual history. See Richard Kearney, 'The Irish Mind Debate', in *Navigations: Collected Irish Essays 1976–2006* (Dublin: Lilliput Press, 2006), p.26.
6. Stephen J. Brown SJ, 'What is a Nation? *Studies*, 1913, 1.3, 496–510; Stephen J. Brown SJ, The Question of Irish Nationality', *Studies*, 1913, 1.4, 634–55.
7. J. Sugden and A. Bairner, *Sport, Sectarianism and Society in a Divided Ireland* (Leicester: Leicester University Press, 1993), p.29.
8. Kearney has retrospectively depicted the Irish Mind project rather differently from as first outlined in *The Crane Bag*. Initially, it was depicted as a Jungian collective consciousness. As portrayed in 2006 it was a dialectic opposite to the 'colonial slur' he, like Seamus Deane, associated with Matthew Arnold and other Victorian opponents of Irish Home Rule. In this reformulation Kearney inserts his contributions to *The Crane Bag* into a history of contestation of colonial influences that includes Daniel Corkery's *The Hidden Ireland*. Kearney, *Navigations*, pp.17–21.
9. Mark Patrick Hederman, *'The Crane Bag' And The North of Ireland*, 4.2 p.738.
10. As set out in 'The Irish Mind Debate' these four rival hermeneutic models are 1) an Anglo-Irish Ascendancy reading; 2) a nationalist/republican reading; 3) a positivist/enlightenment reading; 4) a socio-economic or materialist reading. Kearney, *Navigations*, p.26.

11. Brown, 'What is a Nation', p.463.
12. O'Rahilly, 'Ideals at Stake', *Studies*, 1915, 4, 16–33, p.26.
13. The article remained unpublished for six years. Francis Shaw SJ, 'The Canon of Irish History: A Challenge', *Studies*, 1972, 61, 117–53, p.119.
14. These are equivalents to two of the four Irish intellectual hermeneutics identified by Kearney ('nationalist/republican' and 'positivist/enlightenment'), Kearney, *Navigations*, p.26. See Jeffery Prager, *Building Democracy in Ireland: Political Order and Cultural Integration in a Newly Independent Nation* (Cambridge: Cambridge University Press, 1986), p.16.
15. Tierney argued that although Herder was not 'a narrow German' nationalist his ideas led not to the wider humanity he had hoped for but to the horrors of the concentration camp. Michael Tierney, 'Nationalism; a Survey', *Studies*, 1945, 34, 474–84, p.482.
16. Ibid., p.479.
17. Michael Tierney, 'A Weary Task: The Struggle in Retrospect', in Tierney (ed.), *Struggles with Fortune* (Dublin: Browne and Nolan, 1954), p.16.
18. Frank O'Connor, 'The Old Age of A Poet', *The Bell*, 1941, pp.7–9, Conor Cruise O'Brien, 'Passion and Cunning: An Essay on the Politics of W.B. Yeats', in A. Norman Jeffares and K.G.W. Cross, eds, *Excited Reverie: A Centenary Tribute to William Butler Yeats, 1965–1939* (London: Macmillan, 1965).
19. Conor Cruise O'Brien, *States of Ireland* (London: Hutchinson, 1972), p.23.
20. Donal Barrington, 'United Ireland', *Studies*, 1957, 46, 379–402.
21. Maurice Goldring, *Pleasant the Scholar's Life: Irish Intellectuals and the Construction of the Nation State* (London: Serif, 1993), p.14.
22. Cited in James Meenan, *George O'Brien: A Biographical Memior* (Dublin: Gill and Macmillan, 1980), p.33.
23. Finola Kennedy, *Cottage to Crèche: Family Change in Ireland* (Dublin: Institute of Public Administration, 2001), p.249.
24. Whyte, *Church and State*, p.376.
25. Tony Fahey, 'The Catholic Church and Social Policy', in Healy, S. and Reynolds, B. (eds), *Social Policy in Ireland* (Dublin: Oak Tree Press, 1998), p.420.
26. On this see Fergahal McGarry, *Eoin O'Duffy: A Self-Made Hero* (Oxford: Oxford University Press, 2005), p. 206.
27. For example, under Article 41.1.2 of the 1937 Constitution: 'The State ... guarantees to protect the Family in its constitution and authority, as the necessary basis of social order and as indispensable to the welfare of the Nation and the State.'
28. Edward Cahill SJ, *Framework of a Christian State* (Dublin: Gill & Son, 1932).
29. Finola Kennedy, 'The Priests, the Family and the Irish Constitution', *Studies*, 1998, 87, 353–64.
30. Michel Peillon, *Contemporary Irish Society* (Dublin: Gill and Macmillan, 1982), p.95.
31. J. Breuilly, *Labour and Liberalism in Nineteenth Century Europe: Essays on Comparative History* (Manchester: Manchester University Press, 1994), p.234.
32. Margaret Preston, 'Discourse and Hegemony: Race and Class in the Language of Charity in Nineteenth Century Dublin', in T. Foley and S. Ryder (eds), *Ideology and Ireland in the Nineteenth Century* (Dublin: Four Courts, 1998), pp.100–12.
33. Bryan Fanning, 'The New Welfare Economy', in B. Fanning and M. Rush (eds), *Care and Social Change in the Irish Welfare Economy* (Dublin: University College Dublin Press, 2006), pp.11–12.
34. W.K. Roche and T. Craddon, 'Neo-corporatism and Social Partnership', in M. Adshead and M. Millar (eds), *Public Administration and Public Policy in Ireland: Theory and Practice* (London: Routledge, 2003), p.73.

Select Bibliography

PRIMARY SOURCES

Administration
Christus Rex
Studies
The Bell
The Crane Bag
Irish Jesuit Archives

Abbott, W.M. (ed.), *The Documents of Vatican II* (London: Chapman, 1967).

Adorno, T.W., Frenkel-Brunswik, E., Levinson, D.J. and Sanforo, R.H. *The Authoritarian Personality* (New York: Harper and Row, 1950).

Allport, G., *The Nature of Prejudice* (Cambridge, MA: Addison-Wesley, 1954).

Akenson, D.H., *Conor: A Biography of Conor Cruise O'Brien* (New York: Cornell University Press, 1994).

Anderson, B., *Imagined Communities: Reflections on the Origin and Spread of Nationalism* (London: Verso, 1983).

Aristotle, *Metaphysics* (Oxford: Oxford University Press, 1995).

Arensberg, C.M., *The Irish Countryman* (London, 1937).

Ayer, A.J., 'Logical Positivism and its Legacy', in Magee, B., *Men of Ideas: Dialogues with Fifteen Leading Philosophers* (Oxford: Oxford University Press, 1978).

Barrington, R., *Health, Medicine and Politics in Ireland* (Dublin: Institute of Public Administration, 1974).

Barrington, T.J., *From Big Government to Local Government: The Road to Decentralisation* (Dublin: Institute of Public Administration, 1975).

Blumer, H., *Symbolic Interactionalism: Perspectives and Method* (Englewood Cliffs, NJ: Prentice Hall, 1969).

Blumer, H., 'Race Prejudice as a Sense of Group Position', *Pacific Sociological Review*, 1.1. 1958, pp.3–7.

Bonaccorso, R., *Sean O'Faolain's Irish Vision* (New York: State of New York Academic Press, 1987).

Booth, C., *Life and Work of the People of London* (London: Macmillan, 1902).

Boyce, D.G. and O'Day, A. (eds), *The Making of Modern Irish History: Revisionism and the Revisionist Controversy* (London: Routledge, 1996).

Brown, T., *Ireland: A Social and Cultural History 1922–2002* (London: Harper Perennial, 2004).

Brown, T., *The Life of W.B. Yeats* (London: Blackwell, 1999).

Browne N., *Against the Tide*, (Dublin: Gill and McMillan, 1986).

Bradshaw, B.,'Nationalism and Historical Scholarship in Modern Ireland', in Brady, C. (ed.), *Interpreting Irish History* (Dublin: Irish Academic Press, 1994), pp.191–211.

Brady C. (ed.), *Interpreting Irish History* (Dublin: Irish Academic Press, 1994).

Breuilly, J., *Labour and Liberalism in Nineteenth Century Europe: Essays on Comparative History* (Manchester: Manchester University Press, 1994).

Burgess, A., *The Wanting Seed* (London: Heinemann, 1962).

Burleigh, M., *The Third Reich: A New History* (London: Pan, 2000).

Cahill, E., SJ, *Framework of a Christian State* (Dublin: Gill & Son, 1932).

Capek, K., *President Masaryk Tells His Story* (New York: G.P. Putnam, 1935).

Carnap, R., 'The Elimination of Metaphysics through Logical Analysis of Language', in Ayer, A.J. (ed.), *Logical Positivism* (Westport, CT: Greenwood, 1959).

Chubb, B. and Lynch, P., *Economic Development and Planning: Readings in Irish Public Administration Volume One* (Dublin: Institute of Public Administration, 1969).

Clancy, P., Drudy, S., Lynch, K., and O'Dowd L. (eds), *Ireland: A Sociological Profile* (Dublin: Institute of Public Adminstration, 1992).

Collini, S., *Absent Minds: Intellectuals in Britain* (Oxford: Oxford University Press, 2006).

Connolly, S.J., 'Culture, Identity and Tradition', in Graham, B. (ed.), *In Search of Ireland: A Cultural Geography* (London: Routledge, 1997).

Cooney, J., *John Charles McQuaid: Ruler of Catholic Ireland* (Dublin: O'Brien, 1999).

Corkery, D., *The Hidden Ireland: A Study of Gaelic Munster in the Eighteenth Century* (Dublin: Gill and Macmillan, 1970).
——, *Synge and Anglo-Irish Literature* (London: Longmans, 1931).
Costello, S.J., *The Irish Soul in Dialogue* (Dublin: Liffey Press, 2001).
Crotty, R., *Irish Agricultural Production: Its Volume and Structure* (Cork: Cork University Press, 1966).
Crotty, R., *Ireland in Crisis* (Dingle: Brandon, 1986).
Curtis, L.P., 'The Greening of Irish History', *Eire-Ireland*, 26.2 1994, pp.23–5.
Day, C., SJ, *Catholic Democracy, Individualism and Socialism* (London: Health, Cranton and Ouesley, 1914).
Duddy, T., *A History of Irish Thought* (London: Routledge, 2002).
Dudley Edwards, R., *Patrick Pearse: The Triumph of Failure* (London: Victor Gollancz, 1977).
Duffy, P.J., 'Writing Ireland: Literature in the Representation of Irish Place', in Graham, B. (ed.), *In Search of Ireland: A Cultural Geography* (London: Routledge, 1997).
Fahey, T., 'The Catholic Church and Social Policy', in Healy, S. and Reynolds, B. (eds), *Social Policy in Ireland* (Dublin: Oak Tree Press, 1998).
Fanning, B., *Evil, God, the Greater Good and Rights: The Philosophical Origins of Social Problems* (New York: Edwin Mellen, 2007).
Fanning B., *Racism and Social Change in the Republic of Ireland* (Manchester: Manchester University Press, 2002).
Fanning, B., 'The New Welfare Economy', in Fanning, B. and Rush, M. (eds), *Care and Social Change in the Irish Welfare Economy* (Dublin: University College Dublin Press, 2006).
Fanning, B. and McNamara T. (eds), *Ireland Develops: Administration and Social Policy 1953–2003* (Dublin: Institute of Public Administration, 2003).
Fanning, B. and McVeigh, T., 'Developmental Welfare Once Again: Growth, Human Capital and the New Welfare Economy', in Hayward, K. and McCartaigh, M. (eds), *Recycling the State: The Politics of Adaptation in the Republic of Ireland* (Dublin: Irish Academic Press, 2008).
FitzGerald, G., *All in a Life: An Autobiography* (Dublin: Gill and Macmillan, 1991).
Flathman, R.E., *The Public Interest: An Essay Concerning Normative Discourse of Politics* (New York: John Wiley, 1966).

Fogarty, M., Ryan, L. and Lee, J.J., *Irish Values and Attitudes: The Irish Report of the European Value Systems* (Dublin: Dominican Publications, 1984).

Foster, R., 'History and the Irish Question', in Brady (ed.), *Interpreting Irish History*, pp.112–45.

Galbraith, J.K., 'Foreword', in Hederman, M. (ed.), *The Clash of Ideas: Essays in Honour of Patrick Lynch* (Dublin: Gill and Macmillan, 1988).

Garvin, T., *Preventing the Future:* Why Ireland Remained so Poor for So Long? (Dublin: Gill and Macmillan, 2005).

Garvin, T., 'The Strange Death of Clerical Politics in UCD', *Irish University Review*, 1998, 28.2, pp.308–14.

Gellner, E., *Nations and Nationalism* (Oxford: Blackwell, 1983).

Goldring, M., *Pleasant the Scholar's Life: Irish Intellectuals and the Construction of the Nation State* (London: Serif, 1993).

Hardiman, T.P. and O'Neill, E.P., 'The Role of Science and Innovation', in O'Muircheartaigh, F. (ed.), *Ireland in the Coming Years: Essays to Celebrate* T.K. Whitaker*'s 80 Years* (Dublin: Institute of Public Administration, 1997).

Harmon, M., *Sean O'Faolain: A Life* (London: Constable, 1994).

Hederman M. (ed.), *The Clash of Ideas: Essays in Honour of Patrick Lynch* (Dublin: Gill and Macmillan, 1988).

Hederman O'Brien, M., 'The Organic Role of Taxation', in O'Muircheartaigh, F. (ed.), *Ireland in the Coming Years: Essays to Celebrate* T.K. Whitaker*'s 80 Years* (Dublin: Institute of Public Administration, 1997).

Hobsbawm, E., *Age of Extremes: The Short Twentieth Century 1914–1991* (London: Michael Joseph, 1994).

Hogan, E., *The Irish Missionary Movement: A Historical Survey 1830–1980* (Dublin: Gill and Macmillan, 1992).

Howe, S., *Ireland and Empire: Colonial Legacies in Irish History and Culture* (Oxford: Oxford University Press, 2000).

Humphries, A.J., *The New Dubliners: Urbanisation and the Irish Family* (London: Routledge and Kegan Paul, 1966).

Hutchinson, J., 'Irish Nationalism', in Boyce, D.G., and Day, A. (eds), *The Making of Modern Irish History: Revisionism and the Revisionist Controversy* (London: Routledge, 1996).

Inglis, T., *Moral Monopoly: The Catholic Church in Modern Irish Society* (Dublin: Gill and Macmillan, 1987).

Inglis, T., 'Sacred and Secular in Catholic Ireland: A Review Article of *Irish Values and Attitudes: The Irish Report of the European*

Value Systems Study by Micheal Fogarty, Liam Ryan and Joseph Lee (Dublin: Dominican Publications, 1984)', *Studies*, 73.293 (1984), 38–46, pp.40–1.

Jeffares, A.N., and Cross, K.G.W. (eds), *Excited Reverie: A Centenary Tribute to William Butler Yeats, 1965–1939* (London: Macmillan, 1965).

Kane, E., 'The Power of Paradigms: Social Science and Intellectual Contributions to Public Discourse in Ireland', in O'Dowd, L., (ed.), *On Intellectuals and Intellectual Life in Ireland* (Dublin: Royal Irish Academy, 1996), pp.132–55.

Kearney, N., 'Social Work Training: Its Origins and Growth', in Kearney, N. and Skehill, C. (eds), *Social Work in Ireland: Historical Perspectives* (Dublin: Institute of Public Administration, 2005).

Kearney, R., (ed.), *The Crane Bag Book of Irish Studies 1977–1981* (Dublin: Blackwater Press, 1982).

——, *Dialogues with Contemporary Continental Thinkers: Paul Ricoeur, Emmanuel Levinas, Herbert Marcuse, Stanislas Breton and Jacques Derrida: The Phenomenological Heritage* (Manchester: Manchester University Press, 1984).

——, *Postnationalist Ireland: Politics, Culture and Philosophy* (London: Routledge, 1997).

——., 'Post-modern Ireland', in Hederman, M. (ed.), *The Clash of Ideas: Essays in Honour of Patrick Lynch* (Dublin: Gill and Macmillan, 1988), pp.112–41.

——, *Navigations: Collected Irish Essays 1976–2006* (Dublin: Lilliput Press, 2006).

Keenan, M., 'Child Sexual Abuse: The Heart of the Matter', *The Furrow*, 2003, pp.597–605.

Kennedy, F., *Cottage to Crèche: Family Change in Ireland* (Dublin: Institute of Public Administration, 2001).

Kennedy, K.A. and Dowling, B., *Economic Growth in Ireland: The Experience Since 1947* (Dublin: Gill and Macmillan, 1975).

Kennedy, S. (ed.), *One Million Poor? The Challenge of Irish Inequality* (Dublin: Turoe Press, 1981).

Keogh, D., *Jews in Twentieth Century Ireland* (Cork: Cork University Press, 1998).

Kettle, T., *The Open Secret of Ireland* (London: W.J. Ham-Smith, 1912).

Lee, J.J., *Ireland 1912–1985* (Cambridge: Cambridge University Press, 1989).

Levin, H. (ed.), *The Essential James Joyce* (London: Penguin, 1963).
Leo XIII *Rerum Novarum: On Capital and Labour* (1891), http://www.vatican.va.
Lynch P. et al., *Investment in Education: Report of a Survey Team Appointed by the Minister for Education in Conjunction with the OECD* (2 vols) (Dublin, 1965, 1966).
Lynch, P. and Carter, C.F., *Planning For Economic Development* (Dublin: Mount Salus Press, 1959).
Lynes, T., *Welfare Rights* (London: Fabian Society, 1969).
Lyons, J.B., *The Enigma of Tom Kettle: Irish Patriot, Essayist, Poet, British Soldier* (Dublin: Glendale Press, 1983).
McCormack, D., 'Policy Making in a Small Open Economy', in Hagan, J.W. (ed.), *The Economy of Ireland: Policy and Performance* (Dublin: Irish Management Institute, 1984).
McCormack, W., *The Battle of the Books* (Mullingar: Lilliput, 1986).
McDermott, T. (ed.), *Thomas Aquinas: Selected Philosophical Writings* (Oxford: Oxford University Press, 1993).
McGarry, F., *Eoin O'Duffy: A Self-Made Hero* (Oxford: Oxford University Press, 2005).
McRedmond, L., *To the Greater Glory: A History of the Irish Jesuits* (Dublin: Gill and Macmillan, 1991).
Maguire, J., 'The Case for a New Social Order', in Hederman (ed.), *The Clash of Ideas*, pp.61–88.
Manning, M., *James Dillon: A Biography* (Dublin: Wolfhound, 2000).
Marcuse, H., *One-Dimensional Man* (London, Abacus, 1964).
Maritain, J., *The Rights of Man and Natural Law* (London: Centenary Press, 1944).
Meenan, J., *George O'Brien: A Biographical Memior* (Dublin: Gill and Macmillan, 1980).
National Social and Economic Council, *NESC Report No. 26: Prelude to Planning* (Dublin: Dublin Stationery Office, 1976).
Newman, J., *Studies in Political Morality* (Dublin: Sceptre, 1962).
O'Brien, C.C. *Maria Cross: Imaginative Patterns in a Group of Modern Catholic Writers* (London: Burns and Oates, 1954).
O'Brien, C.C., *States of Ireland* (London: Hutchinson, 1972).
O' Brien, C.C., *Memoir, My Life and Themes* (London: Profile Books, 1998).
O'Cathain, S., *Secondary Education in Ireland* (Dublin: Talbot Press, 1958).
O'Connor, F., 'Preface' to Brian Merriman, *The Midnight Court* (Dublin: O'Brien Press, 2000).

O'Connor, S., *A Troubled Sky: Reflections on the Irish Scene 1957–1968* (Dublin: Education Research Centre, 1986).

O'Connor, S., *The Workhouses of Ireland: The Fate of Ireland's Poor* (Dublin: Anvil, 1995).

O'Dowd, L.(ed.), *On Intellectuals and Intellectual Life in Ireland: International, Comparative and Historical Contexts* (Dublin: Royal Irish Academy, 1996).

O'Driscoll, F., 'Social Catholicism and the Social Question in Independent Ireland: The Challenge to the Fiscal System', in Cronin, M. and Regan, J., M., *Ireland: The Politics of Independence 1922–49* (London: Macmillan, 2000).

O'Faolain, S., *The Great O'Neill: A Biography of Hugh O'Neill, Earl of Tyrone* (London: Longmans, 1942).

O'Faolain, S., *The Vanishing Hero* (Boston: Little, Brown, 1957).

O'Faolain, S., *The Irish* (London: Pelican, 1969).

O'Faolain, S., 'A Portrait of the Artist as an Old Man', *Irish University Review*, 1976, 6.1, p.11.

O'Faolain, S., *King of the Beggars: A Life of Daniel O'Connell, the Irish Liberator, in a Study of the Rise of Modern Irish Democracy 1775–1847* (Dublin: Poolbeg, 1980).

O'Faolain, S., *A Bird Alone* (Oxford: Oxford University Press, 1985).

O'Leary, O., and Burke, H., *Mary Robinson: The Authorised Biography* (London: Hodder and Stoughton, 1998).

O'Muircheartaigh, F. (ed.), *Ireland in the Coming Years: Essays to Celebrate* T.K. Whitaker's *80 Years* (Dublin: Institute of Public Administration, 1997).

Peillon, M., *Contemporary Irish Society* (Dublin: Gill and Macmillan, 1982).

Pierce, C.S., *Writings of Charles S. Pierce: A Chronological Edition Vol. III 1872–1878*, edited by the Pierce Edition Project (Bloomington: Indiana University Press, 1993).

Popper, K., *The Open Society and its Enemies* (London: Routledge, 2002).

Prager, J., *Building Democracy in Ireland: Political Order and Cultural Integration in a Newly Independent Nation* (Cambridge: Cambridge University Press, 1986).

Preston, M., 'Discourse and Hegemony: Race and Class in the Language of Charity in Nineteenth Century Dublin', in Foley, T. and Ryder, S. (eds), *Ideology and Ireland in the Nineteenth Century* (Dublin: Four Courts, 1998).

Raftery, M. and O'Sullivan, E., *Suffer Little Children* (Dublin: New Ireland, 1999).

Regan, J.M., *The Irish Counter Revolution 1921–1936* (Dublin: Gill and Macmillan, 1999).

Ricoeur, P., *The Symbolism of Evil* (Boston, MD: Beacon Press, 1969).

Riordan, S., '"A Political Blackthorn": Sean MacEntee, the Dignan Plan and the Principle of Ministerial Responsibility', *Irish Economic and Social History*, XXVII (2000), pp.44–62.

Roche, W.K. and Craddon, T., 'Neo-corporatism and Social Partnership', in Adshead, M. and Millar, M. (eds), *Public Administration and Public Policy in Ireland: Theory and Practice* (London: Routledge, 2003).

Ross, E.J., *Basic Sociology* (Milwaukee, MI: Bruce Publishing Company, 1960).

Sagovesky, N., *Between Two Worlds: George Tyrell's Relationship to the Thought of Matthew Arnold* (Cambridge: Cambridge University Press, 1983).

Scaff, L., *Fleeing the Iron Cage: Culture, Politics and Modernity in the Thought of Max Weber* (Berkeley: University of California Press, 1989), pp.225–6.

Scheper-Hughes, N., *Saints, Scholars and Schizophrenics: Mental Illness in Rural Ireland* (Berkeley: University of California Press, 1979).

Sennett, R., *Respect: The Formation of Character in an Age of Inequality* (London: Penguin, 2003).

Share, P. and Tovey, H., *A Sociology of Ireland* (Dublin: Gill and Macmillan, 2000).

Siggins, L., *Mary Robinson: The Woman Who Took Power in the Part* (London: Mainstream, 1977).

Sigmund, P.E., *St Thomas Aquinas on Politics and Ethics* (New York: Norton, 1988).

Skidelsky, R., *John Maynard Keynes: The Economist as Saviour 1920–1937* (London: Macmillan, 1992).

Smyth, G., *Decolonisation and Criticism: The Construction of Irish Literature* (London: Pluto, 1998).

Sugden, J. and Bairner, A., *Sport, Sectarianism and Society in a Divided Ireland* (Leicester: Leicester University Press, 1993).

Tierney, M., 'A Weary Task: The Struggle in Retrospect', in Tierney, M. (ed.), *Struggles with Fortune* (Dublin: Browne and Nolan, 1954).

Townsend, P., *Poverty in the United Kingdom* (London: Penguin, 1979).

Tyrell, G., *Medievalism* (Tunbridge Wells: Burns and Oates, 1994).

Watson, T., *Sociology of Work and Industry* (London: Routledge, 1987).

Max Weber, *Essays in Sociology*, ed. Gerth, H.H. and Wright Mills, C. (London: Routledge, 1948).

Witoszeck, W. and Sheeran, P.F., 'Irish Culture: The Desire for Transcendence', in Keneally, M. (ed.), *Cultural Contexts and Literary Idioms in Contemporary Literature* (Colin Smythe: Gerrards Cross, 1988).

White, J., *Minority Report: The Protestant Community in the Irish Republic* (Dublin: Gill and Macmillan, 1975).

White, L.M., 'Peadar O'Donnell, "Real Republicanism" and *The Bell*', *The Republic*, vol. 4 (June 2005), pp.80–99.

Whyte, J., *Church and State in Modern Ireland* (Dublin: Gill and Macmillian, 1971).

Whitaker, T.K., *Economic Development* (Dublin: Stationery Office, 1958).

Whitaker, T.K., *Interests* (Dublin: Gill and Macmillan, 1984).

Yeats, W.B., *The Letters of W.B Yeats*, ed. Wade, A. (London: Rupert Hart-Davis, 1954).

Young, M. and Willmott, P., *Family and Kinship in East London* (London: Pelican, 1962).

Index